SNA:
Architecture,
Protocols, and
Implementation

J. Ranade IBM Series

ISBN	AUTHOR	TITLE
0-07-006551-9	K. Bosler	CLIST Programming
0-07-044129-4	H. Murphy	ASSEMBLER for COBOL Programmers: MVS, VM
0-07-006533-0	H. Bookman	COBOL II
0-07-051265-5	J. Ranade	DB2 Concepts, Programming and Design
0-07-054594-4	J. Sanchez	IBM Microcomputers Handbook
0-07-002467-7	M. Aronson	SAS: A Programmer's Guide
0-07-002673-4	J. Azevedo	ISPF: The Strategic Dialog Manager
0-07-009816-6	M. Carathanassis	Expert MVS/XA JCL: A Complete Guide to Advanced Techniques
0-07-017606-X	P. Donofrio	CICS: Debugging, Dump Reading and Problem Determination
0-07-018966-8	T. Eddolls	VM Performance Management
0-07-033571-0	P. Kavanagh	VS COBOL II for COBOL Programmers
0-07-040666-9	T. Martyn, T. Hartley	DB2/SQL, A Professional Programmer's Guide
0-07-050054-1	S. Piggot	CICS: A Practical Guide To System Fine Tuning
0-07-050691-4	N. Prasad	IBM Mainframes: Architecture and Design
0-07-051144-6	J. Ranade, G. Sackett	Introduction To SNA Networking: A Guide to VTAM/NCP
0-07-051143-8	J. Ranade, G. Sackett	Advanced SNA Networking: A Professional's Guide For Using VTAM/NCP
0-07-054528-6	S. Samson	MVS Performance Management
0-07-054529-4	S. Samson	MVS/ESA Performance Management (ESA/390 Edition)
0-07-032673-8	B. Johnson	MVS: Concepts and Facilities
0-07-046263-1	P. McGrew	On-Line Text Management
0-07-071136-4	A. Wipfler	Distributed Processing In The CICS Environment
0-07-071139-9	A. Wipfler	CICS Application Development Programming
0-07-051244-2	J. Ranade	VSAM: Concepts, Programming and Design
0-07-051245-0	J. Ranade	VSAM: Performance, Design and Fine Tuning
0-07-007252-3	K. Brathwaite	Relational DataBases: Concepts, Design & Administration
0-07-009820-4	M. Carathanassis	Expert MVS/ESA JCL: A Guide to Advanced Techniques
0-07-023682-8	G. Goldberg, I. Smith	The Rexx Handbook
0-07-032674-6	B. Johnson, D. Johnson	DASD: IBM's Direct Access Storage Devices
0-07-040763-0	M. Marx, P. Davis	MVS Power Programming
0-07-057553-3	D. Silverberg	DB2: Performance, Design, and Implementation
0-07-069460-5	A. Werman	DB2 Handbook for DBAs
0-07-017607-8	P. Donofrio	CICS: A Programmer's Reference
0-07-054597-9	J. Sanchez, M. Canton	Programming Solutions Handbook for IBM Microcomputers
0-07-002553-3	P. Artis, G. Houtekamer	MVS I/O Subsystem: Configuration Management and Performance Analysis

SNA: Architecture, Protocols, and Implementation

Atul Kapoor
Kaptronix, Inc.
Haworth, New Jersey

McGraw-Hill, Inc.
New York   St. Louis   San Francisco   Auckland   Bogotá
Caracas   Lisbon   London   Madrid   Mexico   Milan
Montreal   New Delhi   Paris   San Juan   São Paulo
Singapore   Sydney   Tokyo   Toronto

Library of Congress Cataloging-in-Publication Data

Kapoor, Atul.
    SNA : architecture, protocols, and implementation / Atul Kapoor.
        p.   cm. — (J. Ranade IBM series)
    Includes bibliographical references and index.
    ISBN 0-07-033727-6
    1. SNA (Computer network architecture)   I. Title.   II. Series.
TK5105.5.K36   1992
004.6′5—dc20   91-37675
                                                                    CIP

1 2 3 4 5 6 7 8 9 0   DOC/DOC   9 7 6 5 4 3 2 1

ISBN   0-07-033727-6

*The sponsoring editor for this book was Jerry Papke, the editing
supervisor was Joseph Bertuna, and the production supervisor was
Donald F. Schmidt. It was set in Century Schoolbook by
McGraw-Hill's Professional Book Group composition unit.*

Printed and bound by R. R. Donnelley & Sons Company.

*Dedicated to Sunita, Sapna, Anuj,
and of course Frostie*

Contents

Part 3   Upper Layers, PU/LU Types, Control Sequences

Preface

IBM announced System Network Architecture (SNA) in 1974, with the first reasonably complete implementations appearing around 1980. Since then SNA has become the most widely implemented data communications architecture and a de facto standard. Starting as an awkwardly defined, mainframe-oriented architecture, it has since evolved into a very elaborate and rich architecture with extensive support for multihost networks and capabilities to interface between independently defined networks. Also, with the Logical Unit (LU) 6.2, otherwise known as Advanced Program to Program Communications (APPC), you can even implement host-independent distributed processing. Then there has been the addition of applications architectures such as SNA Distribution Services (SNADS) and Distributed Data Management (DDM). In 1974 no one could have visualized the impact of personal computers. SNA is still evolving to bring PCs in the mainstream of SNA networks.

The primary purpose of this book is to explain SNA to practicing professionals—people who have to implement SNA, provide interfaces to it, or work around it. The focus of the book is on the "real world," and the topics selected reflect that bias. The material is based upon extensive personal hands-on experience in designing, implementing, and diagnosing SNA networks. This hands-on experience is further augmented by years of consulting and teaching about SNA.

One problem in writing a book on SNA is in trying to maintain an accuracy of terminology. And here again IBM documentation is frustrating and inconsistent. As SNA has evolved, IBM has published new manuals to document new features.

However, the terminology in the new manuals is not always the same as in the earlier manuals, and nowhere is explained the reason for the inconsistency or whether a change in terminology implies a change in the architecture itself.

Good cases in point are the *SNA Format and Protocol Architecture Logic Manual* and the *LU-LU Session Types* manuals. Even the basic layers of SNA as described in these manuals differ from the layers described in the current version of *SNA Technical Overview* and the *LU 6.2 Format and Protocol* manuals. As a specific example, while the earlier manuals describe a layer called NAU_SERVICES_MANAGER, the latter manuals make no reference to this layer and present a new layer called TRANSACTION_SERVICES. Does the layer called NAU_SERVICES_MANAGER no longer exist? IBM documentation does not provide any elaboration. Similarly, there is lack of coordination between products documentation (e.g., manuals on CICS, ACF/VTAM, etc.) and architecture documentation (e.g., *SNA Format and Protocol Logic Manual*). While there have been improvements, the product manuals still handle architectural issues in vague or confusing terms.

A frequent question about the architecture itself is: Does SNA have to be so complex? The answer takes us into some fairly complex issues in the theory of networking architectures. Some complexity is to be expected since SNA is trying to solve a fairly complex problem. But the degree of complexity in SNA may have had something to do with the fact that SNA was IBM's first foray into the world of networking. SNA is certainly not an architecture that can be rationalized in the context of simple networks.

In any case, this book represents a modest attempt in explaining a very complex subject matter. To prevent the book from running into several thousand pages, certain compromises had to be made. Which topics to include and what to exclude was the most difficult question. The primary criteria used were that the book must provide a solid foundation of SNA fundamentals and that it should give a sense of completeness about the topics covered. Equally important was to keep the subject matter current. Even as this book was being written, a number of significant announcements were made by IBM in the areas of network management, LU 6.2, AS/400, OS2 EE, SAA, OSI support, new front processors, 3174 controllers, Token Ring interfaces—all within the two years that the book was being written. A revision every six months was the norm. Well, life under SNA is never dull!

The book is organized in five sections.

Part 1 consists of Chaps. 1 and 2 and deals with historic background and evolution of IBM products leading up to SNA. The section also introduces concepts of a formal network architecture, layers, headers, and basic SNA terminology (SSCP, PU, LU, domains, subareas, etc.). This section should prove sufficient for any one needing only a high-level view of SNA.

Part 2, Chaps. 3 and 4, deals with the transport mechanism, the path control network, in SNA. This section covers the lowest three layers of SNA: physical, data link control, and path control. Here is also your first introduction to the turbidity in terminology in SNA: the path control *network* is *not* the same as path control *layer*.

Part 3, Chaps. 5 to 7, deal with Network Addressable Units (NAUs): SSCP, PU, and LU and higher layers in SNA. Protocols from transmission control and data flow control layers are discussed along with different PU/LU types. Functions pertaining to LU 6.2, PU 2.1, and transaction services layer are discussed in Part 5 under advanced architectures.

Part 4, Chaps. 8 to 10, deal with implementation, operation, and network management issues. ACF/VTAM and ACF/NCP are used as the implementation environment. Considerations for multiple systems networking (MSN) and discussion of network management products such as NetView are also covered in this section.

Part 5, Chaps. 11 to 14, covers gateways and later developments in SNA such as SNA-SNA and SNA-X.25 gateways. SNA distributed processing, LU 6.2 (APPC), PI 2.1 (LEN), and APPN are discussed in great amount of detail. Also included in this section are the latest developments in IBM support for international standards.

Acknowledgments

Of course, no book on SNA could be written without referring extensively to IBM publications. A bibliography is included in the book that cites important IBM manuals and papers referred to in the preparation of this book.

Thanks to all the students who attended all those SNA seminars conducted by the author and who, with their constant badgering and sharp questions, helped refine the methods of explaining SNA.

Thanks also to Joseph Bertuna and McGraw-Hill's Professional Book Group for their work in editing, designing, and producing this book.

But most of all thanks to IBM, "Big Blue." Without you none of this would have been possible.

The book is also dedicated to all those programmers and analysts, as well as all those technical support, sales, marketing, and management professionals who slogged for so long through all those IBM manuals and public seminars before realizing that the expert consultant was only an acronym ahead!

Atul Kapoor

About the Author

Atul Kapoor has been an SNA integrator, developer, and implementer since 1974. He is the founder of Kaptronix, Inc., a firm specializing in LAN/WAN software development, training, and consulting.

Background and Introduction

1

IBM and the Evolution of Teleprocessing

1.1 INTRODUCTION

SNA is the strategic architecture developed by IBM to unify its tele-processing systems and products under a single set of protocols. Even though the roots of SNA are in mainframe-based systems, it now in-cludes communications with minis (e.g., AS/400, Systems 36 and 38), micros, and local area networks. Acquisition and departure of Satel-lite Business System (SBS) and Rolm may reflect some miscalcula-tions and missteps, but, overall, IBM's commitment to provide inte-grated telecommunications solutions remains intact and would be reflected in future SNA developments.

SNA, as we know it today, did not happen overnight. Since its an-nouncement in 1974, it has evolved and changed significantly. At each major step in its evolution IBM has either added more functions or provided new products to implement the architecture. A common theme in this evolution has been the accommodation of new applica-tions in areas where IBM had historically, at best, a very feeble pres-ence.

SNA is undoubtedly the most dominant architecture today and is supported by all major vendors. Outside the United States, other ar-chitectures such as CCITT's Recommendation X.25 and International Standards Organization's Open System Interconnect (OSI) are major alternatives to SNA. These architectures are becoming more signifi-cant in the United States, too, along with other standards such as Transmission Control Program Internet Protocol (TCP/IP). IBM al-ready provides gateways from SNA to these systems. There has also been extensive speculation about the future impact of Integrated Ser-vices Digital Networks (ISDN), software defined networks, and high-speed switched digital facilities on SNA. IBM has major projects under way to evaluate how SNA may accommodate such emerging technologies.

Reflecting rapidly evolving communications technology, SNA too has been in a perpetual state of evolution. It keeps changing. It is elaborate and complex. It certainly uses some unusual terminology. For a new student of SNA, that presents a problem: Where to begin?

First of all one has to have a good understanding of the basics of data communications before undertaking a study of SNA. In addition, to understand implementations of SNA, a knowledge of IBM products is also required. To understand the idiosyncrasies of SNA (such as a major dependence on the host machine), it is also necessary to understand the evolution of IBM teleprocessing software and historic limitations of pre-SNA systems.

To understand SNA is to understand the world of IBM. Since the intent of this book is to satisfy the needs of a broad cross section of readers, the first part of this chapter deals with some rudimentary facts about data communications and introduces basic IBM products and terminology. Readers familiar with this subject matter may skip Sec. 1.2. Following Sec. 1.2 is a review of major IBM system software products and their limitations. This is an important topic and gives a very good insight into the objectives of SNA.

1.2 NETWORK COMPONENTS

Figure 1.1 shows a simple IBM mainframe-based network. Using this as a reference, we identify major components of an IBM mainframe-based network. Actually we have an additional motive in discussing this network: to introduce common IBM acronyms and terms that are used extensively in the book.

Figure 1.1 shows terminals on the right side connected over modems and a telecommunications link to the *front end processor* (FEP). The FEP, also known as a communications controller, is connected to the host computer over an I/O channel. Major software components shown in the host include the operating system, access method, *teleprocessing monitor* (TP monitor), applications, and other subsystems. The term *subsystem* refers to major IBM software products outside the access method that are used to support communications applications.

1.2.1 Terminals

A typical terminal may be a display station with a keyboard, a printer, or a typewriter-style device. Terminals can also be devices such as card readers or minicomputers. Then, of course, there is the

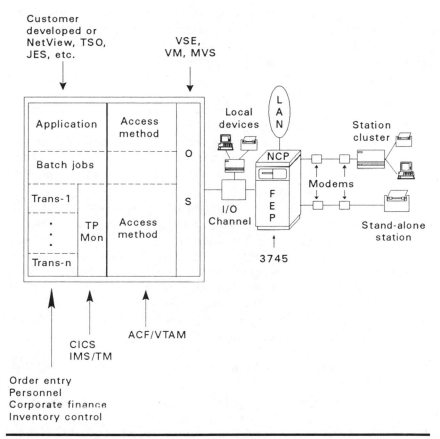

Figure 1.1   IBM teleprocessing environment (TP Mon = teleprocessing monitor).

ubiquitous PC, which is rapidly becoming the universal terminal (workstation).

One important characteristic of a terminal is whether it is a "clustered" or a "stand-alone" terminal. With a cluster, a number of terminals can be attached to a common cluster controller, and each terminal can be used by a different user. The terminals on a controller have to be within a certain distance (which can be as far as 5000 feet in some models) from the controller. The IBM 3270 family represents the most eminent example of these terminals. The cluster controllers are beginning to provide many more functions than simple clustering of terminals. The IBM 3174 (and competitive products) can also attach asynchronous terminals and communicate with X.25 and IBM Token Ring *local area networks* (LANs). Though not shown in the picture, LANs are rapidly becoming the preferred mode of connecting devices within a building or campus. Both display stations and printers can be attached to the same controller. Asynchronous and card-reader-type (batch) terminals typically come in stand-alone mode only.

From a link protocol point of view, terminals come in two classes: asynchronous and synchronous.

Asynchronous terminals are sometimes also known as *teletypes* (TTY) or ASCII terminals. Asynchronous protocols are not a part of SNA, and devices using them cannot be connected to an SNA network without some form of protocol conversion. Traditionally, teletypes were used in low-speed [less than 1.2 kilobits per second (KBPS)] applications. Lately, speeds as high as 9.6 KBPS have become possible with asynchronous protocols.

Synchronous terminals have two major categories: Binary Synchronous Communications (BSC) and Synchronous Data Link Control (SDLC). BSC terminals are not architected under SNA (i.e., they are not a part of SNA). SNA defines only SDLC as the link protocol. Nevertheless, there are SNA products (note the distinction between SNA *architecture* and SNA *product*) that support selected BSC terminals without going through any protocol conversion. Prior to the advent of SNA, BSC terminals were the most common in IBM networks. Examples of major BSC terminals include:

IBM 3270 family with 3274 and 3174 controllers, 3277 display stations, and 3287 printers

2780/3780/3770 card reader, printer terminals with console (commonly used in remote job entry applications)

The third link protocol for terminals is SDLC, which is the only one that SNA supports. Both the IBM 3270 family and the 3770 terminals are also available in SDLC models. Another SDLC terminal is the IBM 3767, which is a stand-alone typewriter-style terminal. The 3770 and 3767 are no longer manufactured by IBM. IBM minicomputers, such as AS/400, and micros also support SDLC in addition to other protocols. A number of products are available that allow PCs to act as asynchronous, BSC, or SDLC terminals.

We also need to make a distinction between *locally* connected terminals and *remote* terminals. The distinction is based on the mode of host attachment, not the distance of a terminal from the host machine. A local device could possibly be more distant from the host than the so-called remote device.

Remote devices, by definition, go through a front end processor (FEP), whereas the local devices are connected directly to the host I/O channel. The physical interface for locally attached devices does not require a modem and uses IBM System 370/390 I/O channel interface. Local devices can transfer data at 1–3 million characters per second and use the S/370/390 channel protocols instead of SDLC (or BSC). Local devices are also referred to as channel attached and remote devices as link attached.

1.2.2 Modems/DSUs

Modems convert binary data from a computer or a network device to a signal form that is compatible with common voice-grade telephone lines by modulating the binary bit streams into analog waveforms (*modulation-dem*odulation function, thus the name *modem*). For digital transmission facilities, the instrument used is called a Digital Service Unit (DSU) and its primary difference from a modem is that it uses a technique different from modulation-demodulation for bit translation before transmission. However, both modem and DSU provide the same standard interface to the attached terminal equipment. There are basically two categories of modems: synchronous and asynchronous. (The term *synchronous* comes from the fact that in synchronous systems a master bit synchronization clock is provided. No such clocking mechanism is used with asynchronous transmission systems.) With synchronous modems, the modem typically provides the clock for bit synchronization. Within each category, modems are further divided into switched (dial-up) and private line (leased line) categories.

In Fig. 1.2, the interface between the modem (DSU) and the communications device (terminal or FEP) is controlled via signals exchanged between the two. The interface consists of a multipin cable with the function of each pin defined by well-established standards. The best-known standards for this interface are the Electronic Industries Association's standard number RS232 (EIA RS232) or the CCITT V.35 for data rates above 19.2 kilobits per second (KBPS). RS232 is a

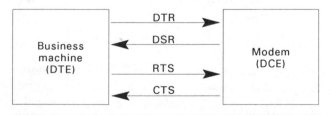

Figure 1.2 Modem and business machine interface, selected leads.

24-pin interface. An understanding of at least some of the signals on this interface is important for appreciating the performance issues discussed later in the book.

When discussing the RS232, the term *data terminal equipment* (DTE) refers to the business machine (terminal or front end) side of the interface, and the term *data communications equipment* (DCE) refers to the modem side of the interface. (There is some confusion in terminology here due to the CCITT use of the term *DCE* to refer to a public network node rather than a modem. To keep terminology straight we use the term *modem* rather than the EIA term *DCE*.)

The following definitions refer to Fig. 1.2.

Data terminal ready (DTR):   This signal is generated by the DTE to indicate its power-on status to the modem. This signal stays on in a constant state (rather than a pulse) while the DTE is active.

Data set ready (DSR):   This constant-state signal is presented to the DTE by the modem when modem power is on. The DTR-DSR exchange is the first handshake between the modem and the DTE indicating that both are active. In most private line configurations these signals are automatically exchanged when power is turned on.

Request to send (RTS):   After the DTR-DSR exchange, the RTS signal is used by the DTE to inform the modem that it has a bit stream for transmission and requests the modem for permission to present this stream, one bit at a time, to the modem.

Clear to send (CTS):   The modem presents this signal to the DTE in response to the DTE's RTS signal to indicate that the modem is ready to accept the data stream.

Both RTS and CTS remain constantly on for the duration of bit stream transmission. After presenting the last bit to the modem, the DTE drops its RTS, at which time the modem also drops its CTS signal.

On multipoint lines, only one station should transmit at a time, i.e., only one station may raise RTS at any given time. Later we see how this is achieved by link protocols.

1.2.3   Links

Links are typically common-carrier-provided facilities. The primary attributes of a link that are of interest to us are dial-up versus private (leased) links; line speed; line type (full versus half duplex); and point to point versus multipoint.

With switched links you have to dial a number to connect with the computer or the terminal (from the host end). This arrangement has been very popular with PCs and in asynchronous communications. A private line, on the other hand, is permanently in place. With private lines, the common carrier vendors (telephone companies) can use special techniques (called conditioning the line) on voice telephone lines to improve their quality and achieve speeds higher than 9.6 KBPS. Until very recently, 1.2 KBPS was the highest speed one could attain on dial-up lines. With the improvements in the modem technology, 9.6 KBPS line speeds are becoming quite commonplace on dial-up lines these days. Technology is already available to implement 56 KBPS digital switched lines, but it requires upgrading of common carrier central offices before this service can be offered. ISDN provides 64 KBPS digital switched service as a standard feature.

Another attribute of interest is the mode of operation of a link—half duplex (transmissions in one direction only at a time) versus full duplex (simultaneous transmission in both directions). The mode of operation is determined collectively by the physical link, the modems, and the station equipment on the line. Each of these components has to be capable of full-duplex mode for a full-duplex operation. Half-duplex operation is not only less efficient, it is also more complex to implement from a link control protocol point of view.

Finally, a link can be point to point or multipoint (i.e., multiple stations on the line). Multipoint configuration is possible only with a private line. One of the stations on the line is designated as a control or the primary station (typically the front end processor), which controls other stations called secondary stations.

Polling is used on multipoint lines to ensure that only one secondary location transmits bits (i.e., only the polled station on the line should raise its RTS signal to its modem) at any given time. As the primary station polls each station on the link, only the polled station responds to the poll. When the primary station has a message to be sent to the network, the primary identifies the station on the line which is to receive the message. Although all stations look at the message, only the station identified as the destination assembles the message. To identify stations on the line, each station on a multidrop line is assigned a unique identification. If the station represents a clustered arrangement, additional identification must be assigned to each device attached to the cluster controller. Device IDs have to be unique within a cluster. Figure 1.3 shows a line configuration and unique IDs assigned to various stations. Often these IDs are referred to as the *hardware IDs*. In SNA, the station ID is called the link station ID and the device is known as the local ID (i.e., it is understood locally by the

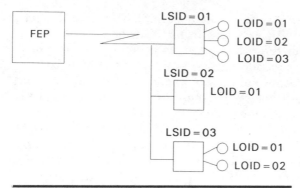

Figure 1.3 Multipoint line addressing (LSID = Link Stations ID, LOID = Local ID).

cluster controller only and has no meaning to other stations on the line).

1.2.4 Link and Link Protocols

Link protocols are procedures used to manage and control a link. The polling function just described was an example of a link protocol function. Similarly, rules for assigning link station IDs are also a part of link protocol specifications. Assignment of local IDs within a station is not a part of the link protocol, as local IDs are internal to a station and not a part of link management. Other link protocol functions include logical initialization of a station, recovery from link errors, etc. Units of transmission are called blocks and frames in BSC and SDLC, respectively.

As mentioned in Sec. 1.2.1, common link protocols include asynchronous, BSC, and SDLC. A terminal itself, attached to a cluster controller such as the IBM 3174, does not understand or implement these protocols. The link protocol terminates at the cluster controller.

1.2.5 Front End Processor (FEP)

A front end processor is a special-purpose computer that acts as a termination point for network facilities. In formal usage, IBM refers to these processors as communication controllers. However, the term *communications controller* means several different things in common usage, and the term *FEP* is more commonly understood to mean the IBM communications controller. In any case we would use the term *FEP* to refer to the IBM communication controllers. Lines are terminated through their modems at the FEP "ports." The DTE end of the modem interface (e.g., RS232) is provided by the port hardware. Depending on the front end model, different types of port hardware may have to be configured to support different protocols and line speeds.

In addition to providing line terminations, the FEP also off-loads some of the communications overhead from the host machine. For example, FEPs handle all line transmission errors. The SDLC header and trailer are also formatted by the FEP. The FEP buffers data from telecommunications lines and sends it over the high-speed I/O channel to the host computer.

An FEP can be attached to a host computer over the I/O channel, or it can be configured as a network concentrator. In the latter case the front end configuration is called a remote FEP.

Starting with the nonprogrammable 270X series controllers (2701, 2702, and 2703 models) the IBM front end processor line has evolved to the 37XX line, where the current model is the IBM 3745 machine. Older models such as 3705, 3720, and 3725 are still around and are being replaced by the new machines. All IBM FEPs are capable of supporting SNA and non-SNA networks.

Front end software.   The capabilities of an FEP are really determined by the type of software running in it. The IBM front ends support two basic software configurations: Emulation Program (EP) and Network Control Program (NCP). The Emulation Program is the older of the two and supports only asynchronous and BSC protocols. EP does not support SNA. NCP supports both SNA and non-SNA configurations. It should be noted that the term *network control program* is also a generic term for communications control software. In this book when we use the term *Network Control Program* we refer to a specific IBM product, not to the generic term.

1.2.6   I/O Channel

The term *channel* is somewhat of a misnomer since it raises the image of a communications facility—a passive path. That would be misleading. A more appropriate term for the IBM I/O channel would be the *I/O processor*. The primary function of an I/O channel is to transfer information between the host main storage and I/O devices such as disk drives, tape drives, printers, local terminals, and the FEP.

The I/O channel is capable of executing its own commands and programs. The commands for the channel are generated by host resident system software and access methods (see the following sections), and do not require any direct involvement of applications programmers.

1.2.7 Host/Mainframe Processor

In IBM terminology and throughout this book, the term *host* refers specifically to an IBM mainframe from the System 370 or the newly announced (September 5, 1990) System 390 family. Each family consists of a range of processors. S/370 processors consist of the 9370 at the low end, the 4300 series in the mid-range, and the 93XX processors at the high end. The S/390 family consists of series 9000 processors.

1.2.8 Operating System

The operating system is the main control software in the host. It schedules all the work on the mainframe and manages its resources. IBM's host operating systems, however, do not play a major role in support of communications or SNA. It has been observed that IBM operating systems are not communications oriented since most communications functions are performed outside the operating system in the access method (see the following).

In any case, there are three major operating systems available from IBM for the System 370/390 machines.

Disk Operating System/Virtual Storage Extended (DOS/VSE): Typically used on small to mid-sized machines. Supports software for both SNA and non-SNA networks. It is commonly referred to simply as VSE.

Multiple Virtual Systems (MVS): For large users, supports SNA and non-SNA software. Within MVS, the largest installed version is the MVS Extended Edition (MVS/XA). The latest version of MVS is the MVS Enterprise System Architecture (MVS/ESA).

Virtual Machine (VM): Used by small and large users. Allows VSE and MVS (or multiple copies of the same operating system) to run on the same machine concurrently. Until 1985 this operating system had no direct support for SNA.

1.2.9 Teleprocessing Access Methods

Before discussing teleprocessing access methods, let's describe access methods in general.

The access method serves as a software interface between the host computer and its peripherals. It governs the sequence of operations required to get data from an external device into the computer's memory and vice versa.

Since different types of devices are attached to a mainframe (disk drives, card readers, FEPs, etc.), different types of control sequences are needed to communicate with them, and consequently different types of access methods are required.

Teleprocessing access methods assist in moving information to and from the network over the I/O channel. These access methods at minimum provide commands for the I/O channel and to control and manage the front end. Three major access methods for teleprocessing applications include:

Basic Telecommunications Access Method (BTAM)

Tele-Communication Access Method (TCAM)

Virtual Telecommunications Access Method (VTAM)

Of the three, only VTAM is a "current" product.

BTAM.   A basic and simple access method, BTAM always ran as a part of the program using it. BTAM was the earliest of the IBM TP access methods and it had no support for SNA. It worked only with an FEP in an Emulation Program (EP) mode and supported only asynchronous and BSC protocols.

VTAM and TCAM.   Unlike BTAM, these access methods run as independent jobs. Both VTAM and TCAM support SNA and require Network Control Program (NCP) in the front end for SNA functions. In addition, TCAM can also support non-SNA devices with front end running in an EP mode. Today VTAM is the only current access method for SNA.

1.2.10   Teleprocessing (TP) Monitors

This additional layer of control software sits between an application program and the access method. The original reasons for developing teleprocessing monitors had to do with the limitations of the BTAM/EP environment and the need to provide a transaction management environment in the host.

With teleprocessing monitors it becomes possible to run multiple applications (transaction programs) under the control of the monitor rather than the operating system. Teleprocessing monitors also simplify application development and thereby reduce the cost of software development.

The two major teleprocessing monitors from IBM are Customer Information Control System (CICS) and Information Management

System/Data Communications (IMS/DC). (The latter was renamed IMS Transaction Manager, IMS/TM, on September 5, 1990.)

1.2.11 Database Management Systems

This software component, very important for application programs, is generally ignored in SNA discussions since it does not directly get involved in data communications functions. In the future, with more extensive support for distributed processing, IBM relational database, Database/2 (DB/2) will gain more importance even in an SNA context. Except for passing references, we ignore this component.

1.2.12 Applications (Transactions Processing)

This is the reason for buying the computer in the first place. Not surprisingly, with all the other control software in the host, the applications do not seem to get much of a chance to use the CPU. In large IBM shops it is not surprising to see applications getting less than 40 percent of the CPU time.

In the following section we discuss how IBM products have evolved from the pre-SNA BTAM environment to today's VTAM environment.

1.3 IBM PRODUCTS AND THE EVOLUTION OF SNA

The evolution of SNA has been a continuous learning experience, both for its implementors and inventors. A look at IBM products at different points in time is very helpful in understanding some of the functional objectives behind SNA. The products also give us a more tangible understanding of SNA in contrast to the architected layers, which are often too abstract.

1.3.1 The BTAM Era

This was the age of simple systems, which started with low-speed teletype (TTY) devices, mostly in dial-up configurations. Synchronous devices and multipoint private networks came later as devices such as the IBM 3270 BSC were invented. Mainframe machines were small and software had to be efficient, complex and, thus, difficult to modify. When it first became available in the late 1960s, BTAM worked with nonprogrammable IBM 270X FEPs, which were replaced by programmable and more flexible 3705 front ends. However, since BTAM could work only with the 270X FEPs, the 3705 FEP had to run under the EP software—emulating the old 270X front ends and providing no new intelligence.

To make up for the lack of intelligence in the FEP, BTAM and application programs had to control the network. Additionally, all software interfacing with BTAM had to be written in assembler language. The application programmer was responsible for all aspects of the system—the business application and the technical details of communications. Thus, the same programmer had to be knowledgeable in business functions, BTAM, and network devices. Major software changes were needed to support new devices and protocols. Given the state of the art in software engineering, these were not modifications that one took lightly.

Figure 1.4 shows a simple BTAM/EP environment (remember that BTAM does not work with NCP). The diagram shows two applications, order processing and inventory management. Observe that there are two copies of BTAM, one in each system. (Certain routines in BTAM could be made shareable to reduce storage requirements.) Each appli-

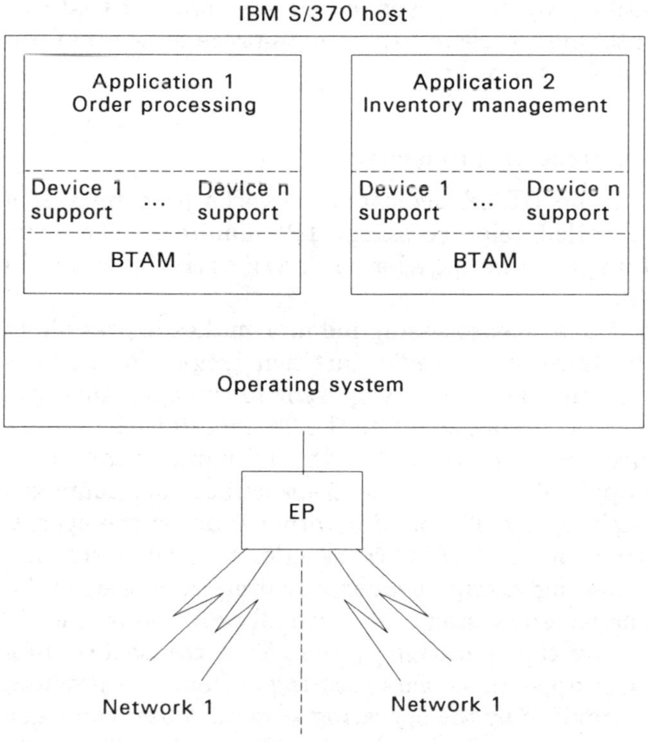

Figure 1.4   Early BTAM networks.

cation also has a full set of code to handle device-dependent considerations. Our focus for now is the way in which lines and terminals are
allowed access to the two applications shown in Fig. 1.4. The IBM operating systems allow a link (and all of its terminals) to be allocated to
(owned by) only one job at a time, which means that for a link allocated to the order processing job, all terminals on that line can only
access (or logon to) the order processing system. A user who needs to
access the inventory management application would need another terminal attached to a line allocated to the inventory management job.
In effect, under BTAM a *dedicated network* was required for each application. A person needing access to multiple applications would need
multiple terminals. The number of links required was thus much
greater than justified by traffic requirements alone.

Often these systems were developed by separate programming
teams working independently of each other. When it came to software
engineering, each team came up with its own message formats, coding
conventions, and unique operational considerations (the "better
mouse trap" syndrome). The final result was inefficient and expensive
networks, high software development cost, high maintenance overhead, and incompatible systems. It was in this environment that corporate managements were pressing their data-processing organizations for more and more on-line systems.

1.3.2 The Rise of Teleprocessing Monitors

The first solution to the BTAM dedicated networks problem was a
software invention called teleprocessing (TP) monitors. The term
transaction control programs perhaps better describes the function of a
TP monitor.

As shown in Fig. 1.5, a teleprocessing monitor makes it possible to
run multiple applications in a single partition (region or address
space) as a single job in a manner transparent to the operating system. The lines (network) are allocated to the TP monitor job, and all
applications running under the control of the TP monitor can share
the network. The application programs (transactions) are managed
and controlled directly by the TP monitor rather than by the operating system. Functions such as loading transaction programs, starting
their execution, managing storage usage, providing interfaces to database and file management systems, etc., are all provided by the TP
monitor rather than by the operating system. To a transaction program, the TP monitor appears as the operating system and provides
functions normally provided by the operating system. A user can logon
to any transaction program controlled by the TP monitor. This tech-

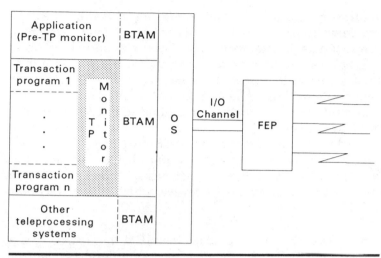

Figure 1.5 Teleprocessing monitors.

nique gets us around the operating system restrictions on sharing lines across programs and significantly improves resource utilization.

Additional benefits include separation of communications and business functions in the software. Communication functions are implemented within the TP monitor, and applications (transactions) have to handle primarily business functions such as order processing and inventory management. With most TP monitors it also becomes possible to write application code in high-level languages such as COBOL or PL/1 instead of assembler as was needed with BTAM.

From a software development point of view, this approach provides a low-cost, low-risk entry into real-time transaction processing. As more and more users started migrating to popular TP monitors, there developed communities of interest and user groups using the same TP monitor. There was an incentive for TP monitor vendors to keep their products compatible with new technologies (or lose market share). Another implication was the de facto evolution of programming standards, as all organizations using a given TP monitor had to use the same programming conventions. You could even hire trained personnel off the street for popular monitors.

Customer Information Control System (CICS) and Information Management System/Data Communications (IMS/DC) are the two teleprocessing monitors available from IBM.

CICS. It has perhaps the largest installed base as a TP monitor worldwide. Through its task management capabilities, CICS allows multiple on-line applications to share a common network. The applications may be written in COBOL and PL/1 in addition to assembler.

CICS supports simple file structures using standard IBM access methods, as well as database systems through interfaces with other well-known systems such as IBM's Database/2 (DB/2) and Information Management System (IMS), Adabase (Software, A. G.), and IDMS/R (Cullinet Corp.). Other features include handling of errors, security, and priority transactions.

By using the Basic Mapping Support (BMS) feature of CICS, an application can be written without detailed knowledge of technical aspects of a terminal such as message formatting characters, device sense/status information, and error recovery, which are entirely managed by CICS.

IMS/DC.   This is the other major product from IBM that can be used as a TP monitor. IMS was originally developed as a database management system (its original name was DL/I and later became IMS/360). Communications capabilities were added later to provide a comprehensive database/data communications (DB/DC) package. IBM does not provide any significant criteria for selecting IMS/DC over CICS or vice versa. CICS does seem to provide better performance and is, generally, ahead of IMS in implementing new communications features. IMS/DC is not available for VSE environments.

While the concept of TP monitors and products such as CICS go a long way in solving the dedicated networks problem with BTAM, they provide only a partial solution. It is neither necessary nor always desirable to run all applications under the control of a single TP monitor. For whatever reasons, if any applications run outside the control of the TP monitor, they still need *separate networks*. In addition, there are teleprocessing systems, including some from IBM, that cannot be run under a TP monitor. Specific examples are IBM products such as Time Sharing Option (TSO) and Job Entry Subsystem (JES). If an organization has a combination of these systems, it would still require a separate network for each system. In addition, TP monitors are of no help at all in allowing access to applications running in different hosts.

1.3.3   Emergence of New Access Methods

If the objective was to have any-to-any connectivity in a network, it became obvious that TP monitors were not going to provide this capability. Ideally, one would have liked an operating system that could directly dispatch messages to the correct transaction. For IBM to provide this function at the operating system level would mean a radically new operating system that would be incompatible with billions of dollars worth of customers' investment in software built around existing operating systems. So IBM provided a solution that was implemented outside the operating system, thereby protecting the compatibility of existing software at the operating system level and yet solving some of the BTAM and TP monitor problems.

The solution was a new set of teleprocessing access methods. These new access methods were Virtual Telecommunications Access Method (VTAM) and Tele-Communications Access Method (TCAM). The proper names for these products have the prefix *ACF* for Advanced Communications Function. The prefix had some meaning in the late 1970s and is redundant now. We refer to these products (and ACF/ NCP) throughout this book without the prefix.

In any case, the major difference between BTAM and these new access methods is their relationship to application programs. Whereas BTAM can run only as a part of an application and is in effect "owned" by the application, the new access methods run independently of the applications as independent jobs under the operating system. Figure 1.6 illustrates this structural distinction.

Conceptually it is helpful to think of the network as if owned by the access method. However, unlike BTAM, no application owns these new access methods, which also have some TP-monitor-like capabilities. For a logon or session establishment, a terminal must first be logically connected to (i.e., be in session with) the access method. This logical connection with the access method can be initiated only by the access method, not the end user. Following the connection with the access method, the user can request the access method to establish a logon with a specific subsystem such as CICS, IMS/DC, or TSO, etc. By so doing we make it possible for a terminal user to log onto any application in the host (so long as all applications run under VTAM or TCAM) with or without a TP monitor and eliminate the problem of dedicated networks in a single host environment. Later we also look at functions that allow a user to access any application in any host for true any-to-any connectivity.

Compared with VTAM, TCAM had a very rich set of built-in functions. Examples of two such capabilities are message queuing and message switching. But TCAM was also the most complex and difficult to deal with. In any case, merits of TCAM over VTAM are a moot point since IBM has phased out TCAM leaving VTAM as the only access method for SNA.

VTAM does raise one interesting question: Why would one still use TP monitors if their sole purpose was to allow access to multiple applications? To the extent that TP monitors are used for this purpose, yes, they are redundant. But as TP monitors have evolved, access to

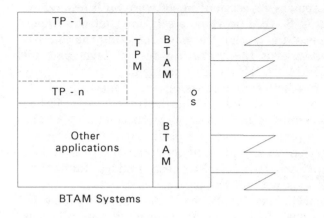

BTAM Systems

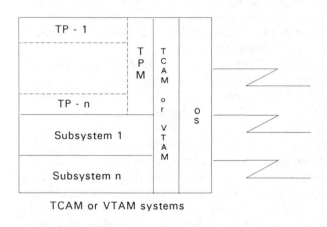

TCAM or VTAM systems

Figure 1.6 BTAM versus VTAM and TCAM (TPM: teleprocessing monitor).

multiple applications is not the only function they provide. Tasks such as data mapping (message formatting), file recovery, and database interfaces are other important functions provided by TP monitors. The VTAM application programming interface allows only assembler language and is really meant for highly technical programmers. TP monitors make the access method interface totally transparent to the applications. One could migrate from BTAM to VTAM without rewriting a single line of application code if the applications were running under a TP monitor. Finally, TP monitors also implement certain SNA protocols that would otherwise have to be implemented in an application.

Thus, TP monitors make SNA transparent to applications. So we will continue to see TP monitors in extensive use even if one of their original functions is not important anymore.

1.3.4 Parallel Developments: The Front End Evolution

Hardware FEPs. When nonprogrammable front ends first became available, they fulfilled the following needs:

1. To provide a standard interface to the host I/O channel on behalf of the network

2. To partially make up for the speed mismatch between the host channel and the network

3. To provide EIA (or equivalent) interface for each line and buffer line data

4. To provide selected data link control (DLC) functions and check for transmission errors

Some of their major limitations, above and beyond capacity, were: (1) lack of flexibility; (2) need for vendor personnel to make changes to the network configuration—expensive for both vendor and customer; and (3) centralization of network management, control, and protocols in the host.

Programmable FEP with Emulation Program (EP). As IBM grew more experienced in data communications, it developed its first family of larger and programmable front ends, the 3705 family.

Initially, however, these new machines did not provide any functions different from the earlier hardware machines in order to maintain compatibility with the existing host (BTAM-based) systems. These machines emulated the old hardware FEPs through their control software, Emulation Program (EP). As with the hardware controllers they replaced, FEPs with EP supported only asynchronous and BSC protocols.

Some of the non-IBM front ends that became available around this time not only provided complete EP capabilities, but also additional features, such as speed/code conversion. Capabilities such as Multi Access Facility (MAF) from NCR/COMTEN provided multiple application access without requiring a TP monitor in the host or a VTAM or TCAM as an access method.

Programmable FEP with Network Control Program (NCP) (VTAM and TCAM only). With SNA came the need to off-load network functions out of the host and thus the NCP. Even though the host is still the "center of the universe," some functions such as DLCs (asynchronous, BSC, and SDLC, tracking status of physical circuits and terminals) are now performed by the FEP with NCP. Additional NCP functions allow a front end to act as a concentrator and an SNA routing node. Finally, NCP is also capable of staying operational even when the owning host is lost—a critical requirement in a multiple-host networking environment. The current versions of NCP also provide gateways to Token Ring LANs and X.25 networks.

Partitioned Emulation Program (PEP).   There is one final option for the front end software called the Partitioned Emulation Program (PEP). In this configuration, shown in Fig. 1.7, a single front end runs both EP and NCP software concurrently. During the system generation procedures, lines can be individually assigned for processing by EP or NCP. Normal configuration rules still apply (i.e., SDLC lines cannot be assigned to EP, and data processed by EP must be transferred to the host to an EP compatible system, BTAM or TCAM; and the NCP traffic to NCP compatible software, VTAM or TCAM). The major advantage of PEP is that it allows the handling of both SNA and non-

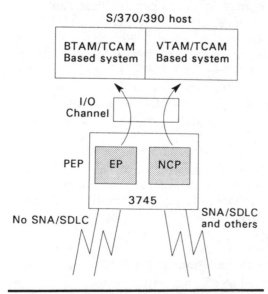

Figure 1.7   Partitioned Emulation Program (PEP).

SNA data by the same front end for organizations with hybrid networks.

1.3.5 The Future

In the last few pages we have taken a simple BTAM environment and migrated from it to SNA (VTAM/NCP) without actually mentioning SNA by name. Figure 1.8 summarizes this evolution. The overall issues are actually much larger than the product-oriented narrow viewpoint that we have taken so far. Surely with VTAM and NCP it is possible to attain complete any-to-any connectivity, but there are still the areas of network management, distributed processing, accommodating international standards, integration of LANs, interfaces with

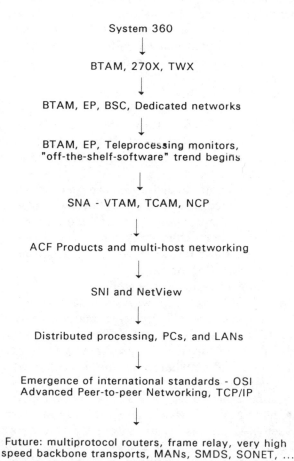

System 360
↓
BTAM, 270X, TWX
↓
BTAM, EP, BSC, Dedicated networks
↓
BTAM, EP, Teleprocessing monitors,
"off-the-shelf-software" trend begins
↓
SNA - VTAM, TCAM, NCP
↓
ACF Products and multi-host networking
↓
SNI and NetView
↓
Distributed processing, PCs, and LANs
↓
Emergence of international standards - OSI
Advanced Peer-to-peer Networking, TCP/IP
↓
Future: multiprotocol routers, frame relay, very high
speed backbone transports, MANs, SMDS, SONET, ...

Figure 1.8 IBM teleprocessing evolution: summary.

PBX, and the impact of ISDN. A number of these requirements are already being met by IBM. In other areas, we are already beginning to see new emphasis from IBM and expect to see more IBM products to address these needs. A number of these areas are discussed in more detail in the following chapters.

1.4   NETWORK ARCHITECTURES AND SNA

To introduce the concept of a formal network architecture, we have to look at the data communications environment in its entirety and attempt to define a comprehensive solution touching on all aspects of our network. When discussing teleprocessing or data communications systems, there are often implied assumptions about what we call a network. Obviously, a collection of transmission facilities alone without additional protocols is not a functional network. A set of "locally" interconnected terminals (consoles) and machines (disks, tapes, printers, etc.) within one computer center can be called a network, but these are not included in teleprocessing discussions since they do not involve telecommunications.

Sometimes networks are classified based on whether they are fixed in place (using leased lines) or transitory (using dial-up lines). In some cases it is possible to identify a network in terms of applications using the network, e.g., inquiry/response, remote job entry, timesharing, data entry, etc. In any significant system one will find a simultaneous mix of several of these functions.

However, one critical characteristic to distinguish these networks is the manner in which the host machine exerts control over the system. In the *older* "teleprocessing" systems, there was only one host and it supported many terminals in a hierarchical way. There could be only two levels in the hierarchy, host and terminal. A four-level hierarchy involved host, FEP, cluster controller, and terminals.

In all cases, the system control resided in *one* host.

As the number of single-host systems grew, it became desirable to consolidate communications networks. There were many situations within the same community of users in which different hosts (often different types) provided different application programs and services to different types of terminals over nonshared communication lines often operating well below capacity.

Consolidation of single-host networks gave rise to networks with multiple coequal hosts, none of which was single-handedly in control of the total network. Each of these hosts could interact with others to provide resources to its applications and terminals on demand. This latter type of environment with multiple hosts is often referred to as a computer networking environment to distinguish it from traditional, terminal-oriented (i.e., single-host) systems.

Once the concept of computer networking took hold, it became obvious that the advantages of such an environment far surpassed the reduction in line costs. Performing code conversion and providing alternate routes became natural extensions of such a system. As viewed by the user community, such a networking environment could provide more powerful options such as complete freedom for any terminal to access any CPU or any CPU to access any other CPU. Such a set of objectives gives rise to a generalized definition of *computer networking* as "a set of autonomous, independent computer systems, interconnected to permit interactive resource sharing between any pair of endpoints."

However, this broad definition raises communication issues far more extensive and complex than those of achieving increased utilization at a lower cost. There is the need for common definitions, message formats, and protocols between different data-processing systems communicating with each other and between data-processing systems and remote devices. These issues also involve complex regulatory matters in the United States that infringe on the scope of the regulated carriers' involvement in the networking solutions.

Network management itself presents a complex problem. Some of the questions that come up are: Which operations center is going to be responsible for which part of the network? How can one provide backups? How do various hosts coordinate their activities with each other? Distribution of databases is a whole new area that needs a separate discussion. A great amount of research and development effort is being spent in this area. The rewards of such efforts still seem a few years away.

So, while networking environments with resource sharing and distributed processing offer an attractive set of advantages, their design and installation is too complex for in-house development by customers. There are two basic approaches to implementing complex networking systems: private networks using vendor proprietary (or a standard architecture), or the use of shared public networks. We discuss these two approaches next.

1.4.1 Private Networks

SNA-based networks and private packet networks are two examples of such networks. A private network in this context does not mean a network built exclusively with private or leased lines; switched lines are very much a part of it. These networks are private in the sense that they are deployed, managed, used, and controlled by an enterprise for its own private use. The network still consists predominantly of common carrier facilities. In this sense most existing customer networks in the United States today are private networks.

A customer may use an architecture such as SNA to build a private network. It would be the customer's responsibility to select appropriate SNA compatible terminals, front ends, and host system software and applications. The customer would also be responsible for the physical network design (number of private and switched lines, use of satellites, speeds, location and number of drops, etc.), modem selection, attaining response time objectives, and backup and recovery of system failures. Network management, operation, and technical support would also be a customer responsibility.

Somewhere along the way the customer would also have to understand what SNA formats and protocols mean, which in itself may cause some problems.

The customer could also use public architectures such as CCITT X.25 to build a private network, but that does not change the scope of the aforementioned problems. If anything, the customer has one additional problem in that X.25 does not define the internal architecture of the backbone network, and the customer would still have to use some proprietary architecture on the backbone.

1.4.2 Shared Public Networks for Computer Communications

An increasingly attractive option for a number of customers may be not to do any deployment on their own, but rather connect into existing data networks available for public access for a fee.

Such networks, called the shared public networks, are being provided by a number of vendors who may use common carrier facilities for actual transmission media. Billing to customers is based primarily on usage and some fixed monthly charge—not the distance that data have to travel. Some other names for such networks are public data networks (PDNs), public packet switched data network (PPSDN), and value added networks (VANs). Currently some of the available offerings in the United States are Tymnet, Telenet, Accunet Packet Service (AT&T), and IBM's SNA-based Information Network. Canada has the oldest public data network, Datapac.

A customer using a public network does not have to worry about network management, operation, and recovery of the network. Most of these networks also provide features (called values—thus the name VANs), such as code, protocol, and speed conversions, which make it possible to support a diverse range of terminals without requiring support software in the customer host for each terminal type.

Public networks, because of their complexity, provide a big challenge to vendors. Maintaining security and message integrity are two of the major concerns of PDN users. On the other hand, PDNs also provide ready-made data networks that one can use with minimal effort in a manner similar to using voice networks. While the VAN concept is here along with a few basic offerings, it would probably be a few years before PDNs become an ubiquitous force in the United States.

It should also be noted that private and public networks are not mutually exclusive. Comprehensive solutions of the future would include a combination of both public and private networks along with local area networks (LANs) and emerging technologies such as integrated services digital networks (ISDN).

1.5   DEFINING A FORMAL ARCHITECTURE

Whether we use a public or private network, someone still has to define the architecture. The architecture definition starts with a detailed analysis of the network functions and services.

Once the functions and services of a network have been thoroughly analyzed, the next step is to describe them in a formal and precise manner. The level of detail should be sufficient so that the implementors do not have to guess the architect's intent. A common technique is to describe the architecture as a hierarchical set of layers and protocols. The concept of layers is rooted in the basic principles of systems analysis. If a problem is complex, decompose it into smaller parts. The layers or levels represent various subdivisions of the architecture. Network components (we use the term *component* in a functional sense here, not as a physical component) performing similar functions should have the same set of layers implemented in them. If we define our layer specifications carefully so that they are not biased toward any specific product, we can make our architecture independent of underlying products or implementation. The advantage, of course, is that dissimilar machines, minicomputers and mainframes from different manufacturers using different operating systems, can communicate with each other if they use a common networking architecture. One additional component needed is the definition of semaphores or signals that these otherwise incompatible machines need to inform each other of the processing to be done on the unit of information exchanged. And that brings us to protocols. Protocols define control information formats and

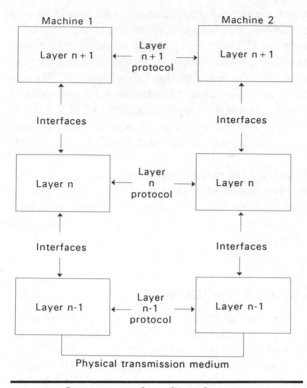

Figure 1.9 Layers, protocols, and interfaces.

processing steps to be taken by a layer for a given unit of information. This concept is illustrated in Fig. 1.9.

As shown in Fig. 1.9, a process in layer $n + 1$ in machine 1 can converse with its equivalent process in layer $n + 1$ in machine 2 even if the two have different hardware and software architectures. The protocols used by the two processes in this case would be called layer or level $n + 1$ protocols.

For peer layer communications, the information has to flow through the underlying layers, over the physical transmission medium, and through the lower layers in the destination node. To distinguish between adjacent layer and peer layer communications, the procedures used between adjacent layers are called interfaces instead of protocols. Protocols are rigorously defined since they can involve dissimilar machines. *Interfaces* generally represent functions performed within a machine and conform to the local operating system and computing environment. Interface implementation may differ from machine to machine.

Architecture designers must take care, though, to ensure that the functions in one layer are independent of other layers. In an ideal situation, changes to level n will have no effect on levels $n - 1$ and $n + 1$. This approach reduces the effort and expense of implementing changes as the architecture evolves. The interdependence between layers can be minimized by allowing an independent header for each layer where the header is used by a layer to specify protocols for its peer communications. The header used by a layer is meaningful only to its peer layer, and other layers should have no need to interpret it to perform their functions. This concept is illustrated in Fig. 1.10.

As an application data unit passes through each layer in the sending machine, the layer attaches a header to it and passes it to the next layer. As the data unit moves up the layer hierarchy in the receiving machine, each layer, as it processes the data unit, strips its header and passes the data unit to the next layer. When a layer receives a unit of data it is in exactly the same form as was created by its peer in

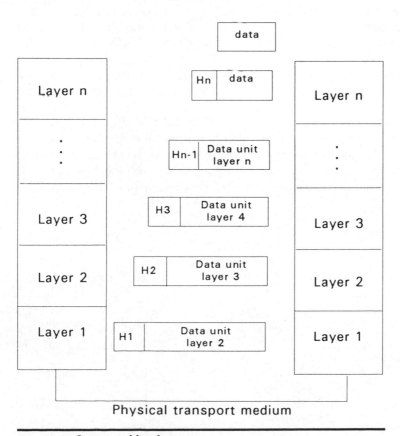

Figure 1.10 Layers and headers.

the sending machine. IBM, ISO, and CCITT use this common technique for defining their architectures.

1.5.1 Formulating Layers

Before we look at the layer structure in SNA, it is helpful to develop an intuitive feel for how network functions can be partitioned in major groups.

As shown in Fig. 1.11, at a high level, we can classify network functions in two broad categories, application functions and network internal functions. Applications (or end users) are users of the network and use the network to establish a session (logon), to send, receive, and process messages. An end user should be able to perform these functions without requiring detailed knowledge of the network topology, transmission media, or routing structures. These latter functions are shown in Fig. 1.11 as internal functions of the network. The network functions represent the lower layers in an architecture, and application functions form the higher layers. Another way of looking at it is to suggest that two end users communicate with each other using higher layers. The higher layers, in turn, use the lower layers to transport information across the network. The lower layers, for that reason, are also referred to as the *transport component* of an architecture.

Figure 1.12 is a rearrangement of Fig. 1.11 to illustrate this relationship between application-oriented functions and the transport network. The higher we go in the architecture, the stronger is the application orientation. The lower we go, the greater is the pure telecommunications nature of functions. By further partitioning applica-

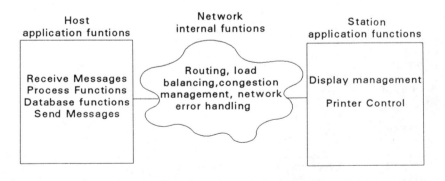

Figure 1.11 A functional view of a network.

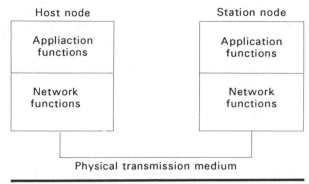

Figure 1.12   Starting layer formulation.

tion- and transport-oriented functions we can develop additional details for the architecture.

1.6   SNA LAYERS

As shown in Fig. 1.13, SNA is defined as a set of seven major layers. [Actually SNA is an eight-layer architecture, where the eighth layer, as shown in the *SNA Format and Protocol Logic Manual,* is called the Network Addressable Unit (NAU) Services Manager. It specifies functions relating to system control, management, maintenance, and configuration services. For whatever reasons, IBM does not show this layer in its later documents even though the function still exists.] The lowest three layers form the transport network in SNA. Levels 4 through 6 provide predominantly application and session support functions. Level 4 represents the delineation between application and the network-oriented functions. Levels 7 through 5 generate data units and pass them on to level 4. Level 4 passes those data units to the transport network in the right priority and sequence for delivery across the network.

As we go through various chapters, we discuss protocols associated with these layers in detail. For now we take a high-level look at their functions.

1.6.1   Physical Control Layer

The physical layer represents the physical interface with the transmission medium. Modems and DSUs typically implement this layer. SNA does not architect any new standard for this layer. IBM does sell a family of diagnostic modems, and protocols used by these modems are not a part of SNA. Prevailing standards such as EIA RS232, V.24,

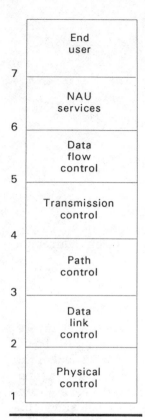

Figure 1.13 SNA model.

X.21, etc. are used for this layer. Since there are no SNA-unique considerations for this layer, we do not discuss it in any detail.

1.6.2 Data Link Control

This layer provides procedures for managing a link and transferring error-free bit streams across the link. Procedures include half- and full-duplex transmission management, error recovery from link errors, control of multipoint lines, and link level flow control. The SNA protocol for link control is Synchronous Data Link Control (SDLC). In addition System 370/390 channel protocols are also supported for I/O channel-attached devices.

1.6.3 Path Control Layer

This layer provides protocols for routing data through the network and managing and controlling network routes and congestion. The layer also provides for a protocol called segmentation, which allows large messages to be sent as multiple segments and reassembled by the path control element in the receiving node.

1.6.4 Transmission Control

The transmission control layer provides for checking of message sequence numbers for each session (each session has its own sequence number series). It also provides procedures for controlling a maximum number of messages released in a session at any given time through a protocol called pacing. Encryption and decryption of data are also done in this layer.

1.6.5 Data Flow Control

This layer provides protocols for controlling the flow of data within a session. It is bad terminology for IBM to have named a layer "data flow control" since all layers in SNA contain flow control protocols. The protocols defined under the DFC layer have a meaning within a specific session only and have no effect on other sessions. Some of the protocols provided follow.

Chaining.   This protocol allows session partners to limit the size of the longest message that can be exchanged in the session. Messages exceeding this limit can be "chained" into a multiple-element chain where each element is equal to or less than the limit specified. Each session decides its own chain element size at session initiation based on the storage capacities of session partners.

Session responses.   These are end-to-end responses between session partners. End-to-end responses are not mandatory in SNA and have to be requested when needed.

Session flow control.   SNA sessions can be defined as full or half duplex and this layer provides protocols for supporting these functions. Controlling the volume of data flow, however, is in the transmission control.

Session sequence number assignment.   When supported, the DFC layer also assigns sequence numbers to messages being sent in a session. Sequence number protocol gives us an opportunity to make two additional observations about SNA. First, we started this paragraph with "when supported." This should point out to us that not all architected protocols are supported by all implementations (products). Second, sequence number validation is a function of transmission control and generation is done in DFC. So here we have a protocol, sequence numbering, whose management involves two layers—DFC and TC. This is contrary to the objective that layers should be partitioned in such a way that no layer should have to interpret the work done by another level.

1.6.6 Network Addressable Unit (NAU) Services

We formally define the term *Network Addressable Unit* later in the book and its definition is not important to understanding functions of this layer.

The NAU services layer has undergone significant changes since the announcement of SNA in 1974. The layer is still evolving, and IBM has made its architecture open-ended with the intention of adding new services to this layer as needed.

The functions defined in this layer include session presentation services, which deal with data formatting considerations and the programming interface between the end user and the services layer. Transaction services define a framework for distributed transactions and special services such as document distribution. The layer also includes a services manager to manage services provided by the layer. Transaction services apply only to program-to-program communications.

1.6.7 End User (or Application)

This layer represents the user of the SNA network and, on the host end, customer-written business applications or other subsystems.

1.7 SNA DATA STRUCTURES

User data and headers used by various levels are shown in Fig. 1.14.

1.7.1 Request/Response Unit (RU)

RU is the official name for user data units flowing through an SNA network. More precisely, user data is a Request RU because it may request an end-to-end SNA response. Another form of RU contains SNA session level response and is called a Response RU. The third class of RUs contains SNA control information such as commands and network management data. The Control RUs are also Request RUs. The three information types are mutually exclusive, and a single RU may contain only one of the three. The RU field may even be absent in

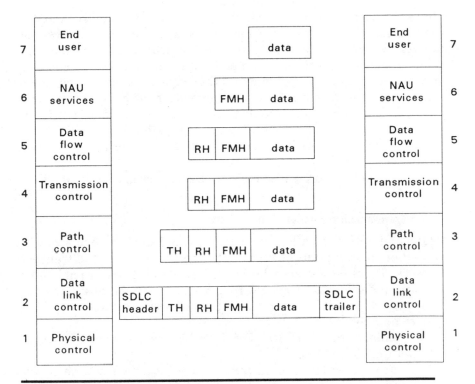

Figure 1.14 SNA layers and headers.

certain information units; for example, certain end-to-end positive responses may not contain any RUs.

1.7.2 Function Management Header (FMH)

This is an optional header and its use depends on the type of entities engaged in the session. For card-reader/printer–type terminals, this header is used to identify a specific component (card reader, printer, punch, or console) of the terminal. This header is also used in support of distributed transactions to coordinate their work.

1.7.3 Request/Response Header (RH)

In simple words, the purpose of the RH is to describe the RU that follows it. Bits in the RH indicate whether the RU is a user-data request, an SNA command, or a Response RU. Response RUs also contain sense data for error responses. Other details in the RH depend on the type of RU. For SNA commands, the RH also identifies the class of SNA command. For user-data RUs, RH has the data flow control layer protocol indicators such as the use of chaining. This header is also shared by the transmission control layer for protocols such as session level pacing. As we mentioned earlier, this aspect of SNA, two layers sharing a common header, is not desirable as it raises potential for changes in one layer affecting the design of another layer. We mentioned earlier that session sequence numbers management involves two layers, DFC and TC. However, these numbers are not carried in the RH—the header associated with the two layers. They are carried in the transmission header (see the following section), the header associated with the path control layer.

RH/RU combination is also called a Basic Information Unit (BIU).

1.7.4 Transmission Header (TH)

Associated with the path control layer, this header contains routing and other information to transport traffic and manage the transport network. TH also indicates whether the enclosed RU is a complete RU or only a part of a multisegment RU. A segment is the closest analogy to a "packet" in SNA. When supported, TH also contains the RU sequence number.

The combination of TH, RH, FMH, and RU is also known as a Path Information Unit (PIU).

PIUs are passed to the data link control layer by the path control layer for transmission over the link. The form in which PIUs are sent to the link control are called Basic Transmission Units (BTUs). A BTU may contain several PIUs blocked together. Maximum BTU size is constrained by the availability of buffers in the link level entity. Figure 1.15 shows the relationship between BIUs, PIUs, BTUs, and link level frames.

1.7.5 SDLC Header and Trailer

This header and trailer enclose a BTU and form an SDLC frame. The SDLC header contains link management, flow control, and frame sequence numbers. The link trailer contains error-checking information for the frame.

The physical control layer does not have any headers associated with it.

1.8 SNA VS. OSI LAYERS

Figure 1.16 shows OSI architecture, which also consists of seven layers similar to SNA. Although SNA and OSI appear similar at a high level, the two architectures are very different.

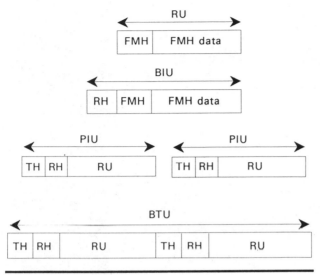

Figure 1.15   SNA BTU.

OSI uses X.25 packet interface for wide area network access. SNA has no exact equivalent of X.25 packets or packet level acknowledgments. Nor does SNA have any equivalent of X.25 permanent or switched virtual circuits. While CCITT and OSI do not define the internal architecture of the transport, the internal architecture forms a major part of SNA. The two architectures have completely different header, flow control, and command structures.

In terms of layer comparison, levels 1 and 2 in the two architectures define equivalent functions using similar protocols. As a matter of fact, level 2 protocol HDLC in OSI was adopted from SNA's SDLC.

Level 3 in both architectures provides similar functions but each architecture uses a different set of protocols. SNA also defines internal protocols for the backbone.

At level 4, in OSI terms, SNA is a connection-oriented network with an assumed reliable transport. SNA does not provide connectionless services and does not really have any layer that is equivalent to OSI level 4. Levels 4 and 5 in SNA contain functions that are mostly defined in OSI level 5. At level 6, presentation services in both architectures have the same intent but different protocols. SNA Transaction Services are closer to functions defined for the application layer in OSI. SNA's Service Transaction Programs (STPs), which provide transaction services, are very much like OSI applications such as FTAM and X.400. End users in SNA are nonarchitected entities except for the interface between a transaction program and NAU Ser-

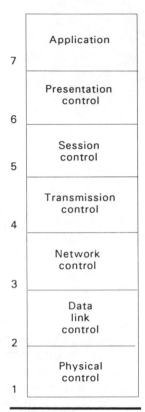

Figure 1.16   OSI layers.

vices, which is called the Advanced Program to Program Communications Applications Programming Interface (APPC API) and is similar to the OSI transaction program API.

1.9 SUMMARY

Corporate managements today have vastly different expectations from their information management organizations. Vendors have further raised these expectations by claiming capabilities or solutions that at best exist only in the marketing brochures. After about fifteen years of "let us do it, patch it, scrap it, do it again...," the age of ad hoc systems seems to be finally ending. Given the complexity of networks and services to be provided, both customers and vendors have to have a strategic plan—whether buying or designing systems. All major vendors at least claim some sort of uniform architecture across their product line. Given the dominance of IBM in the mainframe business,

SNA should maintain its preeminence in the foreseeable future. SNA may not be the most elegant architecture, but it certainly is the most complete from an implementation point of view. The layers and headers, presented briefly here, represent an architect's view of the network. For practicing professionals that is not necessarily the most helpful view. In the following chapters we also look at more pragmatic issues as we add to our details of SNA.

SNA Logical Structure

2.1 INTRODUCTION

In this chapter we investigate further the nature of origination and destination points in SNA—entities that provide end-user interface, control functions, and "domains" of control. We also look at the addressing scheme in SNA and, finally, we take a high-level look at multiple-host networks. But we do so from an architect's point of view. To an architect, tangible entities become abstractions. A terminal is no longer a terminal, a controller no longer a controller. Each is treated as an entity representing a set of functions and services.

For an architect it is not necessary, in fact it is undesirable, to specify whether a set of functions should be implemented in hardware or software or some specific combination thereof. Thus, as technology changes, e.g., a terminal is replaced by an intelligent PC, the architecture does not and should not change.

The problem that an architect runs into is one of terminology: what to call these abstract models. Since they may not always represent access methods, front ends, or terminals, etc., we do not want to use these product-oriented names. So an architect invents broader names that reflect the intent of functions rather than imply specific products.

SNA is not unique in coining its own terms to refer to architected entities. The problem is the choice of terms—SNA uses terms that have long-standing, other meanings associated with them—terms such as *physical and logical entities* or *virtual routes*. As we introduce SNA terms, the reader has to be careful not to assume similarities between SNA terms and words in the English language or in data communications.

2.2 NETWORK ADDRESSABLE UNITS (NAUs) AND PATH CONTROL NETWORK

Entities that can originate or receive messages (RUs) are called Network Addressable Units in SNA. All origination and destination points must be assigned unique addresses and therefore the name NAU.

NAUs represent the outermost boundaries of SNA. As shown in Fig. 2.1, end users, such as host applications or terminal operators, access SNA services via the NAUs that assist them in setting up sessions. Certain other NAUs are responsible for managing other NAUs attached to them. NAUs reside in SNA nodes and the nodes are connected with each other via the transport network which, in the case of SNA, is called the *path control network*. The path control "network" consists of the path control layer plus all the layers below it, i.e., PC, DLC, and physical control layers. (We may use the word *network* with any layer name to refer collectively to a given layer plus all other lay-

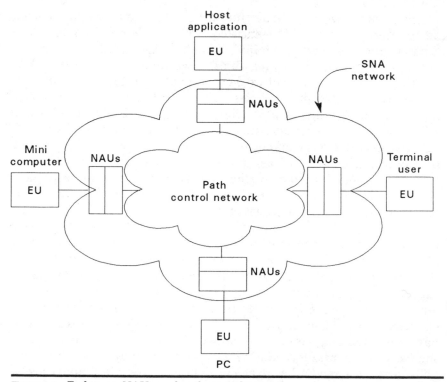

Figure 2.1   End users, NAUs, and path control network.

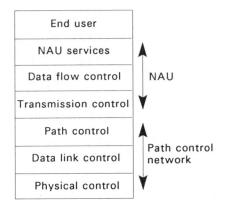

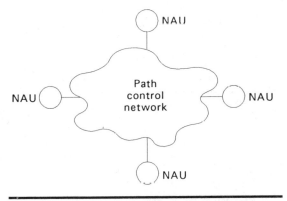

Figure 2.2 NAUs, path control network, and SNA layers.

ers below it. DFC network, for example, consists of DFC, TC, PC, DLC, and physical layers.)

As shown in Fig. 2.2 we can now define an SNA network as a set of NAUs interconnected by a path control network. Figure 2.2 shows the relationship among NAUs, path control network, and SNA layers.

2.3 NAU TYPES

There is a vast range of devices that send or receive data on a network. As shown in Fig. 2.3a, examples include host applications, access methods, FEPs, cluster controllers, and terminals. The NAU is a broad term that includes all of these. To clarify the specific role of an NAU, divide them into three classes:

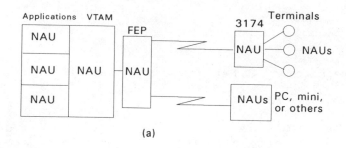

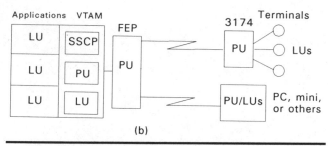

Figure 2.3   (a) NAUs in a network; (b) NAU types.

Logical Units (LU)

Physical Units (PU)

System Services Control Point (SSCP)

Figures 2.3a and 2.3b show NAUs and NAU types in a network.

2.3.1   Logical Unit

This NAU type is used by end users to access SNA services. Therefore, LUs are also described as "ports" or "windows" into the SNA network. For a terminal user, the LU functions are provided by microcode or software in the terminal. On a minicomputer, an LU may be software that sets up communications between local programs and other network users.

As shown in Fig. 2.4, in the host machine the end users are the application programs, and LU functions are provided by a TP monitor such as CICS. An organization that does not use TP monitors would have to write (or acquire) its own software to provide LU functions for host applications. Subsystems such as TSO and JES also represent LUs in a host. From an implementation point of view, any software

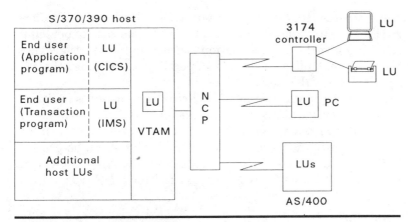

Figure 2.4   Logical Units and selected products.

that interfaces directly with VTAM represents a host LU to VTAM. In addition, VTAM also contains an LU within itself.

Logical Units also represent a wide variety of capabilities—from a dumb typewriter-style terminal to a major subsystem such as CICS with PCs and minicomputers in the middle. To allow various degrees of intelligence in LUs, they are divided into various classes. Currently, major LU types are 0, 1, 2, 3, and 6.2. If the progression of numbers seems strange—it is, because LU classification has evolved in a trial and error manner, and some categories were never announced and others have been retired since their announcement.

Qualitatively speaking, we can associate LU types with generic products. LU Type 0 is a general-purpose, catch-all category that is allowed to use any combination of LU protocols. LU Types 1 and 3 represent batch-type terminals such as card readers and printers. Type 2 LUs are associated with interactive devices such as keyboard-display units. LU 6.2, also known as the Advanced Program to Program Communication (APPC), is the most advanced LU and is associated with software-based systems. On a mainframe, LU 6.2 is available through CICS and VTAM. IBM and a number of other vendors provide LU 6.2 software for minicomputers and PCs.

In the case of the IBM 3270 family, the location of LU functions may or may not be in the display station, depending on the hardware model. Even though SNA documentation (and this book) always associates LU functions with a display station, the actual microcode for LU functions is in the cluster controller for 3278-type display stations. These terminals are referred to as the Control Unit Terminals (CUTs). The more intelligent display stations such as the IBM 3291 provide

LU functions within the display station. These display stations are called Distributed Function Terminals (DFTs). In the case of personal computers running with 3270 Emulation Cards, the LU functions may be in the cluster controller or the PC, depending on whether the PC emulates a CUT or a DFT device.

A mainframe subsystem such as CICS actually represents multiple LU Types. When communicating with a display station, it acts as an LU Type 2 and at the same time acts as LU Type 1 or 3 with a printer and as LU 6.2 on a session with another CICS system. To be precise we should use the term *LU-LU session types*, not *LU types*. However, we follow the precedent set by IBM and use the term *LU types*.

2.3.2 Physical Units

This class of NAUs have no direct interface with the end users and represent network management, and control functions in a node.

A Physical Unit represents a distributed control element in a network and manages and controls resources directly attached to it. As shown in Fig. 2.5, each LU in an SNA network is attached to a PU that manages and controls it.

The term *node* is used specifically to describe a network component that provides Physical Unit functions. A cluster controller node, for example, manages and controls attached LUs (display stations and printers). Another important function of a PU is to provide a directory of locally resident NAUs.

An FEP represents a more significant Physical Unit function—it manages and controls attached lines, cluster controllers, and terminals. It should be pointed out that lines too are assigned unique addresses in SNA for identification purposes but are not considered NAUs because lines do not originate or receive messages.

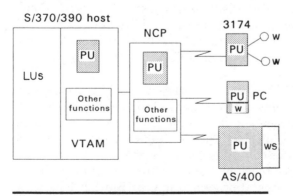

Figure 2.5 Physical Units and selected products.

There is also a Physical Unit in the host to manage SNA resources in the host. The host PU provides the global directory for the network and is also responsible for managing locally attached resources. In a multihost network, each host has its own directory.

It is important to note that the term *Physical Unit* does *not* represent a physical or tangible component; but rather a list of functions. Wherever these functions are performed in an SNA network, therein lies a Physical Unit. The host PU, for example, is a set of routines within VTAM in addition to other SNA and non-SNA functions of VTAM.

For stand-alone terminals such as the IBM 3767 or a PC with a 3270 Emulation Card there is no cluster controller. In these cases both the PU and LU functions are included within the software or microcode in the terminal. For CUT devices, described in the previous section, both PU and LU functions are in the cluster controller. However, in all cases, functionally and for addressing purposes, PUs and LUs are considered distinct entities.

Physical Units are divided into five categories: Types 1, 2, 2.1, 4, and 5. PU Type 5 is represented by the host PU that resides in VTAM. PU Type 4 is represented by the NCP in the front end. PU Types 1, 2, and 2.1 are associated with network stations. IBM 3174 Cluster Controller is a PU Type 2. In the case of network devices such as the 3174 we should also point out that the cluster controller includes more than its PU functions. At a minimum it would also include link control (such as SDLC) and other functions associated with SNA layers 1 through 3. These lower-level functions are distinct from the PU functions in the controller. For that reason, a cluster controller is assigned two addresses: One is a link level address, which is transparent to the PU, and the other is the PU level address, which is transparent to the data link control.

Certain IBM documents refer to Type 2 PU as cluster controller nodes and Type 1 as terminal nodes—which is unfortunate since Type 1 PUs have also been implemented in cluster controllers (e.g., IBM 3271, models 11 and 12) and Type 2 PUs in nonclustered nodes (e.g., IBM 3770). In any case, PU Type 1 is now obsolete and irrelevant in practical terms.

PU 2.1 is a relatively new enhancement to SNA and is required to support certain LU 6.2 functions. It is discussed in more detail later in the book.

That leaves us with the question of PU Type 3. As far as IBM documentation is concerned, there is not even an acknowledgment of a missing number in the PU classification sequence. In the early days of SNA, PU Type 3 was a topic of much speculation, but nothing came of it and no such PU is expected to be announced.

The terms SNA *node type* and *PU type* are used synonymously, e.g., T2 node refers to a PU Type 2.

2.3.3 System Services Control Point

System Services Control Point (SSCP) is responsible for the overall management and control of the network and sessions. In addition to the Type 5 PU, the SSCP functions, too, are implemented in VTAM. (TCAM, too, can provide SSCP functions, but not the complete set of functions provided by VTAM. In the rest of this book we would consider only VTAM as the SNA access method and often use VTAM, SSCP, and access method as interchangeable terms.) The SSCP performs its functions through the cooperation of the Physical Units in the network. For example, an SSCP does not directly activate a line—it sends an activation command to the NCP to which the line is attached, and it is the NCP that activates the line.

SSCP is the most important of the NAUs, and its placement in the host is what gives SNA its strong host dependence and orientation. Some of the functions performed by the SSCP include:

Activating or deactivating network resources

Processing logon (session) requests

Receiving all network management information from various PUs

Executing control operator commands

Network management applications such as NetView do not receive their network management information directly from the network. All information goes to the SSCP (VTAM) first, and it is the SSCP that forwards this information to NetView. Similarly, all NetView operator commands for network control and surveillance are forwarded to the SSCP, which actually executes them.

2.3.4 SSCP and Domains

In a multihost network there are multiple SSCPs, one per VTAM. To allow for systematic control and management of the network, each SSCP is assigned a "domain" for which it is responsible. An SSCP "owns" all FEPs, lines, controllers, terminals, and host subsystems in its domain. Channel-attached or local devices are always owned by the host to which they are attached. A network with a single host is, of course, called a single-domain network, and in this case a single VTAM owns everything in the network. Figure 2.6 shows a three-domain network.

In the figure, VTAM-1 owns NCP1, VTAM-2 owns NCP2, and

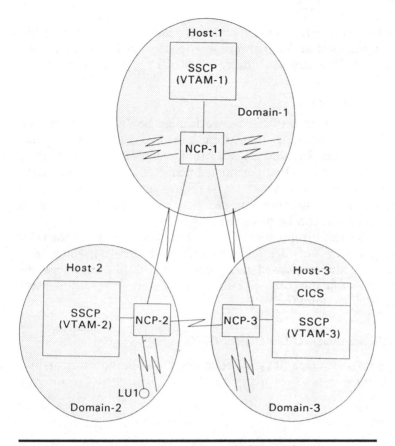

Figure 2.6   System Services Control Point (SSCP) and domains.

VTAM-3 owns NCP3. In this example we assume that all resources attached to an NCP are owned by the VTAM that owns the NCP even though SNA does permit resources attached to an NCP to be owned by an SSCP other than the one that owns the NCP. Leased lines and FEPs can have multiple concurrent owners. For resources in its domain, only the owning VTAM can:

   Activate or deactivate a resource

   Retrieve and display status of a resource

   Receive alarms and management information from them

   Process all logon (session) requests

Ownership, however, does not place any constraints on who can log onto whom. For example, LU 1 in the VTAM-2 domain can log onto

CICS in Host-3; such a logon is called a *cross-domain logon*. A number of additional protocols and definitions are needed for cross-domain sessions. Chapter 9 discusses multidomain operations in more detail.

2.3.5 Subarea Numbers

Each SSCP and NCP in an SNA network must be assigned a unique number called its subarea number; thus, the hosts and NCPs are also called subarea nodes. In contrast, all other terminals, clusters, PCs, minicomputers, etc. are called peripheral nodes. In a multiple-domain network, the subarea numbers must be unique across all domains. In Fig. 2.6, if we assign subarea number 4 to NCP2, no other NCP or SSCP in any domain can be assigned this number.

The reason for the uniqueness of the subarea numbers is that they are used to generate network addresses for NAUs and for routing in SNA. Duplicate subarea numbers would cause duplicate addresses and ambiguous routing tables. Subareas do not represent control boundaries such as domains.

2.4 SUBAREAS AND NAU ADDRESSING

An NAU address consists of two components, a subarea number and an element number, as shown in Fig. 2.7. We can draw an analogy

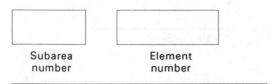

Subarea   Element
number   number

Figure 2.7 SNA addressing: subareas and elements.

between an area code in a telephone number and the subarea number, with the element number being somewhat similar to the last seven digits in the North American telephone number. The subarea numbers are unique across the totality of an SNA network, and the element numbers are unique within a subarea. The subarea numbers are assigned by a system programmer during system generation. Each SSCP and NCP assigns element numbers to NAUs in its subarea. SSCP assigns element number 1 to itself and 0 to the host PU.

The NCP system generation process assigns element numbers to the Physical and Logical Units attached to it, based on the order of definitions in the NCP system generation tables. Even though lines are

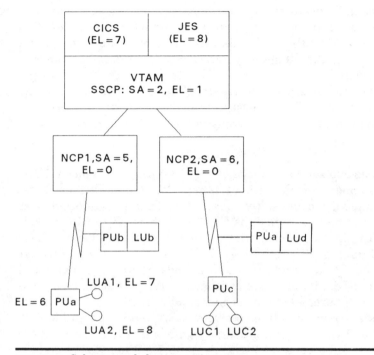

Figure 2.8 Subareas and element assignments.

not NAUs, they too are assigned element numbers for identification purposes. The NCP PU itself is assigned element number 0.

Figure 2.8 shows a network with two NCPs attached to a host. The host subarea number is 2 and the two NCPs are subareas 5 and 6. As in this example, the subarea assignments do not have to be sequential. We have two LUs in the host, CICS and JES (job entry subsystem). The example assumes that VTAM assigned element number 7 to CICS, and 8 to JES. Other element numbers may have been assigned to other subsystems not shown in the example.

Also shown are assumed element numbers for PUs and LUs for various NAUs attached to each NCP. In this case we represent the SNA address for CICS as (2,7), where 2 is the subarea number and 7 is the element number.

2.4.1   Addressing, Peripheral Nodes, and Boundary Nodes

Peripheral nodes do not understand the subarea-element form of addressing. Physical Units and Logical Units work with their own local addresses. For example, in the case of an IBM 3270 Cluster Controller, each device attached to the controller is assigned a one-byte hexadecimal number as its address as a part of the 3X74 (3274 or 3174) controller configuration definitions. Local addresses do not necessarily match the element number in the associated subarea-element address. Therefore, when SNA traffic is delivered to peripheral nodes, the address is in the local address form and not the subarea-element form. To understand how these addresses are converted between local IDs and subarea-element form, we need to define the term *boundary node*.

Boundary nodes and address translation. A *boundary node* for an NAU is the subarea node to which it is attached. For channel-attached stations, the boundary node is the host. For stations connected over SDLC links, the boundary node is the NCP where the SDLC link is terminated. In Fig. 2.8, the boundary node for PUa and PUb and their LUs is NCP1, and for PUc and PUd it is NCP2. The link that attaches a peripheral node to a boundary node is called a route extension. Local addresses are used only on route extensions. Traffic between subarea nodes uses the subarea-element format of addressing.

Let us look at communications between LUA1 and CICS in Fig. 2.8. Assuming that LUA1 has an element number of 7, its proper NAU address will be subarea 5, element 7—or (5,7). When CICS gives a message to VTAM for LUA1, VTAM will attach a transmission header (TH) that will show the destination as (5,7) and pass it to NCP1. NCP1 will look at the destination subarea number, 5 in this case, and recognize that the message is for one of the NAUs in its subareas; i.e., NCP1 is the boundary node. NCP1 will now do a table lookup to translate this address into a link station ID for the controller and a local LUID for LUA1, and send the message on the route extension. Conversely, the boundary node will also convert the origination address of LUa for the host-bound traffic from its local ID to subarea-element format.

2.4.2 Network Address Format

So far we have discussed the contents of a network address. Now let us look at its format and size. Three formats for network addresses have evolved from the original 16-bit address shown at the top of Fig. 2.9. In all three formats, the address consists of two components, the subarea number and the element number. In the 16-bit format, which has since been phased out, the number of bits allocated to each component was a decision made by the system programmer based on the highest subarea number that would be used in the network. If the

Boundary fixed by system programmer

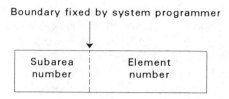

(a) Original SNA addressing, 16 bit format

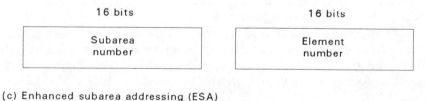

(b) Enhanced network addressing (ENA)

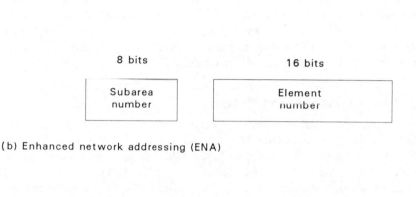

(c) Enhanced subarea addressing (ESA)

Figure 2.9 SNA addressing formats.

highest subarea number used was 12, 4 bits would be allocated for subarea number and 12 bits for elements. In this case the highest subarea number could actually be 15, and for each subarea we could support up to 4095 elements. All SSCPs and NCPs in an SNA network had to use the same subarea-element structure to interpret addresses generated by each other. By increasing the bits for subarea addressing, we could accommodate a higher number of hosts and NCPs in the network, but at the expense of the number of terminals that could be supported by each FEP. If the bit structure needed to be adjusted, it was changed in all subarea nodes in the network at the same time.

This addressing format was found deficient by a number of users with large networks, for whom SNA just ran out of addressing capacity—a much-discussed topic in the early days of SNA. In 1984, IBM announced an expanded network address format as Enhanced Network Addressing (ENA). The ENA format with 16-bit addressing is shown in Fig. 2.9*b*. With ENA, the size of subarea and element fields is constant and fixed at 8 and 16 bits, respectively, and the implementors no longer have to plan where to fix the subarea-element boundary. With ENA, we can support a maximum of 255 hosts and NCPs with 65,536 elements in each subarea. This range should be able to accommodate most private networks. In any case, as of 1988 even this range was extended to 65,536 subareas as shown in Fig. 2.9*c*. If one should exhaust even this addressing capacity, SNA can support still larger networks using the SNA-SNA gateway. This feature is described in more detail in Chap. 11.

2.4.3 NAU Address Type and TH Type

The element part of a subarea-element address, used by subarea nodes, can change as new devices are added, deleted, or moved in an FEP configuration. Having two-level addressing, subarea-element and local IDs, makes it possible for the local IDs to remain the same even as element numbers change. This alleviates the need to reconfigure microcode (or software) in each station any time changes occur in the NCP or VTAM configuration.

This two-level addressing also impacts the structure of the transmission header, TH, which carries these addresses. We need a bigger TH for carrying the full subarea-element address. This bigger TH is known as format ID 4 TH or, written in short, as FID 4 TH. Other types of THs include FID 0, FID 1, FID 2, FID 3, and FID F. FID type and TH type are synonymous terms. FIDs 0, 1, and 3 are being phased out, and FID F is a special-purpose FID. For practical purposes, we need deal only with FID 4 and FID 2 TH, which are used as follows:

1. FID 4 TH carries full subarea-element addresses and is used between subarea nodes (VTAM to NCP, NCP to NCP). In other words, FID 4 is used within the transport networks.

2. FID 2 TH carries addresses in the local ID form and is used between a subarea node and peripheral devices.

2.5 SNA SESSIONS

When two NAUs are communicating with each other, they are said to be in a session. Setting up a session requires an exchange of handshakes, permissions, and verification that the two NAUs are capable of understanding each other (i.e., that they support the same subset of

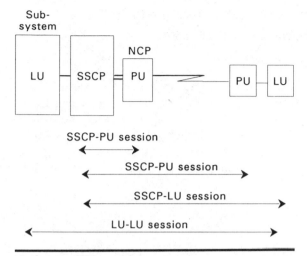

Figure 2.10 SNA sessions.

SNA protocols). SNA sessions are classified by the types of NAUs involved in a session.

Figure 2.10 shows a simple network with various types of sessions. For a multihost network there will be additional sessions between SSCPs, which are discussed later in Sec. 2.7 on multidomain operations.

2.5.1 SSCP Sessions

When SSCP (VTAM) activates an NAU, it is said to have set up a session with the NAU. SSCP sessions are set up predominantly at the network startup. For those resources that are not activated at startup, the SSCP session can be set up later by using the ACTIVATE command from the network control station. These sessions, once established, stay active for as long as the network stays up. One reason for the loss of an SSCP session can be a network or device malfunction, e.g., turning the power off on a terminal or a controller, or an NCP failure. The session can be recovered by reactivating, if possible, the failing resource. A resource that is not in session with the SSCP, i.e., has not been activated, cannot use the network.

Some of the activities that occur during activation of a resource include establishment of a route to the resource being activated and verification that the device is "willing and able." There is a hierarchical order in which SSCP sessions occur, e.g., a cluster controller must be activated before terminals attached to it can be activated. A complete hierarchy for activating a terminal would include:

SSCP-PU session with each NCP in the route to the LU

SSCP-PU session with the peripheral node

SSCP-LU session with the terminal

In Fig. 2.11, VTAM (SSCP) first sets up an SSCP-PU session with the NCP. Next, the link connecting the NCP with the peripheral PU is activated. Activation of a link is not called a session since the link is not an NAU. Following the link and PU activation, each LU is activated individually. Each of these activations requires exchange of one or more SNA commands and corresponding responses. In a large net-

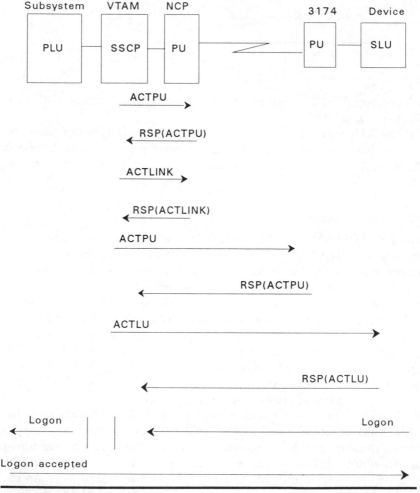

Figure 2.11 Simplified SNA activation sequence.

work that can mean a long startup time (as much as 20–30 minutes with a few thousand terminals). In any case, due to the internal processing structure of VTAM, it is not desirable to activate a very large number of resources at the same time.

Finally, our diagram does not show an SSCP-LU session between host LUs and the SSCP. Functionally, a handshake does occur between the host LU and the SSCP. However, this handshake does not use the same SNA command sequence that is used to set up an SSCP-LU session with a network LU. The session establishment between host LUs and SSCP is initiated by the host LU, not by the SSCP.

2.5.2 LU-LU Sessions

In its most common form, an LU-LU session is a user logon to a host application, where the host application is a subsystem such as CICS, IMS, TSO, or JES, etc., or a customer-written or non-IBM VTAM application (a VTAM application is any software that interfaces with VTAM using a VTAM application program interface). While SSCP sessions represent management and control functions, LU-LU sessions represent application work. Only after an SSCP-LU session has been established with a terminal can a terminal user request an application logon. A terminal user has no awareness of the SSCP-LU session, and no action is required on his or her part to get this session started. Activation of an LU is totally controlled by VTAM (SSCP) or the control station operator.

Earlier in this chapter we had mentioned that LUs are divided into various categories. Only alike LUs can participate in a session. During logon processing, the host subsystem (LU) would verify whether or not it is capable of communicating with the network LU. If the host application finds itself incompatible with the network LU, it will reject the session (logon) request (see BIND processing in Sec. 2.6). In practice, though, this should never happen since no one would knowingly install terminals in a network that are incompatible with the host applications. However, in new networks or after network reconfigurations, it is not unusual to see session setup failures due to incorrect LU definitions or mismatch of definitions with terminal types. On the network side, the LU protocols are handled by the device microcode or software and are transparent to the person using the terminal.

Primary and Secondary LUs (PLU and SLU).   During each LU-LU session one of the two LUs must play the role of a Primary LU (PLU) and the other that of a Secondary LU (SLU). The terms *PLU* and *SLU* have a meaning within a session and the roles hold for the duration of the session. Certain SNA protocols for LU-LU sessions apply differently for Primary and Secondary LUs. Ignoring LU 6.2 for a moment, the differences between Primary and Secondary LUs are discussed in the following paragraphs.

The Primary LU always resides in the host and a network device is always an SLU. A host LU can also act as a secondary but only when in session with another host LU which is acting as a primary for that session.

A Primary LU can support multiple concurrent sessions, whereas a Secondary LU can have only one LU-LU session at any given time. In practical terms that means that a subsystem such as CICS can have a large number of users logged on to it at any given time but we can communicate with only one application at a time from a display station or a printer. For simple stations one session at a time is not an unreasonable restriction. Multiple programs cannot use the same printer at the same time, anyway. Similarly, a terminal user cannot have a dialogue with more than one application simultaneously using the same display screen. However, if we have a display station with "windowing" capability, a user could communicate with multiple applications concurrently if only we could get around the single-session limit.

A number of products are available that make it possible to support multiple concurrent sessions from a single display station, essentially by appearing to VTAM as multiple LUs on behalf of a single terminal. The IBM 3174 provides this function through its Multiple Logical Terminal (MLT) feature. PCs acting as DFT devices can also emulate multiple LUs to support multiple concurrent sessions. In addition there are host-based software packages that simulate multiple LUs on behalf of network display stations to allow them multiple concurrent sessions. In a larger sense, the Secondary LU session limit also presents a problem for distributed processing environments where an SLU may be a multitasking minicomputer or a personal computer. These machines are too powerful to be wasted as single-session-at-a-time LUs. With LU 6.2, intended to support these intelligent machines, SLUs are no longer restricted to only one session at a time. LU 6.2 is discussed in more detail in Chaps. 12 and 13.

2.6 SNA SESSION ACTIVATION COMMANDS

Setting up an SNA session requires an exchange of SNA commands and responses between VTAM and the resource being activated. Figure 2.11 shows a simplified exchange of these commands and responses. The figure does not show all commands as our objective is to develop a high-level understanding only. Chapter 7 contains a comprehensive discussion of these exchanges.

Once VTAM starts running in the host, its SSCP component initiates an activation sequence due to one of two reasons. Either the resource has been marked in the system generation tables for automatic activation at startup, or the control operator has entered an ACTI-VATE command for that resource. Irrespective of the mode of activation, the command sequence stays the same. For activating an NCP, the SSCP would exchange identification with the NCP and then send an activate PU (ACTPU) command over the I/O channel to the NCP. If the NCP software is operating properly, it will respond with a positive response to indicate to the SSCP that it is operational. At this time the establishment of the SSCP-PU session with the NCP is complete.

A link is activated by the activate link (ACTLINK) command. This command is needed once per line. Upon receiving the command, the NCP activates the link and informs the SSCP by sending a positive response to the ACTLINK command.

Following the activation of a link, the SSCP sends the ACTPU command to the PU in the network station (SDLC initialization is completed before sending ACTPU). The ACTPU command is sent individually to each PU. The receiving PU responds to ACTPU with a positive response to confirm its readiness. Following that, the SSCP sends one activate LU (ACTLU) command per LU. The LU receives the ACTLU command, verifies its own readiness for use, and sends an appropriate response to the SSCP.

At this time our activations are complete and users can submit logons from active Logical Units. As a part of the logon message, the user identifies the host LU (subsystem) that he or she wants to log onto. The SSCP passes the logon request to the identified Primary LU (provided that the PLU is running at the time. If the PLU were not running, VTAM could not start it and the logon would fail). The host LU at this time has the choice of verifying the LU type of the terminal where the logon originated. When a terminal user submits a logon to a host subsystem, transparent to the user, VTAM would provide the profile of the LU implemented in the terminal to the host LU. If the host LU finds that it cannot support a session with this LU type, it will reject the logon. If the session can be supported, the PLU will issue a BIND command to the SLU indicating that it is binding or accepting the session request. The microcode or software in the SLU sends a positive response to the BIND command to acknowledge a successful LU-LU session establishment. It is during the BIND command-response exchange that the PLU and SLU agree on the protocols to be supported during the session.

2.7 MULTIDOMAIN NETWORK

Multidomain networks are called multiple systems networking (MSN) in SNA. As discussed in Sec. 2.3.4, in the MSN environment each SSCP is responsible for activating and controlling all of its own re-

sources and for routing an LU-LU session request to another SSCP if
the session involves a Logical Unit in another domain. Sessions between LUs in different domains are called cross-domain sessions.

Figure 2.12 shows a two-domain network. The dotted vertical line in
the middle shows the domain boundary. Domain A is owned by
VTAM-A, subarea number 2; and domain B is owned by VTAM-B,
subarea number 3. In this example, we have a logon request from
LUA in domain A for CICS which resides in domain B. When this request arrives at VTAM-A, it will discover, via a table lookup, that

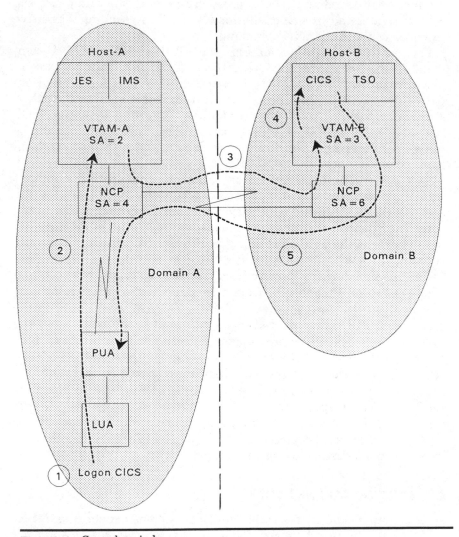

Figure 2.12   Cross-domain logon.

CICS is a cross-domain LU residing in domain B. VTAM-A will route this logon request to VTAM-B. VTAM-B will submit this request to CICS. To the Primary Logical Unit, CICS, it is irrelevant where the logon request originated. The PLU will process this logon as any other intradomain logon. After CICS accepts the logon, the session traffic does not have to flow through host A. Actually owning VTAM plays no role after the session has been established—so much so that an LUA to CICS session can continue even if the host A goes down.

2.8 SUMMARY

We covered extensive SNA terminology in this chapter. The concepts of Network Addressable Units, path control network, SSCP, PU, and LU are fundamental to the understanding of SNA. Many of these functions do not map into products cleanly.

We also introduced the concept of the domain of control associated with an SSCP and how sessions must be established with the controlling SSCP before LU-LU sessions can be established. VTAMs (hosts) and NCPs (FEPs) are assigned unique subarea nodes and are called subarea nodes. In contrast, all other devices in the network are called peripheral nodes. SNA addresses consist of a subarea number and an element number. Finally, we also looked at a cross-domain logon.

Transport Architecture in SNA

Physical Control and Synchronous Data Link Control (SDLC)

3.1 INTRODUCTION

Physical control ensures that a physical transmission medium is available and transmits (receives) data on the medium in a serial, one-bit-at-a-time, manner. SDLC, one level above the physical control, provides logical procedures for controlling the link and recovering from link level errors.

3.2 PHYSICAL CONTROL

The physical control layer provides specifications for DTE to modem (or Digital Service Unit) interface. SNA accepts existing standards, such as EIA RS232, CCITT's V.24, and X.21, etc., for this layer. A brief description of selected EIA RS232 procedures was provided earlier in Chap. 1. There are a number of well-written references available on various standards and modems. The physical control layer is not discussed any further in this book.

As we leave the topic of modems, we would like to mention IBM's microprocessor-based diagnostic modem series 36XX, 56XX, and 76XX. Functions implemented in the host, NCP, and the modems to provide these diagnostic services are collectively known as the Link Problem Determination Aid (LPDA) where the current level of functionality is called release 2 or LPDA-2. Protocols used for LPDA functions are IBM proprietary and not defined by SNA. The IBM diagnostic modems do not establish any sessions with the SSCP. Modems report their management data to the NCP to which they are attached using special SDLC frames, and the NCP forwards this information to the host where it can be forwarded to network management applications such as NetView for recording or further analysis.

3.3 FUNCTIONS OF A LINK CONTROL PROTOCOL

Before discussing SDLC specifically, it would be helpful to develop an appreciation for the functions of a link protocol in general. Broadly speaking, the functions of a link protocol can be divided into four categories as follows.

3.3.1 Synchronization

This process allows a machine on the link to assemble bits received into complete messages. The most basic level of synchronization is the bit level synchronization. Bit synchronization procedures enable sending and receiving machines to keep their bit clocks in synchronization (the clock may be provided by the modem or the terminal). The two clocks must not only run at the same speed but also be in proper phase to capture all the bits on the line. Different link protocols use different procedures for obtaining bit level synchronization. Sampling at correct speed but incorrect phase can cause loss of bits as shown in Fig. 3.1.

Link protocols prior to SDLC, such as asynchronous and Binary Synchronous Communications (BSC), were character oriented; i.e., they had to assemble bits into characters and interpret the characters to perform link control functions. Character assembly requires character level synchronization so that the receiving link control can delineate a continuous bit stream into individual characters.

BSC protocol, for example, uses control characters PADs and SYNs to obtain bit and character level synchronizations. These additional

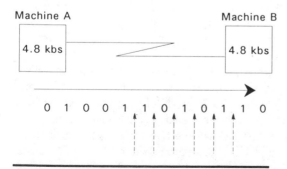

Figure 3.1 Bit level synchronization. Bit loss with correct clock speed but out of phase oscillators. Dotted arrows show bit sampling at correct speed but improper phase.

control characters have to be stripped from a transmission to assemble a message in its original form.

Additionally, to reduce the probability of transmission errors, protocols divide long messages into multiple blocks and transmit each block individually. In some protocols, e.g., BSC, the receiving link control may assemble message blocks into a complete message before processing them or passing them to application programs. In such cases we also need block assembly (synchronization) procedures.

3.3.2 Link Level Error Recovery

The error-handling procedures allow the link protocol to recover from transient transmission errors. The objective of link level error recovery is to provide the appearance of an error-free link to higher levels. A common scheme for recovering from transmission errors is for the transmitting station to attach a parity or check field to the bit stream being transmitted. The algorithms for computing the check field ensure that it is a unique value for the bit stream being transmitted.

The receiving station computes its own check field independently as it receives the bit pattern and compares it with the check field received with the message. If the two check fields do not match, it is assumed that the bit pattern got altered during its passage over the link and has errors in it. The check mechanisms typically used are the *longitudinal redundancy check* (LRC) or *cyclical redundancy check* (CRC) and permit only the discovery of an error but do not pinpoint a specific bit or bits in error, nor do they provide error correction capability. For recovery from a transmission error, the receiver requests a retransmission of the block or blocks in error.

Figure 3.2 illustrates this process. Depending on the specific protocol in use, multiple blocks (or frames) may have to be transmitted for recovery.

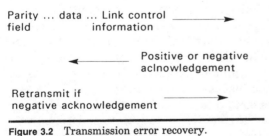

Figure 3.2 Transmission error recovery.

3.3.3 Controlling Multipoint Links

As mentioned in Sec. 1.2.3, procedures are also required for controlling multipoint links. To uniquely identify each station on the link, we need an addressing scheme. These addresses are level 2 (DLC) addresses and are meaningful on a given link only. As information is transmitted by the FEP, each station on the link compares the destination address in the message with its own. The station with the matching ID assembles the message bit stream, and others ignore it. When transmitting to the FEP, the link station puts its own address in the message.

3.3.4 Half-Duplex Management

For half-duplex links, procedures must be provided to ensure proper send and receive states for link stations. This is achieved by designating the front end as the primary or the control station and other stations as secondaries. A secondary station enters a send state only when explicitly invited (polled) to do so. The secondary station goes back to the receive state after it has transmitted all of its frames. The FEP is responsible for ensuring that each secondary station on the link gets a fair amount of service.

Polling is also necessary for managing multipoint lines even when they are full duplex to ensure that multiple secondary stations do not start sending data at the same time.

3.4 ASYNCHRONOUS OR START/STOP PROTOCOL

This is the earliest of the link protocols in data communications, and, surprisingly, it is still in extensive use—especially outside the IBM world.

The word *asynchronous* comes from the fact that there is no master synchronization clock on the link and each station provides its own clock. It does *not* mean that synchronization at bit or higher levels is not necessary. Each character is transmitted individually with its own synchronization control and parity. When no characters are being transmitted there is a constant idle, or stop, signal on the line. As a station prepares to transmit bits in a character, it signals the other station by sending a start signal preceding the data bits. The receiving station, upon seeing a stop-to-start transition, starts its clock and assembles bits from the line at the agreed clock rate. Bit assembly is stopped when the next stop signal is observed on the line. Bits received between start and stop bits form a character.

Architecturally, asynchronous protocols can accommodate any number of bits in a character. ASCII code with 7 data bits and 1 parity bit is the most common character size. Stop-to-start transition provides bit and character level synchronization. The end of a complete message is indicated by a *carriage return* (CR), *line feed* (LF), or implementation-chosen control character.

Parity information is a 1-bit field with each character and can be set to provide no parity information or an even or odd number of bits set to 1 in a character. This primitive scheme works only if an odd number of bits get altered in a character due to transmission errors. In asynchronous protocols, generally, there is no acknowledgment or recovery when an error is detected. IBM does not support asynchronous stations in a multipoint configuration; thus, no link level addressing is necessary.

Finally, asynchronous stations are supported only on switched lines in IBM systems. Asynchronous link protocols are not supported under SNA and require protocol conversion to access SNA networks.

3.5 BINARY SYNCHRONOUS COMMUNICATIONS (BSC)

Before SNA, BSC was the most common link protocol in the world of IBM. It uses control characters for bit, character, and message level synchronization. The character code used is 8-bit EBCDIC to give a character set of 256 characters. Transmissions are in a block mode instead of one character at a time. The protocol also provides a block check field and an acknowledgment mechanism so that blocks with errors can be retransmitted. Multipoint operations are also supported.

Figure 3.3 shows a typical BSC exchange. To provide bit level synchronization, one or more PAD characters can be used ahead of the user data stream. By observing signal variations on the line provided by the PAD characters, the receiving station can bring its clock in synch with the bit stream. *Synchronous characters* (SYN) are provided to assist in identifying 8-bit characters (for character level synchronization). To delineate text characters from control characters such as PAD or SYN, the text is preceded by the *start-of-text* (STX) control character. Certain BSC functions require the use of a BSC header and, when used, its presence is indicated by the *start-of-header* (SOH) character preceding the header.

To reduce the probability of transmission errors, long messages are divided into multiple blocks. The most common block size in BSC is 256 characters. A small message not requiring blocking is enclosed between an STX and the *end-of-text* (ETX) character. For a long message, all blocks except the last one are terminated by *end of text block* (ETB) instead of ETX, and the last block carries an ETX indicating the end of a complete message. There is no block level sequence numbering to protect against lost blocks. Figure 3.3*a* shows a single block message and Fig. 3.3*b* shows a message being transmitted as three blocks.

Also, as shown in Fig. 3.3, each block of data is explicitly acknowledged before the next block can be transmitted. In BSC there is never

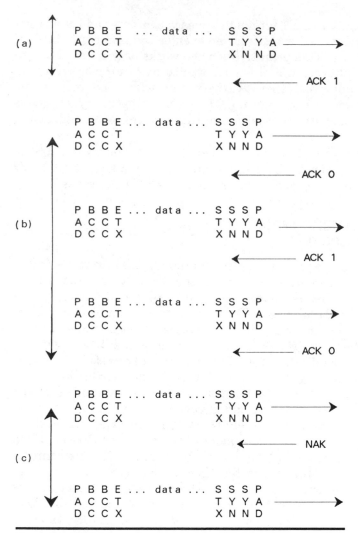

(a)
```
P B B E ... data ... S S S P
A C C T               T Y Y A  ———————>
D C C X               X N N D

                          <——————— ACK 1
```

(b)
```
P B B E ... data ... S S S P
A C C T               T Y Y A  ———————>
D C C X               X N N D

                          <——————— ACK 0

P B B E ... data ... S S S P
A C C T               T Y Y A  ———————>
D C C X               X N N D

                          <——————— ACK 1

P B B E ... data ... S S S P
A C C T               T Y Y A  ———————>
D C C X               X N N D

                          <——————— ACK 0
```

(c)
```
P B B E ... data ... S S S P
A C C T               T Y Y A  ———————>
D C C X               X N N D

                          <——————— NAK

P B B E ... data ... S S S P
A C C T               T Y Y A  ———————>
D C C X               X N N D
```

Figure 3.3   BSC data exchange.

more than one unacknowledged block. An acknowledgment can be positive (ACK) to indicate the reception of an error-free block, or negative (NAK) to indicate an error in the data block. The block check field is two characters in size, is called the *block check character* (BCC), and follows the ETX or ETB character. To further enhance the integrity of the recovery process, positive acknowledgments are provided in two forms—type 0 and type 1—which must be alternated. Two successive type 0 or type 1 positive acknowledgments indicate a lost acknowledgment and trigger error recovery procedures.

On negative acknowledgments, as shown in Fig. 3.3c, the block of data in error is transmitted again.

3.5.1 Half-Duplex Management in BSC

BSC is a half-duplex protocol with one exception for multileaving remote job entry (RJE) stations on point-to-point lines. There are three classes of procedures in BSC to enforce half-duplex control: BSC1, BSC2, and BSC3. BSC1 and BSC2 are also known as contention BSC, and BSC3 as polled BSC.

Contention (BSC1 and BSC2) protocol can be used only on point-to-point lines. The only difference between BSC1 and BSC2 is that BSC1 applies to dedicated lines, and BSC2, to switched (dial) lines. Once the physical connection is complete, there is no difference between BSC1 and BSC2.

In the contention protocol, Fig. 3.4, a station at either end of a point-to-point link can attempt to seize the line for transmitting data without prior permission of the primary. The line is seized by sending the ENQ control character. In this context ENQ is also called the bid character since the sender of the ENQ is bidding for the use of the line. The receiving station responds with an ACK 0 to accept the bid. The bidder can now send the text.

However, as shown in the lower half of Fig. 3.4, it is possible that both stations are ready to transmit data at the same time. In this case, when the primary sends its bid, the secondary responds with a bid of its own rather than with an ACK 0. We now have "contention" for the use of the line. To resolve contention, the designated primary persists with its bid and the secondary drops its bid. Now the normal message exchange can take place.

In polled or BSC3 protocol, the FEP is always the primary and in total control of who may send or receive data. The FEP polls a station by transmitting the polling ID of the station, and only the station with a matching ID responds. Even though BSC3 was designed for multipoint lines, it can also be used for point-to-point lines.

As shown in Fig. 3.5, the FEP starts the polling process by transmitting an *end-of-transmission* (EOT) character, which puts the line in control mode in preparation of the poll. Assuming that the FEP wishes to poll station B, it transmits the ID of station B. Station B interrogates its terminals to see whether there are any data to be sent.

If none of the terminals at station B has any data to send, station B responds with an EOT indicating that it has no data. EOT is, therefore, also known as the negative response to poll. If an EOT is indeed sent by station B, the poll is complete and the FEP can poll the next station in its polling list.

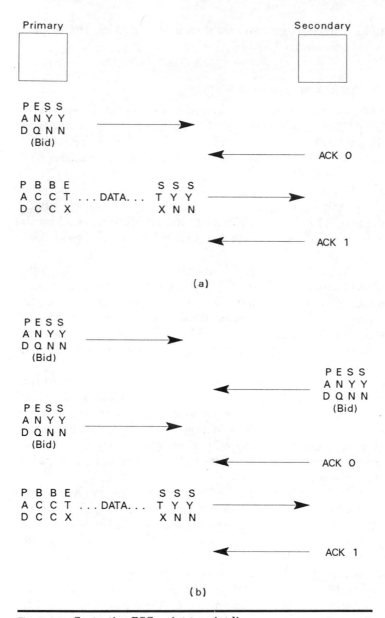

Figure 3.4   Contention BSC, point-to-point lines.

On the other hand, if one or more of the terminals on station B have data, the station responds with a message. Assume that the message was from terminal T4 in this case. The FEP acknowledges the text received. Upon receiving the acknowledgment, the station will continue sending more blocks of data, including from other terminals, until it

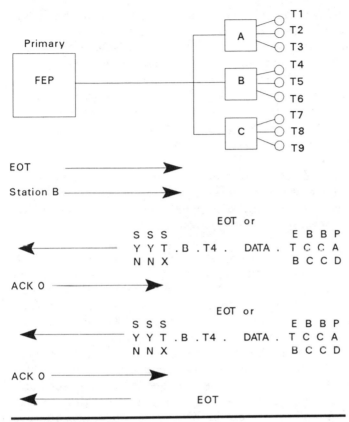

Figure 3.5 BSC3 polling.

has exhausted all blocks. At this point station B would send an EOT to complete the poll cycle.

3.6 INTRODUCTION TO BIT-ORIENTED PROTOCOLS

The next generation of link protocols that replaced BSC were the so-called bit-oriented protocols. IBM's entry in this family was the Synchronous Data Link Control (SDLC), which was adopted with some modifications by CCITT as LAPB, and by ISO as High Level Data Link Control (HDLC). Given the current state of the three, LAPB and SDLC both are subsets of HDLC. Before looking at their technical details, let us review some of the limitations of BSC that these protocols overcome.

Character set and code sensitivity. The BSC protocol was designed to transmit a predefined character set. Data characters not in this set or binary data matching control characters required special handling; i.e., BSC did not provide data transparency. Control characters had different representations in ASCII and EBCDIC disallowing devices supporting different codes on the same multipoint line.

Control and text modes. BSC had separate modes for poll operation and text transfer. This required extra overhead for polling in addition to the associated propagation delay and additional modem turnaround delays due to the half-duplex nature of BSC.

One block at a time. In BSC protocol, each block is individually acknowledged and no subsequent blocks can be sent until the previous one is acknowledged. Each acknowledgment causes a propagation delay and a line turnaround.

Device dependencies. The inclusion of certain functions in BSC, such as specific terminal poll and the reporting of device sense-status via link protocol messages, introduced device dependencies in the protocol. Not only did it mean changes to the protocol as device technology evolved, but you could not connect different types of BSC stations, e.g., IBM 3270 and IBM 2780, on the same multipoint line.

In bit-oriented protocols, by treating user data as a bit stream rather than a character set, the protocol can carry any data bit stream, irrespective of the character set embedded in the user data. These protocols use a header for control functions rather than control characters. The functions of control bits do not change whether EBCDIC or ASCII code is used for data encoding, making these protocols independent of the data-coding scheme.

The new protocols can also transmit multiple data blocks, or frames as they are called, without intervening acknowledgments—a single acknowledgment can acknowledge multiple frames. This provides an efficiency on good links that can be greater than that of BSC by several orders of magnitude.

Also, in the newer protocols there is no distinction between text and control mode for polling. Polling function can be combined with text through the use of the poll bit in the link header. This eliminates the overhead of extra transmissions for polling.

For device-dependent issues, SNA and OSI both provide higher-level procedures to report device errors and sense-status information. Protocols such as SDLC have no need to know device characteristics, nor are they affected by them. SDLC can support an IBM 3270, an RJE station and a typewriter station, or any other mix of SNA stations on the same multipoint line.

Finally, while BSC was a half-duplex protocol, the new protocols are capable of supporting full-duplex operations.

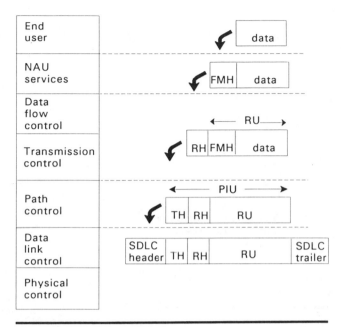

Figure 3.6 SDLC frame structure.

3.7 SDLC

SDLC, the link control protocol in SNA, can support point-to-point, multipoint, half-duplex, full-duplex, dedicated (leased) line, and switched line configurations. All SNA and user data are enclosed within an SDLC header and a trailer, where header and trailer fields contain SDLC control information. Figure 3.6 illustrates the relationship between SDLC control information and data units (PIUs) from higher layers.

SDLC procedures do not split PIUs into multiple frames. Higher layers must ensure that PIUs passed to the link layer do not exceed the size of the local link entity buffer or the link buffer of the target link station.

Not all SDLC frames carry PIUs. Frames for certain SDLC control functions carry only the header and trailer and no PIU.

3.7.1 Polling in SDLC

SDLC is an unbalanced, normal response mode subset of HDLC, which means that, unlike X.25 LAPB (balanced), where either end of a link can be the primary, the NCP is always the primary link station and only the NCP is capable of issuing link commands. The NCP controls the secondary link stations by using polling in a manner similar to BSC protocol.

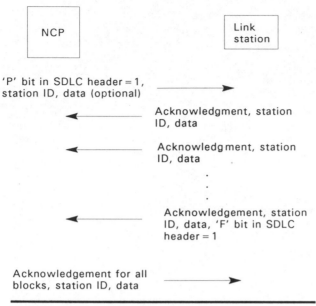

'P' bit in SDLC header = 1,
station ID, data (optional)

Acknowledgment, station
ID, data

Acknowledgment, station
ID, data

Acknowledgement, station
ID, data, 'F' bit in SDLC
header = 1

Acknowledgement for all
blocks, station ID, data

Figure 3.7   Polling in SDLC.

Figure 3.7 shows an illustrative sequence between an NCP and a secondary link station. The NCP uses a bit called the poll (P) bit in the SDLC header. It sets P bit to 1 in the header of a frame following which it wishes to receive frames from a secondary link station. The frame also contains the address of the link station being polled.

The target link station responds to the poll by sending one or more frames. Each frame from the secondary link station also acknowledges the last good frame that it has received so far. If the secondary has multiple frames, it does not have to wait for an acknowledgment from the primary after each frame sent. To indicate that the secondary has sent all of its frames, the secondary sets a bit called the final (F) bit equal to 1 on the last frame. Upon receiving the frame with F bit equal to 1, the primary acknowledges the frames received so far. The primary can also include a PIU in the acknowledgment frame.

For half-duplex operation, poll and final bits act as line turnaround signals.

In contrast to BSC operation, observe that we can combine poll, data transmission, and acknowledgments in a single transmission.

3.7.2 SDLC Frame Numbering and Modulo

SDLC uses frame sequence numbers to keep track of frames carrying PIUs. Each secondary link station maintains two counters: one for frames sent and the other for frames received. The primary link station maintains one pair of sequence numbers per secondary link station connected to it. These sequence numbers are inserted in the SDLC headers when PIUs are sent as SDLC frames. The two sequence numbers are called the Nr and Ns. The Ns sequence number (s for send) identifies the frame being sent, and Nr (r for receive) is the frame sequence number that a station expects to receive *next* from the other link station. The maximum Nr or Ns value can be a 7 or 127 (modulo 8 or modulo 128), after which it goes back to 0 and the cycle repeats.

Figure 3.8 shows an illustrative sequence with Nr and Ns sequence numbers changing as frames are exchanged. The illustration shows a half-duplex communications mode, typically used by secondary link stations in SNA (this is more of a product restriction than an architectural constraint).

When the primary initializes the secondary station (the SDLC initialization command is discussed later), the primary and second-

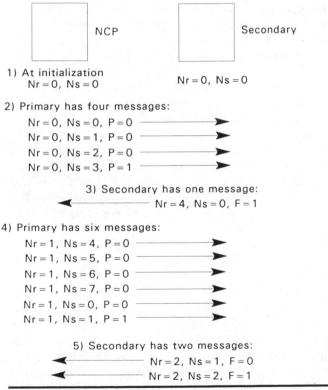

Figure 3.8 Assigning sequence numbers to SDLC frames: Nr and Ns counts.

ary set their Nr and Ns sequence numbers to 0; i.e., the station at each end of the link is expecting to receive frame 0 next (Nr = 0), and the first frame either station would send would also be numbered 0 (Ns = 0).

At this time let us assume that the primary has accumulated four frames to be sent to the secondary. The first frame being transmitted is assigned sequence number 0 (Ns = 0). The primary also indicates to the secondary that the next frame expected from the secondary is a frame with sequence number 0 (Nr = 0). Since the primary has more frames to send, it maintains its send mode by setting the poll bit equal to 0 (P = 0).

On the next frame transmitted, the primary assigns a sequence number of 1 (Ns = 1). Since the primary has not received any frames in the meantime from the secondary, it is still expecting the frame to be frame number 0 (Nr = 0). The primary still has more frames to send, so the P bit is again set to 0.

The last frame in this sequence is the fourth frame. It is identified as frame number 3, Ns = 3 (remember that the count starts with a 0, not 1). No frames have been received from the secondary, so the Nr stays at 0. The primary has no more frames to send so it sets P = 1 to poll the secondary and cause a line turnaround.

In the meantime, the secondary station has been incrementing its own Nr value internally as it has been receiving these frames. As the last frame received by the secondary was frame number 3, its Nr value would at this time equal 4; i.e., it would expect the next frame from the primary to carry a sequence number of 4.

In step 3, as secondary transmits a frame, the frame is numbered as 0 (Ns = 0). The secondary Ns value must equal the Nr value of the primary and vice versa, or an error condition is implied. (Error handling is discussed later.) In our example, though, the Ns value of the secondary does match the Nr value of the primary. At this time the secondary must confirm to the primary if it has received the four frames sent by the primary earlier. The secondary does so by setting Nr = 4 in the frame being transmitted. The secondary has only one frame to send at this time, so it sets final bit 1, F = 1, on this frame, causing a line turnaround.

From this point the process keeps repeating as shown in steps 4 and 5 of Fig. 3.8. One additional item of interest is the count wraparound. In this example we have assumed a modulo 8 system; i.e., our system is capable of counting frames 0–7, after which it starts again with number 0. This is illustrated in step 4 of our example. The count keeps going until Ns = 7 when we reach our modulo 8 capacity and the next frame sent is Ns = 0. The secondary would also internally set its own Nr equal to 0 after receiving frame number 7 from the primary.

As of the writing of this book, only NCP-to-NCP and NCP-to-IBM 3710 communications are capable of supporting modulo 128. Other SNA terminals support only modulo 8.

3.7.3 Nr and Ns Sequence Numbers and SDLC Frame Types

SDLC defines three types of frames: unnumbered, supervisory, and information frames. Of these, only information frames carry SNA PIUs and are counted in the Nr and Ns sequence numbers. Supervisory and unnumbered frames have no effect on SDLC sequence numbers. The three frame types are discussed in more detail in Secs. 3.8.3–3.8.6.

3.8 SDLC HEADER AND TRAILER

In Fig. 3.9, the SDLC header and trailer are 3 bytes each in length. The header has two 1-byte fields: flag and address, and a control field that can be 1 or 2 bytes long. The trailer has a 2-byte field, the frame check sequence, and a 1-byte trailing flag. These fields are discussed in detail in the following sections.

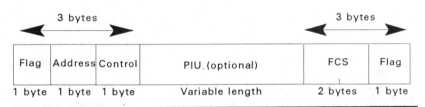

Figure 3.9   SDLC header and trailer.

3.8.1 SDLC Flags

Flags enclose an SDLC frame. The leading flag indicates that the next byte contains the address field, and the trailing flag indicates that the previous two bytes were the FCS field. A frame may have multiple leading or trailing flags. A trailing flag may also serve as the leading flag for the next frame following it in a continuous bit stream.

The flag field has a fixed hexadecimal value of X'7E' (binary 0111 1110). A bit configuration representing X'7E' must not occur anywhere within the frame as it would be erroneously interpreted by the receiver as a trailing flag terminating the frame. SDLC has a built-in procedure to prevent such an occurrence in a manner transparent to

SDLC users. A user can present any bit stream to SDLC, including flag patterns. The technique used by SDLC to handle flag patterns within a frame is called *bit stuffing*.

Preventing flags with a frame.   The SDLC microcode and software in a station transmits continuous flags while a link is idle. As it prepares to send a frame, it turns on its bit-stuffing logic *after the last leading flag* but *before* the SDLC address field is transmitted.
    Starting with the address field, the bit-stuffing logic monitors the

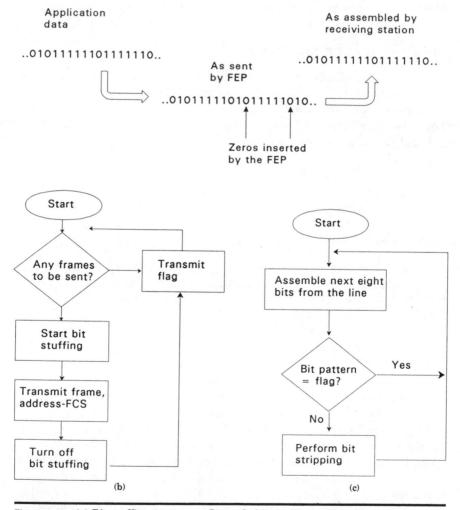

Figure 3.10   (*a*) Bit stuffing to prevent flags; (*b*) bit stuffing—sending rotation; (*c*) bit stripping—receiving station.

bit pattern in the frame for occurrences of five consecutive 1s. For every five consecutive 1s, an extra 0 is inserted (stuffed) in the data stream. After all bits in the frame have been transmitted, including the FCS, bit stuffing is turned off. The trailing flag is sent following that.

The receiver, on the other hand, must remove the inserted 0s to assemble data bits in their original form. Figure 3.10a illustrates this process. Figure 3.10b and 3.10c summarizes the logic for sending and receiving stations.

3.8.2 SDLC Address Field

This 1-byte hexadecimal field carries the address of the *secondary* SDLC station. The valid range of addresses is 01-FE. Address FF is reserved for the broadcast function. In May of 1989, IBM announced a new extension to the SDLC architecture called a *group* address which allows any *one* of a group of stations to respond to a poll. The group poll feature is intended for use with remote 3174 controllers acting as Token Ring gateways and is not used with normal SDLC operation.

On a multidrop line, each drop must have a unique link station ID. The terms cluster controller ID and link station ID both refer to this address. *Link station* is a formal SNA term and refers to the microcode or software that implements SDLC in a station. This definition is important so that we can distinguish between SDLC (link station) and PU functions, both of which may be located within the same device but have distinct addresses and functions. SDLC and PU/LU addresses are contrasted in more detail in Sec. 4.4.

Figure 3.11 shows an SDLC link with two drops, STNA and STNB, each with multiple LUs. STNA has a link ID of 01; and STNB, 02. The top part of Fig. 3.11 shows the NCP sending and receiving information from STNA. Note that the SDLC address field always contains the address of the secondary station, STNA (this is different from LAPB). To summarize, the SDLC address field contains the destination link station address for the outbound (leaving the primary station) traffic and the source address for the inbound (going to the primary station) traffic. The lower part shows similar exchanges with STNB.

3.8.3 SDLC Control Field

This field contains most of the intelligence associated with SDLC. The structure of this field is determined by the SDLC frame type. There are three types of SDLC frames and, thus, three formats of control byte.

3.8.4 Unnumbered (U) Frames

These frames are used for performing SDLC-level initialization/ termination of a station and for reporting other than transmission

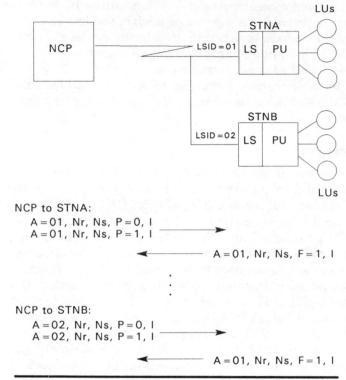

NCP to STNA:
  A = 01, Nr, Ns, P = 0, I
  A = 01, Nr, Ns, P = 1, I ———————→

          ←——————— A = 01, Nr, Ns, F = 1, I

              .
              .
              .

NCP to STNB:
  A = 02, Nr, Ns, P = 0, I
  A = 02, Nr, Ns, P = 1, I ———————→

          ←——————— A = 01, Nr, Ns, F = 1, I

Figure 3.11 Link station addressing (A = link station address, F = final bit, I = information frame, LS = link station, P = poll bit).

(FCS) errors. Unnumbered frames never carry any user data (PIUs). Structure of the control byte for unnumbered frames is shown in Fig. 3.12. Selected unnumbered commands and responses are discussed in the following. Unlike LAPB, all SDLC commands are issued by the primary (NCP) station only.

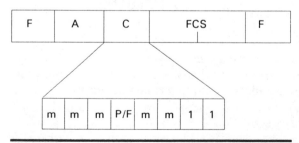

Figure 3.12 Unnumbered frame—control byte (m = modifier bits, command/response codes; see Table 3.1 for specific values).

Set normal response mode (SNRM). This command is used by the primary link station to initialize a secondary link station. It is during the SNRM exchange that both the primary and secondary set their Nr and Ns sequence numbers to 0. The primary would start polling a station only after a successful SNRM exchange. No information or supervisory frames may be exchanged prior to that. An NCP issues an SNRM to a station when a control operator or VTAM issues an activation command for the station.

Unnumbered acknowledgment (UA). UA is the response to SNRM or DISC (see the following sections) to indicate successful processing (positive response) of the command.

Disconnect mode. This is the default mode of a station when it is powered on. No supervisory or information frames can be exchanged in this mode. The primary station can change the state of the secondary from the disconnect to normal response (or information exchange) mode by executing the SNRM command. Once a station has been put in the normal response mode, it stays in this mode unless there is a reinitialization of the station. A reinitialization can occur due to power off/on sequence, station internal hardware/ microcode/software errors, or a DISC (see the following section) command from the primary.

Response to all frames other than an SNRM is DM during disconnect mode.

Disconnect (DISC). This command is used by the primary to put a secondary station in disconnect mode. Valid responses to DISC are UA or DM.

Figure 3.13 shows examples of the foregoing commands.

Frame reject (FRMR). This is an error response frame for other than FCS errors. FRMR response is used when a frame is received with a good FCS field and yet cannot be processed. The reason for an unacceptable frame can be invalid control byte, invalid Nr, frame too long, or an I field present in a noninformation frame. FRMR response contains an I field describing the reason for rejection. Figure 3.14 shows the format of the FRMR command.

There is a 3-byte information field included with FRMR. The first byte, shown as C′ in the figure, contains a copy of the control field from the frame being rejected. The next field contains the Nr and Ns values as they are currently in the station transmitting the FRMR. In a modulo 128 system each of the first two fields is 2 bytes long. The

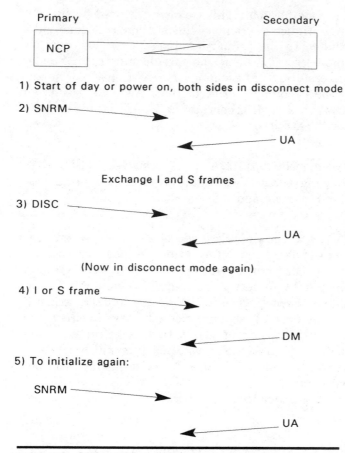

Figure 3.13 Link station initialization (activation) and termination.

third byte in the information field contains a reason code in the low order 4 bits, shown as bits z, y, x, and w. The meaning of these bits is as follows:

z: 0 = no error

        1 = received Nr disagrees with transmitted Ns

y: 0 = no error

        1 = buffer overrun—I field is too long

z: 0 = no error

        1 = rejected frame contains an I field where none is allowed

x: 0 = no error

        1 = invalid SDLC command received

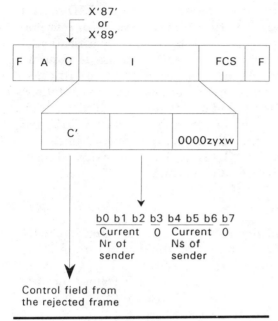

Figure 3.14   Frame reject (FRMR).

A secondary station cannot get itself out of the FRMR state and requires a new SNRM from the primary to continue communications.

UI (unnumbered information):   As a command or a response, a UI frame is for transmitting unnumbered information.

RD (request disconnect):   This request is sent by a secondary station desiring to be disconnected (by a DISC command).

RIM (request initialization mode):   An RIM frame is transmitted by a secondary station to notify the primary station of the need for an SIM command.

SIM (set initialization mode):   This command initiates system-specified procedures for the purpose of initializing link level functions such as down-loading software to a remote NCP. UA is the expected response. The primary and secondary station Nr and Ns counts are reset to 0. No SNRM is required if SIM is used.

TEST (test):   As a command, a TEST frame may be sent to a secondary station in any mode to solicit a TEST response. If an information field is included with the command, it is returned in the response. If the secondary station has insufficient storage available for the information field, a TEST response with no information field is returned.

XID (exchange station identification):   As a command, XID solicits the identification of the receiving (secondary) station. An information field may be included in the frame to convey identification of the transmitting (primary) station. An XID response is required from the secondary station. An information field in the response may be used for identification of the responding secondary station.

The XID command has multiple formats and is one SDLC command that is also used over the I/O channel between VTAM and NCP for exchanging identification information during initialization. For peripheral PU2 nodes, XID is used only on switched lines, and the relatively new XID Type 3 is used with PU Type 2.1.

3.8.5 Supervisory (S) Frames

S frames are used to acknowledge receipt of I frames (and implicitly report frames with FCS error) and to control the flow of I frames. The structure of the control byte for S frames is shown in Fig. 3.15. As in U frames, no information field is permitted with S frames, nor are they counted in Nr/Ns sequence numbers. There are three types of S frames and they can be used as commands or responses.

Receive Ready (RR).   Sent by either a primary or secondary station, an RR confirms error-free receipt of numbered frames up to a sequence number of $Nr-1$ and indicates that the sender of RR is ready to receive additional information frames.

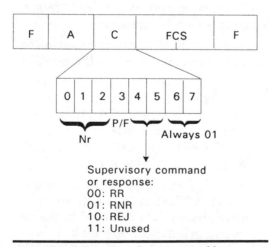

Figure 3.15 Supervisory frame—control byte.

Receive Not Ready (RNR). Sent by either a primary or secondary station, RNR indicates a temporarily busy condition due to buffer storage or other internal constraints. During this state the sender of the RNR cannot receive any I frames.

As a command or response, RNR also confirms error-free receipt of numbered frames up to $Nr-1$ and indicates the frame expected next.

A station reports the clearing of an RNR condition by transmitting an I frame with the P/F bit on or an RR or REJ frame with the P/F bit on or off.

Only information frames can be declined via an RNR. A station must always be capable of receiving supervisory or unnumbered frames.

Reject (REJ). This command/response may be transmitted to request retransmission of one or more information frames. REJ confirms frames up to $Nr-1$ and requests the retransmission of information frames starting at the Nr contained in the REJ frame. The REJ condition is cleared when the requested frame(s) or a mode-setting command has been correctly received.

Since transmission errors can be reported by any frame carrying an Nr sequence number (RR, RNR, REJ, or I frame), the use of the REJ frame is optional under SDLC and a number of products do not support it.

3.8.6 Information (I) Frames

These are the only frames that carry SNA PIUs (data, SNA commands or responses). The structure of the control byte for I frames is shown in Fig. 3.16. Bits 0-2 contain the Nr sequence number. Bit 4 is always the poll/final bit. Bits 4-6 contain the Ns number, and bit 7 is always 0 in I frames, which identifies the frame as an I frame. The figure also

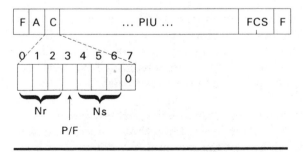

Figure 3.16 Information frame—control byte.

TABLE 3.1   SDLC Control Byte Summary

Format	Binary configuration			Hex P/F off	P/F on	Command mnemonic
Unnumbered	000	P/F	0011	X'03'	X'13'	UI
	000	F	0111	X'07'	X' 7'	RIM
	000	P	0111	X'07'	X'17'	SIM
	000	F	1111	X'0F'	X'1F'	DM
	001	P	0011	X'23'	X'33'	UP
	010	F	0011	X'43'	X'53'	RD
	010	P	0011	X'43'	X'53'	DISC
	011	F	0011	X'63'	X'73'	UA
	100	P	0011	X'83'	X'93'	SNRM
	100	F	0111	X'87'	X'97'	FRMR
	101	P/F	1111	X'AF'	X'BF'	XID
	110	P/F	0111	X'C7'	X'D7'	CFGR
	111	P/F	0011	X'E3'	X'F3'	TEST
	111	F	1111	X'EF'	X'FF'	BCN
Supervisory format	RRR	P/F	0001	X'?1'	X'?1'	RR
	RRR	P/F	0101	X'?5'	X'?5'	RNR
	RRR	P/F	1001	X'?9'	X'?9'	REJ
Information format	RRR	P/F	SSSO	X'??'	X'??'	Numbered information

(P = poll bit, F = final bit, RRR = Nr sequence number, SSS = Ns sequence number, ? = don't care)

shows the bit structure for modulo 128 systems where the control field is 2 bytes long.

Table 3.1 summarizes the format of the control byte for the three frame types. A question mark (?) in the table indicates that any value is possible in these positions, also known as "don't care" values.

3.9   ERROR HANDLING IN SDLC

3.9.1   Transmission Errors

The *frame check sequence* (FCS) field is used to determine occurrence of transmission errors. The acknowledgments are provided implicitly via the Nr sequence number in supervisory or information frames. Unnumbered frames cannot be used for acknowledging I frames. Unlike BSC, multiple frames can be acknowledged with a single acknowledgment.

Figure 3.17 shows four error-free frames being acknowledged by a single acknowledgment. The example assumes that communications on the link were established some time ago and a number of frames have already been exchanged. The example picks up a sequence of

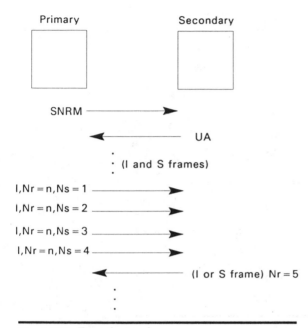

Primary   Secondary

SNRM ———————————▶

◀——————————— UA

⋮ (I and S frames)

I,Nr = n,Ns = 1 ———————————▶

I,Nr = n,Ns = 2 ———————————▶

I,Nr = n,Ns = 3 ———————————▶

I,Nr = n,Ns = 4 ———————————▶

◀——————————— (I or S frame) Nr = 5

⋮

Figure 3.17   Error-free exchange.

frames, numbered 1 through 4 ($Ns = 1$ to $Ns = 4$), being sent by the primary.

The secondary station, upon receiving each frame, increments its internal Nr number if the frame is free of transmission errors. In this case all frames are assumed free of errors and, thus, the next I or S frame from the secondary contains an Nr of 5 acknowledging frames 1-4 as having arrived free of errors.

Figure 3.18 shows the same exchange but with errors this time. In this example, frame 1 was good and caused the secondary to increment its Nr to 2 internally.

The next frame from the primary (primary $Ns = 2$) is assumed to have transmission errors and is discarded by the secondary. Since this frame was discarded, the internal Nr count of the secondary stays at 2 ($Nr = 2$); i.e., it is still expecting to receive frame 2.

From this point on, the secondary *discards all frames,* including good frames, until it receives another error-free frame 2. In this example, frames 3 and 4 are also discarded. When the secondary gets a

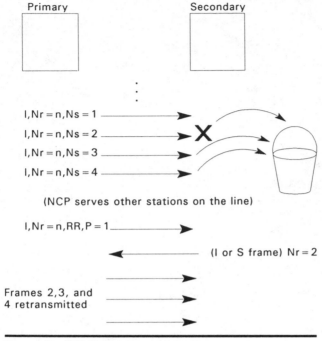

Primary

Secondary

I,Nr = n,Ns = 1

I,Nr = n,Ns = 2

I,Nr = n,Ns = 3

I,Nr = n,Ns = 4

(NCP serves other stations on the line)

I,Nr = n,RR,P = 1

(I or S frame) Nr = 2

Frames 2,3, and
4 retransmitted

Figure 3.18 SDLC error recovery.

chance to send an acknowledgment, it sends an Nr = 2, telling station A that it is still expecting frame 2.

Station A in this case would retransmit frames 2, 3, and 4. Later in this chapter we see that the worst case retransmissions can be 7 or 127 (depending on the modulo). The implication is that, while SDLC provides a significantly superior performance than BSC on good links, the performance can actually be much worse than BSC on bad lines. The expectation, of course, is that the links are predominantly good.

One final observation about retransmissions: What if even the retransmitted frame is bad? The retransmissions will be continued until either the frame is received free of errors or a designated retransmit limit is exhausted. In the latter case no further protocol level recovery is possible, the line would be taken out of service by the NCP, and the control operator would be informed of the out-of-service line. It would now be up to the operator to run further diagnostics on the line or to reactivate it.

3.9.2 Time-Out Errors

SDLC responses must be received within a designated period (NCP has a default value of 2 seconds). A response is due every time a frame with a P bit = 1 is sent. If the response is not received within that duration, another request for a response (an RR with P = 1) is sent. After the designated maximum number of retries, the station is assumed to be out of service.

3.9.3 Frame Reject

The unnumbered response FRMR, as discussed earlier, is used to report non-FCS errors. See Sec. 3.8.4 for details.

3.10 LINK LEVEL MODULO AND WINDOW

SDLC protocol has an inherent capacity to count a maximum of 8 frames, 0-7 (modulo 8); or 128 frames, 0-127 (modulo 128). For modulo 8 systems, the control field is 1 byte long, and for modulo 128 it is 2 bytes long.

The maximum number of *unacknowledged* information frames that can be outstanding at any time must not exceed modulo minus 1 but may be lower. The number of frames after which an acknowledgment must be forced is called the *link level window*. A maximum window of modulo minus 1 is necessary to maintain unambiguous acknowledgments. The following illustration makes this point clear.

Figure 3.19 shows an example of an ambiguous acknowledgment. In this case we have violated the "modulo minus 1" rule and transmitted a full modulo, frames Ns = 0 through Ns = 7, in a modulo 8 system. The acknowledgment, Nr = 0, from station B in this case can mean one of two things:

Station B received all frames, 0-7, free of errors and is expecting to receive a new frame with sequence number 0.

Station B had received frame 0 with errors and has discarded all frames and is expecting a retransmission of all frames, 0-7.

Station A at this point has no way of knowing which of the foregoing is true. To resolve this dilemma, the maximum number of unacknowledged frames is restricted to modulo minus 1.

With that restriction, station A would have requested an acknowledgment after the seventh frame, Ns = 6. If all frames were received free of errors, station B would respond with Nr = 7. To contrast with

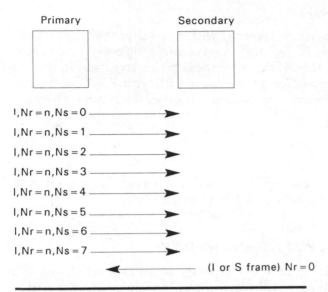

Figure 3.19 Ambiguous acknowledgments.

the previous case, if the very first frame, Ns = 0, was bad, the acknowledgment from station B would be Nr = 0.

The link level window also represents the worst case of retransmissions due to FCS errors. To reduce the worst case retransmissions, the window size can be set to a value of less than the maximum permissible (modulo minus 1). However, on good links it is desirable to use the largest permissible window for the most efficient link operation. Larger window size is also desirable for high-speed links—for example, modulo 128 is especially appropriate for T1 or satellite links.

3.11 INTERPRETING SDLC FRAMES

This section describes techniques for interpreting SDLC data in hexadecimal format. We use Table 3.1 as our primary reference.

For unnumbered frames, the only entities to be decoded are the command/response and the value of the P/F bit.

For supervisory frames, we have to decode the command/response, the value of the P/F bit, and the value of the Nr sequence number.

For information frames we have to decode the Nr/Ns numbers and the value of the P/F bit.

As shown in Fig. 3.20, the control byte consists of two hex digits, X_1 and X_2. For information frames, X_2 is always an even digit such as 2, 6, C, E, etc. This is indicated by the notation '?EVEN' for the

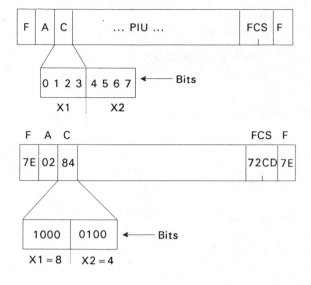

Figure 3.20 Interpreting SDLC frames.

I frame in Table 3.1. The question mark stands for "any value" or "don't care."

For supervisory frames, X_2 must have a value of 1, 5, or 9; and X_1 is a "don't care" value as shown in the table.

All other values represent an unnumbered command/response or an invalid frame.

Our algorithm for analyzing the control byte is as follows:

1. Locate control byte.

2. Is second hex digit X_2 an even value?

    Yes, go to I frame, Step 9.
    Else,

3. Is X_2 = 1, 5, or 9?

    Yes, go to S frame, Step 7.
    Else,

4. Unnumbered or invalid frames: Find a match with an unnumbered entry in the table.

5. Match found?

    No, invalid frame, exit.

Else,

6. Unnumbered frame:

   Table gives command/response and P/F bit.
   Exit.

7. Supervisory frame:

   X_2 = command/response code

8. Divide X_1 by 2.

   Quotient = Nr, remainder = P/F
   Exit.

9. Information frame:

   X_2 divided by 2 = Ns (remainder is always 0)
   Divide X_1 by 2.
   Quotient = Nr, remainder = P/F
   Exit.

Examples

1. 7E 02 93 ——7E

   In the foregoing partial frame shown, 7E is the leading flag, 02 is the address of the secondary station, and 93 is the control byte. X_1 = 9, X_2 = 3

   Since X_2 is neither even nor a supervisory command, a comparison with unnumbered definitions in Table 3.1 shows that this is an SNRM with poll bit = 1.

2. 7E 7E 7E 04 D5 ——7E

   In this example we have multiple leading flags. The secondary station address is 04. The control byte is D5. X2 is an odd value; so it is not an information frame.

   Table 3.1 shows a match with supervisory command RNR.
   Hex D is a 13 in decimal.

   $$13 \text{ divided by } 2 = 6, \text{ remainder } 1$$
   $$Nr = 6, P/F = 1$$

3. 7E 7E 04 94 ——7E

   We have two leading flags. Address = 04 and control byte = 94. Since 4 is an even digit, this must be an information frame. To compute Nr and Ns:

   $$4 \text{ divided by } 2 = 2 \text{ (Ns)}$$
   $$9 \text{ divided by } 2 = 4 \text{ (Nr), remainder } = 1 \text{ (P/F)}$$

3.12 SUMMARY

In this chapter we discussed levels 1 and 2 of SNA architecture. We really did not say much about level 1 since SNA does not architect any new physical control layer protocol.

SDLC, the layer 2 protocol, is a bit-oriented protocol with extensive similarities to X.25 LAPB, but, unlike LAPB, it is an unbalanced protocol requiring a primary station that controls the link. SDLC has three types of frames: unnumbered, supervisory, and information. Only information frames carry SNA PIUs, and these are the only frames acknowledged in SDLC. Unnumbered and supervisory frames perform control functions.

4

SNA Path Control Layer

4.1 INTRODUCTION

Path control, or level 3, in SNA forms the highest layer in the SNA transport network. As shown in Fig. 4.1, it is through this layer that NAUs interface with the transport network in SNA. The functions of this layer include routing of traffic and general management of the transport network. PU Type 2.1 has some special transport considerations and we discuss these in Chap. 12.

The path control layer also provides procedures for managing congestion in the transport network and ensures that the PIUs do not exceed the PU buffer in the destination peripheral node. The transmission header (TH) carries all path control information.

4.2 NODE TYPES AND PATH CONTROL

Overall, SNA nodes are divided into subarea nodes and peripheral nodes. From a routing point of view, subarea nodes are further divided into two categories: boundary nodes and intermediate nodes. As introduced in Sec. 2.4.1, boundary nodes are the subarea nodes to which session partners are attached. All other subarea nodes in the session path are called the *intermediate network nodes* (INNs). Consider the session between LUb and CICS in Fig. 4.2.

For LUb, SA8 is the boundary node, and for CICS, SA2 is the boundary node. On this session, SA4 is an intermediate node. Unless session partners are within the same boundary node (application-application or application-local LU), a session involves at least two boundary nodes for routing.

4.3 TRANSMISSION HEADER TYPE AND SNA NODES

The transmission header is the path control layer header. It is with the TH that we see most clearly the relationship between PU-Type

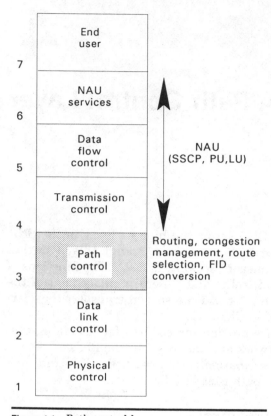

Figure 4.1 Path control layer.

and path control elements. Not all SNA nodes support the same level of path control functions. As discussed in Sec. 2.4.3, SNA permits multiple TH types, each identified by its unique *format identification* (FID). We discuss the relationship between FID type and subarea and peripheral nodes in more detail in the following sections.

4.4 BNN TO PERIPHERAL NODES PATH CONTROL

The two types of transmission headers used with peripheral nodes are FIDs 2 and 3. Information carried in a TH consists of:

Destination address and origination address

Session sequence number (FID2 only)

Segmentation indicators

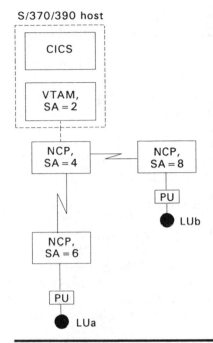

S/370/390 host

Figure 4.2 Boundary and intermediate network nodes (BNNs and INNs).

4.4.1 Peripheral Nodes, BNN Routing, and Addressing

So far we discussed three types of addresses in SNA:

1. SDLC link station addresses

2. Subarea-element addresses for NAUs

3. Peripheral node local IDs

Let us review them before we look at addressing used with peripheral nodes.

Link station address. This SDLC level address identifies a particular link station on a circuit and is relevant on that link only. The link station address may change from link to link if a message has to travel over multiple links to reach its final destination. This address is relevant only to SDLC software or microcode in a station, and PUs and LUs do not deal with the address and are not aware of it.

Subarea-element address. This format is used by VTAMs and NCPs to identify resources in the network. It is used only in FID4 TH. Subarea-element addressing is not understood by peripheral nodes.

PU/LU local IDs.   Local IDs are used by peripheral PUs and LUs and by the boundary subarea node serving them. Local IDs are used in FID2 and FID3 transmission headers.

FID2 and FID3 THs contain two fields called destination and origination address. However, only one of the two fields contains an address—outbound PIUs (BNN to peripheral node) contain the destination address and inbound PIUs (peripheral node to BNN) contain the origination address. The other address field contains a session type indicator, which is described in more detail in Sec. 6.4.1. The single address in the TH is in the local ID format—a 1-byte hexadecimal value for PU.T2 (FID2), or a 6-bit value for PU.T1 (FID3).

PU local address.   Local ID of a PU is always X'00.'

LU local address.   LU local IDs can be any value in the range 02-FE (00 is for the PU, and 01 and FF are reserved). On the IBM 3174 (and compatibles), the LU address is determined by the cabling arrangements within the cluster controller. The terminal on the lowest port has the lowest LU local ID (i.e., 02, with each successive device being assigned the next sequential number). LU 6.2 uses local IDs differently and is discussed in Chap. 12.

For stand-alone terminals, SDLC, PU, and LU functions are all within the same "box" and all three types of addresses are assigned to the same box.

Figure 4.3*a* shows detailed local addressing for two stations, A and B. The three types of addresses are shown for each—the SDLC address, the PU local ID, and the LU local IDs. We illustrate local addressing by tracing messages to various LUs on these two stations.

Let us look at our first example, Fig. 4.3*a*, with a message going from BNN to LU1 on STNA. Both stations A and B will look at the SDLC address, and station A will assemble the frame and station B will ignore it.

Once station A has assembled an error-free frame (based on SDLC procedures), it will look at the transmission header to determine the local destination. In this case the address field in the TH, the local ID, contains a value of 02, which identifies LU1 as the recipient for this message.

The remaining two examples, Fig. 4.3*b* and 4.3*c*, show messages for the PU in station A and for LU3. Figure 4.3*d* shows a message for LU3 on station B. They can be analyzed in the same manner.

4.4.2   BNN Routing Exercise

We use the sample network configuration in Fig. 4.4 to reinforce SNA addressing concepts. The network consists of a host machine with

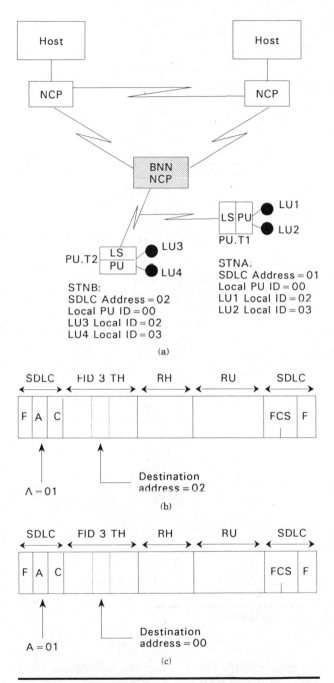

(a)

(b)

(c)

Figure 4.3 (a) Local addressing; (b) addressing traffic to LU1, STNA; (c) addressing traffic to PU, STNA.

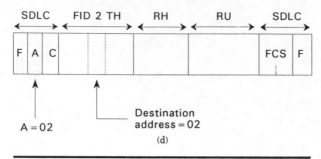

Figure 4.3   (*Continued*) (*d*) Addressing traffic to LU3, STNB.

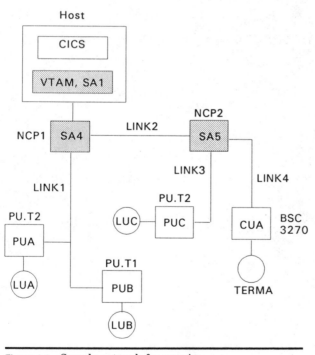

Figure 4.4   Sample network for exercise.

subarea number 3. For this example we consider one subsystem, CICS, in the host. (The specific subsystem type has no effect on addressing.)

There are two front ends in the network. NCP1 with subarea 4 is the channel attached to the host, and NCP2, subarea 5, is a remote FEP connected to NCP1 over an SDLC link. There are four controllers in the network: PUA and PUB, both SNA, stations are connected to NCP1 over a multidrop line. NCP2 has an SNA controller, PUC, and a BSC 3270 controller, CUA (for control unit A), attached to it. PUC and CUA are on separate point-to-point lines.

Partial configuration information for addressing is as follows:

NCP1:   Subarea number 4, primary SDLC link station for LINK2

NCP2:   Subarea number 5, secondary link station ID for NCP2 = X'03'

PUA: Attached to NCP1 over LINK1 (multidrop circuit)

           Associated link station ID = X'01'

LUA: Subarea-element address, assigned by NCP1 = (4,5), i.e., subarea 4, element 5. Local ID = X'02'

PUB: Attached NCP1 over LINK1

           Associated link station ID = X'02'

LUB: Subarea-element address, assigned by NCP1 = (4,9). Local ID = X'02'

PUC: Attached to NCP2 over LINK3

           Associated link station address = X'01'

LUC: Subarea-element address, assigned by NCP2 = (5,4)

           Local ID = X'02'

CUA: BSC 3270 control unit, attached to NCP2 over LINK6

           Controller polling ID = X'40' and selection ID = X'60'

TERMA: BSC terminal, subarea-element address, assigned by NCP2 = (5,9)

           BSC device ID (BSC analog of local ID) = X'40'

Configuration discussion.   The foregoing configuration information is incomplete and includes only the facts necessary to understand addressing aspects of SNA. For example, element addresses for VTAM, NCP1, and NCP2 are not shown. We do not need these to do the exercise, but we know that the default element number of an SSCP is 1 in its subarea number and each PU.T4 (i.e., NCP) is element 0 in its own subarea. We have not shown subarea-element addresses for various cluster controllers as we do not need to know them for this exercise.

During the system generation, the system programmer only assigns the subarea number and is therefore aware of it. The element numbers are created by the software; to find the complete subarea-element address of an NAU, we would have to look at assembled generation tables of the boundary node to which the NAU is attached (or we could display network configuration information on the network control terminal using the IBM network management product NetView).

We have also included a BSC 3270 Cluster Controller to illustrate how these stations are addressed in an SNA network.

Exercise requirements. For this exercise we consider various message flows, one at a time, from host subsystem CICS to each of the
four terminals shown in Fig. 4.4. Our intent is to show what various
SNA addresses look like as traffic moves from link to link in the
network.

Host subsystems pass messages to VTAM, without any RH or TH,
which are attached by VTAM. For the purposes of this example we
ignore RH since it does not contain any addressing information.
Our primary interest would be the TH and, where applicable, the
SDLC header. In FID4 TH, even though we would show the address
in the form (subarea, element), the two components of this address
are carried in different parts of FID4. Appendix A contains a detailed description of FID4.

From CICS to LUA.   The message path is from VTAM to NCP1 over the
I/O channel to PUA over LINK1.

Over I/O channel

FID Type = 4

Destination address in TH = (4,5)

SDLC does not apply over an I/O channel.

As NCP1 receives this PIU, it interrogates the FID4 destination address. Since the destination subarea number is that of NCP1, NCP1
recognizes itself as the boundary node for this message. NCP1 interrogates configuration information provided in the system generation
tables to locate information associated with PU and LU for address
(4,5). The tables would identify the link station (SDLC) address, PU
type, and LU local ID.

Over LINK1.   NCP1 will strip the FID4 TH, replace it with an FID2
(for PU.T2), and add the SDLC header and trailer. The SDLC header
address field would contain link station ID, X'01' in this case, and
FID2 TH would contain the local ID of LUA, X'02'. To summarize:

FID Type = 2

TH destination address = X'02'

SDLC address = X'01'

Using similar analysis, addressing for other destinations is summarized in the following.

From CICS to LUB.   The message path is VTAM to NCP1 to PUB.

Over I/O channel

FID Type = 4

TH destination address = (4,9)

SDLC address = not applicable

Over LINK1. NCP1 is the boundary node; it would do the FID conversion and attach SDLC information.

FID Type = 3 (PUB is PU.T1)

TH destination address = X'02'

SDLC address = X'02'

From CICS to LUC. The message path is VTAM to NCP1 to NCP2 to PUC.

Over I/O channel

FID Type = 4

TH destination address = (5,4)

SDLC address = not applicable

Over LINK2 (NCP1 to NCP2). When the aforementioned PIU arrives in NCP1, it compares destination subarea 5 with its own subarea number, 4. Since the destination is different, NCP1 forwards the PIU to the next node, NCP2, using routing tables.

FID Type = 4

TH destination address = (5,4)

SDLC address = X'03' (The SDLC address is that of NCP2 since NCP2 is the destination for this frame on LINK2.)

Over LINK3. NCP2 would recognize destination subarea 5 as its own, do the FID conversion, and rebuild the SDLC header and trailer.

FID Type = 2, TH destination address = X'02'

SDLC address = X'01'

From CICS to TERMA (BSC terminal). The message path is from VTAM to NCP1 to NCP2 to CUA.

Over I/O channel

FID Type = 4

TH destination address = (5,9)

SDLC address = not applicable

Over LINK2 (NCP1 to NCP2)

FID Type = 4

TH destination address = (5,9)

SDLC address = X'03' (link station address of NCP2)

Over LINK4. No SNA/SDLC data streams can be used on this link. SDLC, TH, and RH information is converted to a BSC data stream by NCP2, the boundary node.

The sequence of BSC exchanges would be as shown in Fig. 4.5. Those not familiar with BSC should refer to other sources for an explanation.

4.4.3 Session Sequence Numbers

SNA supports session level sequence numbers to keep track of PIUs flowing on a session. For PU.T1-attached LUs, no sequence numbers are supported.

Sequence numbers are *not* a path control protocol. As discussed earlier (Sec. 1.6.5), generation of sequence numbers is the responsibility of the data flow control (DFC) layer, but we discuss them here because they are carried in the TH.

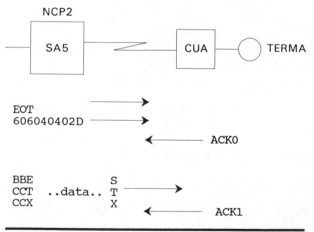

Figure 4.5 Boundary node to BSC data stream. NCP2 to BSC traffic on LINK4 (ACK=positive acknowledgment, ETX=End of text, EOT=End of transmission, STX =Start of text; PADs and SYNs not shown).

In FID2, sequence numbers are 2 bytes long. The highest sequence number that can be carried in a 2-byte field is 64K; after that sequence numbers start with 1 again. Each session partner maintains its own sequence number based on the number of PIUs sent by it. For a clustered station, each of its LUs has its own sequence number series.

Session level sequence numbers have nothing to do with SDLC frame numbers. A single PIU may be transmitted as multiple SDLC frames, depending on its length. In this case each frame will contain a new SDLC frame sequence number in the SDLC header, but the TH in all these frames will carry the same session sequence number. Figure 4.6 shows two examples of how session sequence numbers and SDLC frame numbers are incremented.

Figure 4.6a shows PIUs numbered 1 and 2 being sent by LUA to its session partner LU, LU1. For each frame, we also show the Ns part of the SDLC header in parentheses. LU1 responds with three PIUs, numbered 1-3; and LUA responds with a PIU numbered 3. Note that in all cases that SDLC sequence numbers are maintained independently of PIU sequence numbers. The last PIU is from the LUA to LU2 and carries a sequence number 1 (assume it is the first PIU on this session), but its SDLC frame number is sequential from the previous message since the frame is between the same two link stations.

Figure 4.6b shows a long PIU, PIU number 1074, being transmitted as three frames. In this case, the FID2 TH will contain the same sequence number, 1074, for all three frames. SDLC has no knowledge that these three frames are related. Indication that these are related frames is found in the TH. In the first two frames, the TH will carry flags to indicate that they are partial PIUs. The TH in the last frame will indicate that it is the last of the partial PIUs.

4.4.4 Segmentation

Segmentation is a BNN-to-peripheral-node protocol to ensure that PIUs do not exceed the size of the buffer in the destination PU. Before transmitting a PIU, the boundary node interrogates the destination PU buffer size to determine whether the PIU would fit in the destination PU buffer. If the PIU exceeds the PU buffer, it is "segmented" into multiple PIUs. Conversely, the peripheral node PU would also use segmentation on traffic sent to the BNN.

In SNA there is no direct limit on the size of the SDLC frame (there is no equivalent of the HDLC/LAPB "k" parameter). The frame size is indirectly limited by the segment size. A segment is never broken into multiple frames; in other words, SDLC must always be capable of handling the largest possible segment.

For segmentation protocol to work, the boundary node has to know

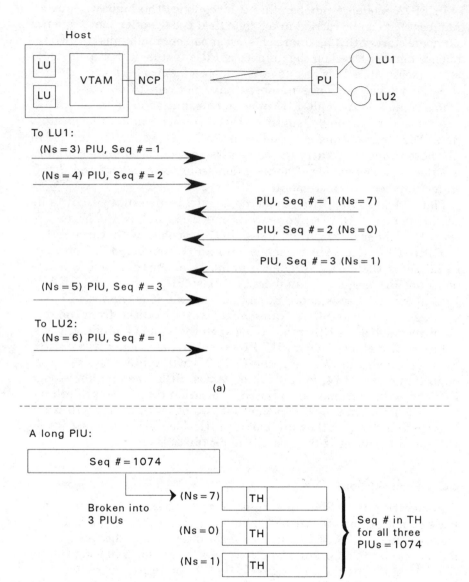

Figure 4.6   (a) Sequencing PIUs in each direction on LU-LU sessions; (b) breaking one PIU into multiple PIUs.

the buffer size of the peripheral PU. This information is provided to the boundary NCP in the system generation tables. The most prevalent PU buffer size is 265 (PU.T2) or 261 (PU.T1). The reason for the odd-looking numbers is that they also include TH and RH. In both of the foregoing cases, RU size is 256.

For PU.T1:
$$256(RU) + 3(RH) + 2(FID3\ TH) = 261$$

For PU.T2:
$$256(RU) + 3(RH) + 6(FID2\ TH) = 265$$

These norms are not SNA-defined, but product-defined, constraints. The case against too long a segment is basically that it requires a large SDLC frame, which in turn increases the probability of transmission errors and also requires larger buffers.

Segmentation is not the only SNA protocol involved in message sizing. *Chaining protocol* defines session level maximum RU size. Chaining protocol is discussed in Sec. 5.4, which also discusses the relationship between chaining, segmentation, and sequence numbers.

4.5   INN PATH CONTROL

Intermediate network node (INN) path control forms the backbone network in SNA and is responsible for all routing and for managing network level congestion. All control information associated with INN functions is carried in FID4 TH.

4.5.1   INN Connectivity

Routing and flow control are, of course, based on the physical topology of the network. In this section we review the major physical connectivity options for interconnecting subarea nodes, including both channel and SDLC connections.

4.5.2   Host-to-NCP Connectivity

A host computer is connected to an FEP over an I/O channel. Other than establishing a maximum of 64K subareas, SNA places no restriction on the number of NCPs that can be channel-attached to a host. The practical limit is determined by the I/O channel capacity and other I/O devices configured on the machine. Depending on the CPU model and the I/O channel configuration, multiple FEPs can even be configured on the same I/O channel.

Figure 4.7a shows a configuration with three FEPs attached to a

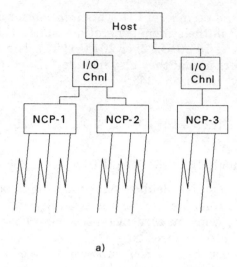

a)

b)

Figure 4.7   (*a*) Single-host, multiple-channel-attached FEPs; (*b*) host-to-NCP connection.

host. Two of the FEPs, NCP1 and NCP2, are on the same I/O channel, with a third FEP, NCP3, on a separate I/O channel.

Conversely, a front end can be channel-attached to more than one host. Again, there is no SNA limitation on the number of hosts that can be attached to an FEP over the I/O channel. The hardware design of an IBM 3725 FEP restricts attachment to a maximum of 4 I/O channels, or an IBM 3745, to 16 I/O channels.

Figure 4.7b shows an FEP attached to three different hosts over four subchannels. The two attachments in the middle go to the same host but could have been to different hosts.

Host-to-network connectivity without FEPs. For low-end mainframe computers such as 43XX and 9370 processors, it is possible to attach a network without a separate front end processor. Very often these machines have only a few circuits to support and the cost of a full FEP (a minimum configuration starts at around $50,000) cannot be justified. In such cases the FEP functions can be provided by communications hardware integrated within the host. As shown in Fig. 4.8, such hardware is called the Telecommunications System Controller (TSC) for the 9370 processors and the Integrated Communications Adapter (ICA) for 43XX series processors.

Of course, if you do not have an FEP, you do not have an NCP either. In the configuration shown in Fig. 4.8, functions normally provided by NCP are provided by VTAM. Until a few years ago a special version of VTAM called VTAM-Extended (VTAME) was required to support these configurations. However, this support is a standard part of the current VTAM releases.

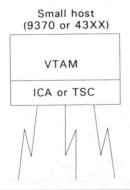

Small host
(9370 or 43XX)

VTAM

ICA or TSC

Figure 4.8 Integrated communications adapters—small host.

4.5.3 Host-to-Host Connectivity

Figure 4.9 shows some of the possibilities for physical connectivity between host machines. Most machines located in close proximity can be connected directly over I/O channels using channel-to-channel (CTC) adapters. In Fig. 4.9, hosts H1 and H2 are connected via I/O channels. Hosts that are too distant to be connected over I/O channels can be connected via NCPs over SDLC links. Hosts H1, H3, and H4 are connected via NCPs and SDLC links. We also have channel extenders available from corporations such as Network Systems Corporation and Paradyne that allow channel-to-channel connectivity over the T1 carrier system. IBM also provides two products, IBM 3737 and IBM

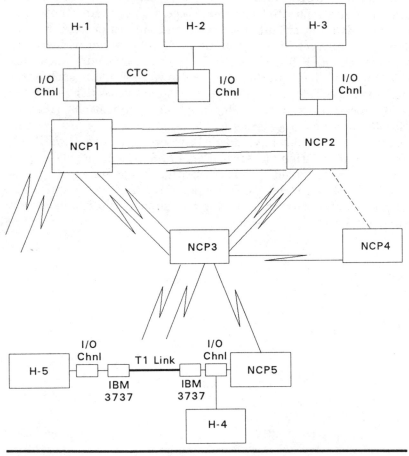

Figure 4.9 INN connectivity: host-to-host connection.

3172, that allow I/O channels to be connected over T1 links. Hosts H4 and H5 are connected via a channel extender.

4.5.4 FEP-to-FEP Connections

FEPs are connected to each other over SDLC links. A front end can be attached to another host-attached front end or to a remote front end.

In Fig. 4.9, NCP1 is connected over SDLC links to a channel-attached front end, NCP2, and a remote front end, NCP3. The term *remote* came into vogue because devices on an SDLC link were generally more distant from the host than were channel-attached resources. An FEP can also be a local and a remote at the same time. In Fig. 4.9, NCP1 is a local FEP to host H1; at the same time it is a remote FEP to host H3.

Also, as shown in Fig. 4.9, NCPs can have multiple, parallel SDLC links connecting them. Besides providing greater bandwidth, parallel links also provide better reliability. To lose direct connection between NCP1 and NCP2 we would have to lose all three links. In this particular example, even if we lost all three links, we could still reach NCP2 via NCP3. The placement of FEPs and the number of links connecting them are important network design decisions involving cost, performance, and reliability tradeoffs.

Transmission groups. Parallel links between NCPs can be further combined in logical groups called transmission groups. A transmission group appears as a single logical link to the rest of the network. Only the NCPs connected by a *transmission group* (TG) are aware of its internal structure. A TG can continue to operate in a degraded mode so long as at least one link is available within the TG.

For terminology purposes, a single link connecting two NCPs is also called a TG even though in this case there is only one link in the TG.

You can also have multiple TGs between two subarea nodes. In addition to higher reliability, it also gives us a load-balancing capability. Each TG can have a different bandwidth, and high-priority traffic can be routed over higher-bandwidth TGs.

The subarea node distributes the traffic automatically over links within a TG. Physical links within a TG should be of the same speed—if not, in certain circumstances, the speed throughout may be equivalent to the lowest-speed link in the TG.

When we have multiple TGs between two subarea nodes, each must be assigned a unique TG number. In our example in Fig. 4.10, we show two transmission groups, TG1 and TG2 between subareas 4 and 8. Also note that the same TG number can be used more than once in

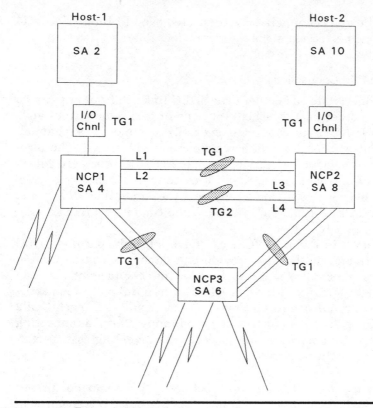

Figure 4.10   Transmission groups.

a subarea node if the TGs using the same number are going to different subarea nodes. In subarea 4 we have three TGs with TG number 1
assigned to them. To specify which TG1 of the three is to be used (routing tables never specify a TG number alone), it is always qualified
with the subarea number toward which it travels.

For terminology purposes, the host I/O channel is always called
TG1.

If you have a single NCP connected over more than one subchannel
to the same host, you would have two TGs with number 1 between the
same subarea nodes, as shown in Fig. 4.11. The host would identify
the specific TG from the underlying subchannel number. The NCP
would distinguish between the two TGs via the channel adapter
through which it is connected to the host.

TG assignment.   Transmission group assignments are made during
NCP system generation. For network in Fig. 4.10, system programmers for both NCP1 and NCP2 must coordinate their system genera-

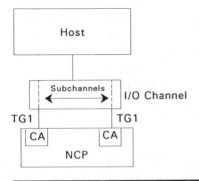

Figure 4.11 Multiple subchannel links between a front end and host computer.

tions to ensure that both sides assign a line to the same transmission group. The statements below in Table 4.1 show parameters that would be necessary to make the proper TG assignment.

Because this is our first look at IBM system generation tables, we describe some of the notations used in Table 4.1. The system generation tables are coded using IBM 370 Macro Assembler syntax. The names in the left column, L1, L1NCP2, L2, etc., can be up to eight alphanumeric characters long and are symbolic names assigned to resources being described. The first link described in the system generation (or sysgen) has been assigned a symbolic name of L1; the only PU on that link has been assigned a symbolic name L1NCP2, etc. Most corporations have well-defined conventions for assigning these names.

Keywords in the second column, LINE, PU, etc., identify the type of definition (resource) that is being described. A LINE entry, for exam-

TABLE 4.1   Assigning Lines to TGs

NCP1	NCP2
:	:
L1 LINE ---	L1 LINE ---
L1NCP2 PU ---, TG = 1, ---	L1NCP1 PU ---, TG = 1, ---
L2 LINE ---	L2 LINE ---
L2NCP2 PU2 ---, TG = 1,---	L2NCP1 PU ---, TG = 1, ---
L3 LINE ---	L3 LINE ---
L3NCP2 PU ---, TG = 2, ---	L3NCP1 PU ---, TG = 2, ---
L4 LINE ---	L4 LINE ---
L4NCP3 PU ---, TG = 2,---	L4NCP1 PU ---, TG = 2, ---
:	
:	

ple, describes attributes of a line. The rest of the statement contains actual attributes describing the resource and may actually run several sentences. Table 4.1 shows partial coding only to illustrate how TG numbers are assigned in an SNA network. Chapter 8 discusses system definitions in more detail.

The TG assignment for a line is defined, not on the line profile, but on the profile of the PU (remote NCP) attached to the line. In the foregoing example, a PU statement with the symbolic name L1NCP2 is associated with the line immediately above it, L1; and the parameter TG = 1 on the PU profile associates line L1 with TG1. In NCP2, the specification TG = 1 on PU entry, with the name L1NCP1, associates line L1 with TG1 and so forth. Note that the system programmers responsible for administering the two NCPs must coordinate their definitions and ensure that a line is defined as a part of the same TG in both NCPs.

Managing traffic over TGs. To keep track of overall traffic being exchanged over a TG between two NCPs, the NCPs use sequence numbers on each transmission group. Transmission group sequence numbers are carried in the FID4 TH and are validated by the receiving NCP. The TG sequence number is in addition to the session sequence number, which was discussed earlier in Sec. 4.4.3. It is possible for a PIU to arrive out of sequence or in duplicate over a TG due to transmission errors and associated retries. The receiving subarea node resequences out-of-sequence PIUs and discards duplicates. The TG sequence numbers go to a maximum of 64K and then wrap around to 0.

When TG sequence numbers wrap around to 0, some additional processing is required. First of all, we must collect any outstanding PIUs since we plan to reuse their sequence numbers. In addition, we must also acknowledge all unacknowledged PIUs. The process of collecting and acknowledging outstanding PIUs is called a TG sweep. TG sweep ensures that no PIUs are lost and that they are acknowledged properly. A special TH type, FIDF, is used to start a TG sweep.

4.6   INN ROUTING

Subarea nodes, i.e., hosts, and NCPs are the routing (switching) nodes in SNA. The objective of INN routing is to get a PIU from the originating BNN to the destination BNN. All information required for routing is contained in the FID4 TH. The subarea number of the destination is used by each node to determine the next node in the message path. Once at the destination boundary node, the BNN uses the boundary node procedures to deliver the PIU to the appropriate NAU in its subarea.

4.6.1 Virtual Routes

The SNA routing algorithm is basically a pass-the-buck method. All that a node knows about a route is the *next* node to which the message is to be passed for a given destination. No subarea node needs to know the complete end-to-end route. The end-to-end routes are called *virtual routes* (VRs).

Consider a session between CICS and LU1, shown in Fig. 4.12. BNN for CICS is host SA2; and for LU1, NCP SA12. As shown in the example, three virtual routes are possible between SA2 and SA12. When multiple routes are possible between two BNNs, each VR must be assigned a unique ID. In addition, traffic on a session can also be assigned one of three priority levels: low, medium, or high. A maximum of 16 virtual routes, VR0–VRF (hex F = decimal 15), can be provided between each pair of subarea nodes in SNA.

Virtual route and session priority are established at session setup and do not change for the duration of the session. There is no congestion-based adaptive routing in SNA. Alternate routes can be defined but are used only in case the route currently in use fails. Session continuity is not maintained across route failures.

For the CICS-to-LU1 session in Fig. 4.12, if we assume TG1 between SA6 and SA12 to be of greater bandwidth than TG2, we can

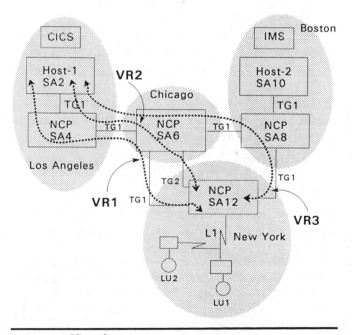

Figure 4.12 Virtual routes.

specify VR1 as the primary route and VR2 and VR3 as being the first and second backups, respectively.

VR1 in this case goes from SA2 to SA4 over TG1; SA4 to SA6, over TG1; and SA6 to SA12, over TG1, i.e.,

$$VR1 = SA2 \text{------} TG1 \to SA4 \text{------} TG1 \to SA6 \text{------} TG1 \to SA12$$

$$VR2 = SA2 \text{------} TG1 \to SA4 \text{------} TG1 \to SA6 \text{------} TG2 \to SA12$$

$$VR3 = SA2 \text{------} TG1 \to SA4 \text{------} TG1 \to SA6 \text{------} TG1 \to SA8$$
$$\text{------} TG1 \to SA12$$

A virtual route must traverse the same physical path in both directions (therefore, there is no adaptive routing).

Since the routing algorithm is responsible for identifying only the next node in the message path, routing tables for VR1, VR2, and VR3 for Fig. 4.12 are defined as follows in various nodes:

1. *Host SA2:* In this case all three routes traverse the same physical component, the I/O channel, to get to the next node, SA4. The routing table for destination BNN 12 would specify that all traffic for routes 1, 2, and 3 should be forwarded to adjacent subarea node SA4 over TG1 (I/O channel).

   SA2 does not know (nor does it care) how the next node will determine the next hop in the message path.

2. *In SA4:* Here again, the three routes traverse the same physical components. The routing table for destination BNN 12 would specify that all traffic over routes 1, 2, and 3 should be passed to adjacent SA6 over TG1.

3. *In SA6:* It is in subarea 6 that the three routes diverge and map into different physical components. The routing table for destination BNN 12 would specify the following:

   For route1, forward traffic to SA12 over TG1.
   For route2, forward traffic to SA12 over TG2.
   For route3, forward traffic to SA8 over TG1.

4. *In SA8:* Only route 3 for BNN 12 traverses SA8, so the routing table would only define route 3 and specify that traffic for this route should be forwarded to SA12 over TG1.

   Once traffic arrives in SA12, the routing process is complete. The SA12 NCP would now use BNN-to-peripheral-node procedures (Sec. 4.4) to deliver the PIU to LU1 over route extension L1.

   This simple example considered traffic routing from SA2 to SA12. Similar tables would be required to move traffic back from SA12 to SA2.

As an example of routing for the host-bound traffic, routing tables in SA12 for routing traffic to BNN SA2 would specify:

For route1, forward traffic to SA6 over TG1.
For route2, forward traffic to SA6 over TG2.
For route3, forward traffic to SA8 over TG1.

The routing tables that we discussed so far provide only for routing to and from SA2 and SA12. Additional routing tables would be required to cover each other possible destination in the network.

Inputs to the routing algorithm are the destination subarea number (element numbers play no part in routing) and a route number (and a transmission priority number that does not affect the physical path) that are carried in the FID4 TH. Using these fields in the TH, the subarea node determines the next node and TG number from the routing tables. Routing tables are coded for each VTAM and each NCP individually as a part of the system generation of these software systems.

4.6.2   Virtual Routes and Explicit Routes

A virtual route is a bidirectional route with a forward and a reverse direction. For directional purposes, it helps to consider the host to be the starting point of the route (in subarea-based routing with no APPN network nodes, one end of a route is always the host). When traffic is leaving the host (outbound) it is traveling on the forward route, and when the traffic is going toward the host (inbound), it is said to be traveling on the reverse route.

The forward and reverse routes underlying a VR are called *explicit routes* (ERs). In other words, an end-to-end bidirectional VR always maps into a forward ER and a reverse ER (RER). To draw an analogy with a north-south highway, southbound and northbound lanes would be the two explicit routes constituting the highway or the virtual route.

Detailed route descriptions provided in Sec. 4.6.1 are actually the forward ERs associated with VR1, VR2, and VR3. The two explicit routes underlying a VR are also assigned numbers to identify them. It is generally intended that the two ERs associated with a VR should have the same number as that of the VR containing them. In certain network configurations, routing tables can get into conflict with each other, and it becomes necessary to assign a number to an underlying ER that is different from the number assigned to the associated VR. This methodology for resolving routing conflicts appears to be the primary motivation for providing a somewhat confusing two-level ER-VR structure in SNA. An example of conflicting routes and their resolution is shown in Sec. 4.6.4.

For the network shown in Fig. 4.12, we can restate VRs 1, 2, and 3

TABLE 4.2   Forward and Reverse ERs for VRs 1, 2, and 3 for Fig. 4.12

VR1:

Forward ER1:   SA2 ――― TG1 → SA4 ――― TG1 → SA6 ――― TG1 → SA12
Reverse ER1:   SA12 ――― TG1 → SA6 ――― TG1 → SA4 ――― TG1 → SA2

VR2:

Forward ER2:   SA2 ――― TG1 → SA4 ――― TG1 → SA6 ――― TG2 → SA12
Reverse ER2:   SA12 ――― TG2 → SA6 ――― TG1 → SA4 ――― TG1 → SA2

VR3:

Forward ER3:   SA2 ――― TG1 → SA4 ――― TG1 → SA6 ――― TG1 → SA8 ―――
                TG1 → SA12
Reverse ER3:   SA12 ――― TG1 → SA8 ――― TG1 → SA6 ――― TG1 → SA4 ―――
                TG1 → SA2

---

in terms of their underlying ERs, as shown in Table 4.2. In this example we use the same numbers for underlying ERs as for the associated VR.

Translating a VR number into its underlying ER number is done in the host by VTAM. The ER number in FID4 is the one used for routing, not the VR number. As a consequence, only the host (VTAM) deals with virtual route numbers; NCPs deal only with underlying ERs.

4.6.3 VTAM and NCP PATH Tables

Routing information is provided to each host and NCP by the customer system programmer as a part of the system generation tables. The actual coding structure of routing tables—called the PATH tables—is defined by IBM products VTAM and NCP, not by SNA. (VTAM has another table that also uses the term PATH to define details of switched lines, but that has nothing to do with routing.)

The system programmer must define a set of PATH tables in each subarea node to cover all possible destinations. For each possible destination, VTAM PATH tables include information to map each VR into its underlying ER number and the TG number for the adjacent node to which the PIU is to be passed next. NCPs have the same information except the VR number since NCPs do not get involved in VR-to-ER mapping.

Figure 4.13 shows the structure of a PATH statement. Numbers I, II, and III are shown for reference purposes only to discuss the manner in which the statement is processed.

The name field assigns a unique name to the PATH statement being described.

Section I, DESTSUB = (---,---,---), enumerates one or more destination subareas covered by this PATH statement.

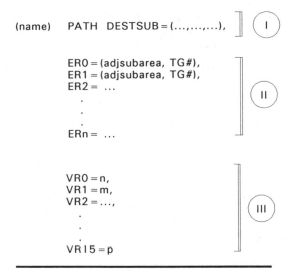

(name)   PATH   DESTSUB = (...,...,...),   I

ER0 = (adjsubarea, TG#),
ER1 = (adjsubarea, TG#),
ER2 = ...
.
.
.
ERn = ...

II

VR0 = n,
VR1 = m,
VR2 = ...,
.
.
.
VR15 = p

III

Figure 4.13   SNA PATH table for routing.

When a subarea node receives a PIU, it first searches for a PATH statement that covers the subarea number in the destination address part of the FID4 TH. Having located the appropriate PATH statement, in case of VTAM, it looks at section III next for the VR number selected at the session establishment time. The numbers n, m, -, -, p, etc., where n-p can be 0-15, identify the underlying ER number for each available VR. Only as many VRs and ERs are coded as the actual number of routes available in the network. In our example, VR0 = 0 tells VTAM to use ER0 whenever VR0 is selected. A specification of VR0 = 2, for example, would map virtual route 0 into explicit route 2.

Once the ER number is known, section II is used to determine the next subarea to which the PIU is to be passed and the TG to be used. The adjacent node and TG number must be specified even if only one node and TG are possible. Figure 4.14 shows how PATH tables would be coded in various nodes to define three VRs between host SA2 and NCP SA12 for the network shown in Fig. 4.12. Note again that VRs are defined only in the host, SA2. Additional PATH tables would be needed in each subarea node to cover other destinations in the network.

For host SA2. P212 on the left is the name assigned to this PATH statement. It is a unique name within SA2 tables.

DESTSUB = (12) identifies this as the statement containing information about all routes defined to destination subarea 12. A given destination can be defined only in one PATH statement.

1) In Los Angeles host, SA2, partial VTAM tables:

```
P212    PATH  DESTSUB=(12),ER1=(4,1),ER2=(4,1),
              ER3=(4,1),VR1=1,VR2=2,VR3=3
```

2) In Los Angeles front-end, SA4, partial NCP tables:

```
Forward path:
Pxx     PATH  DESTSUB=(12),ER1=(6,1),ER2=(6,1),
              ER3=(6,1)
Reverse path:
Pyy     PATH  DESTSUB=(2),ER1=(2,1),ER2=(2,1),
              ER3=(2,1)
```

3) In Chicago front-end, SA6, partial NCP tables:

```
Forward path:
Pxx     PATH  DESTSUB=(12),ER1=(12,1),ER2=(12,2),
              ER3=(8,1)

Reverse path:
Pyy     PATH  DESTSUB=(2),ER1=(4,1),ER2=(4,1),
              ER3=(4,1)
```

4) In Boston front-end, SA8, partial tables
   (only ER3 passes through Boston SA8):

```
Forward path:
Pxx     PATH  DESTSUB=(12),ER3=(12,1)

Reverse path:
Pyy     PATH  DESTSUB=(2),ER3=(6,1)
```

5) In New York front-end, SA12, partial NCP tables
   (only reverse path needed to return to SA2):

```
Pyy     PATH  DESTSUB=(2),ER1=(6,1),ER2=(6,2),
              ER3=(8,1)
```

Figure 4.14   Partial routing tables for network in Fig. 4.12; Pxx and Pyy can be any names assigned by the system programmer.

The last three parameters, VR1 = 1, VR2 = 2, VR3 = 3, define three virtual routes to destination SA12.

VR1 = 1 specifies that for VR number 1, the underlying ER is ER number 1.

VR2 = 2 maps VR2 into ER2.

VR3 = 3 maps VR3 into ER3.

ER1 = (4,1) specifies that for traffic on route 1 the PIU should be forwarded to subarea 4 over TG1 (I/O channel). In this case ER2 and ER3 also specify the same values since there is only one way to get from SA2 to SA4; i.e., all three routes map into the same physical components over this part of the network.

In summary, host SA2 will forward all traffic for SA12 for all three ERs (VRs) to SA4 over TG1.

For NCP SA4. Here again the three routes have the node SA6 as the next hop over TG1, and therefore ER1, ER2, and ER3 all equate to (6,1), i.e., forward the PIUs to SA6 over TG1.

For NCP SA6. It is at this point that the three routes diverge, and this divergence is coded in the PATH statement.

ER1 = (12,1) specifies that if the ER number is 1 (and DESTSUB = 12), send this PIU to adjacent SA12 over TG1.

ER2 = (12,2) would cause traffic on ER2 also to be sent to subarea 12, but over TG2.

ER3 = (8,1) would cause traffic destination SA12 over ER3 to be forwarded to SA8 over TG1.

In NCP SA8. Of the three routes between SA2 and SA12, only ER3 passes through SA8; therefore, only ER3 is defined to SA8.

ER3 = (12,1) specifies that the traffic for SA12 over ER3 is to be passed to subarea 12 over TG1.

Since ER1 and ER2 are not defined to NCP SA8, any changes in those two routes (due to changes in network topology) would be transparent to NCP SA8.

The reverse ER statements for each node are also shown and can be analyzed in a similar manner.

4.6.4 Routing Conflicts and Their Resolution

In the previous example we considered only a partial set of routing statements which covered a single destination, SA12. The process must be repeated in each node for each possible destination subarea in the network. It is the coverage of additional routes to other destinations that can give rise to conflicts that must be resolved by adjusting the ER number for the underlying ERs.

To illustrate an example of a conflict and its resolution, let us review VR2-ER2 between SA2 and SA12 for network shown in Fig. 4.12.

Specifically, the reverse ER2 statement in NCP SA12 directs NCP SA12 to route traffic for SA2 on ER2 to SA6 over TG2.

Let us put that aside for a moment and look at the routing needed for IMS-CICS sessions between SA10 and SA2 in Fig. 4.15. From an SA10 vantage point, the most efficient route would be SA10 → SA8 → SA6 → SA4 → SA2 shown as VR1 with underlying ER as ER1.

In case we lose TG1 connecting SA6 and SA8, we would also like to define an alternate VR2-ER2 as SA10 → SA8 → SA12 → SA6 → SA 4 → SA2.

Let us focus on how this ER2 would be defined to SA12. The necessary routing statement, would have to specify that, for destinations

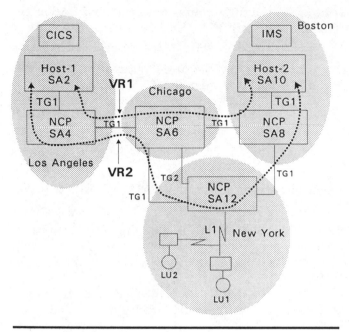

Figure 4.15 Explicit routes conflicts.

SA2 and ER2, forward the PIU to SA6 over TG1. We have created a conflicting requirement.

Let us compare ER2 in Fig. 4.16 with ER2 in Fig. 4.15. The reverse ER2 in Fig. 4.16 requires that, for destination SA2, if the ER number is 2, forward PIU to SA6 over TG1. Our old ER2 (Fig. 4.15) requires that for the same destination (SA2) and the same ER (ER2) PIU is to be forwarded to SA6—but over TG2.

To resolve this conflict, we can either change the VR number in SA10 to a new number such as VR4, or keep the same VR number (VR2) and change the number of the underlying ER to something other than ER2—say ER4. For this example, we change the underlying ER number.

To accomplish this, routing tables in SA10 and SA12 (and other INN NCPs) would be coded as follows:

In host SA10

```
---     PATH    DESTSUB = (2), ER1 = (8,1), ER4 = (8,1),
                VR1 = 1, VR2 = 4
```

In NCP SA12

```
---     PATH    DESTSUB = (2), ER1 = (6,1), ER2 = (6,2),
                        ER4 = (6,1)
```

4.7 ALTERNATE ROUTES AND CLASS OF SERVICE

Earlier in Sec. 4.6.1 we mentioned the ability to assign priorities to traffic on primary and alternate routes. Priorities and alternate routes are defined through the SNA class of service.

To understand the class of service concept, let us assume that in Fig. 4.13, LU1 is an interactive display station and LU2 is a batch terminal; and we wish to assign more efficient routing to LU1 than LU2. Assuming that TG1 between SA6 and SA12 has a greater bandwidth than TG2, we would like to assign VR1 to traffic associated with LU1, and VR2 for LU2. Should VR1 break down, we would like to use VR2 as a backup, but with a higher priority for LU1 traffic than for LU2. To accomplish this objective we would need to set up two classes of service. Classes of service (COS) are created by defining a COS table in VTAM. In our example, we need only two entries in the COS table—but as large a COS table can be established by a user as is necessary to fulfill network performance objectives.

As shown in Table 4.3, we have arbitrarily chosen to call the two classes of service COS1 and COS2. Each entry in the table enumerates all virtual routes available for that COS and traffic priority for each route. Up to 16 unique VR numbers, 0-15, can be specified, and each VR can be specified up to three times, each with a unique priority level—0, 1, or 2. The "VR = ---" operand lists the available routes. The first entry represents the primary route for a given class of service and each subsequent entry represents an alternate route. An alternate route is used if all VRs preceding it in the list break down. If all VRs in a class of service are unavailable, no new sessions can be established within that class.

In our example, Table 4.3, for COS1, the first VR to be used is VR1 with VRs 2 and 3 available as first and second backups. However, VRs 2 and 3 are also used by COS2, which is meant for lower-priority traffic. The second number in paired entries in parentheses represents the *transmission priority number* (TPN). Note that traffic in COS1 is as-

TABLE 4.3   Class of Service Table

Format of table entries:

(name) COS VR = (list of virtual routes and priority numbers)

Example:

COS1	COS	VR = [(1,2),(2,2),(3,2)]
COS2	COS	VR = [(2,1),(3,1)]
		VR# transmission priority number

signed a higher priority of 2 (the greater the number, the higher the priority) when it shares the same routes, VR2 and VR3, with traffic from a lower class of service, COS2.

4.7.1 COS Selection

The class of service used for a session is selected at logon. The COS name is included in a table called the bind image table in VTAM. The bind image specifies the session parameters and protocols for each SNA session and is discussed in more detail in Chap. 6. Parameters in the bind image can be changed by the host LU to specify particular values. In addition, the SNA system programmer can also code a virtual route selection exit routine in VTAM to attain a more dynamic control of VR and COS selection. The exit routine is invoked by VTAM for each logon request received from the network.

4.8 CONTROLLING DATA FLOW IN THE PATH CONTROL NETWORK

Flow of PIUs is primarily controlled via a pacing protocol, which involves defining a pacing window of, say, n PIUs. With such a specification, only n PIUs are released at a time by a transmitter, which then awaits a pacing response from the receiver. Upon receiving the pacing response, the transmitter can send n more PIUs. The receiver can slow down the transmitter by withholding pacing responses during congestions (buffer shortage).

The pacing protocol is used in two distinct modes in SNA: session level pacing and virtual route pacing.

Session level pacing affects flow of traffic only for a specific session and is directly controlled by the session partners. Session pacing is not a path control protocol and is discussed separately in Chap. 6. Virtual route pacing is used to manage global flow on a VR and affects all sessions on the route. The VR pacing involves the subarea nodes and requires no participation by peripheral nodes.

The VR pacing works within a minimum and a maximum pacing window. The minimum default window size n is the sum of TGs in the VR. Maximum default window size is $3n$. Pacing requests and responses are exchanged between endpoints of a virtual route. Let us consider a virtual route connecting SA2 and SA6 in Fig. 4.16. Since this virtual route has two TGs, the minimum VR pacing window n in this case would be 2 and the maximum window would be 6 (3×2).

4.8.1 Window Expansion

Assume that SA2 has a large number of PIUs destined for peripheral nodes attached to SA6. Since the window size is 2, SA2 releases 2

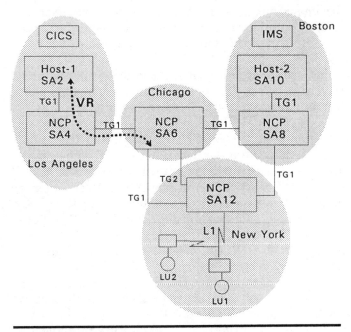

Figure 4.16   Virtual route pacing.

PIUs, reduces the window by 2, and awaits a pacing response from
SA6. SA2 has additional PIUs pending but cannot send them since the
pacing window is down to 0. The VR is considered *blocked* at this time.
The transmitter, SA2, can increase the window size by 1 and keep on
increasing each subsequent window until one of the following occurs:

1. The window is no longer the bottleneck, but the network cannot
   transmit any faster (due to bandwidth limitations). In this case the
   VR is not considered blocked nor is the window expanded.

2. The window has reached a maximum of $3n$.

3. The pacing response indicates that the network is beginning to get
   congested (CWRI bit, discussed in the following section, is set to 1
   in FID4 TH).

4.8.2   Window Contraction

The VR pacing window can be contracted to a smaller number in re-
action to network congestion. For window control purposes, the
network can be considered severely or moderately congested. The definition of severe or moderate congestion is left up to specific implementations but is generally tied in with the availability of free
buffers in a subarea node. A specific VR can get congested due to an

increase in activity on specific sessions using it, or the node itself can get congested due to accumulative traffic on all VRs passing through it. In the latter case, all VRs in the node would require that their windows be contracted.

A mild congestion is indicated by setting the bit *change window reply indicator* (CWRI) in FID4 TH to 1. A severe congestion is indicated by another bit in the FID4 TH called the *reset window indicator* (RWI) to 1.

When mild congestion occurs (CWRI = 1), the transmitter reduces the window by 1 unless minimum window n is reached when no further reductions are made to the window size. If the receiver is still congested, it can withhold the VR pacing response entirely, thereby completely stopping the transmitter from sending any further PIUs. One additional window may get transmitted before a CWRI-induced effect takes hold.

For severe congestion (RWI = 1), the window size is immediately reduced to minimum window n by the transmitter. The VR pacing window size is exchanged as a parameter of the ER activation command. VR itself is not activated via any commands but is considered active when the underlying ER has been successfully activated.

To summarize, various bits in the FID4 TH control VR pacing.

VR pacing request (VRPRQ):   This bit is set to 1 by the transmitter to request a pacing response. VRPRQ is set to 1 in the first PIU in a window.

VR pacing response (VRPRS):   This bit is set to 1 by the receiver to allow the transmitter to send an additional window of PIUs.

Change window reply indicator (CWRI):   When set to 0 by the receiver, the transmitter may increase the window by 1 if the VR is blocked.

When set to 1, the transmitter must reduce the window by 1 (unless it is already at minimum).

Reset window indicator (RWI):   When set to = 1 by the receiver, the transmitter must immediately reduce the window to the minimal value n.

Any node on the VR can set the CWRI or RWI flag to 1 depending on its internal condition.

4.9 SUMMARY

SNA path control functions are divided between two distinct sets: BNN-to-peripheral-node protocols and subarea-node-to-subarea-node protocols. BNN-to-peripheral-node protocols do not use subarea-element-type addressing and employ shortened versions of TH—FID2 and FID3.

Subarea nodes form the backbone of the SNA network and use FID4 TH. End-to-end routing structures are called virtual routes and map into underlying explicit routes. Alternates can be defined to back up failing routes but not for congestion-based adaptive routing. Virtual route pacing protocol is provided to manage PIU volume through the backbone.

Upper Layers, PU/LU Types, Control Sequences

5

NAUs and Higher-Level
Protocols in SNA

5.1 INTRODUCTION

Part 2 of this book, Chaps. 3 and 4, dealt with levels 1–3 in SNA, which form the transport network called the path control network. The users of the path control network are the higher layers in SNA which form the Network Addressable Units (NAUs). Three classes of NAUs—System Services Control Point (SSCP), Physical Unit (PU), and Logical Unit (LU)—were defined in Chap. 2.

To the NAUs, the path control network is a utility with which they communicate among themselves. With some exceptions, NAU protocols are transparent to the path control network, and, conversely, NAUs do not get involved in the path control protocols.

In this chapter we explore in more detail protocols used by NAUs to communicate among themselves. In the first part of this chapter we discuss protocols for controlling maximum PIU sizes, session sequence numbers, and session level flow control. The second part of the chapter deals with additional protocols for LU-LU sessions. While the LU-LU session protocols discussed in this chapter also apply to LU 6.2 sessions, the focus here is primarily terminal-type LUs. LU 6.2 is discussed as a separate topic later in Chaps. 12 and 13.

5.1.1 Sessions and Half Sessions

Within a session context, each session partner is also referred to as a half session since each LU represents one "half" of a complete session and the protocols implemented in each LU are also referred to as the half session protocols.

5.2 NAUs, PATH CONTROL NETWORK, AND SNA LAYERS

Sections 2.2 and 2.3 defined Network Addressable Units and their relationship to the path control network and SNA layers. Figure 5.1 illustrates these relationships. The functions of three NAUs types are as follows:

System Services Control Point (SSCP) is the overall control and management point in an SNA domain, where a domain is the part of an SNA network owned by an SSCP. SSCP function is implemented in VTAM.

A Physical Unit assists the SSCP in the management and control of the domain by managing resources attached to it and reporting their state to the SSCP.

While SSCP and PU provide management and control functions,

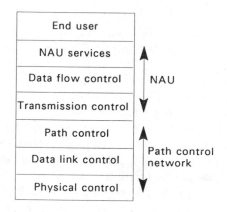

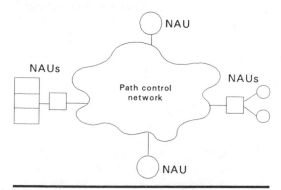

Figure 5.1   NAUs and path control network.

Logical Units provide support for end-user-to-end-user communications where end users can be terminal operators or host applications.

Flows on SSCP-PU and SSCP-LU sessions represent network activations, deactivations, and other network management tasks. Some of these flows are documented in Chap. 7. The protocols discussed in this chapter apply primarily to sessions involving Logical Units.

5.3 MESSAGE SIZING AND LU-LU SESSION FLOW CONTROL

Two protocols, chaining and session pacing (not to be confused with VR pacing), are used to ensure that LU buffers are not exceeded by the PIU volume. In addition, session level sequence numbers are used to ensure that the session PIUs do not get lost in transit. VR sequence numbers in FID 4, discussed in Chap. 4, are in addition to these session level sequence numbers. LUs maintain their own session sequence numbers, which apply only to PIUs flowing on a specific LU-LU session.

With message sizing and flow control our primary objective is to ensure that neither the PU nor the LU buffer is exceeded by data at any given time. To understand message sizing and flow control protocols we need to understand assumptions made regarding the structure of buffers in PUs and LUs. For the purposes of these protocols it is irrelevant whether PU and LU are in the same device as may be the case for a stand-alone device such as an IBM 3767, a PC, or an AS/400; or in separate devices such as in a clustered arrangement in the IBM 3270 family. Although our focus is primarily on LU protocols, we also look again at the segmentation protocol that was introduced in Sec. 4.4.5.

As shown in Fig. 5.2, PU buffers tend to be fairly small. In our example, we assume the PU buffer size to be 250 bytes to keep it a round number.

The LU buffer size is dictated by the type of terminal supported by the LU. For example, the LU buffer in a display station should be at least the size of the display area. For display stations with 24 rows and 80 columns, the LU buffer should be about 2000 characters (2K) to accommodate full screen display and control characters. For printers, basically, bigger is better; 3-4K buffers for printers are quite common.

Given finite-sized buffers, SNA protocols assist in ensuring that a session partner does not create PIUs that would exceed the receiving NAU's buffer. It is the responsibility of the boundary node PU to ensure that peripheral PUs' buffers are not exceeded by any single PIU. Ensuring that the LU buffers are not exceeded is a joint responsibility of the partner LU and the boundary subarea node.

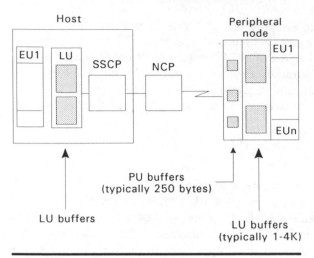

Figure 5.2   PU/LU buffers (PU/LU buffers may or may not be in the same physical device). EU = end user.

In Fig. 5.3, assume that a host application program is transmitting a 4000-character (4K) report to LU3, and that LU3 has a printer buffer of 2K. The partner LU for LU3 would be a host subsystem such as CICS, IMS, JES, etc. The host LU, to ensure that no individual PIU exceeds the receiving LU's buffer size, will break the 4K report into 2 PIUs, 2K each.

The subsystem passes these two PIUs to VTAM, which in turn, using path control routing, passes them to the boundary subarea node NCP. As the boundary NCP prepares to transmit the first 2K PIU, it realizes that it is too big to fit in the PU buffer. So the boundary NCP breaks each 2K PIU further into 8 PIUs, or segments of 250 bytes each, and transmits them to the PU. Segmentation was discussed in more detail in Sec. 4.4.4 and the reader should take a moment to review that material. The PU is responsible for recognizing and reassembling multisegment PIUs before passing them to the LU.

5.4   CHAINING

Chaining is the name for the LU-LU protocol to size messages down to the destination LU buffer size. In our example in Fig. 5.3, the host LU took the 4K report and broke it into a two-element chain, where each PIU in the chain was 2K long. To indicate to the destination LU that the message consists of multiple elements, 2 bits in the RH, called *begin chain* and *end chain,* are used.

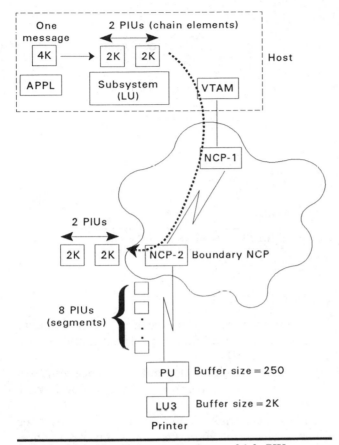

Figure 5.3 Breaking long messages into multiple PIUs.

The begin chain bit when set = 1 indicates the first element in a chain, and the end chain bit = 1 indicates the last element in a chain. Elements between the first and the last element are called middle elements and have both BC and EC bits set to 0 as shown in Fig. 5.4a for a multielement chain.

If a message is small enough to fit in the destination LU buffer, it is sent as a single-element chain, also referred to as the only element in chain, and has both BC and EC bits set to 1. This is illustrated in Fig. 5.4b.

For chaining protocols to work, each session partners have to know the buffer size of its partner LU. The terminal buffer size is defined during the VTAM system generation as a part of the LU profile and is made available to the host LU by VTAM during logon processing. The buffer sizes are transmitted to the SLU during bind processing.

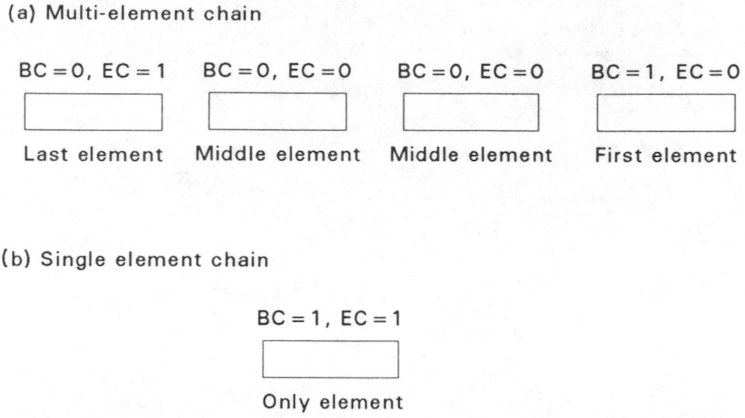

(a) Multi-element chain

BC = 0, EC = 1   BC = 0, EC = 0   BC = 0, EC = 0   BC = 1, EC = 0

Last element   Middle element   Middle element   First element

(b) Single element chain

BC = 1, EC = 1

Only element

Figure 5.4   Chaining indicators in RH (BC = begin chain, EC = end chain).

5.5   SESSION SEQUENCE NUMBERS

The purpose of sequence numbers is to keep track of chain elements being transmitted on a session. Each session partner maintains its own sequence number independently.

In Fig. 5.5, each PIU is a distinct chain element. Sequence numbers start with a value of 1 at session startup and then wrap around every 64K.

In our example, the PLU sends a chain element with sequence number 9 after sequence number 5. Since the chain element is out of sequence, the receiving LU responds with a sequence number error response.

5.6   SESSION PACING

Chaining protocol alone is not sufficient to prevent overflowing of LU buffers. In Fig. 5.3 a two-element chain is being sent to printer LU3 which is going to take a few seconds to print the first element. If the boundary node were to release the second element before the previous element had been printed, it could cause the first element to be overlaid by the second element. To prevent that from happening, we use pacing protocol between the boundary node and the SLU.

The pacing protocol involves a pacing window and a pacing request/response exchange in a manner similar to virtual route pacing discussed in the previous chapter.

The window specifies the number of chain elements n that can be released by the boundary node without exceeding the SLU buffer. After sending n chain elements, the boundary node must wait for a pac-

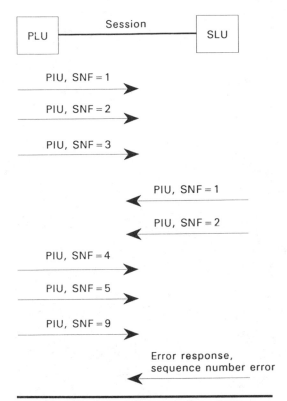

Figure 5.5 Session sequence numbers (SNF = sequence number field).

ing response from the SLU before it can send the next window of n chain elements. The pacing response must be requested by the boundary node by setting the pacing bit to 1 in the RH. The window size itself is defined to the boundary node during system generation or established at logon time by the PLU, based on the chain element size that the PLU intends using.

For Fig. 5.3, the chain element size equals the LU buffer size; therefore the pacing window must be specified as 1 and the boundary node would release only one chain element at a time and request a pacing response with each element. The next PIU would not be released until the printer sends the pacing response for the previous PIU. The secondary LU uses implementation-defined criteria to decide when to send a pacing response.

For printers with large buffers, e.g., 4K, even though very large chain elements can be created, smaller elements may have to be used to prevent the printer from monopolizing the PU buffer or the line on

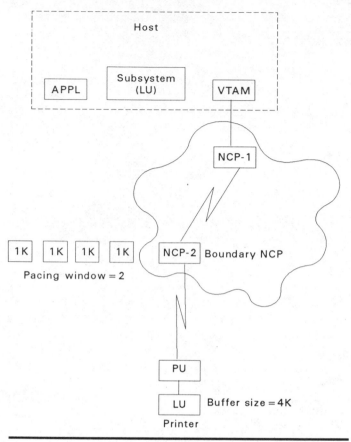

Figure 5.6 Session pacing example.

a multidrop link. In this case we have to balance printer performance with overall service to other users on the line. Another tradeoff would be the number of pacing responses. One should prevent excessive pacing responses since each pacing response adds to the traffic load.

In Fig. 5.6, we have a printer with a 4K buffer, yet we are chaining at 1K level with a pacing window of 2, i.e., filling half the printer buffer while the printer could be printing the other half and thus overlapping print function with the transmission of chain elements.

5.6.1 Multistage Pacing (VPacing)

Pacing between a boundary node and the secondary LU can cause large queues to build in the boundary node. If a boundary node has a number of printers connected to it (or minis and personal computers receiving files), large chains can sit in its buffers, which cannot be quickly transmitted due to pacing restrictions. This can cause serious performance degradation for the boundary node and prevent it from servicing other peripheral nodes.

To prevent this from occurring, pacing protocol can be applied in multiple stages starting with the host LU. The host LU, instead of transmitting a complete chain, can use a pacing window with VTAM; and VTAM can, in turn, pace the boundary node. The pacing window between host LU and VTAM and between VTAM and boundary node can be different from the window between boundary node and the destination LU.

In Fig. 5.6 we could use a pacing window of 4 between host LU and VTAM and between VTAM and boundary node. With this procedure, both VTAM and boundary node can limit printer-bound chain elements to a maximum of four chain elements at any given time.

If the report in our example in Fig. 5.6 were going to a hundred printers, we would have a separate session and therefore a separate pacing window for each printer, and even with pacing we could release a total of 400K worth of PIUs at any given time for all printers combined. This could still cause a large number of VTAM buffers to fill up, making them unavailable to other sessions and causing serious performance degradation.

In 1988, IBM announced adaptive pacing capability for LU-LU sessions. Adaptive pacing allows pacing window control in a manner similar to the VR pacing discussed in Chap. 4. However, LU-LU adaptive pacing is controlled via the RH, not the TH as was the case with VR pacing. With session level adaptive pacing, a newly architected control message, called the *isolated pacing message* (IPM), can be sent by a node on the congested session. The IPM message can specify a new window size as well as reset the current window (a reset means that any remaining PIUs in the current window must be withheld and sent as part of the next window). After sending an IPM, the originator of the IPM must receive an acknowledgement of its IPM. Upon receiving the acknowledgement, the originator of the IPM sends another IPM with a next window size if the original IPM had set the next window size equal to 0.

In VTAM documentation, host-LU-to-VTAM and VTAM-to-boundary-node pacing is called VPacing.

5.7 SEGMENTATION AND HIGHER-LAYER PROTOCOLS

In Fig. 5.3 we reviewed how segmentation protocol worked in addition to chaining. To illustrate how pacing and these protocols interact, let us look at an example in Fig. 5.7.

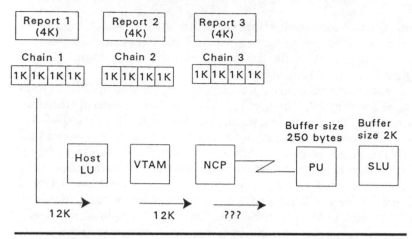

Figure 5.7 Segmentation and higher-level protocols.

In this example we have an application program with three reports to be printed at a printer. Each report consists of 4 pages, and each page contains 1000 characters. The programmer has created each report as a separate chain. The printer buffer is 2K, but the programmer has decided to make each page as an individual chain element, i.e., chain element = 1K.

The PU buffer size is 250 bytes and the last sequence number used in this session for outbound traffic was 50.

For this scenario we answer the following questions:

1. What is the highest pacing window that can be specified?

2. What would be the final sequence number associated with these reports?

3. How many segments would it take to transmit the three reports?

Pacing window. For pacing window, we need to ask how many chain elements 1K big would fit in an LU buffer of 2K size? Since only 2 elements would fit in the LU buffer, the maximum pacing window that can be specified is 2.

Remember that segments are not counted in a pacing window—only chain elements are.

Sequence numbers. For sequence numbers, again, only chain elements are counted, not the segments. Since the last sequence number for outbound traffic was 50, the first chain element in the three chains would be 51, the next 52, etc. Since there are 12 chain elements, the final sequence number on the last element of the third chain would be 62.

Segments. Each 1K chain element would be divided into 4 segments. Since there are 12 chain elements, the total number of segments would be 48.

Finally, Fig. 5.8 shows how chaining and segmentation flags are carried along with sequence numbers.

Chain 1 is shown in detail with TH and RH showing sequence numbers and chaining indicators. The first element in chain 1 carries a sequence number 51 and indicates that it is the first element in chain (BC = 1) and that more elements follow (EC = 0). The next two elements carry sequence numbers 52 and 53 and indicate that they are middle elements (BC = EC = 0). The fourth element in the first chain carries a sequence number of 54 and indicates that it is the last (EC = 1) element of a multielement (BC = 0) chain.

The bottom part of the diagram shows the first element after it has

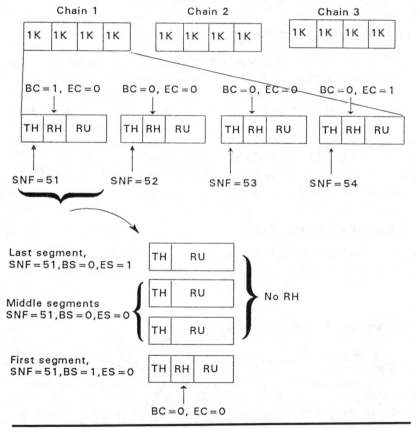

Figure 5.8 Chaining, sequence number, and segmentation indicators (BS = begin segments, ES = end segments, SNF = sequence number field).

been broken into four segments. All four segments carry the sequence number 51 as they are all part of the same chain element. The first segment has the begin segments flag set to 1 (BS = 1) and indicates that more segments follow (end segments, ES = 0). The segment also contains the RH and as many RU bytes as would fit in the segment. The remaining three segments carry the TH with sequence number and segmentation flags and RU bytes. Only the first segment carries an RH, not the subsequent segments.

5.8   SESSION PIU SIZING AND FLOW CONTROL SUMMARY

A good way to summarize chaining, segmentation, sequence numbers, and pacing is to compare segmentation and chaining. Table 5.1 provides this comparison. The remainder of this chapter deals with selected DFC protocols associated with LU-LU session.

5.9   LU-LU DFC PROTOCOLS

Once an LU-LU session has been established, protocols used during the session are primarily determined by the data flow control layer. Some of these protocols are shown in Fig. 5.9. As a matter of fact, chaining and session sequence generation discussed earlier in this chapter are part of the DFC layer. Additional protocols that we discuss now are used to control the direction of data flow and to provide session level LU-LU acknowledgements. Specifically bracket, full-duplex, half-duplex contention and flip-flop, and except and definite responses are discussed.

5.10   BRACKET PROTOCOLS

Bracket protocol was invented so that one could "bracket" a transaction or unit of work in order to delineate its beginning and end clearly.

TABLE 5.1   Segmentation versus Chaining

Segmentation	Chaining
Based upon PU buffer size	Based upon LU buffer size
Done by the PU (boundary NCP or peripheral node)	Done by LU (host subsystem or device LU)
Has no effect on sequence numbers	Each chain element causes sequence number to be incremented by
Segments not counted in pacing	Chain elements are counted in pacing

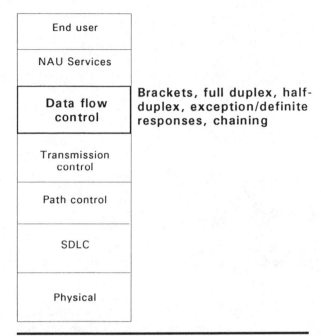

End user	
NAU Services	
Data flow control	Brackets, full duplex, half-duplex, exception/definite responses, chaining
Transmission control	
Path control	
SDLC	
Physical	

Figure 5.9 DFC LU-LU protocols.

The terms *transaction* and *unit of work* are used very broadly here and could involve any number of PIUs exchanged between the session partners while the session is in a bracket state. The unit of work to be executed within a bracket state is generally uninterruptable or, in some other sense, critical to the session partners. SNA leaves it to implementations to define a unit of work or transaction.

As shown in Fig. 5.10, bracket protocol is implemented by 2 bits in the RH—the *begin bracket indicator* (BBI) and the *end bracket indicator* (EBI). A session can be put in bracket state by either session partner by sending a PIU with the BBI set to 1. The bracket state is terminated when a PIU with EBI = 1 is exchanged.

The criteria used to initiate or terminate bracket state, or the number of PIUs exchanged within a bracket state, are not defined by the architecture and are left up to individual implementations. Various IBM products have used bracket protocol for different purposes; three examples follow.

5.10.1 Brackets to Prevent Unsolicited Data

IBM 3270 and 3770 printers use bracket protocol to prevent unsolicited data from interrupting a print task that is currently in

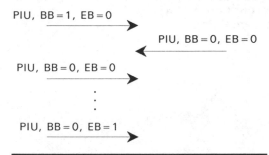

Figure 5.10 Bracket protocols (BB = begin bracket, EB = end bracket).

progress. These printers require that a bracket state be started successfully (BBI = 1) before any data would be accepted. No new bracket attempt is accepted until the current bracket state ends. Figure 5.11 shows an example.

As illustrated in Fig. 5.11, in step 1, program A requests its LU to send a report to a printer, and the LU initiates a bracket by sending a PIU with BBI = 1 in the RH. Assuming that the printer is not already in a bracket state, the printer accepts the BBI and the accompanying PIU. As program A is continuing with the rest of its data, in step 2 of the diagram program B attempts to send a message to the same printer causing the host LU to initiate another bracket state. Since the printer is already in a bracket state, it rejects the BBI attempt by program B by sending a negative response to the PIU that had BBI = 1 on it.

When program A terminates its bracket state with the printer (presumably at the end of the report), step 3 of the diagram, program B can start a bracket state and send its report as shown in step 4 of the diagram.

A similar application for 3270 devices prevents printer disruption from a local print function. On 3270 clusters, display stations can obtain a hard copy of the display by pressing the local print key. The local print key causes the cluster controller to print data in the display station buffer on the printer designated for local print functions. To prevent a local print function from disrupting the printer, which may be in session with a host application, the controller would attempt a bracket state initiation with the printer. If the printer rejects the BBI attempt, the local print function is postponed until the printer finally

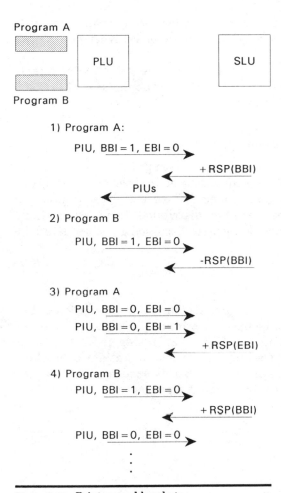

Program A

PLU

SLU

Program B

1) Program A:

PIU, BBI = 1, EBI = 0

+ RSP(BBI)

PIUs

2) Program B

PIU, BBI = 1, EBI = 0

-RSP(BBI)

3) Program A

PIU, BBI = 0, EBI = 0

PIU, BBI = 0, EBI = 1

+ RSP(EBI)

4) Program B

PIU, BBI = 1, EBI = 0

+ RSP(BBI)

PIU, BBI = 0, EBI = 0

Figure 5.11   Printers and brackets.

accepts a bracket state. For 3270 stations, printers can be defined to
the cluster controller as shareable when not in LU-LU session or
when out of a bracket state.

5.10.2 Brackets and Recoverable
Unit of Work (LU 6.0)

LU 6.0, the predecessor of LU 6.2, used bracket protocol to define a
state during which distributed transaction programs updated their
files related to a single business transaction (e.g., order processing).
Completion of a bracket state (successful BBI/EBI exchange) meant
that all files associated with the transaction had been successfully up-

dated. A transaction failure within a bracket state meant that files may have been updated only partially and error recovery procedures were initiated.

LU 6.2 does not use bracket protocol as a basis for file recovery. Since LU 6.0 represents a defunct LU type, this application of bracket protocol is only of historic interest.

5.10.3   Brackets and Conversations (LU 6.2)

For two transaction programs to exchange data units in an LU 6.2 environment they must establish a conversation and terminate the conversation at the end of their exchanges. LU 6.2 uses bracket protocol to bound a "conversation" between two distributed transactions. Conversations and LU 6.2 environment are discussed in more detail in Chaps. 12 and 13.

5.10.4   Brackets and BID Command

BID is an optional SNA command (an LU "bids" for permission to begin a bracket state) that can be used with bracket protocol. The use of the BID command is illustrated in Fig. 5.12. In step 1, LUA sends a BID command to LUB requesting permission to initiate a bracket. LUB grants permission to begin the bracket by sending a positive response, or declines the request by sending an exception response. In a

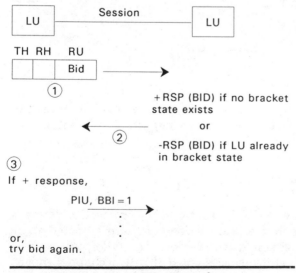

Figure 5.12   Brackets and BID command.

sense, BID command is redundant since one could always start with step 3 in Fig. 5.11. If the destination LU were already in a bracket state, it would reject the BBI attempt and maintain proper protection.

5.10.5 Ready to Receive (RTR)—Recovery from Bracket Rejection

When a bid or begin bracket is rejected, the loser can retry the operation after an arbitrary amount of time. To make this recovery more methodical, a ready to receive (RTR) command can be used.

For such sessions where RTR command is supported, rejection of BBI or BID is accompanied by a sense code indicating whether or not an RTR will follow the rejection. The rejecting LU can then send an RTR when it is ready to accept a new BBI or a BID. Upon receiving RTR, the bidding LU can send a new BID or a PIU with BBI = 1.

5.11 FDX, HDX CONTENTION, AND HDX FLIP-FLOP—CONTROLLING THE DIRECTION OF SESSION FLOW

Within a bracket state, additional procedures can be used to control the session that can send data at any given time.

5.11.1 Full-Duplex Sessions

In full-duplex (FDX) sessions no prior permission is required by either end to transmit a PIU, and consequently no flags or bits are needed in the RH to regulate transmissions. From a control point of view, FDX sessions require no protocol. However, LUs supporting FDX sessions need procedures to manage their input and output buffers and for correlating PIUs with their responses.

None of the common IBM terminals (3270, 3770, 3767) or LU 6.2 support FDX sessions.

5.11.2 Half-Duplex Sessions

There are two options available within the HDX protocol.

Half-duplex contention. In contention half-duplex, either LU can send data at any time without prior permission. The data transfer is considered successful unless the other LU initiates a transfer at the same time. When both LUs initiate transmission at the same time, it is considered a case of contention.

To resolve contention, one of the two LUs is designated contention winner at session setup. The designated winner responds with an ex-

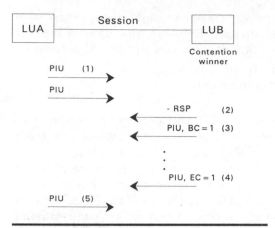

Figure 5.13 HDX contention session (BC = begin chain, EC = end chain).

ception (negative) response to the designated loser and continues with its own PIUs. Figure 5.13 illustrates such an exchange. In step 1 LUA attempts to initiate a send operation which is rejected by LUB in step 2. LUB, the designated winner, transmits its PIUs in steps 3–4. In step 5, LUA successfully initiates a send operation.

Half-duplex flip-flop.   In flip-flop half duplex, one of the two LUs is always in a send state and the other in receive state. The sending station gives up its right to send or changes the direction of flow by sending a PIU with the *change direction indicator* (CDI) bit = 1 in the RH. When the session is established, one of the two LUs is designated as the first speaker, and the first speaker has the right to send when session starts. From then on the direction of flow flip-flops as change direction indicators are exchanged.

Occasionally a half session in a receive state has a need to send data. It can request the LU in send state for a CDI by sending a SIGNAL command. The SIGNAL command is an expedited command and can be sent even while a half session is in receive state.

Figure 5.14 illustrates half-duplex flip-flop control. The exchange is initiated by the first speaker with a begin bracket and the direction of flow from then is controlled via CDI. Note that positive response to SIGNAL only acknowledges the reception of the command and does not imply CDI. The CDI must still be sent on a subsequent PIU. Normally, an LU would transmit a complete chain before sending CDI.

Termination of bracket state (EBI = 1) always implies a change of direction.

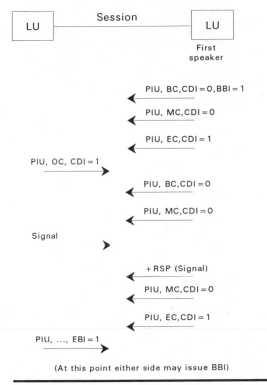

Figure 5.14 Half-duplex flip-flop session.

5.11.3 Brackets, Half-Duplex, and Display Stations

DFC protocols are managed by the LU microcode (or software) in the display station and are transparent to the person operating the station. These protocols do have an effect on locking and unlocking the keyboard.

For the 3270 family display stations, any time the terminal accepts a PIU with BBI = 1, it locks the keyboard, the presumption being that more data are going to come from the host. The keyboard is unlocked when a CDI is received from the host to allow the operator to enter data, since it is now the terminal LU's turn to send. Figure 5.15 illustrates the effect of bracket and half-duplex flip-flop protocols on the keyboard operation for a 3270-type display station.

When the terminal user completes data entry and presses a data transmission key (ENTER, PF, CLEAR, etc.), step 1 in Fig. 5.15, the terminal logic builds a PIU (or a chain of PIUs) with CDI = 1 on the last or the only element in chain and locks the keyboard. The keyboard gets

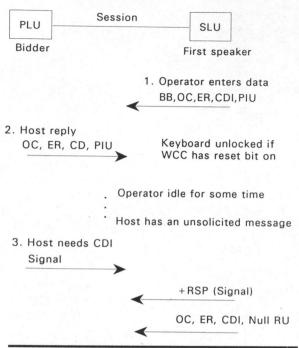

Figure 5.15   Effect of CDI on keyboard (WCC = write control character, a 3270 control character).

released on receiving the next CDI from the host, step 2 [actually, the keyboard is released through the reset bit in the 3270 control character called the *write control character* (WCC)]. The terminal operator, during the time when the keyboard is locked, can cause the terminal logic to send a Signal by pressing the attention key. (Operationally, contention half-duplex would differ from flip-flop in that the keyboard would never be locked and there would be no need to exchange change direction or signal.) Alternatively, the host can send a SIGNAL, too, as shown in step 3 of the diagram.

5.12   LU-LU RESPONSES

Session level responses are exchanged to confirm that session is proceeding without errors. For each chain element transmitted, the sender can request a session level response. Unusual conditions and errors are reported as *exception* responses. The definition of exception conditions is left up to the individual implementations. IBM product technical descriptions list exception conditions for each SNA product.

Most exception responses are also accompanied by a sense code in the RU, which further describes the cause of the exception. Sense codes supported by various SNA products are described in the corresponding product manuals.

The sender of a request RU or chain element (see Chap. 2 for definition of a request) can specify one of three options for a response:

1. No response is necessary—whether PIU is successfully processed or a failure occurs. This is more of a theoretical option since we do want to know if a failure occurred and none of the implementations allow this as an option.

2. A response *must* be sent whether the request was processed successfully or not. This is called the *definite response* option and in this case each chain element causes a response RU to be transmitted. This option may generate excessive response traffic and degrade network performance.

3. A response is required only if an exception occurs. This is the most optimal option in most cases.

By judiciously mixing definite and exception response options we can assure session integrity without generating excessive responses. One of the problems with exception responses is the duration that the sender of the request should wait for an exception response before assuming that everything must have gone well and therefore no response would come back (in SNA there are no session level timers). To solve this dilemma, we can use techniques illustrated in Fig. 5.16. In this example we are sending a multielement chain. On all elements except the last we ask only for exception responses; i.e., a response is due only if an error condition occurs. On the last element we ask for a definite response. Since responses are never sent out of sequence, we know that the whole chain was processed successfully when we receive a positive response to the last element in the chain. Responses also carry the sequence number of the chain element to which the response belongs—thus, in case of an exception response, we also know the chain element that failed.

In a multielement chain, only one outstanding definite response is allowed at a time. SNA does not define recovery procedures when an exception occurs. The recovery, if any, is left up to the implementation.

5.12.1   Response Bits in RH

Bits 0, 2, and 3 in byte 1 of the RH in conjunction with bit 0 in byte 0 define the response protocol for a session. Bits 0, 2, and 3 in byte 1 are called ER, DR1, and DR2, respectively. ER stands for exception response, and DR1 and DR2 stand for definite response types 1 and 2.

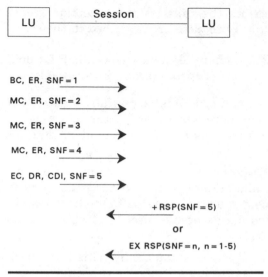

Figure 5.16 Using exception and definite responses.

The interpretation of these three bits depends on whether they are being used with a request or a response RU as follows:

Request RU: (RH, byte 0, bit 0 = 0)
On a request RU, ER takes precedence over DR1 and DR2; i.e., if ER = 1, response is necessary *only if* an exceptional event occurs, irrespective of the setting of DR1 and DR2. No response is due if no exception occurred.
If ER = 0 and DR1 or DR2 or both are set to 1, a response must be sent, whether positive or exception.

Response RU: (RH, byte 0, bit 0 = 1)
ER = 0 means a positive response and ER = 1 means a negative response. The values of DR1 and DR2 are copied from the original request to which this response applies.

Table 5.2 summarizes all possible requests and responses. Other than the foregoing definitions, SNA does not define any additional functions for DR1 and DR2. Certain SNA commands, LU 6.0, and LU 6.2 require specific use of DR1 and DR2 in some cases. Otherwise, the usage of these bits is left up to the implementation. DR1 and DR2 usage is agreed between the session partners at session establishment time.

TABLE 5.2   Request/Response Protocols

Request structure			Possible responses			Comments
ER	DR1	DR2	ER	DR1	DR2	
0	0	1	0	0	1	Positive response
			1	0	1	Exception response
0	1	0	0	1	0	Positive response
			1	1	0	Exception response
0	1	1	0	1	1	Positive response
			1	0	0	Exception response
1	0	1	1	0	1	Exception response (No response sent if positive)
1	1	0	1	1	0	Exception response (No response sent if positive)
1	1	1	1	1	1	Exception response (No response sent if positive)
1	0	0	1	0	0	These two options permitted by architecture but not
or						
0	0	0	0	0	0	implemented in any product

Note: Three types of positive and three types of exception responses are possible.

5.13   REQUEST AND RESPONSE MODES

Request and response modes further define rules that control the timing and order of responses. Modes are defined separately for the requester and the responder. The PLU and SLU can have different modes in a session depending on their capabilities.

5.13.1   Request Modes

These apply to the sender of a request. Two modes are defined.

Immediate control mode.   The LU or the half session operating in this mode can send only single-element chains, and each chain must request a definite response, DR1 or DR2 or both. This mode is generally appropriate for SNA commands only and not for user data.

Delayed control mode.   This mode allows transmission of multiple-element chains. Two suboptions are available for requesting responses:

1. *Immediate request mode:*   On each chain we can ask for no response, an exception response, or a definite response (on the last element only). If a definite response is requested, no additional chains are sent until a response to the outstanding chain is received; i.e., only one definite response is outstanding at any given time.

2. *Delayed request mode:* Multiple definite responses (to multiple chains, there is still only one definite response allowed per chain) are permitted to remain outstanding and they can arrive in any order.

The immediate request mode is used most commonly in SNA products.

5.13.2 Response Modes

These define the role of the responder (the receiver of the request) and are the complement of the request mode. Two response modes are defined:

Immediate response mode. In this mode the responses are sent in the same order as the requests are received. This mode is used when the sender is operating in immediate control or immediate request mode.

Delayed response mode. The receiver operates in this mode when the sender is operating in a delayed control mode and allows the receiver to send responses in any sequence. The only way to assure that all outstanding responses have been received in this mode is for the requester to follow up with the SNA command CHASE. The CHASE command requests the receiver to send all outstanding responses and is typically used for cleanup purposes in preparation of session termination.

5.14 DFC COMMANDS

For BID, RTR, and SIGNAL, see Secs. 5.10.4 and 5.10.5.

5.14.1 Stop Bracket Initiation (SBI) and Bracket Initiation Stopped (BIS)

SBI is no longer a supported command. Its description may be found in earlier SNA documents and it was used in LU 6.0 sessions. SBI has been replaced by *change number of sessions* (CNOS) protocol in LU 6.2, which is discussed later in the book. *Bracket initiation stopped* (BIS) is used to confirm that no new bracket states (BBI = 1) will be initiated in this session. It is typically used in preparation of session termination.

5.14.2 Cancel

This command is used to terminate a partially transmitted chain (probably due to some error condition).

5.14.3   Chase

See Sec. 5.13.2.

5.14.4   LUSTAT (Logical Unit States)

This command is used by an LU to send 4 bytes of SNA- or user-defined status information to its session partner. An example of LUSTAT would be status sent by a display station after recovering from a power loss (component now available). LU 6.2 usage for this command is described in Chap. 12.

5.14.5   Quiesce at End of Chain (QEC), Quiesce Complete (QC), and Release Quiesce (RELQ)

QEC is used by a half session to request its partner to stop sending any further normal flow (e.g., user data) chains at the end of the current chain. A half session may request QEC due to shortage of resources such as buffers or in preparation of session termination.

QC request is sent by a half session after receiving QEC to confirm that it would not send any more chains, i.e., it has quiesced. A half session in quiesced state is released from this state when its session partner sends it a RELQ.

5.14.6   Shutdown (SHUTD) and Shutdown Complete (SHUTC)

SHUTD request is sent by the PLU to SLU to quiesce the SLU, most likely in preparation of session termination.

The SLU responds to SHUTD with a SHUTC. The session can again be taken out of this state with RELQ request from the primary. (Note that SHUTD and SHUTC are asymmetric; i.e., the former is PLU-SLU and the latter SLU-PLU and never vice versa.)

Request shutdown (RSHUTD) too is an asymmetric command, SLU to PLU only, to indicate that the SLU is ready for session termination. The proper reply to RSHUTD is the session termination command, UNBIND (discussed in Chap. 6), and not SHUTD.

5.14.7   Ready to Receive (RTR)

RTR informs the bidder (whose earlier BBI or BID was rejected) that it may now initiate a bracket. See Sec. 5.11.2 for more details.

5.14.8 Signal

Sent by a half session to request a change direction from its session partner in half-duplex flip-flop session. See Sec. 5.11.2 under "Half-duplex flip-flop" for more details.

5.15   PROTOCOL AND COMMAND USAGE

It is important to note that not all LUs support all the protocols and commands described in this chapter. Specific product information should be consulted to determine which subset from the foregoing is supported. As we see in Chap. 6, the specific subsets supported differentiate various LU types (or LU-LU session types) from each other.

5.16   SUMMARY

With the exception of segmentation protocol, discussed in Chap. 4 and reviewed here again, all other protocols discussed in this chapter were from the transmission control and data flow control layers and govern the rules of LU-LU sessions. (Actually some of these protocols can, theoretically, also be used on other sessions such as SSCP-PU or SSCP-LU sessions, but they are rarely used.) Sequence numbers are carried in transmission header, and the usage of all other protocols is indicated in the RH. All commands are carried in the RU.

6

Peripheral PU and LU Types

6.1 INTRODUCTION

Network Addressable Units (NAUs) in SNA define the endpoints of
the SNA network and communicate with each other using the Path
Control Network. There are three classes of NAUs: SSCP, PU, and
LU. Each peripheral node in SNA contains one PU and one or more
LUs.

SNA implications of network stations are fully defined by their PU/
LU types. Another way of looking at PU/LU types is used as a methodology to partition SNA stations into various levels of intelligence. In
more practical terms, compatibility with SNA means ability to emulate a specific PU and LU type.

6.2 PERIPHERAL NODES
AND PU/LU TYPES

Peripheral nodes in SNA represent terminals, clusters, minicomputers and PCs, i.e., any devices attached to an SNA network other than
mainframes and FEPs. As shown in Fig. 6.1, the characteristics of a
peripheral node map into two types of NAUs: a PU type and one or
more LU types. Multiple LU types can be associated with a node if the
node represents multiple devices.

The three PU types defined in ascending order of intelligence are 1,
2, and 2.1. Various LU types include 0, 1, 2, 3 and 6.2. The missing
numbers in LU types represent LU types that have now been abol-
ished or were never announced.

Figure 6.2 shows some of the common IBM terminals and their associated PU/LU types. For the IBM 3270 family, the 3174 cluster controller represents a PU.T2. Each attached terminal represents an LU.
For remote job entry devices such as an IBM 3770 or 3790, the PU and

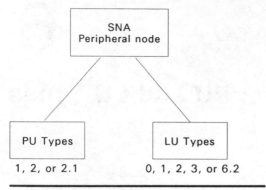

Figure 6.1 Peripheral nodes and PU and LU types (*Note:* Obsolete LU types not shown).

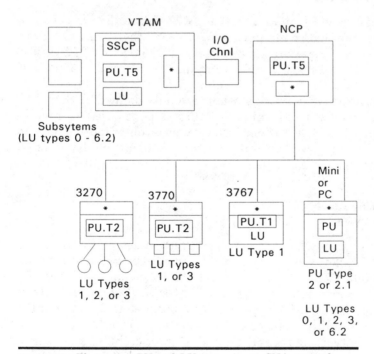

Figure 6.2 Illustrative PU and LU types in an SNA network (* = path control network functions).

LU functions are represented by a single hardware device. IBM 3767, though no longer available but often emulated in protocol converters, represents a PU.T1 and LU Type 1 in a stand-alone machine. PS/2 and AS/400 are capable of supporting PU 2 and 2.1 and multiple LU types.

6.3 PERIPHERAL NODE PU FUNCTIONS

Overall functions provided by a PU are specified in an architected entity called the PU Services Manager. Four categories of services defined for the PU Services Manager include:

Network services: This component processes all SSCP commands and includes functions such as activating and deactivating the physical and internal resources necessary to support session activations requested by the SSCP.

Route management services: These services apply only to subarea nodes and deal with the management of explicit and virtual routes.

Session control services: This component manages the activation, deactivation, and status reporting of the sessions for the node. It is responsible for maintaining control blocks for all sessions supported by the node and the underlying link connecting this node with the subarea node.

Link services: According to the *SNA Format and Protocol Manual,* this component deals with unique aspects of a DLC but its details are not described in any manual.

6.4 NODE TYPES AND FID IMPLICATIONS

Recollect that SNA uses the term *node* to represent a device containing a PU and that the node type for the device is the same as its PU type. One implication of the node type is the Transmission Header (TH) type used. For Type 1 nodes, format identification Type 3 (FID3) TH is used, and FID2 is used for Type 2 nodes. However, the implications of node type go beyond FID type and are discussed in the following section. Node Type 2.1 is discussed as a separate topic in Chap. 12.

6.4.1 Type 2.0 Nodes

FID2, as shown in Fig. 6.3, is used by Type 2.0 nodes and is 6 bytes long. The various fields contained in it are as follows:

Byte 0, bits 0-3: Contain the FID itself and for FID2, a value of B'0010' is contained in these bits.

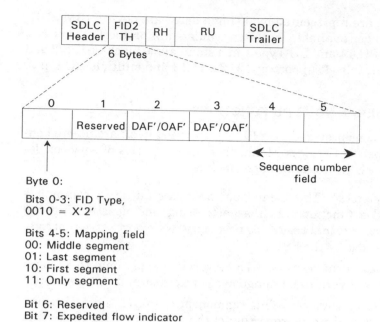

Figure 6.3 FID2 transmission header for PU Type 2 nodes (DAF' = destination address field, OAF' = origination address field).

Byte 0, bits 4, 5:   These bits represent the mapping field (MPF) and contain the segmentation indicators.

Byte 0, bit 6:   Reserved.

Byte 0, bit 7:   Expedited flow indicators (EFI), when set to 1, indicate an expedited PIU. Expedited category is reserved for selected SNA commands.

Byte 1:   Reserved.

Bytes 2 and 3:   These two bytes contain the destination or origination address in a 1-byte local ID format and a session-type indicator.

The local ID of a PU is always X'00'. ID range for attached LUs can be X'02'- X'FE'.

For outbound traffic (boundary node to the device), the destination address field (DAF') is the local ID of the destination PU or LU. The origination address field (OAF') for outbound traffic, IBM terminology notwithstanding, does not contain an address but rather a session-type indicator. VTAM and NCP products can derive the proper origination address from this field. For outbound traffic, for SSCP-LU (and SSCP-PU) session, OAF' = X'00' and for LU-LU sessions OAF' field = X'01'.

For inbound traffic, peripheral node to boundary node, the peripheral node simply switches DAF'/OAF' fields.

Bytes 4, 5: These two bytes contain sequence number for normal flow PIUs on a LU-LU session. Sequence numbers are discussed in detail in Chap. 5.

6.4.2 TYPE 1 NODES

For logical units attached to Type 1 nodes, session level sequence numbers are not supported. In addition DAF' and OAF' fields of PU.T2 are combined in a single byte. Thus, FID3 is smaller than FID2, as shown in Fig. 6.4.

Byte 0: This byte has the same structure as FID2 TH (see Fig. 6.3).

Byte 1:

Bits 0, 1: These two bits contain a session-type indicator where 00 = SSCP-PU, 10 = SSCP-LU, and 11 = LU-LU session.

Bits 2-7: Local ID of the destination. The PU ID is always 0, and the associated LU can have any address in the decimal value range of 2-63.

6.5 PRODUCTS AND PU TYPES

Almost all current IBM network stations, 3270, 3770, AS/400, PS/2, System/3X, and 4600 series financial terminals, support PU Type 2.0. In addition, software-driven systems such as AS/400 and personal

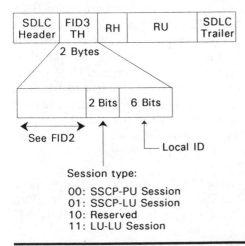

Figure 6.4 FID3 transmission header for PU Type 1 nodes.

computers can also implement PU 2.1 or even non-SNA communications using asynchronous, BSC, or X.25 protocols—depending on the type of software installed.

6.6 LU TYPES—INTRODUCTION

Various LU types represent protocol subsets suitable for particular applications or device types. At the same time, these categories are defined broadly enough so that we do not need too many categories. LU Types 1 and 3, for example, represent batch devices such as printers, card readers, diskettes, and tape devices. LU Type 2 implies a display station and LU 6.2 represents software-based distributed application nodes. LU Type 0 is an unstructured LU that was frequently used in the early days of SNA, to support program-to-program communications, among other things.

Specific session protocols such as chaining, pacing, brackets, etc., supported by an LU are also defined by its LU type.

6.7 LU TYPES AND LU PROFILES

While the basic concept of LU types, as described in the previous paragraph, is straightforward, the SNA methodology used to describe LU types is a little more elaborate.

LU types are defined in terms of two profile numbers—Function Management (FM) profile number and Transmission Services (TS) profile number. To understand FM and TS profiles, we need to review SNA layers associated with LU functions. Figure 6.5 shows the association between a logical unit and SNA layers. As shown in Fig. 6.5, a logical unit represents the top three layers in SNA. The highest SNA layer, NAU services, is referred to as the LU services for this specific NAU type. Within the LU services layer we have a sublayer called the LU Services Manager (generic name NAU Services Manager as shown in Fig. 6.5). The services layer defines services that the LU provides to the end user (application). The protocols that these LUs can support are defined by presentation services (PS), DFC, and TC layers. Since each session partner represents one-half of an LU-LU session, the DFC and TC layers are collectively also referred to as "half session" protocols in a session context. PS protocols supported by an LU are defined in the PS profile.

DFC protocols that can be supported by the half session are specified in a half session profile called the Function Management (FM) profile, which defines usage of protocols such as brackets, HDX F/F, chaining, etc.

TC protocols that can be supported by a half session are specified in

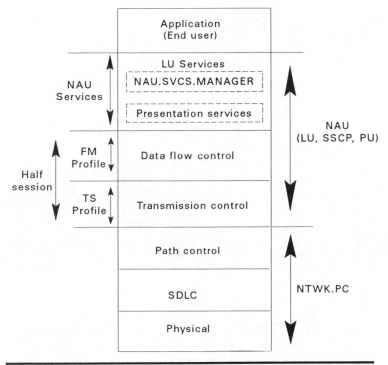

Figure 6.5 SNA layers, LU functions, half sessions, and profiles (*Note:* LU 6.2 also has transaction services).

its TS profile. This profile defines the use of protocols such as pacing and sequence-number-based recovery, etc.

With the concepts of PS, FM, and TS profiles defined, SNA takes it one step further by predefining several PS, FM, and TS profiles and assigning each a number; e.g., FM profiles 2, 3, etc., and TS profiles 2, 3, etc. PS profile number is always the same as the LU type itself. Each profile number represents a unique protocol subset. Each LU type is then assigned a set of profile numbers that can be associated with it.

Table 6.1 summarizes the current LU types and associated profiles. The comments column describes Presentation profile. Brief descriptions of FM and TS profiles are given in the following sections.

6.8 FM PROFILES

Table 6.1 shows available profiles for LU Types 0, 1, 2, 3, and 6.2. As shown in the table, some LU types are allowed multiple profiles and each profile may allow multiple choices in implementing a specific

TABLE 6.1   LU Types Summary

LU type	PS profile	TS profile	FM profile	Comments
0	0	2,3,4,7,*	2,3,4,18,*	Any option desired, open-ended LU
1	1	3,4	3,4	Data streams based on SNA character string or structured fields FM headers (none, or one or more of FMH-1, FMH-2, FMH-3) Data processing media support
2	2	3	3	SNA 3270 data stream No FM headers Display support
3	3	3	3	SNA 3270 data stream No FM header Printer support
6.2	6.2	19	7	Generalized data stream (GDS)

*Note: Profiles 7 and 18 are used with obsolete LU Types 4 and 6.0 and are not described in this book.

protocol. For example, FM profile 3 allows each half session to use definite or exception responses. In such cases the specific option used is implementation defined. Brief descriptions of various FM profiles in Table 6.1 are as follows:

FM profile 3:   This profile allows half-duplex flip-flop sessions, multielement chains, definite or exception responses, bracket protocol, FMHs, and data compression.

DFC commands supported: CANCEL, SIG, LUSTAT, CHASE, SHUTD, SHUTC, RSHUTD, BID, and RTR.
    This profile is allowed for LU Types 0, 1, 2, and 3.

FM profiles 4:   Similar to FM profile 3, this includes additional DFC commands QEC, QC, and RELQ.
    FM profile 4 is primarily of interest in LU Type 0 but may optionally be used with LU Type 1. (FM profile 3 is the norm for LU Type 1.)

FM profile 7:   Described in Chap. 12.

6.9   TS PROFILES

TS profile 2:   Pacing and sequence numbers are supported; CLEAR is supported; SDT, RQR, STSN, and CRV are not supported. TS profile 2 applies only to LU Type 0.

TS profile 3:   Pacing and sequence numbers are supported. CLEAR and SDT are supported, CRV is supported if cryptography is supported, and RQR and STSN commands are not supported. TS profile 3 can be used by LU Types 0, 1, 2, and 3.

TS profile 4:   Pacing and sequence numbers are supported. SDT, CLEAR, RQR, and STSN commands are supported; CRV is supported if cryptography used. TS profile 4 is primarily of interest with LU Type 0 but can be used optionally with LU Type 1. (TS profile 3 is the norm for LU Type 1.)

In all cases, sequence number support also requires that the LU be attached to a PU type that supports sequence numbers, i.e., PU Type 5, 2, or 2.1.

TS profile 19:   Discussed in Chap. 12 under LU 6.2.

6.10   OTHER PROFILE NUMBERS

The profile numbers missing from Table 6.1 have either been phased out in the current implementations or do not apply to LU-LU sessions. Table 6.2 shows usage of profiles for sessions other than LU-LU.

6.11   PRESENTATION SERVICES AND FUNCTION MANAGEMENT HEADER (FMH)

Another feature that distinguishes one LU from another is the support for FMH. Figure 6.6 shows the relationship between FMH and a PIU. The figure also shows various types of FMHs architected in SNA. A number of the FMHs shown were used by LU types that are obsolete now.

Whether or not a session can support FMHs is indicated in the FM profile. Even when FMHs are supported, not every PIU carries an

TABLE 6.2   Profiles for non LU-LU Sessions

FM profile	Session types
0	SSCP-PU, SSCP-LU
5	SSCP-PU
6	SSCP-LU

TS profile	Session types
1	SSCP-PU, SSCP-LU
17	SSCP-SSCP

Note: LUs in the same node as an SSCP use FM profile 6 for SSCP-LU session; otherwise, the LUs use FM profile 0.

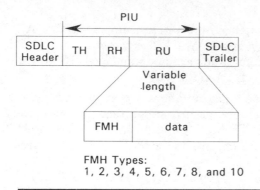

FMH Types:
1, 2, 3, 4, 5, 6, 7, 8, and 10

Figure 6.6   FMH and PIU.

FMH. The presence of a FMH is indicated by format indicator (FI = 1) bit in the RH. A brief description of various FMHs follows:

FMH-1: FMH-1 is used to select a destination within a multicomponent LU. The destination may be a device within an LU or a file on a device. An example of a multidevice LU would be an RJE terminal such as IBM 3770 which can represent a console, printer, card reader or diskette file, and card punch or diskette.

In addition, each destination may have a default data stream type associated with it. FMH-1 can also be used to specify a particular data stream type such as word processing (implementation defined), job (JES), document interchange, etc. Also indicated in FMH-1 is whether compression or compaction is used.

FMH-2: Indicates specific data management activities to be performed at the destination selected by FMH-1. Examples of data management functions include adding and replacing records, creating and deleting files, and providing status information.

FMH-3: It is similar to FMH-2 and specifies data management functions. However, FMH-3 specifies a function that applies to all destinations in both LUs. An example of such a function is a data compaction table that is used to compact and decompact data.

FMH-4: Was used by LU 6.1 to process information for transaction programs. It is not supported by LU 6.2.

FMH-5: Also known as ATTACH FMH (to attach a remote transaction—see Chap. 12 for a discussion of conversations), used by LU 6.2 to establish a conversation between two transaction programs. ATTACH FMH is sent by a LU 6.2 when one of its transaction program issues an allocate request.

FMH-6: Applies to now obsolete LU 6.1. Was used to carry transaction-program-defined commands.

FMH-7: Used by LU 6.2 to report errors during a conversation. The FMH carries SNA sense code and, optionally, an error log record.

FMH-8: Was used by a product-specific (IMS/VS) implementation of LU 6.1.

FMH-9: Was never defined.

FMH-10: Was used by LU 6.1 to prepare the session for a synchronization point. Not used by LU 6.2.

FMH-11: Was never defined.

FMH-12: Used by LU 6.2 to send enciphered password during BIND processing for LU-LU password verification.

6.12 LU TYPES AND PS DATA STREAMS

Presentation Services allow three types of data streams for Logical Units.

1. *3270 data stream:* This product-defined data stream is used by LU Types 2 and 3. The now obsolete LU 6.1 could also support this data stream. The 3270 data stream is described in IBM 3270 publications.

2. *SNA character string (SCS):* SCS is used by LU Type 1 and could also be supported by LU 6.1. SCS defines EBCDIC control codes to format a visual presentation medium such as a printed page or display screen. The control codes also set modes of device operation. Table 6.3 shows control codes defined under SCS.

3. *Generalized data stream (GDS):* This type of data stream is used by basic conversations in LU 6.2. GDS is described in Chap. 13.

6.13 LU PROFILES, BIND IMAGE, AND
BIND IMAGE TABLE

FM and TS profiles associated with each LU in a network are defined in a table in VTAM called the Bind Image table. The table contains one bind image per unique LU type in the domain of that VTAM.

FM and TS profiles are too vague to precisely describe an LU type. Thus, the bind image also contains additional qualifiers to precisely define the protocol behavior of both the PLU and the SLU. In addition, the bind image also contains other information required during the session such as pacing window size and PLU and SLU buffer sizes. Not all of the information required in the bind image need be included at

TABLE 6.3 SNA Character String (SCS) Control Codes

Code (EBCDIC)	SCS control function	Abbreviation
16	Backspace	BS
2F	Bell (Stop)	BEL (STP)
0D	Carriage Return	CR
1B	Customer Use 1	CU1
3B	Customer Use 3	CU3
11	Device Control 1	DC1
12	Device Control 2	DC2
13	Device Control 3	DC3
3C	Device Control 4	DC4
14	Enable Presentation	ENP
36	Expanded Backspace (Numeric Space)	EBS (NBS)
E1	Expanded Space (Numeric Space)	ESP (NSP)
0C	Form Feed (Page End)	FF (PE)
08	Graphic Escape	GE
05	Horizontal Tab	HT
39	Indent Tab	IT
33	Index Return	IR
24	Inhibit Presentation	INP
1C	Interchange File Separator	IFS
1D	Interchange Group Separator	IGS
1E	Interchange Record Separator	IRS
1F	Interchange Unit Separator	IUS
25	Line Feed (Index)	LF (INX)
15	New Line (Carrier Return)	NL (CRE)
00	Null	NUL
34	Presentation Position	PP
17	Program Operator Communication	POC
0A	Repeat	RPT
3A	Required FF (Required Page End)	RFF (RPE)
06	Required NL (Required CR)	RNL (RCR)
41	Required Space	RSP
0450	Secure String ID Reader	SSR
04C1	Select Left Platen	SLP
046n	Select Magnetic Encoder	SME
04C2	Select Right Platen	SRP
28	Set Attribute	SA
2BD1	Set Chain Image	SCI
2BC8	Set Graphic Error Action	SGEA
2BC1	Set Horizontal Format	SHF
2BC6	Set Line Density	SLD
2BD2	Set Print Density	SPD
2BD1	Set Translation Table	STT
2BC2	Set Vertical Format	SVF
0F	Shift In	SI
0E	Shift Out	SO
2BC3	Start of Format	SOF
38	Subscript	SBS
3F	Substitute	SUB
09	Superscript	SPS
2A	Switch	SW
CA	Syllable Hyphen	SHY
35	Transparent	TRN
1A	Unit Backspace	UBS
04	Vertical Channel Select	VCS
0B	Vertical Tab	VT
23	Word Underscore	WUS

Note: SCS control functions are assigned EBCDIC codes as shown above. The control function ID is a one-byte field (for example, 0D for carriage return and 2BC6 for set line density).

the table definition time. Some of the information can be provided at the session setup time by the software.

The bind images are also known as logon mode or simply the logmode definitions. The name is based on the fact that a bind image defines the mode (protocols and other requirements) for a session. Since LU-LU sessions are typically established through a logon procedure, therefore, the term is *logon-mode* or *logmode*.

Figure 6.7 shows the structure of a Bind table. The table shows three partial bind images called RJE3790, IBM32782, and SCS3790. IBM provides a default Bind table as a part of the VTAM product that already contains bind images for the common SNA devices. An SNA user can customize the IBM-provided table by changing, adding, or deleting entries in it or can create an entirely new table.

To illustrate some of the values that can be specified in logmode entry or bind image, we show one entry, IBM32782, in Fig. 6.7 in more detail. Various keywords and entries shown are as follows:

MODEENT indicates the beginning of a new logmode entry.

LOGMODE = IBM32782 assigns the name IBM32782 to this bind image.

FMPROF and TSPROF identify the two profile numbers associated with this LU type.

```
...  MODETAB  ...


...  RJE3790,FMPROF=...,TSPROF=...,...


...  IBM3278,FMPROF=...,TSPROF=...,...


...  SCS3790,FMPROF=...,TSPROF=...,...
                    .
                    .
                    .
```

Bind entry for 3270 display station:

```
(name)  MODEENT  LOGMODE = IBM32782,FMPROF = X'03',
                 TSPROF = X'03',PRIPROT = X'B1',
                 SECPROT = X'90',COMPROT = X'3080',
                 RUSIZE = ...,PSERVIC = ...,
                 SRCPAC = ...,SSNDPAC = ...,...
```

Figure 6.7 Bind or Logmode table.

The remaining values in the table are qualifiers and subsidiary details. A brief description of the remaining fields in our example follows. Appendix B contains a detailed bit level description of bind image.

PRIPROT = X'B1' specifies additional protocol qualifiers for the PLU in session with the SLU being described.

SECPROT = X'90' specifies additional protocol qualifiers for the SLU.

COMPROT = X'03' specifies qualifiers applicable to both PLU and SLU. In the foregoing three parameters, meanings associated with the hexadecimal values can be interpreted using a bit level map of bind image.

RUSIZES defines the largest RUs that would fit in PLU and SLU buffers. This specification is used to determine chain element size.

PSERVIC specifies a number of miscellaneous values such as data stream supported (3270 versus SCS, etc.) display screen size and alternate size, etc.

SRCVPAC and SSNDPAC define send and receive pacing windows for the SLU.

The Bind table, having been coded using the syntax shown in Fig. 6.7, is assembled to convert it into machine code bit map.

6.14 LOGON AND BIND PROCESSING

Two LUs must agree on the bind image before they can form or "bind" an LU-LU session. It is during logon processing (or other session initiation mechanism) that the two LUs analyze the bind image proposed for the session to verify compatibility. The name of the bind image to be used for a particular session can either be provided as a part of the logon message or specified in the system generation tables. The bind image name in a logon message is generally avoided since it is cumbersome to require end users to know the name of a bind image. As an alternative, the default bind image name for each LU maybe defined in the VTAM system generation tables. If there is no name specified in the logon message and none specified in VTAM tables, VTAM uses the very first entry in the Bind table as the default bind image.

We use Fig. 6.8 to describe how bind image is processed during LU-LU session establishment to ensure that both LUs can support protocols in the proposed image.

1. A user at LUX enters a logon message for a host system SUBSYSX.

2. VTAM locates the bind image entry for LUX in the Bind table.

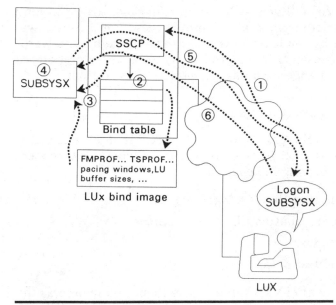

Figure 6.8 LU-LU sessions and bind processing.

3. VTAM passes the logon message to SUBSYSX along with a copy of the bind image for LUX if the subsystem requests it.

4. Subsystem may analyze the details of the bind image to determine whether it can support the session under this mode. The subsystem can accept the bind parameters as they are, modify them, or completely reject the logon request.

   In this example let us assume that the bind image is not rejected.

5. The subsystem, to indicate its willingness to accept the logon, requests VTAM to send SNA command BIND to LUX along with a copy (modified copy if SUBSYSX altered the bind image) of the bind image.

   The BIND command, in effect, says to LUX that SUBSYSX is willing to engage in a session subject to a concurrency by LUX that the bind image is acceptable to LUX too.

6. When the BIND command arrives at LUX, the device microcode validates the contents of the accompanying bind image. If the bind parameters are unacceptable, the Secondary LU responds with an exception response to the BIND command and the session fails. Otherwise, a positive response to BIND is sent and the session gets bound successfully.

   The bind processing is transparent to the terminal user except for the final outcome. Even with a successful bind, the logon may still not be complete from a user's point of view. For a secure system, the next thing would be for the user to go through a password-ID sequence. From an SNA point of view, these latter procedures are user data exchanges and have no protocol implications.

6.15 LOGON MESSAGES IN SNA

All logon messages in SNA are routed to the SSCP that owns the originating LU. When the SSCP receives a logon request, the request must contain the following information:

1. A code indicating that this is a logon request
2. The name of the destination LU (session partner)
3. The bind image name
4. Optionally, some user data

The SSCP component of VTAM must have items 1–3 to process the logon. However, the end user does not necessarily provide all three items. Bind image name, for example, as discussed earlier, can be provided internally by VTAM, based on system generation specifications.

Not only the contents, but the structure of the session initiation request must also conform to a specific form. Depending on their structure, logon messages are classified into one of two categories.

6.15.1 Formatted Logons

This term is used to describe logon messages that conform to the structure of the SNA command for logon called initiate self or INITS. Figure 6.9 shows the format INITS command.

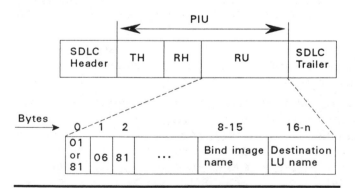

Figure 6.9 Format of INITS command.

The command itself is carried in the first three bytes of RU and has a command code of X'810681'. Starting at byte 8, the command contains alphanumeric names of the bind image and the destination LU.

Formatted logons can be processed directly by the SSCP and do not require any preprocessing in VTAM (LU 6.2 also uses formatted logons but uses the BIND command instead of INITS).

6.15.2 Unformatted Logons

Most SNA stations, such as IBM 3270, etc., are not capable of generating the INITS command, i.e., a formatted logon. For such devices, the only way to submit a logon is through an operator-entered message using an alphanumeric character string. This type of a logon message is called an unformatted logon.

The SSCP cannot process an unformatted logon. VTAM must convert an unformatted logon message to a formatted logon before it can pass the request to the SSCP internally.

Routines and tables within VTAM that are used to convert unformatted logon and logoff messages to a formatted structure are called Unformatted System Services (USS). The tables that describe the details of logon messages for translation are called the USS tables. (USS tables also contain standard messages such as the "welcome" message which is sent to each terminal when the network is started.)

An IBM-defined logon message text comes predefined in the VTAM USS tables. No modifications are required to USS tables if users use the IBM defined logon message.

The structure of an IBM-defined logon message is as follows:

```
LOGON APPLID(application name) LOGMODE(bind image name)
DATA(optional data)
```

This message, however, is generally too cumbersome for a typical user. A customer can define logon messages with a simpler syntax by adding user-defined entries to the USS tables.

As an example, to logon to TSO subsystem, the standard IBM message format would be:

```
LOGON APPLID (TSO) LOGMODE (---)
```

A simplified message could be simply

```
TSO
```

In any case, if a non-IBM unformatted message is used, it must go through a two-step translation procedure as shown in Fig. 6.10. In step 1 the keyword TSO is translated into the standard IBM syntax.

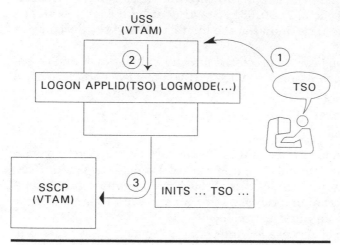

Figure 6.10   Translating unformatted logon messages.

The standard syntax is then converted to a formatted INITS RU and then passed to the SSCP component.

To make the process even more user friendly, a number of host-based software packages are available that display a menu of available applications and the end user can simply select the application to be logged on. IBM products NetView Access Services and SNA Applications Monitor (SAMON) provide such a function.

6.16   LU TYPES SUMMARY

Table 6.4 summarizes attributes of various LU types.

TABLE 6.4   Type Characteristics Summary

LU type	FM profile	TS profile	FMHs	Data stream	Typical implementation
0	0,3,4,7,18	2,3,4,7	Any	Any	—
1	3,4	3,4	1,2,3	SCS	3270 Printers, 3770
2	3	3	None	3270	3270 Display stations
3	3	3	None	3270	3270 Printers, 3770
6.2	7	19	5,7,12	GDS	CICS, VTAM, Systems 36 & 38, Personal computer, Numerous non-IBM products

6.17 SUMMARY: PU AND LU TYPES
AND SNA DEVICES

Ultimately, PU and LU types define rules for connecting and communicating with peripheral nodes (terminals) in an SNA network. When planning connectivity or evaluating compatibility, it may not be sufficient to know the PU/LU type associated with a device since not all devices within a PU or LU type are alike. For compatibility purposes, one must be compatible with a specific IBM product implementations and not just the architecture.

Single-Domain SNA Activation Sequences

7.1 INTRODUCTION

In the previous chapters we referred to various commands when describing activation of network resources and sessions. In this chapter we look at these SNA commands and flow sequences in more detail. Specifically, we look at commands for starting the network, activating links, routes, NCPs, PUs, LUs, and LU-LU sessions.

Since we have not discussed multidomain operation in detail, we look only at a single-host network in this chapter. However, the flows described here would remain the same even in a multihost network. Additional flows for multidomain operations and cross-domain logons are described later in Chap. 9.

7.2 SAMPLE NETWORK FOR ACTIVATION SEQUENCES

Figure 7.1 shows the sample configuration that we use in this chapter for illustrating activation sequences. We have a host with subarea 1 and a subsystem, SUBSYSX. The host is connected to an FEP, NCP1, over the I/O channel, shown as link L1. Link stations associated with L1 are LS1 in the host and LS2 in NCP1. NCP1 is assigned subarea 2.

NCP1 is connected to a remote front end—NCP2, SA3. The two NCPs are connected over a dedicated (nonswitched) SDLC link, L2. LS3 and LS4 are the link stations associated with L2 in NCP1 and NCP2, respectively.

NCP2 has a dedicated link, L3, connecting it to a peripheral node. The peripheral node link station is LS6; its associated PU is PUA; and it contains one LU, LUA.

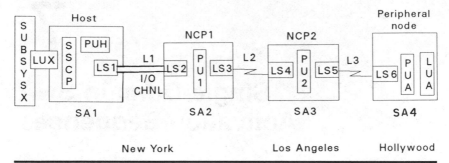

Figure 7.1   Sample network for activation sequences (LS = link station).

7.3 OVERVIEW OF ACTIVATION PROCESS

The activation of a resource requires both physical and logical activation. Physical activation involves turning the power on and loading the software or activating microcode [Initial program load (IPL) or Initial Machine Load (IML)]. Depending on the type of equipment, the software can be loaded in one of three ways:

1. Host can transmit the software.
2. Host can send a command to the node to load the software from an I/O device attached to the peripheral node.
3. An operator at the remote node can load the software.

Methods 1 and 2 can be unattended operations. In any case, once the physical activation is complete, the logical activations can proceed. Logical activation consists of a handshake between SSCP in VTAM and specific network components and proceeds in a hierarchical manner.

For example, in Fig. 7.1, NCP2 in Los Angeles cannot be activated until link L2 connecting it with NCP1 has been activated. Link L2 cannot be activated until NCP1 in New York has been activated, and so forth. In our example, we look at all the activations necessary to ultimately set up an LU-LU session between SUBSYSX residing in the New York host and a terminal, LUA, in Hollywood.

Before looking at SNA command sequences, let us review the order of activations and describe at a high level what happens at each step. We start with the assumption that VTAM has been started in the New York host. SSCP in VTAM initiates all activations. The stimulus for SSCP to activate a resource can come either from the control operator who enters an activation command at the control terminal NetView console or from the automatic activation flag in the resource profile in the system generation tables in VTAM.

The session activation sequence proceeds as follows:

1. *SSCP-PUH session:* This SSCP-PU session is an internal handshake within VTAM and basically involves setting up and initializing control blocks within VTAM. It should be remembered that PUH is going to provide all network addresses to the SSCP for this domain.

   From this point on, the SSCP-LU session between LUX in SUBSYSX and VTAM can be established at any time.

2. *SSCP-NCP1 session:* The link connecting the two, i.e., subchannel L1 on the I/O channel, must be activated first. This requires address assignments for LS1 and L1.

   Following that, since NCP1 is a subarea node, routes must be established with NCP1 and through it to other subarea nodes, and, finally, the session is established between the SSCP and PU1.

3. *SSCP-NCP2 session:* Link L2 must be activated. If NCP1 and NCP2 were connected via multiple physical links in one or more transmission groups, all of them may be activated at this time.

   Once the link or links connecting NCP1 and NCP2 have been activated, SSCP can activate PU2, establishing SSCP-PU session with PU2.

4. *SSCP-PUA session:* Link L3 must be activated and then PUA and LUA are activated establishing SSCP-PU and SSCP-LU sessions.

At this time LUA operator or SUBSYSX can initiate a LU-LU session request.

7.4 COMMAND OVERVIEW

A number of SNA/SDLC commands and their responses are involved in accomplishing the foregoing activations. The responses to SNA commands in many cases return more than just positive or exception responses. Some of the responses provide addressing information to the SSCP; others provide information about explicit route, etc.

A brief description of these commands follows:

ADDLINK (add link). This network services command is used by the SSCP to obtain the network address of a link from a PU. This command is typically followed by ACTLINK.

The response to ADDLINK contains the element number of the link network address.

ACTLINK (activate link). This network services command flows from SSCP to the PU to which the link is connected. The link is identified by its element number (from subarea-element address of the link). The command asks the PU to prepare the link for use. For an I/O channel link, the command causes allocation of appropriate control blocks and an exchange with the operating system for enabling the subchannel. For SDLC links (on an FEP or integrated adapter), the command causes a DTR/DSR exchange on the modem interface.

Response to ACTLINK provides a positive or negative indication of whether the link was prepared successfully for data exchange.

ADDLINKSTA (add link station).   This SSCP to PU network services command is used by the SSCP to obtain the network address of an adjacent link station. The target link station is identified in the command by a locally used identifier. The PU returns the adjacent link station address.

CONTACT.   This network services SSCP to PU command requests the PU to execute a procedure to establish a link level contact with the adjacent link station identified in the command.

Upon receiving the CONTACT command, the NCP causes the local link station to exchange an XID or SNRM SDLC command with the target link station.

Response to CONTACT from the NCP only acknowledges that CONTACT request has been received and does not imply that a contact has been successfully established.

CONTACTED.   This is a PU-SSCP network services command from the NCP. This SNA command (the terminology here gets a little awkward since CONTACTED does not command or request any action but contains only a notification) informs the SSCP that the link initialization process, undertaken due to an earlier CONTACT request from the SSCP, has been successfully completed; or, if not successful, a status field indicates whether an adjacent node needs down-loading of software or that some other error has occurred.

CONTACTED does not require a response from the SSCP.

NC-ER-OP (network control explicit route operative).   This is a PU-PU flow between subarea nodes. This request is exchanged when a link in an inoperative transmission group is activated. Using NC-ER-OP request, a PU informs another PU about the subareas that can be reached through the PU issuing the NC-ER-OP and the explicit routes available to reach these subareas.

NC-ER-ACT (network control explicit route activate).   This network control PU-PU flow is used between subarea nodes to activate an explicit route. NC-ER-ACT command is propagated to the destination subarea over intermediate nodes in the explicit route.

Any intermediate node that has no ER defined to the specified destination will intercept the request and generate a response indicating a route activation failure.

NC-ER-ACT-REPLY (network control explicit route activate reply). This PU-PU flow is used to indicate whether an earlier NC-ER-ACT was completed successfully. If the ER activation request fails, the reply contains a reason such as ER not defined, maximum route length specified in activate request exceeded (the route length is the number of transmission groups in the route), a TG in the route is inactive, or there is no reverse ER defined.

The successful activation response also includes parameters such as the route length, and a list of reverse ERs available.

NC-ACTVR (network control activate VR). This PU-PU flow is used to set up VR attributes such as forward and reverse ERs, maximum and minimum sizes of VR pacing window, and maximum PIU sizes. A virtual route is considered active when the underlying ER has been successfully activated (NC-ACT-ER).

IPLINIT, IPLTEXT, and IPLFINAL. These three network services commands are used by a PU4 or PU5 (VTAM or NCP) to load software in an adjacent PU.T4 (NCP) node.

ACTPU (activate physical unit). This session control SSCP to PU command is used by the SSCP to activate or establish an SSCP-PU session with the addressed PU.

ACTLU (activate Logical Unit). This SSCP to LU session control command is used by the SSCP to activate or establish an SSCP-LU session with the addressed LU.

SDT (start data traffic). This session control command flows from an SSCP to another SSCP or PU and from PLU to SLU. For those sessions that support this command, it is the first command executed after successful session establishment. SDT puts the session in data transfer mode (FM and DFC RUs may now be exchanged).

RNAA (request network address assignment). This SSCP to PU command requests network addresses from a boundary node for PUs and LUs on dial-up lines. It is also used in SNA-SNA gateway to assign alias addresses.

SETCV (set control vector). This network services request is used to transmit several types of system information—each type being identified by a unique key. Examples of some of the information types sent via SETCV include date and time, SSCP-PU and SSCP-LU session capabilities, SSCP name and identifier, NAU address, etc.

7.5 ACTIVATION SEQUENCES

The activation sequences are shown in the same order as they would generally occur in a real network. Though our overall network is the same as in Fig. 7.1, each illustration in this section shows only those parts of the configuration that are relevant to the particular sequence being explained.

7.5.1 Activating Host Node

1. SSCP sends ACTPU command to the host PU, PUH (Fig. 7.2). PUH sends a positive response to the ACTPU to indicate that the host node is active. This activation sequence is an internal flow within VTAM.

7.5.2 Activating Channel-Attached NCP

This flow also applies to two hosts connected via an I/O channel.

This sequence is a continuation of Sec. 7.5.1, and we start with item 2 in Fig. 7.2.

2. ADDLINK: SSCP requests PUH to furnish it with the network address of link L1. PUH returns that address to SSCP.

3. ACTLINK: SSCP requests PUH to prepare link L1 for use. This command contains the network address of L1 obtained in the previous step.

   PUH executes internal procedures and informs SSCP that L1 is usable.

4. ADDLINKSTA: SSCP obtains the network address of LS2 from PUH. LS2 resides in NCP2 but also has an element address assigned to it in subarea 1 by PUH.

5. CONTACT: SSCP requests PUH to initiate a link level contact with adjacent link station, LS2. Response to CONTACT acknowledges that CONTACT request has been received.

6. XID: LS1 (VTAM) sends link level command XID to LS2 (NCP), passing information about the host to NCP1. XID is initiated because of the CONTACT in the previous step.

7. XID: LS2 in NCP1 returns information about NCP1 to the host and informs LS1 that parameters sent in step 6 are acceptable.

8. Channel contact: LS1 completes the logical activation of TG1 (I/O channel) by accepting parameters received in step 7 (channel contact).

9. CONTACTED: PUH informs the SSCP that the contact procedure, initiated in step 5, has been completed.

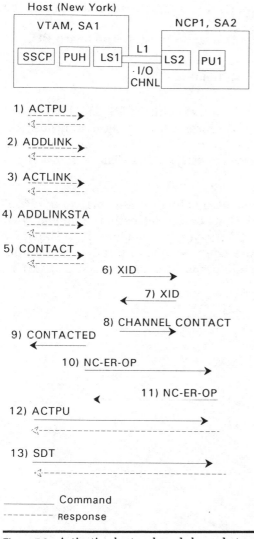

Figure 7.2   Activating host node and channel attached nodes.

10. NC-ER-OP: Physical Unit PUH in VTAM passes to PU1 in NCP1 a list of subareas that can be reached through the host and explicit routes available for reaching those subareas.

11. NC-ER-OP: PU1 in NCP1 returns similar information about destinations and routes that can be reached through NCP1.

12. ACTPU: The SSCP now sends an ACTPU command to PU1, and PU1 responds with a positive response.

13. SDT: SSCP sends this command to enable session data flows for the session.

An SSCP to PU session has now been established with PU1.

7.5.3 Activating Explicit and Virtual Routes to Channel-Attached NCP

Having established a successful contact with NCP1, the host would now activate explicit and virtual routes between the two nodes. Assume that there is one virtual route, VR1, between host SA1 and NCP1. Underlying ER and reverse ER is ER1. The activation sequence is shown in Fig. 7.3.

1. NC-ER-ACT (network control explicit route activate): PUH (VTAM) to PU1 (NCP1). PUH sends ER activation command with ER1 as the route number. ER activation command is initiated by VTAM when the route is needed by VTAM to satisfy a session activation request (in this case in preparation of setting up an SSCP-to-PU session with PU2).

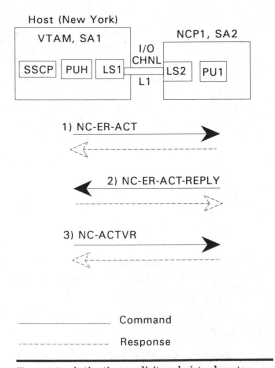

Figure 7.3   Activating explicit and virtual routes.

2. NC-ER-ACT-REPLY (network control explicit route activate reply): PU1 to PUH. PU1 sends a reply confirming ER activation. The reply contains both forward and reverse ER numbers and the route length. In this case there is only one TG, the I/O channel, in this route, and the route length is 1. Route length is used to determine VR pacing window.

3. NC-ACTVR (network control activate virtual route): PUH to PU1. Now that the underlying ERs have been activated, PUH activates the VR when the first session request is received that needs this particular virtual route. PU1 sends a response to NC-ACTVR confirming that the VR is active.

7.5.4   Activating Remote NCP, Part I:
Down-Loading NCP Software

The activation of a remote NCP, NCP2 in our example, involves activating cross-subarea links, down-loading NCP software, activating explicit routes to the remote NCP, and then activating the PU in the NCP.

In the first part we look at the activation of cross-subarea links and the software down-load as shown in Fig. 7.4.

1. ACTLINK L2: SSCP directs NCP1 in New York to activate SDLC link L2 to NCP2 in Los Angeles. Link activation is a local procedure between NCP1 and the modem and does not require NCP2 to be active.

2. CONTACT LS4: SSCP directs PU1 to establish contact with LS4 in NCP2.

3. XID: Link station LS3 (NCP1) sends an XID command to LS4 (NCP2) to verify its ID. In this case we assume that NCP2 software has not been loaded. Since the FEP in Los Angeles is not ready for communication, it rejects the XID command with an SDLC FRMR (frame reject) response.

4. SNRM/RIM: LS3 tries to initialize LS4 with an SNRM and, since LS4 is not loaded with software, it responds with an SDLC response, RIM (request initialization mode) response.

5. CONTACTED: NCP informs SSCP that NCP2 requires a load as a part of the CONTACTED notification.

6. IPLINIT: SSCP sends initial load information to NCP1.

7. SIM (set initialization mode), UA, and IPLINIT: LS2 (NCP1) initializes LS3 for the load and transfers the initial load information as SDLC information frames, which are acknowledged by LS3.

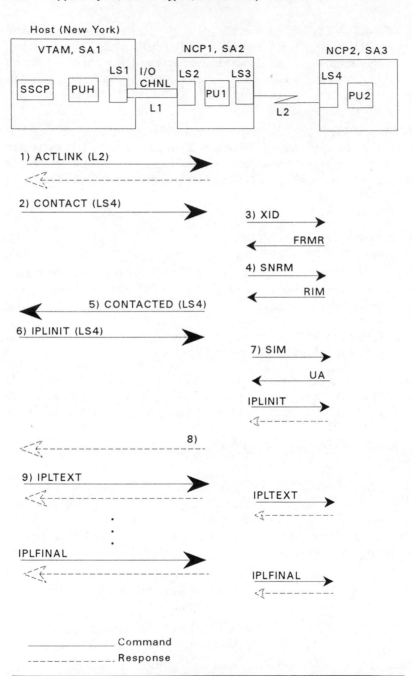

Figure 7.4 Activating remote NCP: Part 1.

8. PU2 informs SSCP that IPLINIT has been accomplished.

9. IPLTEXT through IPLFINAL: SSCP transmits rest of the software to NCP1, which in turn transmits it to NCP2.

After IPLFINAL, NCP2 software has been successfully loaded and its PU can now be activated between NCP1 and NCP2.

7.5.5   Activating Remote NCP, Part II:
Route and Domain Establishment

Since the commands used here are the same as those for the channel-attached NCP discussed in Sec. 7.5.3, they are described only briefly. The sequence is illustrated in Fig. 7.5.

1. CONTACT, XID, SNRM, UA, and CONTACTED: In this phase SSCP directs NCP1 to contact NCP2, causing XID and SNRM exchange between NCP1 and NCP2. After a successful SNRM/UA exchange, NCP1 informs SSCP that it has contacted NCP2.

2. NC-ER-OP: In this phase SSCP, NCP1, and NCP2 determine the subareas that can be reached through NCP2 and the ERs available to reach those destinations.

3. NC-ER-ACT and reply: SSCP activates explicit and virtual routes to NCP2.
   If NCP2 were not to be a part of SSCP (SA1) domain, the initialization would be complete at this time and NCP2 could provide path control network functions for host SA1 and NCP1. Step 4 below is needed if NCP2, in addition, is also to be a part of the host SA1 domain.

4. ACTPU and SDT: SSCP and PU2 exchange ACTPU commands completing the SSCP-PU session. SDT (start data traffic) SSCP-PU2 command, puts the session in data exchange state.

7.5.6   Activating Peripheral Nodes on
Nonswitched Links

Activation of PUA and LUA connected to NCP2 in Los Angeles is illustrated in Fig. 7.6.

1. CONTACT: SSCP sends this command to the PU in the boundary node, PU2.

2. SNRM/UA: LS5 in the boundary node establishes SDLC handshake with LS6 in the peripheral node.

3. CONTACTED: PU2 informs the SSCP that link level communications have been successfully established with the peripheral node.

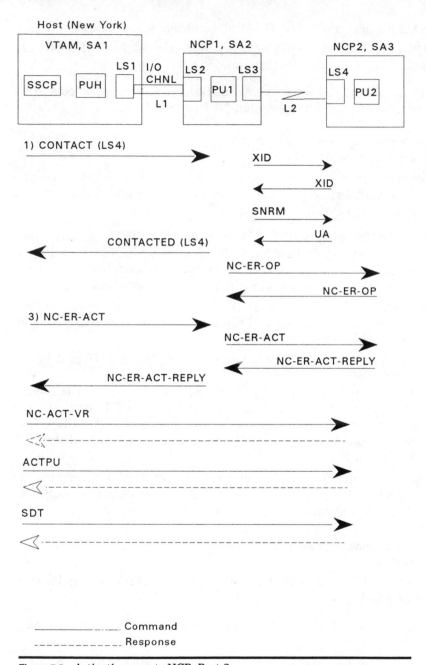

Figure 7.5 Activating remote NCP: Part 2.

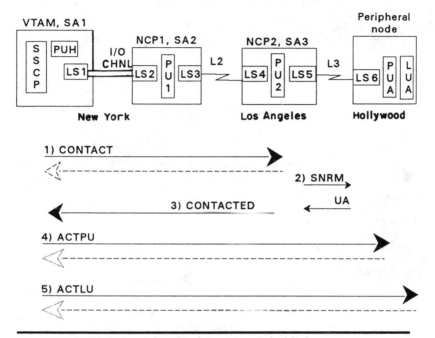

Figure 7.6   Activating peripheral node on nonswitched link.

4. ACTPU: SSCP sends ACTPU command to PUA in the peripheral node and receives associated response.

5. ACTLU: SSCP sends ACTLU command to LUA and receives associated response.

   (In some cases ACTPU and ACTLU commands may be followed by the SDT command.)

7.5.7 Activating Peripheral Nodes on Switched Links

This sequence is illustrated in Fig. 7.7.

1. CONNECT OUT/ACTIVATE CONNECT: These are SSCP-PU commands. CONNECT OUT directs PU2 in NCP2 to dial out (for autodial ports), whereas ACTIVATE CONNECT asks PU2 to activate an autoanswer port for incoming calls.

2. XID and REQUEST CONTACT: After an outgoing or incoming call has been successfully completed, LS5 in NCP2 and LS6 in the peripheral node exchange their identifications via XID commands.

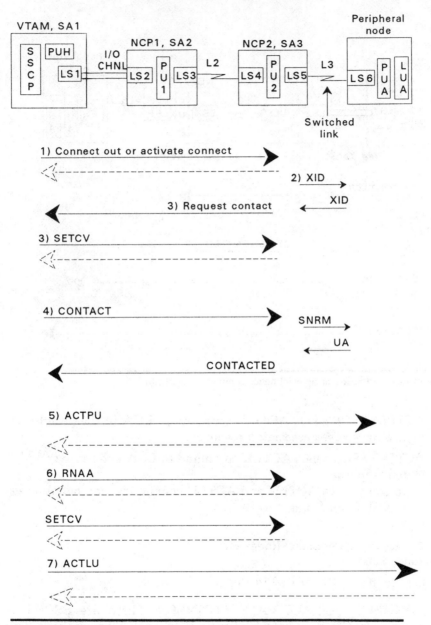

Figure 7.7 Activating peripheral node on a switched link.

Following a successful XID exchange, NCP2 informs the SSCP that it may initiate a contact (REQUEST CONTACT) for the peripheral node. The station identifier of LS6 is also passed to SSCP as a part of REQUEST CONTACT.

3. SETCV: If SSCP recognizes the ID returned in CONTACTED, it passes information about PUA to NCP2 via a SETCV command. Information contained in SETCV is segment size, PU type, etc. NCP2 saves the information received in SETCV.

4. CONTACT, SNRM, UA, and CONTACTED: SSCP sends a CONTACT command to NCP2 and NCP2 goes through a SNRM/UA sequence with LS6 in the peripheral node and informs the SSCP, via CONTACTED, that link level communications have been established with the peripheral node.

5. ACTPU: SSCP now established SSCP-PU session with PUA in the peripheral node.

6. RNAA (request network address assignment) and SETCV: On a switched connection, the LU definitions in the system generation tables are model (dummy) definitions. SSCP uses the RNAA command to tell NCP2 the number of LU control blocks to allocate for the PU just activated.

   Following that, the SSCP uses another SETCV to pass information such as local ID of each LU to the NCP.

7. ACTLU: At this time SSCP and the boundary NCP, NCP2, each have properly initialized control blocks and ACTLU command can be sent to each LU to establish SSCP-LU session.

7.5.8 LU-LU Session

Once network activations, including SSCP sessions are complete, LU-LU sessions can be established. As shown in Fig. 7.8, we consider a session between a host subsystem, SUBSYSX, and a peripheral LU, LUA.

Before we look at the flow sequence, let us review the structure of the host LU. Even though IBM documentation shows host LUs to be in the subsystem, the LU functions are partially implemented within VTAM. Actually, exchanges between VTAM and host LUs use VTAM application program interface and are not in the form of SNA commands and data formats. That is why LUX, representing SUBSYSX, is shown partially in VTAM and partially in SUBSYSX.

1. LUA sends a logon request to SSCP. The logon request can come as INITS (formatted) or, as is the case with most terminals, as a character-coded (unformatted) logon. If the logon comes in

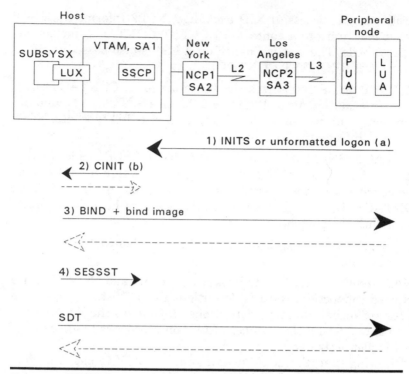

Figure 7.8   LU-LU Sessions. (*a*) Unformatted logon translated by VTAM to INITS format. (*b*) PLU may do bind analysis before sending response to CINIT; negative response may be sent.

unformatted, VTAM would convert it to INITS before passing it to its SSCP component.

2. CINIT (control initiate): SSCP uses this command to inform a PLU that a logon request has been received for the PLU. The LUX component that receives CINIT is within VTAM. VTAM passes this logon request to SUBSYSX over the VTAM application programming interface.

   At this time SUBSYSX has the option of analyzing bind parameters. SUBSYSX returns a value to LUX component in VTAM indicating whether or not the logon should be accepted.

   If the subsystem indicates session acceptance, LUX returns a positive response to the SSCP for the CINIT command.

3. BIND: LUX (VTAM) sends BIND command to LUA. LUA validates the contents of the bind image, assuming that bind image is acceptable, and sends a positive response to BIND.

4. SESSST (session started): LUX informs the SSCP that the session has been bound successfully.

5. SDT (start data traffic): LUX issues SDT putting session in data exchange state.

7.6 SUMMARY

Activation sequences described in this chapter provide a good insight into how various nodes acquire information about each other and, in the case of subarea nodes, about explicit routes. Our intent is to describe overall flows at a sufficiently detailed level to explain why these sequences are necessary. For bit level details and detailed parameters the SNA formats manual should be consulted.

Implementation, MSN, and Management

SNA Implementation

8.1 INTRODUCTION

Implementing a large teleprocessing system is a complex project. It requires a large team of people with varied skills—telecommunications experts, hardware specialists, systems and applications programmers, and network operations and management specialists. In addition, good project management practices and tools are also required. The historic record for implementing large communications systems has not been a good one—significant delays in project completion are the norm rather than the exception.

The major phases in an implementation plan include planning and design of hardware and software components, provisioning common carrier facilities, installing and testing hardware, generation of system software, coding applications, and unit and system testing including stress testing. The project team may consist of anywhere from ten to more than a hundred people depending on the size and complexity of the system. Ongoing support for the network requires similar levels of personnel. Application programming support would be in addition to that.

This chapter deals with software considerations in implementing an SNA network. Topics include system generation tables for VTAM and NCP. The next few paragraphs discuss the overall tasks to be performed in an implementation plan before we get into the details of specific software systems.

8.2 PLANNING AND DESIGN

In most cases a network already exists—pre-SNA or non-IBM—or the implementation involves expansion of an existing SNA network. In such cases, a number of requirements are already known: applications, facility types, physical topology of the network, connectivity requirements (physical and logical), backup and recovery requirements, operating procedures, and management support systems. For a new network everything would have to start from scratch.

Users starting with an existing system would also have to assess the impact of the new architecture and changes on the performance of the existing system and devise a migration plan.

The design process would normally start with a set of requirements established by a planning group. The planning group would in turn be driven by the business needs of a corporation. An application derived from business needs would dictate the selection of terminal type and the definition of response time and reliability objectives, which in turn would dictate network design, operation, and management objectives. Only after the overall system objectives have been defined can the individual teams start with the design or selection of various hardware and software components.

8.3 HARDWARE COMPONENTS

Even though this book does not deal with the selection of hardware components, they form a major part of the overall project and would cost much more than the software. Some of the components involved are discussed in the following sections.

8.3.1 Terminals

There is much more to terminals than the IBM 3270 family. Even within that family, specific display station and printer models have to be selected and customers must know how to configure the cluster controllers and attached devices. For batch-type applications, IBM 3770 or compatible devices can be selected. More often than not, *personal computers* (PCs) are masquerading as terminals, driven by software emulating a terminal type. In such cases users would have to select appropriate emulation software and communications cards.

For industry-specific applications there are specialized devices such as banking and retail terminals and *automatic teller machines* (ATMs).

No matter what terminal type is selected, each requires hardware expertise and has software implications. Not all software packages are created equal when it comes to terminal support—especially at the subsystem level. CICS, IMS/DC, TSO, and job entry subsystem (JES), just to name a few, all support a different universe of terminals.

8.3.2 Modems/DSUs

Historically, modems (or DSUs) did not have any SNA implications. Customers could select from one of several vendors, modems including a management system, to track the health of the physical facilities without any fear of SNA incompatibility. While all those options are still available and will work, we have an additional wrinkle that we may want to consider: the compatibility of modem-based control and management systems with SNA's management services architecture and IBM's host-based NetView product. This could be an important consideration for customers who want to integrate all network management functions in NetView. Beyond that, modems and associated management systems can be selected on their merits without any SNA implications.

[Compatibility with IBM diagnostic modems is not required for integrating non-IBM modem management systems with NetView. Only a capability called Service Point (see Chap. 10) is required in the non-IBM management system.]

8.3.3 Communications Facilities

Ever since the divestiture of the operating telephone companies from AT&T in the United States, the selection of facilities and optimizing tariffs has become a black art. For large users, the problem is further compounded by the use and optimization of large bandwidth systems such as T1 carriers, shared between voice and data. While SNA has no unique requirements for facilities, the use of high-bandwidth circuits does impact the configuration of FEPs. In addition, if facilities management is to be host based, NetView interface could be a consideration.

8.3.4 Other Network Support Systems

A number of other support systems such as matrix switches for FEP backups, protocol analyzers, analog and digital test systems, etc. are critical for quick resolution of network problems and restoration of service.

Host-independent systems are also available for monitoring elements such as response time.

8.3.5 Front End Processors

Front end processor hardware has to be configured based on circuit types, aggregate bandwidth, and response time objectives. Token Ring gateway function requires additional hardware. Both IBM and compatible manufacturers provide assistance in configuring the front end hardware options.

8.3.6 Distributed Application Nodes

With the availability of LU 6.2, distributed processing has become much more feasible under SNA. This also introduces the need to configure distributed processors such as IBM systems 9370, AS/400, and PS/2, or machines from other vendors such as AT&T/NCR, DEC, Tandem, Sun, etc. Each distributed node, besides requiring hardware expertise, also has software implications that must be addressed by the user.

8.4 SOFTWARE CONSIDERATIONS

Various categories of software to be implemented include:

1. *System software:* This includes defining operating system, VTAM, and NCP. Each product has its own definition tables and generation procedures. As described later, VTAM and NCP share a number of common table definitions.

2. *Network management software:* This category includes software such as NetView or NetMaster, and any change, problem, configuration management, or other similar system.

3. *Subsystems:* Included here are software subsystems such as CICS, IMS/DC, TSO, and JES, etc., which are defined as VTAM applications during VTAM system generation. However, each of these systems requires elaborate definitions and procedures to implement them on the host machine.

4. *Applications:* These are business applications that would typically run under a teleprocessing monitor such as CICS or IMS/DC in case of a mainframe. We do not discuss the design or implementation of applications except for their LU 6.2 implications, which are discussed in Chap. 13.

5. *Gateways and interfaces for non-SNA devices:* We would put SNA-SNA gateway, SNA-X.25 gateway, and IBM protocol conversion packages such as Network Terminal Option (NTO) in this category.

8.4.1 Overview of System
Generation Procedures

The purpose of a system generation is to customize a software system to your specific needs and configuration. Typical features customized may include hardware to be supported, optional software features (e. g., dynamic reconfiguration ability), message buffer pool size, performance tuning, error handling, etc. The procedure is

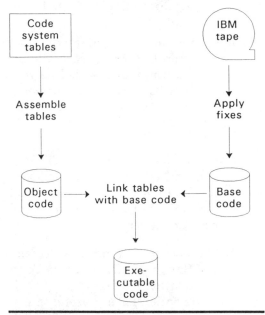

Figure 8.1 Overview of system generation procedures.

illustrated in Fig. 8.1. Before a customer actually starts coding system generation tables, the following tasks must already be complete:

1. Detailed analysis, system design, and specification of network hardware to be installed.

2. Training of system programmers in the use and installation of each system software component to be installed. To illustrate the extent of training required, just to install and support VTAM and NCP, a programmer would need to go through at least a month-long training program to acquire the minimal skills to be functional. Tuition alone for such training at IBM could run about $6000-7000 per person in addition to travel and related costs. Following that, ongoing training would still be required in additional specialized areas and to keep up with new releases of products.

In any case, assuming that these requirements have been completed, we can track the system generation procedure as shown in Fig. 8.1:

1. Customer obtains the IBM program product on a machine-readable medium and transfers the original to a disk. At this time any out-

standing fixes [Programming Temporary Fixes (PTFs)] would also be applied.

2. System programmer(s) codes appropriate tables describing the specific hardware and software configuration to be supported. As an example, just to describe the profile of a communications line you could possibly end up coding more than 30 parameters for each line. The tables are coded using macros and syntax required by the specific product. These tables are then assembled to convert them to an object code format.

3. System generation tables in the object code form are linked with IBM-provided executable code to form a customized working version. Not all tables are necessarily linked with the final version. Some of the tables may be filed separately on a system library and the software may access this information dynamically on a need basis.

IBM does provide customers with the option of ordering a startup system that comes preconfigured from IBM in the form of a facility that IBM calls Solution Pac. With most Solution Pacs, IBM personnel would also install the initial system. This option is very useful in establishing a basic system quickly and without up-front expertise and training. Systems staff can be trained while they gain experience with a basic system already in place.

8.5 OPERATING SYSTEM GENERATION

There are three operating systems of interest for IBM mainframes: the Disk Operating System (DOS), which has no relationship to PC/DOS and is often referred to by its suffix VSE (Virtual Storage Extended); the Virtual Machine (VM), and Multiple Virtual Systems (MVS).

Although programming details for system generation vary from operating system to operating system, the definitions are similar functionally. The system programmer must create system libraries for VTAM and NCP programs and tables. As far as the network is concerned, the operating system does not need to know about the details of FEPs, remote links, and terminals attached to those links. This part of the configuration is defined to NCPs and VTAM. The only configuration information defined to the operating system includes VTAM as one of the access methods and channel and subchannel definitions for channel-attached (local) devices and front ends.

8.5.1   MVS Definitions

Defining VTAM.   In the MVS system, access methods to be installed are defined in the DATAMGMT table on the ACCMETH parameter. VTAM must be specified as one of the access methods.

Local devices. The IODEVICE table identifies each channel and subchannel number and its associated devices on UNIT parameter. Proper definitions for the front end and other local devices must be included.

8.5.2 DOS/VSE Definitions

The current versions of VSE no longer require that VTAM be identified to the VSE Supervisor; the VSE system generation statements already include VTAM support. However, a DOS partition must be defined for VTAM, and this partition must have a higher priority than application partitions.

In addition, the IOTAB table must include definitions for all locally attached stations and front ends.

8.5.3 VM Definitions

The process, again, consists of providing information about VTAM in the VM Control Program (CP) tables. VTAM and an application called VM SNA Console Support (VSCS) must also be defined as authorized virtual machines. [These definitions are provided as a part of defining the Group Control System (GCS) under VM]. Channel-attached terminals and front ends must also be defined in the DMKRIO file for the VM Control Program.

8.6 NCP SYSTEM GENERATION

The system programmer has to create at least one NCP per FEP in the network (the IBM 3745 can run two NCPs concurrently). The NCP generation procedures are run on the mainframe and the software created is placed on a mainframe disk. This software must be downloaded into the FEP before the FEP can be operational. Since the NCP and its attached network must belong to a VTAM domain, a copy of NCP generation tables is also filed on the VTAM system library. Figure 8.2 illustrates this process.

Note in Fig. 8.2 that the definitions filed on the VTAM library are in an unassembled source format, and VTAM interprets these to convert them into an internally usable machine format at execution time. In addition, NCP system generation tables also include parameters that are used only by VTAM and are ignored by the NCP. Such parameters are identified as "VTAM only" values in the following discussions.

Tables coded during the NCP generation can be divided into four major categories:

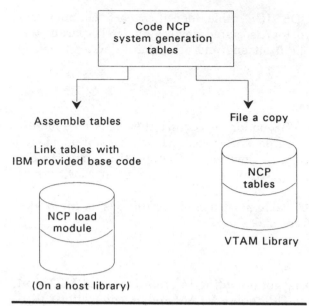

Figure 8.2   NCP system generation overview.

1. Front end hardware, NCP common functions, and host interface parameters
2. Dynamic reconfiguration tables
3. Routing tables
4. Network tables describing lines and terminals

The order in which these tables are coded is important and is described in the *NCP Installation Reference Manual*.

8.6.1   NCP Common Functions and Host Interface

Values coded in these tables apply to the total system and define the profile of the host system attached to the NCP over an I/O channel.

Build table.   This is normally the first table in the system generation and defines global system parameters. Figure 8.3 shows a few selected parameters that can be defined in this table.
      The following definitions refer to Fig. 8.3.

      TYPEGEN: This operand defines the type of front end software being created; applicable options include channel-attached NCP

```
BUILD    TYPEGEN = [NCP, NCP-R, PEP],
         MODEL = [3720, 3745-nnn],
         NEWNAME = name for the new NCP,
         SUBAREA = subarea number,
         BFRS = buffer size,
         SLODOWN = n%,
         TYPSYS = [OS, MVS, DOS, VSE, VM],

            .
            .
            .
```

Figure 8.3   Selected BUILD parameters.

(NCP), remote NCP (NCP-R) or a Partitioned Emulation Program (PEP).

MODEL: Specifies the front end hardware model numbers, e.g., 3745, 3720, etc.

NEWNAME: Specifies the name to be assigned to the NCP load module created by this generation.

SUBAREA: Subarea number to be assigned to the NCP being created.

BFRS: Specifies the size of NCP buffers in the message buffer pool.

SLODOWN: Specifies the percentage of free buffers below which NCP would go into a slowdown mode. During the slowdown, NCP stops noncritical polling and tries to free up its buffers by performing output operations only.

TYPSYS: Specifies the operating system under which the generation process is being run. Options are OS, MVS, DOS, VSE, and VM.

Other operands in the BUILD table define parameters such as the frequency of I/O interrupts to the host, I/O channel timeout value, maximum data that can be transferred to the host in one I/O operation, and information pertaining to running NCP traces and obtaining dump information. In an SNA-SNA gateway configuration, additional parameters are specified about the gateway.

Host table.   This table is coded to describe the interface between the front end and each host with which the front is attached over an I/O channel. A Host table is not needed when generating a remote NCP. For an FEP that is channel-attached to multiple hosts, one Host table is needed per host. Some of the values coded in the Host table are shown in Fig. 8.4.

```
HOST     SUBAREA = host subarea number,
         UNITSZ = host buffer size,
         MAXBFRU = number of host buffers,
         INBFRS = initial number of NCP buffers,
                        .
                        .
                        .
```

(UNITSZ * MAXBFRU = Largest PIU host would accept)

Figure 8.4 Selected parameters for the Host table.

The following definitions refer to Fig. 8.4.

SUBAREA: Identifies the subarea number of the host being described.

UNITSZ: Specifies the size of the buffer units in the host VTAM buffer pool.

MAXBFRU: Defines the maximum number of buffers that VTAM would allocate to receive any RUs from the NCP.

MAXBFRU*UNITSZ is the largest single PIU that the NCP can transfer to this VTAM. The NCP must not accept any PIUs longer than this from the network (also see TRANSFER operand on the LINE macro).

INBFRS: Specifies the number of buffers that NCP must allocate when it initiates a receive operation from the host. If the host continues sending more data after initial allocation of buffers has been filled, NCP must allocate additional buffers dynamically to receive the rest of the data.

8.6.2 Dynamic Reconfiguration Tables

In the early days of SNA it was impossible to change NCP configuration tables without bringing down the part of the network controlled by the NCP. As customers' networks have grown and their businesses become more dependent on the network, it has become important that customers be able to change system configurations without having to shut down the network. With each new release of its products, IBM has been enhancing dynamic reconfiguration capabilities of its products. Some of the tables defined in the NCP to facilitate dynamic reconfigurations include:

PU and LU dynamic pools.   The system programmer can define pools of dummy PUs and LUs—one pool for each. The definitions in these pools are model definitions and are not associated with any line or controller. The PU pool is created by coding a PUDRPOOL (PU dynamic reconfiguration pool) table and the LU pool by coding a LUDRPOOL (LU dynamic reconfiguration pool) table.

In addition to these tables, the system programmer also has to code a reconfiguration data set (a data set in the world of IBM is a file, not a modem) to actually assign these resources to specific lines.

Dynamic reconfiguration data set (DRDS).   This file is defined as a part of the VTAM generation, not the NCP, and works in conjunction with the dynamic pool definitions established during the NCP generation. The DRDS file basically consists of a number of ADD, MOVE, and DELETE statements. The ADD statement can be used to add a PU to a line or an LU to a PU. The DELETE statement can be used to remove PUs and LUs from an existing configuration.

VTAM and NCP dynamic definitions apply to PUs and LUs only and do not allow lines, or non-SNA (BSC and asynchronous) resources to be added dynamically. However, the system programmer can predefine extra resources in the generation tables and activate them only when the resources have been installed in the network.

8.6.3 NCP Network Definitions

The function of network definitions is to define links, PUs, and LUs connected to the front end. In addition, routing tables are also defined during the NCP system generation. The routing tables were discussed earlier in Chap. 4 and are not included in this chapter.

The overall structure of network definitions is as shown in Fig. 8.5.

```
        .
        .
        .
BUILD      ...
HOST       ...
PUDRPOOL   ...
LUDRPOOL   ...
        .
        .
        .
GROUP      ...
LINE       ...
SERVICE    ...
PU         ...
LU         ...
        .
        .
        .
```

Figure 8.5 Selected network definition tables in NCP.

The network tables have to be defined in a hierarchical order, i.e., the Group table first, followed by a line description of each line in the group. Each line entry is followed by a SERVICE entry followed by PU descriptions. Each PU is followed by its associated LUs.

The following definitions refer to Fig. 8.5.

GROUP: This table contains common attributes of a group of lines and attached terminals. Only similar resources can be combined within a common group. From a group definition point of view, the following attributes must be common:

All lines within the same group must be dedicated or all switched. All lines must use the same protocol—SDLC or BSC or asynchronous.

LINE: One LINE statement is coded per physical link attached to the front end. The statement describes a line profile.

SERVICE: Each LINE entry must be followed by a SERVICE table. The SERVICE table defines the order in which the stations on the link are to be serviced. The NCP performs SDLC polling and output operations according to the SERVICE table.

PU: Following the SERVICE entry is one PU entry per station attached to the line being described. The PU entry describes both the PU and SDLC attributes of a station.

LU: Following the PU entry there is one LU entry per LU attached to the PU. LU entry describes the profile of an LU.

Figure 8.6 shows the order of entries for a network with two line groups—BSC and SDLC. Figure 8.6 is meant only to show the order of tables and not all the permissible parameters. The generation defines an NCP with subarea number 4 (BUILD macro). The NCP is channel attached to a host with subarea number 2 (HOST macro).

In Fig. 8.6, G3BSC represents a set of BSC lines. Note that controllers in the BSC group are defined using CLUSTER and TERMINAL entries (for BSC 3270), not PU and LU. We do not discuss BSC definitions any further in this book.

G1SDLC represents a group of private lines with two lines in it, PVTLN1 and PVTLN2.

Defining GROUP parameters.   Figure 8.7 shows some of the parameters that can be coded in a Group table. The following definitions refer to Fig. 8.7.

```
            BUILD    SUBAREA=4, ...
            HOST     SUBAREA=2, ...
                 .
      other tables
                 .
G3BSC     GROUP    ...BSC,...
BSCL1     LINE     ...
          SERVICE
CLSTR1    CLUSTER
TERM1     TERMINAL
                 .
                 .
G1SDLC    GROUP    ...SDLC...
PVTLN1    LINE     ...
          SERVICE ...
PU1       PU       ...
LU1       LU       ...
LU2       LU       ...
                 .
                 .
PU2       PU       ...
LU10      LU       ...
                 .
          (LUs for PU2)
                 .
PVTLN2    LINE     ...
          SERVICE ...
PU4       PU       ...
                 .
          (LUs for PU4)
                 .
                 .
```

Figure 8.6 Ordering of NCP tables.

```
GROUP  LNCTL = [SDLC, BSC, SS],
       DIAL = [YES, NO],
       NPARSC = [YES,NO],
                 .
                 .
```

Figure 8.7 Illustrative parameters for Group table.

LNCTL: Identifies the link protocol for all lines in this group. For VTAM/NCP systems, applicable options are SDLC and BSC.

DIAL: Specifies whether all lines in this group are switched (YES) or dedicated (NO).

NPARSC: Specifies whether this group of lines is to be monitored by host-based IBM NetView Performance Analyzer (NPA). NPA is a host-based performance monitoring product and is not a part of the NetView product.

Line table.   One LINE entry is coded per circuit attached to the front end. Figure 8.8 shows some of the parameters that can be coded on a line profile. The following definitions refer to Fig. 8.8.

ADDRESS: This operand identifies the physical port for the line being described. The address is specified as a relative value; i.e., the line on the lowest physical port is defined as line 0, the next line as relative line 1, etc. The number of ports available on an FEP depends on the hardware model of the FEP.

HDX/FDX: This operand on the ADDRESS parameter, specifies whether the line is to operate in a full- or half-duplex mode. For full-duplex communications, NCP reserves two addresses (or ports) for this line.

SPEED: This operand specifies the data rate for this line. For synchronous lines (such as SDLC), the line speed is generally determined by the modem and this operand serves only a documentation purpose and is ignored by the generation procedures. However, this operand is required if NetView Performance Analyzer (NPA) is to be used to evaluate the performance of the line.

AUTO: This operand is coded if it is a switched, autodial line using an automatic calling unit (ACU). This operand specifies a relative address for the port to which the ACU unit is attached. For lines with ACU, two addresses (ports) are required—the aforementioned ADDRESS operand identifies the data port, and AUTO identifies the port for the ACU.

```
LINE    ADDRESS = [relative port no., HDX|FDX],
        SPEED = bit rate,
        AUTO = port no.,
        CLOCKNG = [EXT,INT],
        CONFIG = [NONSW,SW],
        LPDATS = [YES,NO,Model no.],
        MODULO = [8,128],
        NPACOLL = [YES,NO],
        NRZI = [YES,NO],
        RETRIES = [m,t,n],
        TRANSFER = largest PIU size,
                .
                .
                .
```

Figure 8.8   Illustrative parameters for Line table.

CLOCKNG: This operand identifies whether the NCP (internal) or the modem (external) is to provide the bit clocking for this line. For SDLC lines, clocking is typically provided by the modem (EXT).

CONFIG: This operand applies only to NCP-NCP links and identifies whether the link connecting them is dedicated or switched.

LPDATS: This operand specifies whether LPDA-compatible modems are installed on the line and whether they are LPDA type 1 or 2.

MODULO: Defines the link level modulo that can be used on the line. The modulo values can be 8 or 128. The actual link level window, which can be equal or less than modulo minus 1 is defined in the MAXOUT operand described in the PU table below.

NPACOLL: This operand specifies whether NPA is to collect statistical information on data exchanged on this line.

NRZI: Specifies whether NRZI bit encoding scheme is to be used on this line. Whether or not to use NRZI is determined based on the modem specifications. If a line is designated as an NRZI line, then all stations on the line must also be configured to recognize NRZI encoded bit stream.

RETRIES: Specifies parameters for controlling retry operations in case of SDLC errors, with m specifying the number of retries. If the error still persists, a pause of t seconds can be specified and after each pause the process is repeated a total of n times. If at the end of this retry sequence the error still persists, the error is considered permanent and NCP posts this error to VTAM, which in turn passes it to NetView for displays on the NetView terminal. It is up to the NetView operator to initiate any further recovery. For SDLC lines, default for RETRIES is a single sequence of 15 retries.

TRANSFER: Defines the size of the largest single PIU (chain element or segment) that the NCP can receive from any device on this line. The actual specification is defined in number of NCP buffers required to fit the PIU. TRANSFER operand must be large enough to accommodate the largest PIU from the line, and yet must not exceed the largest PIU that can be transferred to the host (each host has a limit on the largest PIU that it would accept from the network—see UNITSZ and MAXBFRU in the HOST table). Any PIUs that exceed this specification would be rejected with a "PIU too long" sense code.

PU table. One PU table entry is required per station on the line and describes the profile of the PU and SDLC parameters for the associated link station. Figure 8.9 shows selected PU parameters. The following definitions refer to Fig. 8.9.

```
PU      ADDR = link station (SDLC) address,
        ANS = [CONT, STOP],
        MAXDATA = PU buffer size,
        MAXOUT = SDLC window size,
        PUDR = [YES, NO],
        PUTYPE = [1, 2, 4],
        SRT = [number,number],
        SUBAREA = subarea number if T4.0 node,
          .
          .
          .

    (VTAM only parameters follow)
        DISCNT = [YES, NO],
        ISTATUS = [ACTIVE, INACTIVE],
          .
          .
          .
```

Figure 8.9   Illustrative parameters for PU table.

ADDR: Specifies the hexadecimal address assigned to the link station associated with the PU being described. This address is used in the SDLC header address field. The range of valid addresses is X'01'-X'FE'. An address value of X'FD' also is not allowed if LPDA-2 modems are installed on this line. On a multidrop line, each station on the line must have a unique address.

(Each drop on the line also has the PU local ID associated with it, which is always X'00' and is not coded in the table. IBM reference manuals are misleading when they describe the ADDR field above as the PU ID—ADDR value is the SDLC level address and not the PU local ID.)

ANS: The NCP enters an automatic network shutdown (ANS) mode when any of its owning SSCP fails. This operand specifies whether cross-domain sessions for LUs associated with this PU should be stopped (STOP) or allowed to continue (CONT) when the owner of the PU fails.

MAXDATA: This operand is defined for peripheral nodes only and specifies the PU buffer size. The NCP segments larger PIUs to this size before they are sent to the PU.

MAXOUT: Specifies the link level window; i.e., NCP would request an SDLC response from this link station after every MAXOUT number of frames. The MAXOUT value must be less than or equal to modulo minus 1, i.e., 7 for modulo 8 and 127 for modulo 128.

PASSLIM: Specifies the maximum number of PIUs or segments that NCP would transmit to this PU in one service pass. After PASSLIM has been exhausted, the NCP would service other drops on the line and keep remaining PIUs pending for the next service pass. The intent of this parameter is to prevent a single station from monopolizing the line.

PUDR: Specifies whether this PU can be deleted from the network using dynamic reconfiguration function.

PUTYPE: Defines the PU type of the PU being described. Incidentally, PU2.1 is defined as PU2 in the NCP generation.

SRT: This parameter specifies output PIU and error retry thresholds. When either of these thresholds is exceeded, NCP generates a statistics maintenance record, which is recorded by NetView in the performance events database.

SUBAREA: This operand is coded only if the PU being described is a remote NCP and this parameter defines the subarea number of the remote NCP. For remote NCPs, no LUs are defined for the PU.

VTAM-only parameters for PU. The following parameters are ignored by the NCP system generation procedures and used only by VTAM.

DISCNT: Specifies if this PU should be deactivated if all LUs on this PU have ended their LU-LU sessions.

ISTATUS: Specifies whether or not VTAM should activate this PU automatically when it activates the NCP controlling the PU.

LU table. For each LU on the PU described in the foregoing section, one LU entry must be defined to describe the LU profile. Figure 8.10, to which the following definitions refer, shows some of the parameters that are defined.

LOCADDR: This parameter defines the local ID of the LU that is used in the FID2 and FID3 THs. Address range for LUs on PU Type 1

```
LU      LOCADDR = LU local ID.,
        LUDR = [YES, NO],

               .
               .
               .

(VTAM only parameters for LU follow)

        DLOGOMOD = bind image name,
        ISTATUS = [ACTIVE, INACTIVE],
        LOGAPPL = application name,
        VPACING = pacing window size,

               .
               .
               .
```

Figure 8.10   Illustrative parameters for LU table.

is X'02'-X'40' and X'02'-'FE' for PU Type 2. LUs must be defined in the table in the ascending order of addresses. For independent LU6.2, LOCADDR is defined as 0.

LUDR: Specifies whether the LU can be deleted from the network definitions by using dynamic reconfiguration function.

VTAM-only values for an LU. The following parameters are ignored by the NCP generation procedures and are used by VTAM only.

DLOGMOD: Defines the name of the bind image in the VTAM Bind Image table for the LU. VTAM uses this bind image for sessions with this LU if no other bind image name is provided in the logon message.

ISTATUS: This operand tells VTAM whether it should automatically activate this LU at startup (i.e., establish SSCP-LU session). If ISTATUS is not defined as active, the LU has to be activated manually by the control operator via an activation command to VTAM.

LOGAPPL: This parameter can be used to set up an automatic logon between the LU and a host application by coding the name of the host application on the LOGAPPL parameter. VTAM automatically submits a logon to the application when the LU is activated.

VPACING: Specifies pacing window size if VTAM is to pace session traffic for this LU.

NCP summary. The tables discussed in the previous few sections are meant only to provide an overview of the NCP system generation. There are a number of additional tables and parameters that need to be coded to define NCP-NCP links, control service on multipoint links, and overall performance. The performance-related parameters have to be tuned on an ongoing basis based on network statistics. NCP installation manuals should be consulted for additional details.

8.7   VTAM DEFINITIONS

VTAM definition tables are the most elaborate in an SNA network. These tables can be divided into three functional areas:

1. *Domain tables:* List resources that constitute VTAM's domain and include definitions of NCPs, host subsystems, channel-attached terminals, and switched line connections.

2. *Cross-domain tables:* These tables are used to identify other hosts and cross-domain LUs in the network.

3. *Other system tables and lists:* Include routing tables, tables for

translating logon messages, Bind Image table, dynamic reconfiguration statements, checkpoint definitions for warm re-starts, and startup information.

Some of the aforementioned tables are assembled and maintained in an object code format, but most are filed in the VTAM system library in a source form. We discussed bind and USS tables earlier in Chap. 6 and routing tables in Chap. 4. We discuss cross-domain definitions in Chap. 9.

8.7.1 VTAM Domain Definitions and Major and Minor Nodes

VTAM can have five types of resources in its domain:

1. NCPs and their attached networks

2. Host subsystems, such as CICS, JES, TSO, etc., representing host LUs

3. I/O channel-attached SNA stations

4. I/O channel-attached non-SNA 3270 stations

5. Switched link attached resources

Each of these resource types is defined as what VTAM calls a *major node*—for these five resource groupings we have five types of major nodes in VTAM. The use of the term *node* in VTAM has no relation-ship to the term *node* in SNA. An SNA node type is synonymous with PU type, and a VTAM node is a description of a group of one of the five types of resources. The major node name in VTAM is the name of a file in the VTAM library containing system generation definitions.

Individual resources described within a major node are called minor nodes. For example, for a VTAM with 10 NCPs in its domain, we would define 10 NCP major nodes. For each NCP, each of its lines, PUs, and LUs would constitute a minor node. Similarly, each host subsystem would be defined to VTAM as one or more applications in the applications major node. Each subsystem (LU) would then be called a minor application node. All major node statements are filed on the VTAM library in a source code (unassembled) format.

Defining NCP major nodes. NCP major nodes are created by simply fil-ing a copy of NCP generation statements on the VTAM system li-brary. NCP generation statements were discussed in Sec. 8.6. The file name under which NCP definitions are filed in the VTAM library be-comes the major node name of the NCP.

Model:

```
        VBUILD  TYPE = APPL
 name   APPL    ...parameters...
          .
          .
          .
```

Example:

```
        VBUILD   TYPE = APPL
 CICS02 APPL    ...
 IMS01  APPL    ...
          .
          .
 TSO01  APPL    ...
 TSO02  APPL    ...
          .
          .
 definitions for TSO03-TSO19
          .
          .
 TSO20  APPL    ...
```

Figure 8.11   Defining applications major node.

Applications major node. This major node is used to identify various subsystems (host LUs) to VTAM. Figure 8.11 shows the format of statements required to define an applications major node.

VBUILD: This keyword indicates the beginning of a VTAM major node. TYPE = APPL identifies this as an applications major node.

Following the VBUILD statement, one APPL statement is coded per host LU. The number of APPL statements required depends on the number and type of subsystems being defined. The name coded on the left of the APPL statement is the name by which the application is known to VTAM and is specified in the logon message. Subsystems such as CICS and IMS require only one APPL statement (i.e., they are defined as single LUs). TSO on the other hand requires as many APPL statements as the number of users that would be concurrently logged on to it. IBM's NetView product also requires multiple APPL statements. In the example shown in Fig. 8.11, we define a CICS system called CICS02, an IMS system called IMS01, and a TSO system to support a maximum of 20 users concurrently.

Channel-attached (local) SNA resources major node. Figure 8.12, to which the following definitions refer, shows a model statement and an example of defining a local SNA major node.

```
(name)    VBUILD   TYPE = LOCAL

(name)    PU       ADDR = device channel address,
                   PUTYPE = PU type of device,
                      .
                      .
                      .
(name)    LU       LOCADDR = ...,...
             .
             .
(name)    LU          ...
```

Figure 8.12 Local SNA major node (*Note:* T1.0 nodes are not supported as local nodes).

VBUILD TYPE = LOCAL: Identifies this as the beginning of a local SNA major node.

PU statement: Describes the profile of a PU (cluster controller) on the I/O channel. LOCADDR parameter of the PU statement defines channel-subchannel number over which the station is attached to the host. Only PU Type 2 is allowed as a channel-attached station. Since SDLC protocol is not used on the channel, no SDLC parameters are coded.

LU statement: Following the PU statement, one LU statement is coded for each terminal attached to the PU. Parameters coded for the LU are similar to the parameters coded for LUs attached to the NCP, as described in Sec. 8.6.3 under "LU table."

Defining switched major node. NCP generation tables do not contain complete information to support switched lines. Part of the information is specified during the VTAM system generation and is passed to the NCP during the activation of switched connections. Major statements coded in the switched node are shown in Fig. 8.13, to which the following definitions apply.

VBUILD TYPE = SWNET identifies the major node as a switched node.

PU statement: One PU statement is coded per switched port on the NCP. ADDR parameter defines the SDLC address for the station. IDBLK and IDNUM collectively define a block and device identification, which is used as the identification sequence in the SDLC XID frame when the connection is established. IBM product specifications contain recommended values to be coded in the ID fields. Other parameters on the PU profile are similar to the PU statement in the NCP generation, as described in Sec. 8.6.3. under "PU table."

PATH statement: The PATH statement in the switched node has noth-

```
(name)   VBUILD   TYPE = SWNET,...

(name)   PU       ADDR = SDLC address,
                  IDBLK = ...,
                  IDNUM = ...,
                     .
                     .
                     .

(name)   PATH     DIALNO = ...,
                  PID = ...,

(name)   PATH     DIALNO = ...,
                  PID = ...,
                     .
                     .
                     .

(name)   LU       LOCADDR = ...,...
          .       LOGMODE = ...,
          .
          .

(name)   LU         ...
```

Figure 8.13   Defining switched resources to VTAM.

ing to do with the PATH statement for the routing tables, in spite of having the same name. The PATH statement in the switched node is used to define the telephone number for dial-out ports.

DIALNO: This parameter is used to define a telephone number for dial-out ports. Multiple PATH statements can be coded for each PU to define multiple telephone numbers.

Path ID (PID): This parameter assigns a unique number to each path statement. The specific number to be dialed is identified by the control operator in the line activation command via the PID of the PATH statement containing the desired telephone number.

LU statement: One LU statement is coded per device on the switched station. Parameters defined for a switched LU are similar to those of a private line LU, as described in Sec. 8.6.3. under "LU table."

Local non-SNA 3270.   These stations are defined separately in a non-SNA local node. The only non-SNA devices supported by VTAM are the pre-SNA IBM 3270 family. Details of their definitions are not discussed in this book.

8.8   START AND CONFIGURATION LISTS

8.8.1   Start List

A *start list* contains information that VTAM needs to configure itself at startup. Multiple start lists can be defined, but only one can be re-

```
poolname1 = (buffer pool parameters),

poolname2 = (buffer pool parameters),
                    .
                    .
                    .

CONFIG = ...,

HOSTSA = ...,

NODELST = ...,

TNSTAT = ...,
           .
           .
           .
```

Figure 8.14 VTAM start list parameters.

ferred to during each startup. A start list on the VTAM library must have a name conforming to the notation ATCSTRxx where xx can be any alphanumeric string. One should rarely need more than a few start lists. Some of the parameters defined on the start list are shown in Fig. 8.14 and are described below:

poolname = parameters: VTAM uses several buffer pools, each with a unique pool name. For each pool the user can define the buffer unit size, number of buffer units, and an expansion value so that VTAM can expand the pool dynamically should the number of available buffers fall below a designated value. One poolname parameter is coded per VTAM buffer pool.

CONFIG: Identifies the suffix of the configuration list that VTAM is to use to activate major nodes. See Sec. 8.8.2 for further discussion of the configuration list.

HOSTSA: Assigns the subarea number to this VTAM.

NODELST: Specifies the name of the file where VTAM is to maintain the names of all currently active major nodes. This file is used by VTAM during warm restart to reconfigure the network to the same state it was in before the failure.

TNSTAT: Specifies whether tuning statistics for VTAM buffer usage and I/O operations with the channel-attached NCPs should be recorded. In addition to recording statistics on a disk file, they can also be displayed on the system console periodically. The statistics provide very useful information for analyzing and optimizing VTAM buffer utilization and the efficiency of VTAM-to-NCP transfers over the I/O channel.

NCP1, NCP2, APPLS1, LOCSNA1, ...

Figure 8.15   Defining VTAM configuration list.

8.8.2 Configuration List

A *configuration list* simply lists all the major nodes that VTAM is to activate at startup. Multiple configuration lists can be defined in the VTAM library using the naming convention ATCCONxx, where **xx** can be any alphanumeric string.

As shown in Fig. 8.15, the configuration list contains the names of major nodes to be activated at startup. The major nodes listed in the configuration list are NCP1, NCP2, APPLS1, and LOCSNA1.

8.9 AN ILLUSTRATIVE STARTUP SEQUENCE

To illustrate how various system generation definitions interact, we go through a network startup scenario. Figure 8.16 shows the sample network for this example. The host machine has TSO, CICS, and IMS running as subsystems. There is one channel-attached SNA station with one PU and three LUs and one channel-attached FEP. The specific number of lines and terminals on the FEP would not be important for this illustration.

To support this network, the system programmer has created the following major nodes.

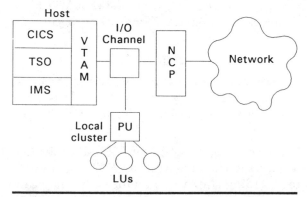

Figure 8.16   Sample VTAM network [Major nodes: APPLS01 = (IMS, CICS); APPLS02 = (TS001, TS002, ..., TSOnn); LCLHQ = 1 PU and 3 LUs for local SNA major node; NYNCPA = describes NCP major node].

APPLS01: This applications major node defines two minor nodes, CICS and IMS.

APPLS02: This applications major node defines multiple host LUs associated with TSO. Note that APPLS01 and APPLS02 could have been combined to form one applications major node—it is up to the system programmer to configure the nodes most suitable to his or her needs.

LCLHQ: This local SNA node defines one PU and three LUs attached locally; the name LCLHQ implies a local cluster at headquarters location.

NYNCPA: Defines an NCP major node. This node would contain GROUP, LINE, PU, LU, etc. statements for the NCP being described.

Figure 8.17 shows a VTAM system library with various definitions. Our intent here is to show various tables figuratively; actual coding

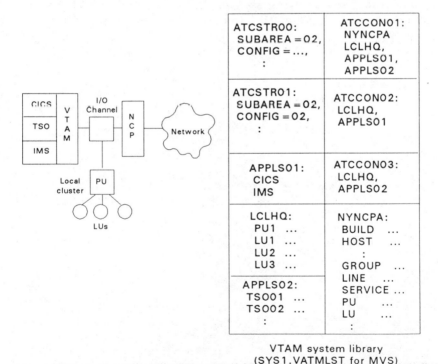

VTAM system library
(SYS1.VATMLST for MVS)

Figure 8.17   VTAM system library.

syntax would be as discussed earlier in this chapter. Each box in the diagram represents a file on the system library.

The diagram also shows two start lists, ATCSTR00 and ATCSTR01, which we would refer to as start lists 00 and 01. We also have three configuration lists ATCCON01, ATCCON02, and ATCCON03.

8.9.1 VTAM Startup

Figure 8.18 shows a startup chronology and the effect of coding various parameters in these tables.

1. The system operator enters the operating system procedure name, NET in this case, to start VTAM. The syntax shown in the diagram applies to MVS systems only. DOS systems would use an EXEC command, whereas VM users would use VTAM START command.

2. The operating system loads a copy of VTAM from the VTAM load library (or phase library in DOS) and VTAM starts initializing itself.

3. VTAM obtains the rest of the parameters on the START command from the operating system. In our example we show only one parameter, LIST = 01. This operand identifies the start list

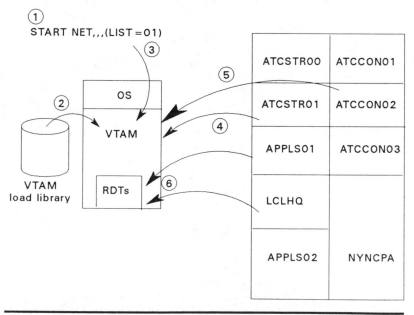

Figure 8.18 VTAM startup sequence (START command syntax shown for MVS).

through its suffix 01 (for ATCSTR01) that VTAM is to use to configure itself.

4. VTAM reads the start list from the system library, assigns itself the subarea number on the start list, allocates buffers, and processes other information on the list. Among the information on the start list is the identification of the configuration list, CONFIG = 02, that contains names of major nodes to be activated.

5. VTAM reads ATCCON02 file from the library. This file tells VTAM to activate major nodes APPLS01 and LCLHQ.

6. VTAM reads files APPLS01 and LCLHQ from the library and translates them to a machine-processable form and builds a Resource Definition table in main memory. Entries in the Resource Definition table, shown as RDTs in the diagram, represent VTAM's view of its domain.

VTAM next interrogates ISTATUS and LOGAPPL specifications on local PU and LU statements and activates sessions automatically if so requested. Note that VTAM cannot start CICS, TSO, or other host subsystems. At this time VTAM only knows that these subsystems exist but would not accept any logons for these subsystems until they tell VTAM to do so. During the subsystem initialization, each subsystem would perform a handshake with VTAM and inform VTAM to accept logons on its behalf.

Figure 8.19 shows a current view of VTAM of its domain.

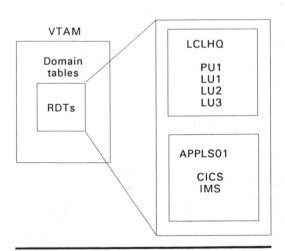

Figure 8.19 VTAM view of its domain when using start list 01 for example in Fig. 8.18.

8.9.2   Modifying the Network

Because of the way we started VTAM in this example, NCP activation was not a part of the initial startup. Of course, the NCP major node, NCP1, could have been made a part of the configuration list, and NCP could have been activated automatically. To illustrate how resources can be activated manually we are treating NCP activation as a separate step. Figure 8.20 shows manual activation of the NCP.

1. The system operator enters a command (VARY) to change the status of a resource to active (ACT) status; the name of the resource is identified as NYNCPA.

2. VTAM analyzes the existing RDTs to check if NCP1 is already a known resource but inactive. In our example, VTAM would not find NCP1 in the existing RDTs because of the way we started VTAM.

3. VTAM goes back to the system library looking for a major node definition called NCP1. Note that VTAM does not know that it is activating an NCP until it reads the NCP1 major node definition from the system library. VTAM adds NCP1 definitions to its RDTs.

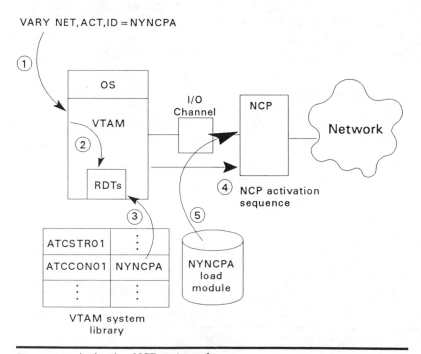

Figure 8.20   Activating NCP major node.

4. VTAM goes through the activation sequence for the front end. As discussed in "Activation Sequences" in Chap. 7, a number of commands and responses are exchanged between VTAM and NCP during activation.

5. In any case, it is possible that the FEP may not have been powered on or loaded with software. In such a case the activation would fail. If the activation sequence fails, VTAM can automatically try to reload the NCP software and attempt activation again if so specified in the generation tables or START command.

Once the NCP has been activated successfully, VTAM would go through ISTATUS and LOGAPPL parameters on PU and LU profiles for automatic activations and establish automatic sessions if any were specified. At this time NCP activation is complete.

8.10   VTAM SYSTEM GENERATION SUMMARY

VTAM system generation is the most elaborate in SNA. In the preceding sections we looked only at the domain definitions and start and configuration lists. Other tables, such as bind, USS, cross-domain, warm start reconfiguration file, and routing tables, are just some of the examples of additional tables needed. Additional multidomain tables are discussed in Chap. 9.

8.11   CONSIDERATIONS FOR SUBSYSTEMS

Each subsystem has its own requirements and tables that need to be coded using product-unique syntax. Teleprocessing monitors such as CICS and IMS would require definitions in the following areas.

1. *Password and ID information:*   These tables include user identification information and access authorization information about operators to control their access to various transaction programs.

2. *Transaction programs:*   For each transaction program (application), a transaction code would be listed along with the name of the program load module. Additional information such as programming language and library information may also have to be provided.

3. *Files and databases:*   TP monitors handle all file and database requests for transaction programs running under their control. Tables would also be defined to identify all files, their attributes (file type, record size, etc.), and file authorizations for access.

4. *Terminal descriptions:* These tables include descriptions of network terminals. It should be remembered that these descriptions are in addition to the profiles already defined to VTAM and NCP. Terminal profiles typically contain terminal name, terminal type (e.g., 3270), and terminal buffer size, etc. Most of this information is used by the subsystems to decide which bind parameters to use in communications with this device. Theoretically one could say that subsystems can obtain most of this information from VTAM since VTAM already has this information in its tables. However, IBM products do not necessarily work that way. So, frequently, adding a terminal to the network requires changing tables in NCP, VTAM, and the subsystem.

In addition to these tables, TP monitors also have tables to manage other system attributes such as buffer pool sizes, maximum concurrent transactions, recoverable transactions, checkpoint and logging files, etc.

8.12 IMPLEMENTATION SUMMARY

Implementing SNA or any other large network is a complex task requiring expertise in both hardware and software systems. Knowledge of the architecture alone is not sufficient—one has to have very detailed expertise in the specific products installed. For SNA networks, at a minimum VTAM, NCP, one or two subsystems, and IBM-3270-type terminals would be involved. Looking into the future, AS/400, PS/2, and gateways to LANs and OSI would also be an integral part of SNA implementations. Given the large size of implementation teams, it is also important to have very good project management and communications procedures in place.

Multiple Systems
Networking (MSN)

9.1 INTRODUCTION

So far in this book we have focused on single-host networks. That, however, is not the primary environment that motivated SNA. The larger intent of the architecture is to provide any-to-any connectivity and distributed processing. In this chapter our focus moves to any-to-any connectivity in a multihost environment with S/370/390 acting as hosts. Connectivity with minicomputers such as IBM systems AS/400 and PCs is treated as a part of distributed processing and is discussed in Chaps. 12 and 13 under LU 6.2.

While discussing distributed processing, let us also make a distinction between distributed control and distributed applications. Distributed control is very much a part of the multihost operations. It is the distributed applications that fall under the LU 6.2 category.

Multihost or multidomain configurations are referred to as Multiple Systems Networking (MSN). As an historic footnote, this function was originally referred to as MSNF—where F stood for feature or facility, depending on which IBM reference you looked at. In any case, when first announced, the so-called MSNF was an extra cost feature in VTAM and NCP and later, when it became a standard feature, IBM dropped the F in MSNF.

MSNF was also the reason for the addition of the prefix ACF (Advanced Communications Function) to VTAM, TCAM, and NCP product names to indicate the support for multihost networks as the advanced function implied in the ACF prefix. Even though the capability is no longer an advanced one, the prefix remains. None of the non-ACF products are current or available from IBM anymore. All references to VTAM, TCAM, and NCP in this book imply their ACF releases even though we do not use the prefix.

9.2   DEFINITIONS AND CONCEPTS

9.2.1   MSN Definition

The MSN capability provides LU-LU sessions between any two LUs in the network irrespective of the domain they belong to. The session could be between a terminal and a host application or a host application and another host application. The LUs participating in such a session do not have to know about each other's owners or location or even the fact that they are participating in a cross-domain session.

As shown in Fig. 9.1, a terminal user at LUD in Los Angeles can log onto CICS system in New York by specifying the name CICS2 in the logon message. To log onto CICS system in Los Angeles, the logon message would identify the Los Angeles CICS as CICS1. This brings up our first requirement for MSN: LU names must be unique across

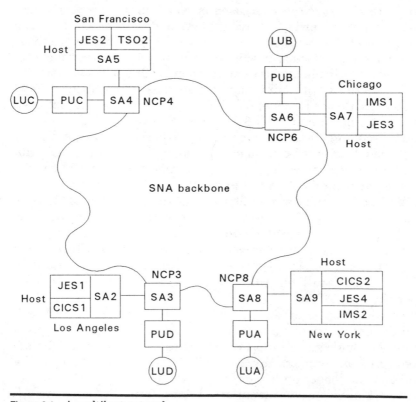

Figure 9.1   A multihost network.

all domains in order to participate in cross-domain logons. A corporation implementing a multidomain network, therefore, must establish a naming convention; and systems programmers in all data centers must conform to it to assure unique symbolic names for all VTAMs, NCPs, applications (subsystems), and network devices.

MSN does not provide LU-LU sessions between peripheral node; at least one of the LUs must be host resident. In our example in Fig. 9.1, sessions would not be possible between any of the LUs from among LUA, LUB, and LUC since none of them is host resident. For such sessions we would need PU 2.1 and LU 6.2. However, PU 2.1 does not use MSN protocols. Chap. 12 discusses LU 6.2 and PU 2.1 in more detail.

9.2.2 Domain and Ownership Implications

We introduced the concept of a domain earlier in Chap. 2, Sec. 2.3.4; to review it—a domain is a set of resources owned by an SSCP. Figure 9.2 shows the same network as in Fig. 9.1, redrawn to reflect the domain boundaries.

Setting up domains is a key design issue and should not be done arbitrarily. To understand some of the factors that influence domain setup, we need to understand ownership implications. Some of these are as follows:

1. All session requests (logons) must go through the SSCPs (VTAMs) that own the LUs involved in the session. If either of the two owning VTAMs is unavailable, the session cannot be established. In Fig. 9.2, if JES2 in San Francisco wants to establish a session with LUA, say a printer where a report is to be printed, the session cannot be established if VTAM in New York is not running, even if NCP, SA8 was operational.

2. Resources in a domain can be activated or deactivated only by the owning SSCP. For example, LUA can be activated only from the New York host.

3. Any error and diagnostic messages from the network and peripheral nodes are sent to the owning host only. The owning host may forward it to other hosts.

4. Remote network testing (e.g., loop-back or self-test, etc.) can be initiated only from the owning host. Where supported, network statistics (response time, error counters, etc.) can only be solicited by the owning host.

In broader terms, only the owning SSCP can set up a session (SSCP-PU or SSCP-LU) with a PU or LU. Therefore, any flows that occur on

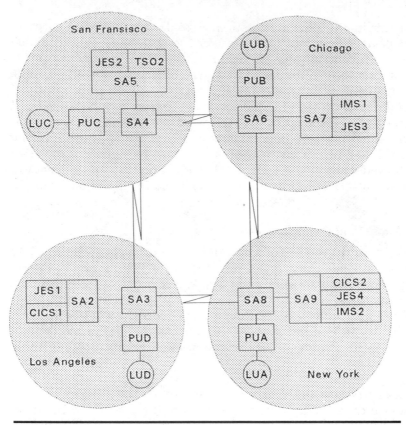

Figure 9.2 A four-domain network.

an SSCP session, of which the four preceding items were examples, can take place only with the owning SSCP.

9.2.3 Setting Up Domains

Considering various factors discussed in Sec. 9.2.2, it becomes apparent that operational issues must be given the most importance when forming domains. For example, in Fig. 9.2, when considering ownership of NCP, SA3, and its attached network in Los Angeles, we should consider which data center would be responsible for down-loading the NCP software or providing hardware and software technical support for this part of the network. Would the end users call the Los Angeles data center when they need assistance? Would the Los Angeles network control center schedule vendor personnel for problem resolution, and who would monitor that part of the network? Whichever data center would have these responsibilities should be the owner of these resources. In our example, we assume that these responsibilities for NCP-SA3, have been assigned to the Los Angeles data center, thus, the NCP-SA3 belongs to the domain of the Los Angeles host.

As with all other things in real life, the domain issues do not always lend themselves to such clearly defined criteria. What if a number of terminal users in Los Angeles are order-entry clerks whose only use of the network is to enter orders and the order-entry application runs under CICS2 in New York? The problem arises in deciding which data center the users should call for help if they are having problems in using the system. If the CICS system is unavailable in New York or users are having difficulty in logging on to the system, the Los Angeles data center cannot help them because it does not operate the New York data center. On the other hand, if hardware support is to be provided from the Los Angeles data center, the users cannot call New York for help with hardware problems. To make matters worse, sometimes it is not clear whether the problem is due to a hardware or software malfunction—and if software, software in which data center? In this case, no matter how you assign the ownership, the network control center at the owning host would not be able to provide complete end-to-end support for the users.

9.2.4 Cross-Domain Resources and Managers

To explain cross-domain logons and flows we have to introduce two new definitions.

Cross-domain resources (CDRSC). From VTAM's (SSCP) point of view, any LUs not in its domain are cross-domain LUs or resources. The cross-domain LUs must be known to VTAM if it is to initiate any sessions with them. As shown in the following paragraphs, these LUs are listed in a table called the Cross-Domain Resources table (CDRSC). Only the cross-domain LUs are defined in the CDRSC table, not the PUs or links to which they are connected.

Cross domain resource managers (CDRM). Cross Domain Resource Manager is an architected component that resides in VTAM and is responsible for handling cross-domain logons. CDRM is an NAU type and has its own element address. Conceptually it helps to view a CDRM as a functional extension of the SSCP. All logons originating in a domain go to the SSCP first. If the logon is intradomain, SSCP handles it completely. If the logon is a cross-domain logon, the SSCP passes it on to the CDRM, which is then responsible for forwarding the logon to the VTAM that owns the destination LU. In addition to the

CDRSC table, each VTAM also has a table called the CDRM table that lists all CDRMs (VTAMs) in the network.

Before any cross-domain LU-LU sessions can be established, the SSCPs in the two domains must establish an SSCP-SSCP session between them. The SSCP-SSCP session is established by either of the two VTAMs automatically at startup or by a command from the control operator.

9.3 SHAREABLE RESOURCES

NCPs and nonswitched SDLC links can have multiple owners concurrently. PUs and LUs may have only one owner at a time. This ability to share NCP and links among domains provides the system programmers with additional flexibility in dividing up domains.

An NCP can have up to eight concurrent owners, of which a maximum of four can be channel attached (the channel attachment of four is a product restriction and not architectural). The system programmer can code special parameters to prevent VTAMs from becoming owners of resources that are not to be a part of their domains. When no restrictions are specified, whichever VTAM activates a resource first becomes the owner.

9.4 NCP-ATTACHED VERSUS CHANNEL-ATTACHED RESOURCES

Resources attached to the NCP do not have to have the same owner as the NCP. Each line can be assigned an owner different from the NCP or other lines on the same NCP. The peripheral nodes on a line, similarly, can have different owners. However, the ownership of an LU cannot be separated from its PU—whoever owns the PU automatically owns attached LUs.

Channel-attached (local) resources and host subsystems, however, must always be owned by the host to which they are attached or where they reside. They cannot participate in the network if their owner is inactive.

9.5 CROSS-DOMAIN LOGON FLOW

9.5.1 SSCP-SSCP Sessions

Let us consider a two-domain network shown in Fig. 9.3, which is a subset of the network shown in Fig. 9.2.

Before any cross-domain LU-LU sessions can take place, either of

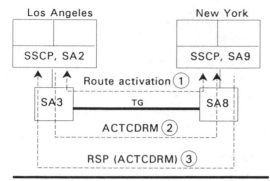

Figure 9.3 Establishing SSCP-SSCP sessions.

the two VTAMs initiates an SSCP-SSCP session. Various steps required to establish SSCP-SSCP sessions include:

1. Activation of virtual and explicit routes between the two hosts. Specific commands for route activation were discussed in Chap. 7.

2. Either of the two VTAMs sending the ACTCDRM command to the other. The command contains information such as the subarea number and the symbolic name of the SSCP issuing the command.

3. The target VTAM returning similar information about itself in the positive response to ACTCDRM command and indicating whether it is ready to accept the SSCP-SSCP session. After the ACTCDRM exchange, both Los Angeles and New York VTAMs have verified each other's identification and subarea numbers. Now cross-domain LU-LU sessions can take place.

9.5.2 Cross-Domain LU-LU Sessions

Consider a logon between LUD in Los Angeles and CICS2 in New York in Fig. 9.4a. Before we look at the actual flows, let us review the information required in the cross-domain tables to process cross-domain logons. In Los Angeles, JES1, CICS1, and LUD will be defined as owned LUs; and CICS2, JES4, IMS2, and LUA as cross-domain LUs owned by a host containing NYCDRM. The CDRM table would further indicate that NYCDRM has subarea number of 9.

The New York host would similarly define CICS2, JES4, IMS2, and LUA as owned resources; and JES1, CICS1, and LUD as cross-domain LUs owned by LACDRM. Table 9.1 shows this information.

Let us now assume that the operator at the terminal LUD enters a logon request for CICS2 as shown in Fig. 9.4b. The logon is routed to the SA2 host, which owns LUD. When this logon arrives at the Los

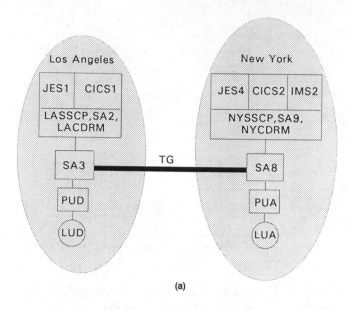

(a)

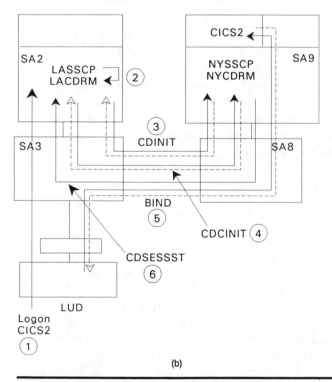

(b)

Figure 9.4 (a) A two-domain network; (b) establishing a cross-domain LU-LU session.

TABLE 9.1   Domain and Cross-Domain Definitions for
Network in Figure 9.3

Definitions for VTAM in Los Angeles host	
Owned	Cross domain
JES1	CICS2;OwnerNYCDRM,SA9
CICS1	JES4;Owner NYCDRM,SA9
LUD	IMS2;Owner NYCDRM,SA9
	LUA;Owner NYCDRM,SA9

Definitions for VTAM in New York host	
Owned	Cross domain
CICS2	JES1,Owner LACDRM,SA2
JES4	CICS1;Owner LACDRM,SA2
IMS2	LUD;Owner LACDRM,SA2
LUA	

Note: Diagram shows functional information, not the actual
structure and syntax for coding these tables.

Angeles host, the SSCP there does not know that CICS2 is not in its
domain. It goes through its domain table (specifically, the applications
major node, see Sec. 8.7.1), shown partially as Table 9.1, looking for
CICS2. When it does not find CICS2 in the applications major node,
the SSCP passes the logon to its CDRM, LACDRM.

LACDRM goes through its cross-domain definitions shown in Table
9.1. The cross-domain definitions indicate that CICS2 is owned by
NYCDRM, which has a subarea number of 9.

At this time it is not known whether CICS2 is really available in
New York, nor is its subarea-element address known. In step 3, Fig.
9.4b, the Los Angeles host sends an SNA command called cross domain initiate (CDINIT) to NYSSCP. CDINIT command contains the
symbolic name and network address of LUD and requests information
about CICS2 from NYSSCP. If CICS2 indeed belongs to NYSSCP domain, NYSSCP returns the network address of CICS2 in a positive response to CDINIT.

LASSCP now has all the information it needs to send the logon request itself in the form of SNA command cross domain control initiate
(CDCINIT). The CDCINIT, step 4, command contains information
such as network addresses of LUD and CICS2 and a copy of the bind
image for LUD. NYSSCP passes the logon request to CICS2.

If CICS2 is willing to accept the logon it causes a BIND command to
be issued to LUD, step 5. LUD indicates its acceptance of the BIND
command by sending a positive response to bind.

At this time, although this is not shown in Fig. 9.4b, CICS2 would
inform NYSSCP that the session has been bound successfully. In step

6 NYSSCP informs LASSCP via SNA command CDSESSST that a cross-domain LU-LU session has been started successfully.

From this point on session traffic does not flow through LASSCP but rather through NCP subarea 3 to NCP subarea 8 directly to the New York host—the path shown for the BIND command in step 5. It does not even matter any more who the owner is—LASSCP host can crash and the cross-domain session between LUD and CICS2 can continue. However, if the LUD operator should log off from CICS2 and LASSCP is still down, LUD cannot initiate any new logons. SNA does permit domain ownership to be reassigned. We discuss domain takeover and host recovery in Sec. 9.8.

9.6 DEFINING CROSS-DOMAIN TABLES—CDRM AND CDRSC MAJOR NODES

The cross-domain descriptions such as those illustrated in Table 9.1 are defined in two VTAM major nodes (in addition to the major nodes discussed in Sec. 8.7): Cross Domain Resource Managers (CDRM) major node and cross-domain resources (CDRSC) major node.

9.6.1 Cross Domain Resource Managers (CDRM) Major Node

This table enumerates all the VTAMs that reside in the network by listing their CDRM names and subarea numbers. Figure 9.5 shows the CDRM major node as it would be defined in each VTAM for the network shown in Fig. 9.1.

In Fig. 9.5, VBUILD TYPE = CDRM tells VTAM that this is the CDRM major node table. Following that, there is one CDRM entry for each VTAM in the network. The name assigned to a VTAM on the CDRM statement must be consistent across the total network, and no two VTAMs may have the same name. In our example, LACDRM is for the Los Angeles host; SFCDRM, for San Francisco; CHICDRM, for

```
          VBUILD   TYPE = CDRM
NYCDRM   CDRM     SUBAREA = 9,...
CHICDRM  CDRM     SUBAREA = 7,...
SFCDRM   CDRM     SUBAREA = 5,...
LACDRM   CDRM     SUBAREA = 2,...
```

Figure 9.5 Cross Domain Resource Managers (CDRM) major node for Fig. 9.1 (this table would be coded in each of the four VTAMs).

Chicago; and NYCDRM, for New York. Each CDRM statement identifies the subarea number of the VTAM being described.

9.6.2   Cross-Domain Resources (CDRSC) Major Node

In addition to the CDRM major node, each host also requires a description of cross-domain LUs. This description is provided in the CDRSC major node.

Figure 9.6 shows the CDRSC statements that would be needed in each host for our sample network. The first major statement in Fig. 9.6, VBUILD TYPE = CDRSC, identifies this table as the CDRSC major node. Following that, there is one CDRSC statement for each cross-domain LU for which logons may originate in this domain. For our sample network, 10 cross-domain LUs are defined in Los Angeles VTAM.

9.7   REDUCING OR ELIMINATING CROSS-DOMAIN LU DEFINITIONS

The example in Fig. 9.6 shows the worst case for LU definition requirements, with all cross-domain LUs defined in each host. In a large network with tens of thousands of LUs, this can be a very burdensome requirement; in reality, it is not necessary. Starting with ACF/VTAM version 2, release 2 (circa 1983), VTAM can discover owners and cross-domain LUs dynamically.

With dynamic definitions capability, a VTAM can find the owner of an LU by asking other VTAMs whether they own a resource whose owner is unknown. Once a VTAM finds the whereabouts of an owner, it notes them in a table so that it does not have to make the search for each new session for the same LU.

9.7.1   Adjacent SSCP (ADJSSCP) Table

To enable efficient searches of unknown owners there is a table in VTAM called the Adjacent SSCP or ADJSSCP table. VTAM would try to find an unknown owner only if an ADJSSCP table is coded as a part of its system generation. The Adjacent SSCP table has two parts to it:

1. Single-default SSCP list
2. Multiple adjacent CDRM lists.

The default list is used when a VTAM does not know the *name* of the SSCP that owns a cross-domain LU. The adjacent CDRM list is used when a VTAM knows the name of the SSCP that owns the cross-

For New York host:

```
        VBUILD   TYPE=CDRSC
LUD     CDRSC    CDRM=LACDRM,...
JES1    CDRSC    CDRM=LACDRM,...
CICS1   CDRSC    CDRM=LACDRM,...
LUC     CDRSC    CDRM=SFCDRM,...
JES2    CDRSC    CDRM=SFCDRM,...
TSO2    CDRSC    CDRM=SFCDRM,...
LUB     CDRSC    CDRM=CHICDRM,...
IMS1    CDRSC    CDRM=CHICDRM,...
JES3    CDRSC    CDRM=CHICDRM,...
```

For San Francisco host:

```
        VBUILD   TYPE=CDRSC
LUD     CDRSC    CDRM=LACDRM,...
JES1    CDRSC    CDRM=LACDRM,...
CICS1   CDRSC    CDRM=LACDRM,...
LUB     CDRSC    CDRM=CHICDRM,...
JES3    CDRSC    CDRM=CHICDRM,...
IMS1    CDRSC    CDRM=CHICDRM,...
LUA     CDRSC    CDRM=NYCDRM,...
CICS2   CDRSC    CDRM=NYCDRM,...
JES4    CDRSC    CDRM=NYCDRM,...
IMS2    CDRSC    CDRM=NYCDRM,...
```

For Chicago host:

```
        VBUILD   TYPE=CDRSC
LUD     CDRSC    CDRM=LACDRM,...
JES1    CDRSC    CDRM=LACDRM,...
CICS1   CDRSC    CDRM=LACDRM,...
LUC     CDRSC    CDRM=SFCDRM,...
JES2    CDRSC    CDRM=SFCDRM,...
TSO2    CDRSC    CDRM=SFCDRM,...
LUA     CDRSC    CDRM=NYCDRM,...
CICS2   CDRSC    CDRM=NYCDRM,...
JES4    CDRSC    CDRM=NYCDRM,...
IMS2    CDRSC    CDRM=NYCDRM,...
```

For Los Angeles host:

```
        VBUILD   TYPE=CDRSC
LUC     CDRSC    CDRM=SFCDRM,...
JES2    CDRSC    CDRM=SFCDRM,...
TSO2    CDRSC    CDRM=SFCDRM,...
LUB     CDRSC    CDRM=CHICDRM,...
JES3    CDRSC    CDRM=CHICDRM,...
IMS1    CDRSC    CDRM=CHICDRM,...
LUA     CDRSC    CDRM=NYCDRM,...
CICS2   CDRSC    CDRM=NYCDRM,...
JES4    CDRSC    CDRM=NYCDRM,...
IMS2    CDRSC    CDRM=NYCDRM,...
```

Figure 9.6 Cross-Domain Resources (CDRSC) major node for Fig. 9.1. [*Note:* This example shows worst case (maximum) number of definitions. In current releases of VTAM these definitions can be reduced or eliminated entirely.]

domain LU but does not know its subarea number, *or* does not have a session with it, *or* has no routing information to reach it. In each of these cases, the adjacent CDRM list provides names of known CDRMs to which VTAM should route the cross-domain logon.

As an example, let us look at Fig. 9.7, which shows partial system generation tables for the New York host to take advantage of the ADJSSCP table.

In the first part of the table in Fig. 9.7, we show the cross-domain LUs table. In this example we identify only LUD and LUB as cross-domain resources and none of the LUs in San Francisco and Chicago.

The second part of the table shows CDRM definitions, where, in addition to New York's own entry, only the Chicago and San Francisco hosts are defined and the Los Angeles host has not been defined.

The third section shows the ADJSSCP table. The first part of the table is the default SSCP table, and the second part is the adjacent SSCP list for specific CDRMs. We illustrate the use of the table through the following example.

9.7.2 Cross-Domain Logon Using ADJSSCP: LU and CDRM Names Known, CDRM Subarea Number Unknown

Consider a request originating in the New York domain for a session with LUD. In New York, the CDRSC major node, the first table in Fig. 9.7, defines LUD as owned by LACDRM. However, the CDRM table in New York, the second table in Fig. 9.7, has no entry for LACDRM— the New York VTAM does not know where LACDRM is in the network. The New York VTAM would go to the ADJSSCP table, the third table in Fig. 9.7.

VTAM would look at the specific CDRM list first to see if there is an entry for LACDRM. In our example, we do have an entry for LACDRM and the second line in that entry, SFCDRM ADJCDRM, tells VTAM to try SFCDRM if the owner is LACDRM. The New York VTAM would forward the session request for LUD to San Francisco. This example assumes that the San Francisco host has Los Angeles defined in its CDRM table, or has its own ADJSSCP table to help it reach Los Angeles. If neither is true, the logon would fail with "owner unknown."

In any case, if the Los Angeles host is reached successfully through San Francisco, the New York VTAM would update LUD profile with the complete information on LACDRM so that the next time there is a request for a session with LUD, New York would not have to search for LACDRM again. In this example, the default SSCP list was not used.

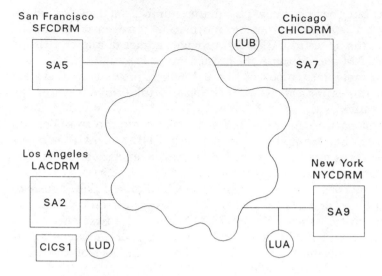

Partial system generation tables for New York:

1) CDRSC definitions:

```
            VBUILD  TYPE = CDRSC
LUD         CDRSC   CDRM = LACDRM
LUB         CDRSC   CDRM = CHICDRM
(No other cross-domain LUs defined in New York)
```

2) CDRM definitions:

```
            VBUILD  TYPE = CDRM
NYCDRM      CDRM    SUBAREA = 9,...
CHICDRM     CDRM    SUBAREA = 7,...
SFCDRM      CDRM    SUBAREA = 5,...
```

3) ADJSSCP table:

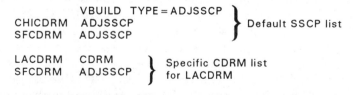

Figure 9.7   ADJSSCP table.

9.7.3 Cross-Domain Logon: LU and CDRM Unknown

Let us next look at a logon request originating in New York for CICS1, which resides in Los Angeles. CICS1 is not defined in the cross-domain LUs (CDRSC) table in New York. In this case the New

York VTAM would try the default SSCP list in the ADJSSCP table. The first entry in the table is the CHICDRM, therefore the logon would be routed to Chicago. If Chicago does not know about CICS1, it would send an exception response to the New York request. New York would try San Francisco next. If San Francisco also rejects the logon, the logon would fail. Otherwise, if LACDRM is defined to Chicago or San Francisco, directly or through its own ADJSSCP table, the logon would be routed to Los Angeles. When Los Angeles responds to the New York logon request, New York would update the profile of CICS1 to reflect that it lives in Los Angeles.

9.8 DOMAIN BACKUP AND RECOVERY

SSCP failure, along with the accompanying domain failure, is a major event in SNA. When an SSCP fails, all sessions with applications in the failing host are terminated, none of the terminals in the domain can initiate any new sessions, and no network management and operations tasks can be performed for that domain.

If the cause of the error is such that it can be fixed and VTAM restored quickly, the domain can be operational again without requiring a backup host. But if a host VTAM cannot be restored within an acceptable time frame (given the complexity of domain failure, domain restoral objectives are typically defined in minutes, not seconds), it may become necessary to use another host to take over the domain of the failed VTAM. However, domain takeover does require planning and training of the operations personnel.

9.8.1 Planning Domain Recovery

Domain recovery costs resources: Do you have a backup host with spare capacity? It should not be assumed that all failures should be automatically recoverable from a backup host. To reduce the cost of backup and recovery, one may even do partial recovery such as critical terminals only.

While discussing recovery for domain failures we also need to make a distinction between host applications recovery and network recovery as follows.

Host applications recovery. Application recovery requires a backup host where the application can be run if the primary should fail. The backup host should have copies of the application software, associated files, and databases available to it. If the primary and the backup host are within the same data center, moving applications and databases may be just a matter of switching disk drives to the backup host. However, if the backup host is at a different site, the problem becomes more complex. Providing copies of application software at the backup site is not difficult. The problem lies with files and databases that keep changing throughout the day as transactions are processed. If the primary host fails during the business day, the backup site would not have the current copies of files and databases. Somehow the current copies of all files must be transmitted to the backup host—but how do you transmit files when your computer is down? One way to solve this problem may be to run all transactions on both primary and backup sites simultaneously in real time. Doing so assures file integrity, albeit at double the CPU and I/O device requirements, and requires synchronization of file updates over multiple hosts, a solvable, but nontrivial, problem. So application backup has to be weighed and justified against business needs and benefits.

In any case, application recovery is not a part of SNA domain recovery protocols but can be implemented using user-defined procedures (which may, optionally, be built on top of LU 6.2 protocols).

Thus, when we talk about SNA domain recovery, we talk only about network recovery as discussed next.

Domain network recovery.   Network recovery pertains only to network components—NCPs, links, PUs, LUs, routes, and sessions—so that they can continue to be active. This recovery requires that a new SSCP take over the domain of the failing host if the failing host is not expected to be available for some time.

Figure 9.8 shows part of the network discussed in earlier examples in this chapter. It is our intent to have Chicago as the backup host for New York and to have Chicago take over SA8 NCP and all of its attached resources when the New York host fails. Domain takeover would work in three phases: definitions in the backup host, the actual failure, and the domain takeover.

9.9   DOMAIN RECOVERY SCENARIO

9.9.1   Definitions in the Backup Host

The Chicago host must know the physical and logical configuration of the NCP in order to take over its resources. A copy of the SA8 NCP system generation tables must be filed at the Chicago host, the backup site.

In addition, we would also have a copy of a set of NCP tables called RRTs (Resource Resolution tables) for NCP, SA8, in Chicago. RRTs are generated during the assembly of the NCP system generation tables.

As shown in the next section, it would be desirable that, even during normal operation, the Chicago host be a concurrent owner of SA8

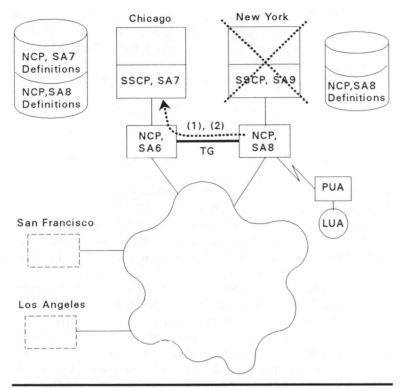

Figure 9.8 Chicago as backup host to New York. From NCP, SA8 to Chicago host: (1) NC-ER-INOP, (2) NC-LCP (if Chicago is coowner of NCP, SA8).

in addition to the New York host (Chicago need own only the NCP/ FEP and not any of the NCP attached resources). The Chicago host can become a concurrent owner by simply setting up an SSCP-PU session (via ACTPU command) with SA8.

At this point the table definition part of our backup planning is complete.

9.9.2 Host Failure Notification and Sessions Termination

Now let us assume that the New York host fails. SA8 NCP would discover the host failure when it tries to transfer data to it over the I/O channel and a host time out would occur indicating a host VTAM failure. At this time SA8 NCP takes the following actions:

1. *Send failure notification:* Two types of error notifications are sent by the NCP.

a. NC__ER__INOP (network control explicit route failure): SA8 sends this RU to each adjacent subarea node (host or NCP) that had an explicit route going to the failed host. Each adjacent subarea node, in turn, forwards the notification to its adjacent nodes until the notification is propagated throughout the whole network.

Each node that receives the NC__ER__INOP RU updates its routing tables to indicate that all routes to the failed host are inactive.

(As an historic footnote, the NC__ER__INOP function was provided in the original architecture by a command called lost sub area (LSA), which was later replaced by an RU called ER__INACT, which then became NC__ER__INACT.)

b. NS__LCP (network services lost control point): This notification goes only to the SSCPs that own the NCP and informs the other owners of the loss of an SSCP. The arrival of the NS__LCP results in each VTAM's sending a message to its control operator about the failure. We suggested in Sec. 9.9.1 that the Chicago VTAM should be a coowner of SA8 for the sole purpose of having it receive this host failure notification automatically.

2. *Terminate sessions:*   A number of sessions are terminated not only by SA8 NCP but also by other boundary nodes. In the New York domain, NCP SA8 terminates all sessions between LUs in its subarea and applications in the New York host by sending an UNBIND command to each such LU. Cross-domain sessions with applications in other hosts continue or are terminated based on system generation specifications.

In other domains, all boundary nodes, on receiving NC-ER-INOP, terminate all sessions—LU-LU or SSCP-SSCP—in their subareas or domains that were using the failed route.

At this time no new sessions can be initiated by or with LUs in the New York domain.

9.9.3 Domain Takeover by the Backup Host

The backup host in our scenario is the Chicago data center. For Chicago staff to initiate the backup procedures they have to know first that the New York host is down.

The Chicago network control center would actually see multiple messages on its VTAM/NetView console due to the New York host failure. First, there would be a message indicating that SA8 NCP had lost its SSCP-PU session with the New York host. Then there would be an explicit route inoperative message due to the NC__ER__INOP generated by SA8 NCP. This route failure notification would cause the Chicago SSCP to terminate its SSCP-SSCP session with the New York host and the Chicago SSCP would display another message on the control operator's terminal indicating the loss of the SSCP-SSCP session. Route failure does not necessarily mean that a host in the network has failed. If route failure was the only notification received by the Chicago VTAM, it would actually try to reestablish a new SSCP-SSCP session with New York over an alternate route if one were available. In our specific scenario, the clearest indication of the New York host failure would be the arrival of the lost control point (NS_LCP) notification in Chicago from SA8 NCP. In addition, the staff in New York may call the Chicago data center to inform them of the failure.

At this time the Chicago operator can initiate the domain takeover procedures. Before taking any action in Chicago, it would be advisable to ascertain from the New York staff the nature of the failure and whether New York expects to restart immediately. Most corporations have or should have clearly defined operational procedures for the backup site to decide whether or not to initiate the domain takeover.

The specific steps to be taken for domain takeover depend on the parameters used in the system generation tables to define domains, and the operators have to be trained accordingly. There are two major options for domain assignment and each one has different backup procedures.

1. *NCP SA8 resources explicitly excluded from ownership in Chicago and Chicago defined as the backup host:* When SA8 NCP system generation tables are defined in Chicago, parameters can be coded to indicate that these resources do not belong to Chicago host but the Chicago host is to act as a backup (BACKUP = YES in system generation tables). Definitions filed in New York do not use BACKUP = YES.

For resources for which the Chicago host is defined as a backup host only, the Chicago host must first "acquire" them to make them a part of its domain before it can activate them. The VTAM/NetView operator enters the ACQUIRE command to VTAM for each resource for which it was designated as a backup. A successful acquisition causes a VTAM to add these resources as part of its Resource Definition table, i.e., a part of its domain.

After acquiring the resources, the Chicago operator would activate the New York resources. For SNA devices with older microcode (those that do not support error recovery procedures, ERP) the activation would terminate their ongoing LU-LU sessions. Most devices, however, do support ERP and can continue their existing LU-LU sessions even as they establish the new SSCP session with the new owner.

At this time the Chicago host has completed the takeover of the SA8 part of the New York domain. However, the Chicago SSCP would lack any knowledge of LU-LU session status of the newly acquired and activated resources. It would not know whether they are in session, or the session partner names, and therefore this information could not be displayed by the Chicago control operator. IBM intends to provide enhancements so that in the future new owners could receive such information from the boundary nodes.

2. *Resources not explicitly excluded from Chicago ownership:* In this case no BACKUP operand is specified in Chicago for the SA8 resources. During normal operation (when the Chicago host is not acting as an owner), the Chicago host simply does not activate resources that it is not supposed to own. When the New York host fails, the Chicago operator can simply activate SA8 resources to make them an active part of its domain and, unlike the first approach, does not have to issue any ACQUIRE commands.

To contrast these two approaches: The first approach is more structured and requires the assignment of a BACKUP operand in the NCP system generation tables. The advantage is that it can prevent inadvertent activation of SA8 resources by the Chicago operators. An SSCP can activate only the resources that it owns—and until the ACQUIRE step is complete, Chicago does not own those resources.

The second approach is more flexible because either the New York or the Chicago host can gain ownership of any SA8 attached station simply by activating it. This method, however, does not provide any protection against the Chicago operator inadvertently or otherwise activating a resource that he or she is not supposed to.

9.9.4 Effect of Domain Takeover on Other than Backup Host

Domain takeover also has operational implications for hosts other than the failing and the backup hosts.

In our scenario, the Los Angeles and San Francisco hosts would also have to perform one function before the backup process is complete.

Prior to the New York failure, all resources attached to SA8 were defined by Los Angeles and San Francisco as owned by New York. Therefore, any LU-LU session requests originating in their domains for the SA8 attached resources were sent to the New York host. However, that may not be done after the New York host has failed and its resources are taken over by Chicago. The new cross-domain session requests for SA8 resources must now be routed to Chicago. To accomplish this, the Los Angeles and San Francisco network control operators must modify their VTAM tables to change the owner name of SA8 resources from New York to Chicago. This change can be accomplished by using the MODIFY CDRM VTAM command in Los Angeles and San Francisco. However, if the New York host is defined in Los Angeles and San Francisco via an ADJSSCP table with Chicago as the adjacent SSCP to reach New York (see Sec. 9.7 for an example of ADJSSCP table), then all logons for New York host would automatically go to the Chicago host when the New York host failed.

9.9.5 Restoring the Failed Host

The last step in our failure and recovery scenario is to restore the failed host in New York. One of the options may be to restart the New York host without regaining the part of the domain that was taken over by Chicago. This may be appropriate if the network is normally brought down overnight and, the next day when the network is restarted, each host starts with its normal domain.

But if it is necessary for the New York host to regain its domain from Chicago as a part of its normal recovery, we would have to undo the domain takeover executed by the Chicago host.

The Chicago network operator would have to be informed by the New York control center that they are ready to take back their domain. The Chicago operator would then deactivate all resources that had been taken over by Chicago. Note that with the ERP feature in peripheral nodes, while the takeover by the backup host can be made totally nondisruptive, reverting to the original host is disruptive. Deactivation of resources by a backup host (in preparation of returning the resources to the original owner) terminates all LU-LU sessions for resources being deactivated. As of 1988 with the availability of VTAM version 3, there is a new deactivation command with TYPE = GIVEBACK option that would allow a backup host to give up its resources without disrupting their LU-LU sessions.

In any case, once the Chicago host has deactivated SA8 resources, New York can regain its domain simply by activating those resources. In addition, VTAM can be implemented so that it maintains the session status of its resources. VTAM periodically writes configuration information to a file to retain the most current session status. After a restart it can restore the session status (except LU-LU sessions) and paths (routing tables) to the same state as recorded in the last configuration record captured before the failure.

9.10 LOSS OF DOMAIN DUE TO ROUTE FAILURE

Not all domain losses are due to host failures. Loss of an NCP, for example, would cause a loss of all resources attached to it. Another rea-

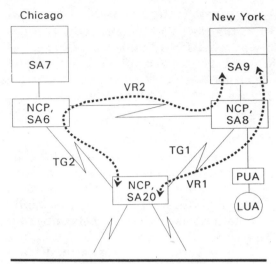

Figure 9.9 Partial domain loss due to route failure and recovery.

son for losing a part of the domain can be the loss of a route over which SSCP had established SSCP-PU and SSCP-LU sessions. (When a route fails, all sessions using it are terminated.) In such cases, the domain recovery can be automatic if there is an alternate route available to the SSCP.

As an example let us look at Fig. 9.9. In this example we have added a remote NCP, SA20, to our network of Fig. 9.1. The SA20 NCP is attached to both the New York NCP, SA8, over TG1 and the Chicago NCP, SA6, over TG2. Resources attached to NCP SA20 belong to the New York host, which uses VR1 as its primary route to reach this part of its domain. VR2 is defined as an alternate for VR1. Should TG1 between SA20 and SA8 fail, all SSCP sessions with resources in SA20 would be terminated along with other LU-LU sessions that use virtual route 1. However, the New York host would automatically reestablish new SSCP sessions along virtual route 2. Any LU-LU sessions lost due to route failure or reactivation (no ERP support) would have to be reestablished.

9.11 SUMMARY

Multiple systems networking, MSN, is a very important part of SNA architecture and has evolved just as the rest of the SNA has. In the early days of SNA all cross-domain definitions were mandatory. For corporations with tens of thousands of terminals and hundreds of applications, implementing MSN was a cumbersome and unwieldy job. With dynamic definitions, default SSCP list, and adjacent CDRM tables, the number of CDRSC definitions can be reduced or completely eliminated. Of course, the tradeoff for a reduced number of cross-domain definitions is that session establishment for undefined LUs or LUs with unknown owners takes a little longer the first time a session is established with them.

Maintaining domain backup is a critical consideration for a number of corporations. Here again, starting with totally disruptive domain takeovers and restorations, we have now come to a stage where, with proper planning, operating procedures, and product levels, domain recovery can be made almost completely nondisruptive.

Network Management and Problem Resolution

10.1 INTRODUCTION

As data networks have grown increasingly complex, so has the need for systems and tools to manage them. Until very recently network management was thought of as a necessary evil, never a part of the overall planning and design process. By and large it was implemented after the fact and in a piecemeal manner. For large corporations who had to have comprehensive management systems, it meant dealing with a number of vendors—each providing only a part of the solution. The users had to integrate these dissimilar and incompatible systems on their own. It was impossible to build a complete network management system strictly with off-the-shelf systems.

Vendors tend to define network management differently to suit their own products. On one end of the spectrum were the mainframe and terminal vendors [or the *customer premises equipment* (CPE) vendors]. To CPE vendors, the network consists of host machines, front ends, and terminals that are interconnected via "transparent" physical links. Mainframe vendors are also concerned about "logical" resources in the network such as the routing structures, network addresses, symbolic names, sessions and domain of control for each host in a multidomain network, etc. CPE vendors provided tools and techniques to manage "their" part of the network. Under this view, network management historically meant network operation, control, and diagnostics. Activities such as system administration and generation; trouble tickets; and problem, change, inventory, and configuration management systems were not considered a part of network management. When present, these systems were mostly user developed, entailing a very high development cost.

In contrast to telecommunications vendors and common carriers, network management typically means managing the physical facilities and services provided by the carrier. With their strong background in managing voice networks, carriers also concentrate more strongly on planning, provisioning, managing changes and moves, and providing good accounting and billing systems. However, common carriers have, traditionally, not provided any management tools to measure performance, test, or diagnose these facilities through systems under customer control. In addition, if the customer used systems such as multiplexers or concentrators to optimize the use of the facilities it was up to the customer to manage these additional network elements.

As of 1992 there are still no seamless integrated, end-to-end network management systems available. What has changed is the recognition, by both customers and vendors, of the importance of network management. In 1990 and 1991, network management was one of the most rapidly developing areas in data communications. Common carriers, too, have recognized belatedly that providing central-office-based testing, measurement, and management capabilities that are accessible to customers, not only is necessary for maintaining their customer base, but can be profitable, too. More significantly, in 1987,

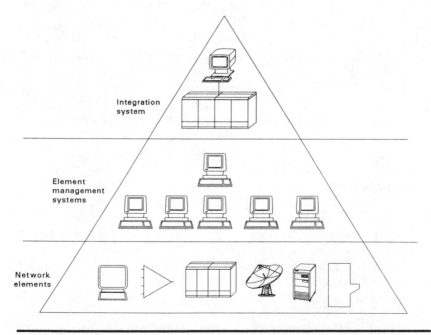

Figure 10.1 AT&T's UNMA view of network management.

AT&T announced its Unified Network Management Architecture (UNMA) based on International Standards Organization's OSI model.

AT&T's UNMA is very helpful in articulating and defining the scope of management process and we use it as a model to discuss network management in general. As shown in Fig. 10.1, UNMA divides network elements into three categories: customer premises equipment (CPE), *local exchange carrier* (LEC) or local-telephone-company-provided services, and facilities and services provided by *interexchange carriers* (IXC) or the long distance (trunk) telephone company. While SNA network management focuses primarily on CPE elements, AT&T's approach is much broader and, at least architecturally, addresses all three levels of network elements—CPE, LEC, and IXC. Another important contribution of UNMA is the recognition that multiple management systems, shown as element management systems, will continue to be a part of network management solutions and also that an integrated management system will not eliminate them. With OSI's Systems Management architecture definitions in final phases of definition, the 1990s should see the development of OSI-based management systems. These are all positive developments for users.

10.2 IBM/SNA OPERATIONS ENVIRONMENT

Figure 10.2 shows various network elements and associated management systems that may be found in a typical network control center to

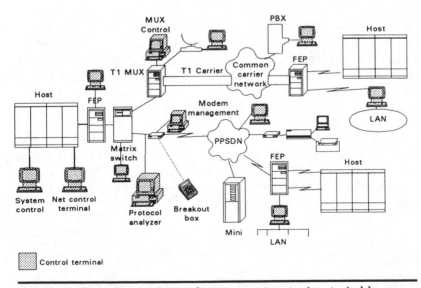

Figure 10.2 Network operations and management center in a typical large multivendor SNA network.

manage mid-sized (thousands of terminals) to large (more than 100,000 terminals) networks. The functions of various components shown in Fig. 10.2 are as follows:

System console: The word *system* here refers to the host computer, not to the network. This console is used primarily for managing the data center operations. The physical device for the console is typically a character-oriented interactive display station with a printer for a hard-copy log. Multiple alternate consoles can be used, and software can be customized so that a console may receive only messages from VTAM (network).

Other control terminals: Typically, host subsystems such as IMS/DC, CICS, etc. require their own control terminals to manage their operation. In addition, one or more terminals are used as NetView consoles to manage VTAM and SNA network operations.

Electronic Matrix Switches (or manual patch panels) are used for switching lines from a primary FEP to a backup in case of an FEP failure. These electronic matrix switches come with their own consoles to manage them. Each FEP has its own management console.

Diagnostic modems have their own network management systems with adjunct processors and consoles. Users of T1 systems have yet additional management systems and consoles.

For corporations subscribing to public data networks, and switched services such as Software Defined/Virtual Private networks, Advanced 800 services, etc., there may be additional control terminals to manage and control these services.

Then there may be other instruments such as line monitors and protocol analyzers, modem interface analyzers, digital and analog link testing equipment, etc. also present in the network control center. All in all, a sophisticated network control center can be quite an impressive site.

Thus, when we talk about centralization or consolidation of network management, it is all of the foregoing capabilities and functions that we are trying to integrate. There are differences of opinion about the right degree of consolidation or integration. Each enterprise must decide for itself the proper level of integration. IBM's NetView, Systems Center's Net/Master, AT&T's Accumaster Integrator, DEC's Enterprise Management Architecture, etc. all attempt to provide integrated network management.

10.3   IBM NETWORK MANAGEMENT
INTRODUCTION

In the pre-SNA days, there was no built-in network management in system software such as Basic Telecommunications Access Method

(BTAM). For each data communication application the user had to develop his or her own network management and control software. With SNA, a single *communications network management* (CNM) interface was provided through VTAM, enabling a single consolidated network control terminal. Subsequently, CNM applications such as Network Communication Control Facility (NCCF) and Network Problem Determination Application (NPDA), etc. were added to provide higher-level (easier to use) interfaces, command languages, and error analysis functions. Over a period of time, a number of data structures and applications evolved under SNA to support network management functions.

In 1986 IBM consolidated many of its host-based CNM applications in a single product called NetView. Additionally, IBM also consolidated various network management data structures and protocols in one document under the title SNA Management Services Architecture. Thus, network management has two aspects under SNA: the architecture and the CNM applications. We discuss both in this chapter.

10.4 SNA MANAGEMENT SERVICES ARCHITECTURE

SNA Management Services (MS) architecture was published in March 1986. It defined various functional areas for network management, control and flow sequences for management data, and the structure of SNA RUs that carry network management data.

The MS architecture defines four categories of functions. However, SNA has not yet defined complete details of many of these functions, nor have they been implemented by IBM in a single integrated product. The four categories of functions are now discussed.

10.4.1 Problem Management

This category includes all tasks related to managing a problem (fault) from the time it is discovered to its resolution. The term *problem* is used very broadly to include any event that may cause loss of a system or an element. Within problem management, specific tasks include:

Problem determination: This is the actual discovery of a loss or an impending loss and the process of identifying the faulty component. Also included here is the assignment of a person or organization for diagnosing the problem.

Problem diagnosis: This is the determination of the precise cause of the problem within a faulty component or system—hardware, software, microcode, etc.—and the action required to fix it.

Once the problem has been diagnosed, a solution can be developed to fix it. While a solution is being developed, it may be necessary to bypass the failing component, if possible. In a large network there may be hundreds of problems that are reported and resolved each day. A database of outstanding problems must be maintained along with a monitoring and reporting system.

10.4.2 Performance and Accounting Management

SNA has chosen to put these two seemingly unrelated functions in the same category.

Performance management is, of course, measuring, reporting, and controlling the responsiveness, availability, and utilization of the network. Performance management requires that measurable objectives be defined for response time and availability. Deviations from the stated objectives must be monitored, measured, and fixed. Although end-to-end performance can be measured easily, it is difficult to measure performance of individual components. To track performance of individual components, we must have network elements that can measure and monitor their internal performance and report these data to a central management system.

Accounting management is the process of defining a basis for charging for network services, then collecting data to compute the usage charges, and, finally, billing the customer.

10.4.3 Configuration and Inventory Management

This function includes tracking and control of physical and logical information about network resources. The physical inventory consists of the number of terminals, circuits, controllers, CPUs, etc.; and their locations, identifications, and other unique information. Additional information about each resource may include items such as the vendor or organization responsible for servicing it, contacts and phone numbers, hardware identification, software or microcode level, etc.

10.4.4 Change Management

This is the process of managing changes to the system including activities such as planning and controlling the change process and the actual application of changes to network configuration, hardware, software, and microcode.

Change management and configuration management are closely related, and it is highly desirable that the two systems post information to each other automatically. Change management is also related to problem management since a solution for a problem normally also triggers a change to the system.

Although the Management Services architecture lists the aforementioned four categories of functions, the detailed specifications deal primarily with event and alarm data structures and some reporting of performance and configuration information. It specifies nothing on databases and management information systems to support these functions. Nor does it deal with the role of expert systems and artificial applications.

10.5 SNA NETWORK MANAGEMENT DATA FLOW

Network management data in SNA flows over SSCP-PU sessions. SSCP forwards CNM data to the CNM application (e.g., IBM's NetView), if one is installed. The component within SSCP responsible for providing management services is called the Control Point Management Services (CPMS), and the corresponding component in the PU is called the Physical Unit Management Services (PUMS). In addition, each LU has a component called LU Management Services (LMS), which is responsible for reporting LU events to its controlling PU, which in turn may report it to the SSCP. SSCP-PU sessions support primitive protocols for flow control and provide no session recovery. IBM has indicated that the network management architecture would use an LU-LU session in the future using LU 6.2 session protocols for network management data flows.

10.5.1 Alerts, Events, and Unsolicited and Solicited Data Flows

Each SNA product is capable of recognizing a number of internal conditions or failures called alerts. An alert, by definition, is a serious occurrence and is reported to the SSCP in an unsolicited manner by the PU controlling the resource. In addition, the SSCP can also solicit certain types of information that are otherwise not sent to the SSCP. For example, the SSCP may request a PU to run a self-test and send the results of the test to the SSCP. Other types of solicited data include activity traces, error logs, and error and response time statistics.

It is also possible to set up certain thresholds within devices for various error or response time statistics. When these thresholds are exceeded, they are treated as alerts and reported automatically to the SSCP as unsolicited management data.

Occurrences that are reported as alerts to the SSCP by network resources are merely events to the host network management applications such as NetView. The user has the option of tailoring the events
that should be considered alerts for the purposes of displaying them on
the control operator's terminal, as well as for recording in the alert
database.

10.5.2 Unsolicited and Solicited Data Flows

Figure 10.3 shows a typical data flow for unsolicited data, as described
in the following.

1. An occurrence associated with an LU is recognized as a reportable
   condition. The LMS component reports this condition and associated data to the PUMS.

2. PUMS converts this information into a Management Services RU.
   There are several RU types defined in SNA for carrying management data (see Sec. 10.6). The particular data structure used depends on the product. In any case, the Management Services RU is
   sent to the host over an SSCP-PU session as a definite response
   RU. SSCP acknowledges the RU by sending a response.

3. What happens next depends on whether a CNM application such as
   NetView or Net/Master is installed. If no network management application is installed, the event is simply forwarded to the VTAM
   log for the host operator to take further action.

   If a CNM application is installed, VTAM forwards the RU to it.
   At this time user-defined criteria would be used by the application
   to decide whether to record or display the event as an alarm.

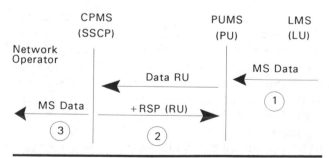

Figure 10.3 Unsolicited network management data flows
in SNA.

Solicited flows.   Figure 10.4 illustrates a solicited data flow.

1. The network operator enters a request for management data from the VTAM console or the CNM application control terminal. The request is forwarded to SSCP.

2. The SSCP converts the request to a management RU and sends it to the PU controlling the resource. The PU acknowledges the request for management data.

3. The PU executes a local procedure for obtaining the requested information from the local LU. Even though we show PUMS and LMS as separate entities, it is possible that both may be implemented in the same microcode or software.

4. PUMS formats requested information into an MS RU and sends it to the SSCP. The SSCP acknowledges the receipt of the RU.

5. The SSCP forwards this information to the CNM application, which displays it on the terminal of the operator who originally requested this information.

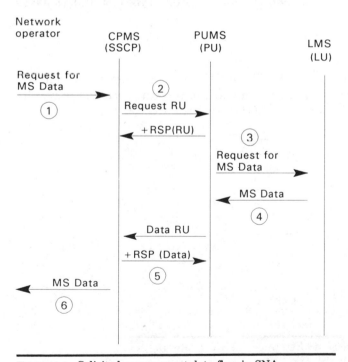

Figure 10.4   Solicited management data flow in SNA.

In steps 1 and 5 information was exchanged between the host management application and the SSCP. This software interface is not defined by SNA and is an IBM proprietary interface within VTAM.

10.6 MANAGEMENT SERVICES (MS) RUs

In previous sections we made a number of references to MS RUs. These RUs are a collection of various data structures that have evolved over a number of years. Each IBM product individually defines the data structures that it supports. The current IBM thrust is to standardize future developments around an RU called Network Management Vector Transport (NMVT). We mention other RU types only very briefly.

The general structure of MS RUs is shown in Fig. 10.5. All Management Services RUs are formatted RUs (i.e., format indicator bit = 1 in the RH) and are identified by a unique network services (NS) header. For our discussion, we break MS RUs into two categories: network management vector transport (NMVT) RUs and non-NMVT RUs.

10.6.1 Non-NMVT RUs

Multiple RU types are defined for different types of functions as follows:

Testing

TESTMODE and RECTR: These RUs flow between SSCP and PU Types 4 or Types 5. They initiate a link test and receive the results of the test in the form of RECTR from the PU.

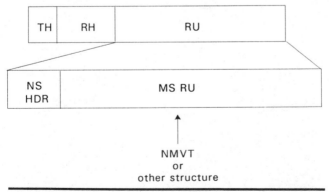

Figure 10.5 Structure of MS RUs (*Note:* NMVT = network management vector transport).

EXECTEST, RECTD: These RUs flow from SSCP to PU Types 5 or Types 4 and are used to initiate tests for a specific PU or LU or link other than those covered in TESTMODE. Results of the test are returned in RECTD RU.

ROUTE-TEST and ER-TESTED: These two RUs are used to test the status of explicit and virtual routes.

REQECHO, ECHOTEST: REQECHO is an LU-to-SSCP RU requesting the SSCP to echo back the enclosed character string. SSCP echoes back the string using ECHOTEST RU.

Tracing

ACTTRACE, DACTTRACE, and RECTRD: ACTTRACE is an SSCP-to-PU RU that requests a PU to start a specified type of trace for one or more resources associated with the PU. DACTTRACE from SSCP requests that the trace be stopped. The PU returns the recorded trace data using RECTRD RU.

Soliciting, recording, and displaying

NMVT: This RU type is discussed in more detail in the next section.

REQMS: This RU is used by the SSCP to request maintenance statistics from a PU. The statistics solicited can be link test results, hardware error summaries, microcode release level, and other implementation-defined information.

RECFMS: Where supported, RECFMS returns parameters in response to REQMS or reports unsolicited alerts and other information from SNA devices that do not support NMVT. This pre-NMVT RU type is to be replaced by NMVT.

DISPSTOR and RECSTOR: DISPSTOR is used by the SSCP to obtain a dump of memory contents from a PU and RECSTOR RU is used by the PU to return the memory dump.

Exchanging system information

SETCV: This a multipurpose RU that flows from an SSCP to a PU Types 4 or Types 5 and can be used for functions such as exchanging date, time, and addressing information and recording network errors in an intensive mode.

10.7 NETWORK MANAGEMENT VECTOR TRANSPORT (NMVT)

NMVT is the most recent MS RU and is expected to replace all of the aforementioned RU types in the future. With NMVT, each major MS data type is defined as a major vector, e.g., alert, response time statistics, trace data, etc. Within each major vector, various fields containing specific details are called subvectors or minor vectors. Figure 10.6 shows the structure of a PIU containing an NMVT RU.

Following the transmission header (TH) and the request/response header (RH), various fields are as follows:

NS Header: This 3-byte field in bytes 0–2 of the RU is always "41038D" and identifies the RU as an NMVT.

Bytes 3-4: Currently unused.

Bytes 5-6: Contain a field called procedure-related ID whose value is implementation defined.

Byte 7: Contains a flag indicating whether this is a solicited or unsolicited RU.

Bytes 8-11: The beginning of the major vector itself, these four bytes are in the form of ll kk where:
Bytes 8-9 are the "ll" and specify the total length of the major vector in hexadecimal.
Bytes 10-11 contain a 2-byte hexadecimal key kk which identifies the major vector type.

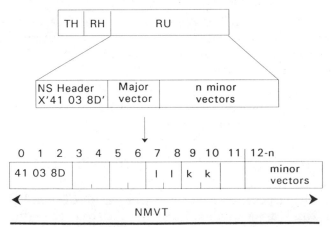

Figure 10.6 Network management vector transport [(NMVT); ll = length, kk = vector key].

Each NMVT contains one and only one major vector. The following major vectors have been defined:

Alerts

Trace data

Problem determination statistics

Response time monitor (RTM) data

Product set ID

Link resource control information

The rest of the NMVT contains details associated with the major vector in the form of a number of subvectors.

Each subvector consists of a field containing subvector length, a key identifying the subvector, and any additional data associated with the subvector. A well-defined set of subvectors is associated with each major vector. There are two types of subvectors—common subvectors and unique subvectors. Common subvectors are allowed in all major vectors and have the same meaning for all of them. Unique subvectors are specific to the major vector for which they are defined and have a meaning only within that major vector. Examples of common subvectors include:

00: Text message

01: Date/time

03: Hierarchy name list

04: SNA address list

05: Hierarchy (resource list)

Appendix C shows various major vectors, subvectors, and subfields in more detail.

10.8   SNA CNM HIERARCHY

The MS architecture is implemented at three levels as shown in Fig. 10.7. The *focal point* is the consolidation point in the host for all network management data and provides centralized network control center support. It is implemented using a VTAM CNM application such as IBM's NetView or Systems Center's Net/Master. We discuss focal point in more detail in Sec. 10.9.

Entry point is a catch-all category for IBM products that are supported by VTAM and NetView, e.g., 3745 FEPS, S/36 and AS/400 minis, and the IBM 3270s, etc. The key characteristic of an entry point

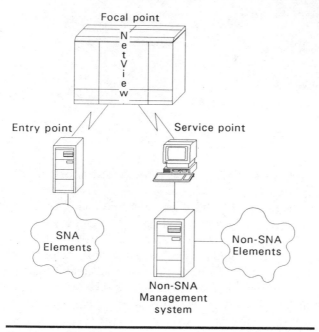

Figure 10.7 Focal point, entry point, and service point.

is that it is inherently compatible with NetView and requires no gateway to communicate with NetView. Specific capabilities of an entry point are implementation defined and vary from product to product. The reader should consult IBM product documentation for information on specific products.

Service point is a network management gateway that converts non-SNA network management data to an NMVT form and forwards it to the focal point. Two of the data structures supported by service point include NMVT and the LU 6.2 data stream. A user or vendor can use IBM NetView/PC product as a foundation to build a service point gateway. Service Point is discussed in more detail in Sec. 10.18.

10.9 FOCAL POINT AND VTAM CNM INTERFACE

VTAM is the recipient of all network management data since it contains the SSCP. It also has a simple operator interface; so, at least theoretically, a user could manage a network using VTAM alone without additional applications such as NetView or Net/Master.

```
IST350I  VTAM DISPLAY - DOMAIN TYPE = STATIONS
IST393I  PU T4/5 MAJOR NODE A03NV4  , SUBAREA =   3
IST396I  LNKSTA     STATUS      CTG GTG    ADJNODE      ADJSA       NETID
IST397I  A03SA      PCTD1        55  55                   0
IST610I                                    LINE A03KA   - STATUS ACTIV-----E
IST397I  A03SB      NEVAC        55  55                   0
IST610I                                    LINE A03KB   - STATUS PALNK
IST397I  A03SC      PCTD1        30  30                   0
IST610I                                    LINE A03KC   - STATUS ACTIV-----E
IST397I  A03SD      PCTD1        31  31                   0
IST610I                                    LINE A03KD   - STATUS ACTIV-----E
IST397I  A03SE      ACTIV----E   70  70    A71NV4        71
IST610I                                    LINE A03KE   - STATUS ACTIV-----E
IST397I  A03SF      NEVAC        70  70                   0
IST610I                                    LINE A03KF   - STATUS IINOP
IST314I  END
```

Figure 10.8 Sample VTAM log.

However, due to the primitive nature of this interface, its use is not recommended.

Figure 10.8 shows a typical VTAM log with various messages for the control operator. All messages from VTAM are preceded by the prefix IST. While some of the information in the VTAM log is fairly straightforward and easy to understand, most of it is difficult to interpret, even with appropriate IBM reference manuals. In Fig. 10.8, examples of such information include keywords such as PCTD1, PALNK, and NEVAC. The CNM application provides value added functions so that users do not have to deal with a VTAM-level operational interface. Later in this chapter we see how NetView helps us in interpreting VTAM log and network alarms.

A focal point application receives all its information from VTAM over two interfaces—program operator interface (POI) and CNM interface as shown in Fig. 10.9. Only applications with proper authorizations can use these interfaces.

10.9.1 Program Operator Interface (POI)

This interface is used by a program (software) operator to submit commands to VTAM and receive unsolicited VTAM messages (messages with IST prefix) that normally go to the system console. There are two types of program operators:

Primary program operator (PPO): VTAM allows only one active PPO at a time. A PPO receives all unsolicited VTAM messages and can also enter VTAM commands.

Secondary program operators (SPO): These programs can submit commands to VTAM and receive replies but do not receive VTAM unsolicited messages.

CNM applications such as NetView and NetMaster run as PPO.

10.9.2 CNM Interface

The POI provides only partial information needed by the CNM application. The network services RUs, such as NMVT, solicited or unsolicited, are presented to the CNM application over the CNM interface. Most of the data used by hardware monitor and session monitor components of NetView also come over the CNM interface.

The CNM RUs are divided into multiple categories. There is a CNM routing table in VTAM that identifies a CNM application for each CNM RU category to which the unsolicited traffic should be forwarded. In reality, these CNM applications are none other than various internal modules of the focal point application such as NetView.

In Fig. 10.9, we show two VTAM interfaces in addition to the POI and CNM interfaces, record mode and APPC APIs, which, too, are used by CNM applications. The VTAM record mode API is used for sending and receiving messages to and from terminals and for using other VTAM services. The LU 6.2 (APPC) API is a relatively new addition to VTAM and is used with recently available applications such as software distribution and file transfers.

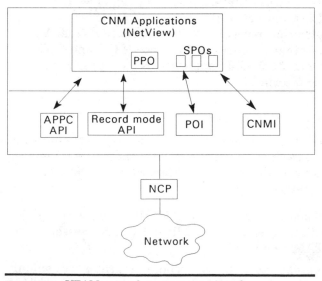

Figure 10.9 VTAM network management interface.

10.10   IBM NETVIEW PRODUCT

NetView is a System 370/390-based program product that provides network control center support for SNA networks. In architected terms, NetView is a focal point product, and to VTAM it is a CNM application that provides PPO and SPO functions.

Prior to NetView IBM had a family of products to provide network management, control, and diagnostics. These products included Network Communications Control Facility (NCCF), Network Problem Determination Application (NPDA), Network Logical Data Manager (NLDM), and Status Monitor (STATMON). In 1986 IBM combined all of these into a single product called NetView to provide comprehensive network management functions. In 1987 NetView was further enhanced to provide mainframe operations support in addition to the network operation. Figure 10.10 shows NetView interfaces with other host components. VTAM-to-NetView interface consists of POI and CNM interfaces. The interface between NetView and MVS is the MVS Subsystem Interface (SSI). In this book we discuss only SNA-related functions of NetView.

Major functional components of NetView are the command facility, hardware monitor, logical data manager, status monitor, and tutorial-help desk.

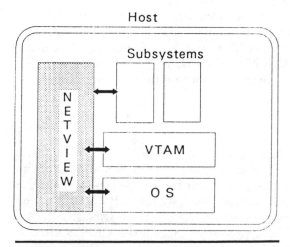

Figure 10.10   NetView introduction.

10.10.1 NetView Command Facility

The command facility provides functions that were provided by the Network Communications Control Facility (NCCF) prior to NetView. Command facility is the foundation function in NetView and is required for all other features. This feature provides the control operator support and executes VTAM/NetView commands entered by the NetView operator. Command facility is also responsible for displaying all network messages to the appropriate control operator to facilitate monitoring of the network.

Two of the most commonly used VTAM commands are DISPLAY or D and VARY or V for displaying and changing the status of network resources. Some examples (using MVS syntax) are as follows:

```
D NET, ID = NCP2
```

The foregoing command (D) requests VTAM (the word NET identifies the command destination as VTAM) to display the status of a resource called NCP2.

If we wanted to activate a cluster controller called XYZ we would enter the command,

```
V NET, ACT, ID = XYZ
```

where V stands for vary, i.e., change, the status; NET again identifies the command as being for VTAM; ACT requests an activation; and ID = XYZ identifies the resource to be activated.

Command list (CLIST) facility. The command list (CLIST) facility is the most powerful feature of the NetView command facility and is used to simplify and automate network and system operation. At a basic level, the command lists can be used to simplify command syntax. For example, the DISPLAY and VARY commands can be simplified by using two CLISTs called DIS (for display) and ACT (for activate), and the two commands can be invoked as follows via CLISTs.

```
DIS NCP2
ACT XYZ
```

For repetitive tasks that take multiple VTAM/NetView commands, a CLIST can be defined to include all required commands and all of the commands in the list can be executed simply by entering the name of the CLIST from a NetView terminal. In addition, we have IBM REXX as the CLIST definition language with operators such as IF, THEN, ELSE, etc., which can be used to build fairly elaborate procedures. CLISTs are created by coding desired procedures and placing them on the CLIST library. NetView interprets CLISTs in real time, as it executes them. Any syntax or logic errors are reported at execution time. CLISTs can be invoked in several ways; several approaches are as follows:

1. *Manual:*   By entering the CLIST name and required parameters from one of the NetView terminals, as illustrated with DIS and ACT in the foregoing examples.

2. *Time based:*   CLISTs can also be defined so that they are invoked based on relative or absolute time. This feature can be useful in automating time-based tasks.

3. *Message driven:*   This is probably the most powerful feature of CLISTs whereby a CLIST gets executed automatically whenever a particular error message is reported. If a user can identify events that require well-defined operator actions, then such event handling can be automated using message-driven CLISTs. This message automation facility is available for network as well as system messages. A user can define a message automation table in which a variable number of criteria can be defined for each message (event) to determine whether or not an automatic response is desirable. Automatic event handling is known as message automation.

By developing an extensive set of CLISTs and a message automation table one can start building a framework for an expert system. For tasks that are too elaborate or too complex for the CLIST language or take too long for execution, NetView command facility also allows for user-written command processors, which can be written in C, PL/1, or assembler language. User command processors are invoked in the same manner as the CLIST by entering the command processor name and associated parameters from a NetView terminal. IBM also sells a NetView Solution Pac that includes several hundred CLISTs and some command processors to automate a significant amount of the routine work in a network control center.

10.11   NETVIEW HARDWARE MONITOR

NetView hardware monitor is an updated version of what used to be Network Problem Determination Application (NPDA). The term *hardware monitor* suggests that it monitors hardware elements and associated failures. Although that is true, the hardware monitor does more than that. It is intended to deal with all physical and other well-defined failures (e.g., program check in microcode or device software). In addition to the monitoring functions, the hardware monitor also assists in diagnosing the cause of a problem and recovering from it.

The hardware monitor records event and alarm information received from the network and displays it to the NetView operator.

Upon operator request, the hardware monitor can also analyze alarm information, identify probable cause, and recommend action for recovery. Since the hardware monitor performs its analysis based on SNA sense and error codes, the analysis can only be as precise as the details available through sense or error codes. As more and more products start implementing NMVT, which has a very elaborate reporting mechanism, the hardware monitor should become an even more powerful tool for resolving physical problems.

10.11.1 Recording and Displaying Alerts

All alerts that meet user-defined criteria are automatically recorded on the hardware monitor alert database. In addition, a one-line message is created for display on the control operator screen. Here again display "filters" can be specified by the user so that a message is actually displayed only if it passes the viewing filter criteria.

Alert messages are the key to network monitoring and troubleshooting. There are various types of detailed display panels that are used by the hardware monitor to assist the operator in diagnosing a problem. To monitor brief, one-line alert descriptions, an operator can call up the Alerts-Dynamic panel which displays alerts as they occur [for a global view of the network in a summary form, the operator can use the Status Monitor (STATMON) feature of NetView]. Once an alert is reported on the Alerts-Dynamic panel, an operator can go through a sequence of steps involving a number of panels to resolve the problem. A typical sequence, described in the next section, takes us from the dynamic display to recent events display to event detail, leading up to probable cause and recommended action.

10.11.2 A Problem Scenario

In this scenario, drawn from the NetView operation manual, we look at a problem from the time it is reported on the Alerts-Dynamic screen to the final step in which the hardware monitor recommends a set of actions to fix the problem. To appreciate how NetView can help reduce the level of expertise required in the network control center, let us assume that this problem is being handled by an operator who is not familiar with modems and facilities.

The scenario starts with the operator observing an alert on the NetView/VTAM log or the Alerts-Dynamic screen or, possibly, the Status Monitor screen. The alert is reported for a line named A71L09. The operator calls up the most recent events reported for A71L09 by entering the following command:

```
events A71L09
```

```
N E T V I E W                         OPER1  01/30/90  16:09:51
NPDA-41A              * MOST RECENT EVENTS *         PAGE   1  OF    1


CNM01          A71NV4     A71L09
              +--------+
DOMAIN       | COMC   |---LINE----
              +--------+
SEL# DATE/ TIME   EVENT DESCRIPTION:PROBABLE CAUSE          ETYP ACT
( 1)  01/30 15:59  DSR ON CHECK:LOCAL MODEM OFF/LOCAL MODEM    PERM  16
( 2)  01/30 15:52  DSR ON CHECK:LOCAL MODEM OFF/LOCAL MODEM    PERM  16
( 3)  01/30 15:34  DSR ON CHECK:LOCAL MODEM OFF/LOCAL MODEM    PERM  16
( 4)  01/30 15:32  MODEM ERROR:LOCAL MODEM OFF/LOCAL MODEM     PERM  26
( 5)  01/30 15:09  MODEM ERROR:LOCAL MODEM OFF/LOCAL MODEM     PERM  26




ENTER SEL# (ACTION), OR SEL# PLUS D (DETAIL) OR P (PROBLEM)

???
CMD--> 1d
```

Figure 10.11   Hardware monitor—recent events.

Figure 10.11 shows the panel displayed by the hardware monitor in response to the foregoing command. The panel shows recent events reported for A71NV4, with the most current event at the top. A simple line diagram shows the physical configuration where A71L09 is attached to an FEP with NCP05 loaded in it. At this point the operator can enter the letter a (for action) for one or more recommended actions by the hardware monitor. Or, to request details of event number 1, the operator can enter:

1 d

where 1 is the event number and d stands for detail.

The details of the event are shown by NetView in Fig. 10.12. The event detail record shows that the probable cause of the error was a modem interface error due to the loss of the data set ready signal. For someone familiar with modems, this provides enough information to take the next step in problem resolution. But if, as we assumed, the NetView operator were not familiar with modems or the meaning of "data set ready," the operator still would not know what to do next. In such a case the operator can request the hardware monitor to recommend an action by entering the letter a for action on the user action line. NetView responds by displaying the panel shown in Fig. 10.13. As shown in Fig. 10.13, the hardware monitor suggests to the operator several options following which either the cause of the problem would be pinpointed or the problem escalated to appropriate support personnel.

Even though this was a relatively simple scenario, it is easy to see here how NetView can help reduce the level of technical expertise required to operate SNA networks. Also, all of the panels in the previous

```
N E T V I E W                        OPER1   01/30/90  16:17:13
NPDA-43B            * EVENT DETAIL FOR SDLC LINE *      PAGE  1  OF  1

CNMO1      A71NV4    A71L09
           +-------+
DOMAIN   | COMC  |---LINE----
           +-------+
DATE/TIME: 01/30 15:32
OPERATION -RUN- INITIATES NORMAL SEND/RECEIVE OPERATIONS ON THE SDLC LINK;
ERROR WHILE SENDING TEXT I-FORMAT


PROBABLE CAUSE - MODEM INTERFACE ERROR
ERROR DESCRIPTION - MODEM ERROR - DATA SET READY DROPPED DURING COMMAND
OPERATION




ENTER A TO VIEW ACTION DISPLAY


???
CMD==> a
```

Figure 10.12   Event detail.

```
N E T V I E W                          OPER1   01/30/90  16:17:07
NPDA-BNIFFE26  * RECOMMENDED ACTION FOR SELECTED EVENT *  PAGE  1 OF   1

CNMO1      A71NV4    A71L09
           +-------+
DOMAIN   | COMC  |---LINE----
           +-------+
USER     CAUSED - LOCAL MODEM POWER OFF
         ACTIONS - D001 - CORRECT THEN RETRY

INSTALL CAUSED - CABLE
         ACTIONS - D022 - CHECK PHYSICAL INSTALLATION

FAILURE CAUSED - LOCAL MODEM
                 LOCAL MODEM INTERFACE CABLE
         ACTIONS - D022 - CHECK PHYSICAL INSTALLATION
                   D002 - RUN MODEM TESTS
                   D005- CONTACT APPROPRIATE SERVICE REPRESENTATIVE



ENTER D TO VIEW DETAIL DISPLAY

???
CMD==> action d001
```

Figure 10.13   Recommended action.

example can be customized to a user's specific preference. For example, in the recommended action panel, Fig. 10.13, a general message such as "Contact Appropriate Service Representative" can be replaced with specific names and telephone numbers.

In addition to the aforementioned functions, the hardware monitor can also be used for running remote tests against devices that support the test feature.

10.12   NETVIEW SESSION MONITOR

This feature is an enhancement of the former IBM product Network Logical Data Manager (NLDM). Whereas the hardware monitor, discussed in the previous section, assists in solving hardware or physical problems, the session monitor assists in solving logical and response time problems. In contrast to a physical problem, in a logical problem there are no reported alerts or breakdowns, and yet communications cannot take place and sessions cannot be established. Logical problems are unpredictable and much more difficult to solve than hardware failures and are generally caused by software or microcode errors or protocol violations. Session monitor can assist the user by gathering and reporting session awareness and response time data.

10.12.1   Session Awareness (SAW) Data

The primary purpose of session awareness (SAW) data is to assist in resolving unexpected or abnormal session terminations. Typically, to solve such problems a trace of activities immediately preceding the failure is needed. For unexpected failures such traces are unavailable because customers avoid running activity traces during normal operation due to the excessive overhead of traces. One approach is to start a trace for a specific session after a problem has been reported; but, due to the unpredictable nature of problems, it may not be possible to recreate the problem. Session monitor helps by automatically recording session awareness data whenever a session terminates, and this information can be analyzed later by the system programmer to pinpoint the cause of the problem. The following information is gathered as a part of the SAW data:

Session initiation data such as partner LU names, SNA addresses, and Primary and Secondary LU configuration information

Bind failure sense code, bind parameters, session configuration data

Session abnormal termination unbind reason code

In addition to the SAW data, the session monitor can also collect session trace data (PIU with partial RU). The number of trace entries saved is defined by the user. Trace data from the SLU end of the session is also collected from the boundary NCP and it provides the last two inbound and outbound PIUs as well as some NCP control block information.

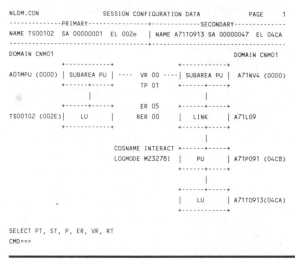

```
NLDM.CON                    SESSION CONFIGURATION DATA              PAGE    1
-------------PRIMARY----------------+-------------SECONDARY-------------
NAME TS00102  SA 00000001  EL 002e  | NAME A71T0913 SA 00000047  EL 04CA
------------------------------------+------------------------------------
DOMAIN CNM01                                                DOMAIN CNM01
             +-------------+                    +-------------+
A01MPU (0000) | SUBAREA PU | ----  VR 00 ----| SUBAREA PU |  A71NV4 (0000)
             +------+------+        TP 01      +------+------+
                    |                                |
             +------+------+        ER 05      +------+------+
TS00102 (002E)|    LU     |        RER 00      |  LINK     | A71L09
             +-------------+                    +------+------+
                                                      |
                        COSNAME INTERACT +------+------+
                        LOGMODE M232781  |    PU     | A71P091 (04C8)
                                          +------+------+
                                                |
                                          +------+------+
                                          |    LU     | A71T0913(04CA)
                                          +-------------+


SELECT PT, ST, P, ER, VR, RT
CMD==>
```

Figure 10.14   Session monitor—session configuration data.

The session configuration information can be displayed on the CNM terminal as shown in Fig. 10.14. Of particular interest should be the information on bind image, class of service, and virtual route specifications—which can be very useful in resolving session-related problems.

10.12.2 Response Time Monitor (RTM)

In addition to SAW, session monitor can also gather session response time information. However, this information can be captured only for those devices that implement the management services RTM feature. For such devices, NetView can also be used to set RTM parameters and to collect and display RTM information.

The RTM feature allows you to define up to four response time categories or counters with an additional overflow category. For example, you could define your response time counters to count transactions at a 3270 display station for response times in the following ranges: 1, 2, 5, and 10 seconds. Every time a transaction has a response time of less than 1 second, the 1-second counter is incremented. If the response time exceeds 10 seconds, the overflow counter is incremented. You can also customize the definition of response time. For example, a peripheral node can be configured to consider a transaction complete as soon as the first character of a reply message is received from the host or when the keyboard is unlocked. In addition to the host, the RTM data can also be viewed at the peripheral device. Specific device documentation should be consulted for RTM features implemented on it.

The host can solicit RTM information on a per-LU basis or for all LUs with nonzero RTM data. In addition RTM information can also be sent to the host at the end of an LU-LU session or when one of the counters overflows.

The session monitor can display RTM information to the host operator as shown in Fig. 10.15. The figure shows response time statistics for a terminal name TEXTAB14 for its session with the host subsystem CICS22A. The figure shows that the user objective in this case is to have 80 percent of the transactions with response times of 5 seconds or less, but only 75 percent of the transactions met that criterion.

IBM has another product, the NetView Performance Monitor (NPM), which is not a part of NetView and provides much more comprehensive information on response time than that provided by the session monitor RTM feature. NPM, using special extensions residing in the NCP, can gather additional data that are not available through RTM. While RTM deals with response time on a per-terminal basis, NPM can provide more global and comprehensive analyses and reports.

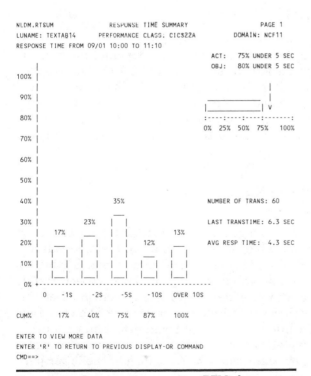

Figure 10.15 Response time monitor (RTM) data.

```
STATMON.NSD(DESC)          NODE STATUS DETAIL (DESCRIPTION)              08:27
HOST: HOST4          *0*      *1*     *2*     *3*     *4*
? NCP51              ACTIVE   PENDING  INACT   MONIT   NEVACT   OTHER
?...20  LINES        ?....8   ?.....  ?....2  ?....1  ?....9   ?.....
------------------------------------------------------------------------
DISPLAY:         |   NODE ID.  DESCRIPTION        NODE ID.  DESCRIPTION
  HIGHER NODE    |
    ? SUMMARY    |  ? K5105     LINE            ? K5110     LINE
    ? DETAIL     |  ? K514003   LINE            ? K5114     LINE
  THIS NODE      |  ? K514103   LINE            ? K5113C    LINE
    ? SUMMARY    |  ? K513222   LINE            ? K5181C    LINE
    ? DETAIL     |  ? K513342   LINE            ? K5112     LINE
                 |  ? K513653   LINE            ? K51NPA    LINE
                 |  ? K5100     LINE
-------------    |  ? K5101     LINE
DETAIL FORMAT:   |  ? K5102     LINE
    ? DESCRIPT   |  ? K5103     LINE
    s ANALYSIS   |  ? K5104     LINE
                 |  ? K5180     LINE
                 |  ? K5108     LINE
                 |  ? K5109     LINE


CMD==>
1=HELP 2=END 3=RETURN 4=BROWSE LOG 6=ROLL        10=VTAM 11=CLIST
```

Figure 10.16 NetView status monitor (STATMON) display.

10.13 NETVIEW STATUS MONITOR (STATMON)

STATMON displays the status of resources in a domain in a summarized manner on a single display, as shown in Fig. 10.16. This display is used by a control operator for general monitoring of a domain. When alerts requiring immediate action occur, the operator can switch to the hardware monitor and look at recent events in order to solve the problem in a manner similar to the scenario described in Sec. 10.11.2.

10.14 NETVIEW BROWSE AND HELP-DESK FEATURES

The NetView browse feature is a general-purpose facility for browsing through system generation tables and files in an interactive manner from a NetView terminal. In addition, extensive help is available on various features of NetView as well as through an interactive tutorial.

The help-desk feature also provides assistance to personnel at the help desk. Figure 10.17 shows a sample screen that can be called up by help-desk personnel while trying to gather information on a user-reported problem. The panel in Fig. 10.17 shows some general questions that the help-desk operator can ask. As shown in the lower part

```
CNMHT1                       THE TERMINAL DOES NOT WORK

1st    Obtain the terminal id/logical unit name (luname).

2nd    Ask the following questions:

       -- Is the terminal plugged in?
       -- Are the key and power switch turned on?
       -- Is the intensity knob turned high enough?
       -- Is the terminal in normal rather than test mode?
       -- Has the terminal ever worked?
       -- Have any changes (such as configuration changes) been made?

3rd    Determine how the terminal is connected and continue below.

           --- Select the number for one of the following ---

1 3274         The terminal is connected to a 3274 controller.
2 4700         The terminal is connected to a 4700 system.
3 8100         The terminal is connected to an 8100 system.

Action===> 1
           PF1= Help  PF2= End  Pf3= Return  PF4= Top  PF5= Bottom
           PF6= Roll  PF7= Backward  PF8= Forward  PF11= Entry Point
```

Figure 10.17   Help-desk.

of the display, the operator can also be prompted to ask questions specific to an equipment type such as IBM 3270, 4700, etc.

10.15   NETVIEW GRAPHIC MONITOR

Starting in 1991 with NetView Version 2, IBM has begun offering a graphics capability with NetView under the NetView Graphic Monitor feature. This feature with the OS/2 EE based GraphicsView 2 product, can display network topology graphically. The initial release of the product can display network resources up to the PU level; LUs cannot be displayed. This release cannot display non-SNA resources whose alarms are reported via NetView/PC (see Sec. 10.18). Using the FIND command, the operator can locate a resource by its symbolic name. To look at the status of LU level resources, a 3270 emulation window can be established on the OS/2 EE workstation and used as a regular NetView terminal. This window can be used to retrieve status of resources and submit commands to NetView. Additional 3270 windows can be established to communicate with other management products such as NetView Performance Monitor, Automated Console Operations, and Target System Control Facility.

The graphic facility can also be configured for a data server environment. In this environment, one OS/2 EE workstation can be configured as a graphical server that can serve multiple client stations acting as graphic monitor stations. The server and client communicate over APPC sessions. This arrangement reduces the number of host connections required for graphical monitors. GraphicsView 2 is purchased separately for each workstation. NetView Graphic Monitor contains the master copy of the code required by the workstation to work with GraphicsView 2. This code can be down-loaded into the workstation with appropriate license authorization.

10.16 REMOTE UNATTENDED OPERATIONS

With the operating system operations support available under NetView, it is now possible to implement unattended remote operations for system 370 and 390 computers. The additional product required for this function is the Target System Control Facility (TSCF). A personal computer is also required at the target site. As shown in Fig. 10.18, we would like to control system B at a remote site from the headquarters site, system A. Human intervention is required at system B to turn on the power at the mainframe and the PC.

The PC at the target site requires two adapters in it. One adapter is required to connect the PC to a channel-attached 3174 controller at the target site. The other adapter is a Token Ring or SDLC adapter required for communications with the controlling host.

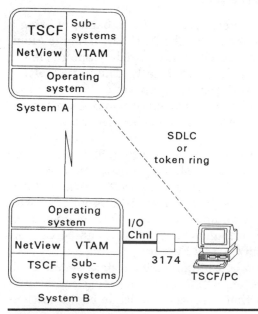

Figure 10.18 Remote operation—TSCF.

The system A operator establishes communications with the PC over the Token Ring or the SDLC link. As a first step, TSCF at system A down-loads the PC component of the TSCF software in the PC at the remote site. At this time the TSCF at system A can send commands to the PC to "boot" system B. Commands sent by TSCF appear to system B as if they were entered by the local console operator. Following the system boot, commands can be sent from system A to start NetView and VTAM on system B. Once VTAM and NetView are running on system B, system A can drop the TSCF connection with the PC and communicate directly with system B using cross-domain sessions over the link connecting the two systems. The two VTAMs can set up an SSCP-SSCP session, following which the two NetViews can set up an LU-LU session between them. Once we have a session between the two NetViews, commands for the operation of system B and its associated network can be sent by NetView-A to NetView-B for total operations management and control.

10.17 COMMUNICATIONS MANAGEMENT CONFIGURATION (CMC) AND FOCAL POINT NETVIEW

Communications Management Configuration (CMC) is a special configuration for centralized management of multidomain networks. One problem with a multidomain network is that it has multiple SSCPs, each receiving alarms and CNM data for its own domain only. One way to view network management information from each domain is to log onto NetView in each host from a single terminal (assuming a terminal with multiple-windows capability). However, this option only provides a view of each domain in a separate window and an ability to send NetView commands to it. It provides neither a consolidated view of all domains nor an integration of alarms and CNM data within a single system or database, but for some users this may be sufficient to meet their needs.

An alternative to the foregoing is to have a single VTAM/NetView own the whole network. In this case all CNM data goes to a single host, providing a better degree of integration, quality of centralized support, alarms and operations automation, and the development of expert systems.

The drawback of having a single owner is that if the host owning the network fails, no users in the network can initiate any new sessions, nor can the network be managed. The reliability of such a host becomes a very important factor. One way to improve the host reliability is to improve the reliability of the control software (hardware failures are few these days). One suggested way of eliminating software problems is to eliminate the software, i.e., run only the operating system, VTAM, NetView, and any other required system software; and eliminate all applications. This configuration, in which a mainframe is essentially dedicated to network management and runs no applications, is called the Communications Management Configuration (CMC) and is illustrated in Fig. 10.19.

In contrast to the CMC host, the other hosts run only applications and are called the data hosts. The one exception that applies is that the CMC host cannot own or manage channel-attached resources and subsystems that must still be owned by the data hosts, and data hosts may choose to use NetView to manage them. So you may still require NetView at the data hosts even though you are using CMC.

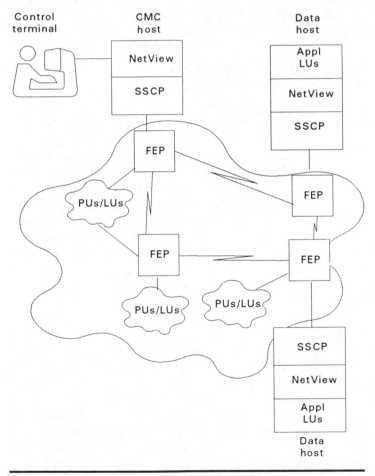

Figure 10.19 CMC configuration.

10.17.1   Focal Point NetView

Starting with NetView, version 1, release 3 in 1989, IBM introduced the concept of focal point NetView. With the focal point capability, the CMC host is designated as the focal point NetView and does not have to own the whole network. Additional copies of NetView are installed in data hosts, each of which owns a part of the network. The identity of the focal point NetView is defined to each distributed NetView. As CNM data arrive at each NetView, it forwards a copy to the focal point NetView automatically, using an LU-LU session. If the focal point NetView fails, distributed NetViews can continue to operate and provide distributed network management. As a further enhancement, one of the distributed NetViews can be designated as the backup focal point. The identity of the backup is defined to all distributed NetViews as a part of the system administration information. When the primary focal point fails, distributed NetViews automatically start forwarding CNM data to the backup focal point, ensuring continuity of the centralized operations.

10.18   MANAGING HYBRID NETWORKS

It is almost impossible to find a large network built exclusively with IBM products. Non-SNA elements typically include diagnostic modems and analog facilities management systems, multiplexers, T1 bandwidth management systems, matrix switches, LANs, etc. Most of them provide their own management systems with unique protocols, data structures, and control sequences. For users desiring a single integrated management system, it becomes necessary to have gateways that would take management information from all these systems and convert it to a format that is compatible with IBM's NetView. Such a conversion system is called a service point by IBM, as discussed in Sec. 10.8. To facilitate the building of a service point, IBM provides a PC-based product called NetView/PC.

10.18.1   IBM NetView/PC

NetView/PC is a foundation software that can be used by a user or vendor to develop applications to convert management data from non-SNA systems to a form compatible with NetView.

Figure 10.20 shows some possible applications of NetView/PC. In the simplest application, alerts and events can be received by NetView/PC from a non-SNA management system, converted to NMVT structure, and forwarded to the host for processing and reporting by NetView. The host NetView operator can also enter commands for execution on the non-SNA system. NetView forwards such com-

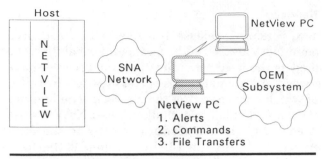

Figure 10.20   NetView/PC applications.

mands to NetView/PC in the form of NMVT. Gateway application in NetView/PC converts and forwards the command to the non-SNA system in its native data structure. The results of the command execution, when received from the non-SNA equipment, are again converted into an NMVT structure by the gateway application in NetView/PC and forwarded to the host.

NetView/PC applications can also transmit files to CICS using IBM's Distributed Data Management (DDM) architecture. Finally, NetView/PC can also exchange management data with other NetView/PCs over public switched facilities.

Figure 10.21 shows the internal architecture of NetView/PC. The current release of NetView/PC runs under OS/2 Extended Edition and requires a PS/2 or AT class machine. IBM Real Time Interface Coprocessor (RTIC) or SDLC or Token Ring adapter is required for host connection. An additional communications port is required to connect the PC to the other vendor's network management system.

NetView/PC functions include:

1. Providing connectivity to the host NetView for alarms and commands

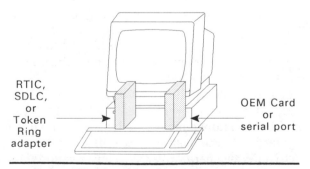

Figure 10.21   NetView/PC architecture.

2. An application programming interface (API) with callable modules for applications to use NetView/PC services

3. Alert displays and monitoring of the non-SNA system

4. File transfers to host

For a vendor planning to use NetView/PC as a service point the most important thing is the development of the application to support the vendor system. Logically the application has two parts: one that handles the interface with the vendor equipment; and the other, with NetView/PC. The vendor must select and provide software to support protocols for communications between NetView/PC and the vendor system. The vendor application program is also responsible for converting non-IBM alarms into an NMVT structure. Then, using NetView/PC application programming calls, the NMVTs can be sent to the host and commands can be received. NetView/PC can also display alerts on the PC and be used as a network management console for other vendors' equipment.

Rolm was the first corporation to develop an application for NetView/PC. Since then a large number of vendors have announced their NetView/PC applications to integrate their network management information with NetView.

10.19   OTHER NETVIEW FAMILY PRODUCTS

While NetView is a product name, the term *NetView* is also used by IBM as a general prefix for a number of network management products, raising much confusion about what is a part of the NetView product and what is a separate product. Some of these related products are described in the following.

10.19.1   IBM Information Management (I/M)

I/M is a general-purpose on-line record-keeping system that lends itself well to managing problem reports (trouble tickets), configuration data, and changes. I/M is the primary IBM product for managing problem reports. A number of customers have also used I/M successfully for maintaining configuration information. I/M uses a NetView software interface called the NetView Bridge, which enables NetView to post alarm information to I/M so that it can automatically create problem reports. The Bridge interface can also be used to develop REXX, C, or PL/1 procedures under NetView to submit database-related transactions from NetView to I/M. This interface is intended to provide better automation and integration of problem management with NetView.

10.19.2 NetView Distribution Services

NetView Distribution Services replaces what was formerly known as the Distributed System Executive (DSX). NetView Distribution Services is intended to become a general-purpose utility for distributing software and system generation tables to remote computers, controllers, and devices. It uses SNA Distribution Services (SNADS) as its underlying architecture. Early applications of this product have been in remote administration and management of IBM 3174 establishment controllers and AS/400 minicomputers.

IBM has a different product, SAA Delivery Manager, to manage software distribution to OS/2 workstations from MVS and VM systems. In addition to software distribution, SAA Delivery Manager can also be used for distributing files, text, source code, and documentation. For managing software distribution, additional features, such as copy limit threshold, license count, and protection against unauthorized copies, are available. The end user interface for the SAA Delivery Manager conforms to SAA Common User Access (CUA) guidelines. IBM expects that NetView Distribution Services and SAA Delivery Manager will be merged into a single product over a period of time.

10.19.3 NetView Access Services

NetView Access Services is IBM's belated response to a genre of software that has come to be known as "session management systems." The NetView Access Services product allows terminal users to maintain multiple concurrent logons (LU-LU sessions)—a function otherwise not allowed in SNA. In addition, in conjunction with another host-based IBM product [SNA Application Monitor (SAMON)], NetView Access Services can provide the status of host applications. It also provides security management by preventing unauthorized access to the network and applications through password/ID verification and management of security information. It also interfaces with host-based security software such as the IBM Resource Access and Control Facility (RACF).

10.19.4 NetView File Transfer
Program (FTP)

NetView FTP is a family of programs, one version each for MVS, VSE, and VM. The program is a VTAM application enabling high-speed bulk data transfers between IBM hosts. The program uses APPC/

VTAM function for communications. It provides an interactive interface for users to define file transfer details. Multiple concurrent file transfers can be initiated, and transfer requests can be queued. Using additional IBM products, data encryption, compaction, and compression can also be supported. FTP provides application programming interfaces in C and REXX. In addition, events associated with the FTP can be reported to NetView and automated via the NetView CLIST function.

10.19.5 NetView Performance Monitor (NPM)

NPM is IBM's most significant product for managing performance and accounting data for IBM networks. It collects performance information, in addition to the RTM data from boundary nodes, and can display network performance graphically. In addition to the SNA network information, NPM can also gather information on Token Ring LAN performance from FEPs equipped with Token Ring interfaces. Information can also be gathered from NetView Access Services. Users can also define performance thresholds, and NPM can automatically send performance-related alarms to NetView when any of the thresholds is exceeded. These performance-related alarms can then be handled by NetView operators or automatically through CLIST-based procedures.

10.20 SUMMARY

The Management Services architecture provides the specifications for network management in SNA. NetView implements the SNA focal point as the centralized, host-based management system. NetView/PC provides a foundation other vendors or users can use to build gateways to consolidate non-SNA network management functions with the host NetView.

Admittedly, network management has come a long way since the early days of SNA. But we still need to go much further in terms of integrated database and reports, trend analysis, expert systems, and graphics. IBM intends to meet these outstanding requirements within the framework of SystemView, a new management strategy announced by IBM in September 1990. The state of the integration in network management is still fairly poor, and, in the absence of international standards, that is a problem that IBM alone cannot solve.

APPC, Gateways, Trends

11

SNA Gateways

11.1 INTRODUCTION

So far our focus in this book has been on moving data within an SNA network. In this chapter we look at the following gateways:

1. SNA-SNA gateway using a feature called SNA Network Interconnect (SNI).

2. IBM Token Ring to wide area SNA gateways.

3. SNA to X.25 gateways. Chapter 14 contains additional information on SNA to OSI gateways.

11.2 SNA NETWORK INTERCONNECT (SNI)

SNI is the official term for the IBM SNA-SNA gateway. SNI is not a product but a function jointly provided by VTAM and NCP; i.e., both are required to build the SNI gateway function. The SNI gateway allows LU-LU sessions between LUs that reside in autonomous SNA networks. By *autonomous* we mean networks that are administered independently, and the system programmers administering the two networks do not have to coordinate their definitions with each other. This would typically be the case in intercorporate communications or communications between independent subsidiaries of the same corporation. Prior to the availability of Enhanced Network Addressing (ENA) in SNA—which allows up to 255 hosts and front end processors (extended to 64,000 with VTAM version 3.2 and NCP versions 4.3 and 5.2) in a single SNA network—several corporations with large networks exhausted SNA's addressing capabilities and had to break up their networks into multiple SNA networks. Even though such networks are not autonomous, SNI function is necessary to allow LU-LU sessions across network boundaries. At one time IBM also viewed SNI as the primary strategy for integrating IBM 9370 networks into existing or new SNA networks.

A common problem in all of the foregoing scenarios is that the autonomous networks can contain duplicate subarea numbers (therefore, duplicate addresses) and duplicate symbolic names. The whole intent of the SNI gateway is to allow communications between such networks without requiring them to maintain unique subarea numbers or names and to minimize the amount of information exchange required between the administrators of the two networks. As we look at various gateway configurations, we discuss information exchange requirements in more detail.

Before we go to the details of SNI, let us point out that for some users an expanded multidomain network may be an alternative solution to SNI. If a corporation had to break up its network into multiple networks in the first place because of addressing limitations in SNA, it may now be possible for them to go back to a unified network with ENA, and an SNI gateway is not necessary.

11.2.1 SNI Structure

SNI is a distributed gateway implemented partially in a NCP and partially in a VTAM, as illustrated in Fig. 11.1. The example shows two networks, NETA and NETB, interconnected via an SNI gateway. We do not show various terminals and applications in the two networks.

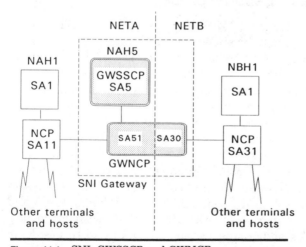

Figure 11.1   SNI: GWSSCP and GWNCP.

VTAM providing the gateway function is called the gateway SSCP or GWSSCP, and the NCP providing the gateway function is called the gateway NCP or GWNCP. Since the SSCP function is implemented in VTAM, we use the terms VTAM and SSCP interchangeably.

GWSSCP and GWNCP are not special products nor are they dedicated exclusively to the gateway functions. Each can continue to perform its normal VTAM and NCP functions in addition to the gateway functions. The GWSSCP can be located in either network and the GWNCP can reside in the same network as the GWSSCP or in another network.

In an internetworking environment we can view LU-LU sessions at three levels: same-domain, cross-domain, and cross-network sessions. All cross-network session initiation requests must be processed by the GWSSCP in addition to the SSCPs that own the LUs involved in the session. However, after the session establishment, the GWSSCP gets out of the picture and GWNCP becomes the important component. All cross-network traffic must flow through the GWNCP.

Only GWSSCP and GWNCP are aware of the presence of multiple networks. To all other SSCPs, the cross-network sessions appear as normal cross-domain networks. To understand how resources in foreign networks appear to each VTAM, let us look at the network shown in Fig. 11.2. Here again we have two networks—NETA and NETB—connected via SNI.

Notice that we have VTAMs and NCPs with duplicate subarea numbers in the two networks—NAH1 and NBH1 both have a subarea

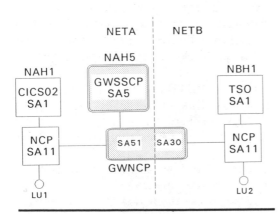

Figure 11.2 Cross-network addressing.

number 1, etc. Since subarea numbers no longer uniquely identify a node, for discussion purposes we use a naming convention that gives us unique names as shown in the following:

```
      N A                      H 5
       ↑                        ↑
       |                        |
       |                        |
 NET ID = NETA          HOST SUBAREA = 5
```

In each host name, e.g., NAH5, the first two characters, NA identify the network, NET A, and the last two characters, H5, identify the subarea number of the host, subarea 5 in this case.

Also observe that the GWNCP—even though a single FEP, is assigned multiple subarea numbers. In this example, the GWNCP is assigned two subarea numbers, 51 and 30. A GWNCP is assigned as many subarea numbers as the number of networks attached to it, for a maximum of 255 networks. However, each network knows of the GWNCP by only one subarea number. In NETA the GWNCP would be known as subarea 51, and as subarea 30 in NETB. The only restriction on the subarea numbers assigned to a GWNCP is that each subarea number must be unique in the network where it is used; i.e., subarea number 51 must be unique in NETA and subarea number 30 must be unique in NETB. It is the GWNCP that hides the presence of other networks from non-GWSSCP VTAMs. All NAUs (SSCPs, PUs, and LUs) are known by their true addresses only in their native networks, and by fake or alias addresses in foreign networks. In our example, CICS02 resides in NAH1. In its native network, NETA, CICS02 has an address of subarea 1 with some element number n, and that is its true address. However, in NETB we cannot define CICS02 as an element in subarea 1 since subarea 1 is associated with host NBH1 in NETB, and all traffic for subarea 1 in NETB is routed to NBH1, which does not know anything about CICS02. Therefore, the GWNCP assigns an alias address to CICS02 from subarea 30 for use in NETB.

Conversely, none of the resources in NETB are known by their true addresses in NETA and are assigned alias addresses by the GWNCP from subarea 51 for use in NETA. As a consequence, all cross-network session requests get routed to the GWNCP, which then reroutes them to the GWSSCP.

The GWNCP uses the two subarea numbers assigned to it as pools of element numbers. Whenever a cross-network session is to be established, the GWNCP assigns a fake address to each session partner for use in the foreign network. When a session terminates, the fake element addresses become free and can be used for other sessions.

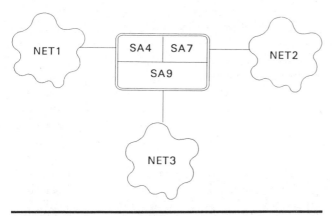

Figure 11.3   Three networks connected to a GWNCP.

In other words, to nongateway entities, all LUs in foreign networks appear as if they were elements in the GWNCP subarea. To summarize this, let us look at Fig. 11.3, where we have three networks connected to the same GWNCP. The GWNCP is known by subarea number 4 in NET1, by subarea number 7 in NET2, and by subarea number 9 in NET3.

In NET1, all origination and destination points (addresses) in NET2 and NET3 appear as elements in subarea 4.

In NET2, all addresses in NET1 and NET3 appear as elements in subarea 7.

In NET3, all addresses in NET1 and NET2 appear as elements in subarea 9.

It is the GWNCP that has to keep track of the real and alias address for each resource. As traffic passes through the GWNCP, it intercepts the traffic and swaps real and fake addresses in the TH and routes the traffic to the true destination.

11.2.2   Ownership of Cross-Network Resources

Cross-network logons appear as normal cross-domain sessions to all VTAMs other than the GWSSCP. It should be recollected that in a normal cross-domain session initiation, the session request always goes from the LU initiating the request to the SSCP that owns the initiating LU. The SSCP owning the initiating LU forwards the request to the owner of the destination (intended session partner) LU. Therefore, to process a cross-domain logon, a SSCP must know the owner of the destination LU. For example, in Fig. 11.2, if it were all a single network, to process a logon request from LU1 for a session with TSO, NAH1 (the owner of LU1) would have to know that TSO is owned by NBH1. If we were to extend this requirement to the SNI environment, it would mean that each host in each network would have to know about all hosts (owners) in the foreign networks in order to route session requests. As networks with large numbers of host computers are interconnected, these definition requirements can be truly imposing. To make matters worse, if any of the networks were to reassign any subarea numbers or change symbolic names, system definitions might have to be changed in all hosts in each network.

SNI does not impose any such requirements. In order to minimize information exchange and the impact of changes, the only host that needs to have detailed knowledge of each network is the GWSSCP.

In our example in Fig. 11.2, NAH1 and NBH1 do not have to be aware of each other or even of the fact that there are two separate networks in existence. To them the whole environment is a normal multidomain network. If such were the case, then how would we define the owner of TSO to NAH1? And, conversely, how would we define the owner of LU1 to NBH1?

From each nongateway VTAM's point view, all foreign LUs would appear as if they were owned by the GWSSCP. The only SSCP that is known in each network is a GWSSCP. In our example, TSO would be defined to NAH1 as if it were owned by the GWSSCP, NAH5. Similarly, to NBH1, LU1 would be defined as if owned by NAH5.

NAH5, itself, the GWSSCP, would be known by its true subarea number, 5, in its native network, NETA, and as an element in subarea 30 in NETB.

For the sample network shown in Fig. 11.4, various ownerships are defined as follows:

In host NAH1. CICS is in the same network as NAH1, and sessions with CICS from LUs in NAH1 domain would be normal cross-domain sessions requiring no SNI functions. CICS would be defined to NAH1 as owned by NAH4, and NAH4 would be identified through its true subarea number, 4.

TSO, JES, and LU2 are cross-network resources to NAH1 (but that would be transparent to NAH1) and would be defined as cross-domain resources and as if owned by the GWSSCP, NBH4. Since NBH4 is in a foreign network, it would not be defined to NAH1 by its true address, but rather as an element in the GWNCP subarea number 21. For these resources, cross-domain tables in NAH1 would be coded as follows (see Chap. 9 for a discussion of cross-domain tables).

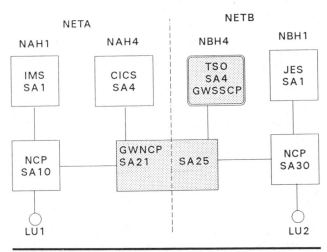

Figure 11.4   SNA cross-network ownership.

Cross-domain managers major node for NAH1

```
         VBUILD   TYPE=CDRM
NAH1     CDRM     SUBAREA=1,...
NAH4     CDRM     SUBAREA=4,...
NBH4     CDRM     SUBAREA=21,...
```

Note that NBH4 is defined through a fake subarea address of 21 and that NBH1 is not defined to NAH1.

Cross-domain LUs major node for NAH1

```
         VBUILD   TYPE=CDRSC
CICS     CDRSC    CDRM=NAH4,...
TSO      CDRSC    CDRM=NBH4,...
JES      CDRSC    CDRM=NBH4,...
LU2      CDRSC    CDRM=NBH4,...
```

Since LU1 is a same-domain resource to NAH1, it is not defined in cross-domain tables.

In host NAH4. IMS and LU1 are normal cross-domain resources and would be defined as owned by NAH1. TSO, JES, and LU2 are cross-network resources; therefore, they would be defined as if owned by the GWSSCP, NBH4. Definitions would be similar to NAH1.

Cross-domain managers major node for NAH4

```
         VBUILD   TYPE=CDRM
NAH1     CDRM     SUBAREA=1,...
NAH4     CDRM     SUBAREA=4,...
NBH4     CDRM     SUBAREA=21,...
```

Cross-domain LUs major node for NAH4

```
        VBUILD    TYPE=CDRSC
IMS     CDRSC     CDRM=NAH1,...
LU1     CDRSC     CDRM=NAH1,...
TSO     CDRSC     CDRM=NBH4,...
JES     CDRSC     CDRM=NBH4,...
LU2     CDRSC     CDRM=NBH4,...
```

Similar rules would apply to network B. Resources that are within NETB would be defined using normal cross-domain definitions, and cross-network resources would be defined as if owned by the GWSSCP—except for the GWSSCP, where true identities of all resources in both networks would be defined.

In host NBH1. For NBH1, LU2 is an owned resource and not defined in cross-domain tables. TSO is a normal cross-domain resource and defined as owned by NBH4. IMS and CICS are cross-network resources; therefore, they are defined as if owned by the GWSSCP, NBH4. But there would be one difference relative to NETA definitions: In NETA, NBH4 was defined through an alias address; in NETB, which is the native network for NBH4, it would be defined through its true address. The definitions would look as follows:

Cross-domain managers major node for NBH1

```
        VBUILD    TYPE=CDRM
NBH4    CDRM      SUBAREA=4,...
NBH1    CDRM      SUBAREA=1,...
```

Cross-domain LUs major node for NBH1

```
        VBUILD    TYPE=CDRSC,
TSO     CDRSC     CDRM=NBH4,...
CICS    CDRSC     CDRM=NBH4,...
IMS     CDRSC     CDRM=NBH4,...
LU1     CDRSC     CDRM=NBH4,...
```

In host NBH4, GWSSCP. The GWSSCP must know the true ownership and identity of all resources. The burden of detailed cross-network definitions falls on the GWSSCP (and GWNCP). At the GWSSCP you can maintain neither the autonomy nor the transparency of a foreign network. The GWSSCP host would list true identities and, therefore, have duplicate subarea numbers in its tables. But these tables would contain an additional statement called NETWORK to differentiate between resources in the two networks. The NETWORK statement is required only in an SNI environment. For NBH4, the definitions would be coded as follows.

Cross-domain managers major node for NBH4

```
        VBUILD    TYPE=CDRM
        NETWORK   NETID=NETA
NAH1    CDRM      SUBAREA=1,...
NAH4    CDRM      SUBAREA=4,...
        NETWORK   NETID=NETB
NBH1    CDRM      SUBAREA=1,...
NBH4    CDRM      SUBAREA=4,...
```

Cross-domain LUs major node for NBH4

```
        VBUILD    TYPE=CDRSC
        NETWORK   NETID=NETA
IMS     CDRSC     CDRM=NAH1,...
LU1     CDRSC     CDRM=NAH1,...
CICS    CDRSC     CDRM=NAH4,...
        NETWORK   NETID=NETB
JES     CDRSC     CDRM=NBH1,...
LU2     CDRSC     CDRM=NBH1,...
```

By segregating resources in a network under the network ID, the GWSSCP can uniquely identify the resources in spite of duplicate subarea numbers.

11.2.3 Use of ADJSSCP Tables

The examples in the previous section represent the worst-case scenarios in terms of number of cross-domain and cross-network LUs to be defined in each host. We did this to illustrate an elaborate example. You can use ADJSSCP tables (Chap. 9) to reduce the number of definitions required.

11.2.4 Three SNI Rules to Remember

Let us summarize the three key rules that we have developed for understanding SNI environment:

1. To nongateway VTAMs, the cross-network LUs appear as if owned by the GWSSCP.
2. The GWSSCP itself is known by its true address in its native network but appears as an element in the GWNCP subarea in a foreign network.
3. The GWNCP appears as the origination/destination subarea for all cross-network traffic.

11.3 INTERCONNECT ALTERNATIVES

A number of configurations can be used to interconnect networks. By having multiple GWSSCPs and GWNCPs we can reduce the amount of information exchange required to implement the gateway and increase cross-network throughput and reliability. Some of the common configurations include:

11.3.1 Single GWSSCP and GWNCP

This is the configuration that we have looked at in the previous examples. As shown in Fig. 11.4, there is a single GWSSCP, NBH4, and a single GWNCP. With this configuration we can connect up to 255 networks and allow LU-LU sessions between any pair of LUs in these networks. The real capacity to interconnect is limited by the traffic handling capacity of the GWNCP.

From an implementation point of view, in NETA, each host has to add GWSSCP, NBH4, in the Cross-Domain Resources Managers table and define all LUs in NETB as if owned by NBH4. Beyond that, any changes in NETB do not effect NETA.

In NETB, hosts other than the GWSSCP have to, at most, define LUs resident in NETA as if owned by NBH4. Any other configuration changes in NETA do not have any effect on system generation tables in NETB hosts.

The bulk of the work for system definitions is done at the GWSSCP host. As we saw in Sec. 11.2.2, in the GWSSCP we not only have to define all the cross-domain managers in NETB, but also identify all hosts in NETA. If any SSCPs in either network were assigned new names or subarea numbers or new hosts were added, tables in the GWSSCP would have to be altered. The number of LU definitions required can be reduced or eliminated by using ADJSSCP tables as discussed in Chap. 9.

11.3.2 Single GWSSCP and Multiple GWNCPs

This configuration is a minor variation on the previous example and is useful when a single GWNCP cannot handle all cross-network traffic. As shown in Fig. 11.5, we can use either GWNCPA or GWNCPB to route traffic between NETA and NETB. Besides providing greater cross-network session capacity, the configuration can also improve the reliability because each GWNCP can act as a backup for the other in case of failure. Through the system generation tables in the GWSSCP we can also control the sessions that are routed through each GWNCP.

11.3.3 GWSSCP and GWNCP in Each Network

This is the most attractive configuration if the objective is to minimize the amount of information to be exchanged or maintained about foreign network configurations in implementing SNI. With multiple

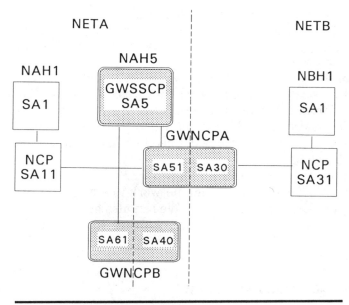

Figure 11.5   Single GWSSCP, multiple GWNCPs.

GWSSCPs, even the GWSSCP in each network does not require de-tailed information about the other network.

Figure 11.6 shows an example. The only definition needed in each network is the addition of a single CDRM to represent the GWSSCP in the foreign network and, of course, the foreign LUs. In our example in Fig. 11.6, the only information needed in NETA about NETB is the

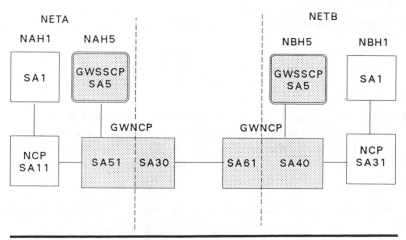

Figure 11.6   GWSSCP and GWNCP in each network.

definition of NBH5 as a CDRM in the NAH5 tables. Conversely, in NETB, only NAH5 is defined as a CDRM and that too only in NBH5. Any moves, changes, or alterations in either network have no effect on definitions in the other network.

In this configuration, the connection between SA30 and SA61, the two gateway NCPs, is called a null network and it contains only alias addresses assigned from subareas 30 and 61. Even the two GWSSCPs are known via alias addresses: NAH5 is defined to NBH5 as if it were an element in subarea 30, and NBH5 is defined to NAH5 as if it were an element in subarea 61.

As a variation on the configuration shown in Fig. 11.6, we can also have multiple GWNCPs within each network in a manner similar to the example shown in Figure 11.5. We can also have sessions that go across more than two networks, i. e., that span multiple gateways.

11.4 ESTABLISHING CROSS-NETWORK SESSIONS

So far we have focused on how cross-network resources appear to various hosts. Now let us look at the details of a cross-network logon.

There are three phases of activities that occur during the establishment of a cross-network LU-LU session:

1. SSCP-NCP session establishment between GWSSCP and GWNCP

2. SSCP-SSCP session establishment between the GWSSCP and the SSCPs owning the LUs for which cross-network LU-LU sessions are to be established

3. Cross-network LU-LU session establishment

The first two sessions need to be established only once, at network startup or any other operationally convenient time, and then they stay up continuously. The LU-LU sessions are established and terminated on a need basis.

In the following example we use the network shown in the top part of Fig. 11.8 and look at session establishment between an application, CICS01, in NETA and a terminal, LU1, in NETB. Before looking at the details let us review the appearance of various resources in each network.

1. LU1 is defined to NAH1 as if owned by NAH5, and NAH5 is known to NAH1 through its true subarea number, 5.

2. CICS01 is defined to NBH1 as if owned by NAH5, and NAH5 itself appears as an element in subarea 7 to NBH1.

3. There will be SSCP-SSCP sessions between NAH1 and NAH5 and between NAH5 and NBH1, but no sessions between NAH1 and NBH1.

Whether LU-LU session request is initiated by CICS01 or LU1, the
owner of the initiating LU would forward the request to the GWSSCP
which, in turn, would forward the request to the real owner. Now the
details:

11.4.1 GWSSCP-GWNCP Session

This session must be established before any cross-network traffic can
flow. The GWSSCP is not identified to the GWNCP in the NCP system
generation tables. It is during the GWNCP activation that the
GWSSCP identifies itself to the GWNCP as the gateway SSCP. The
normal NCP activation sequence was described in Chap. 7. In this section we review the partial activation sequence as shown in Fig. 11.7.

In step 1, a successful contact verifies for the SSCP that the
GWNCP is running. During XID exchange (step 2), SSCP and NCP

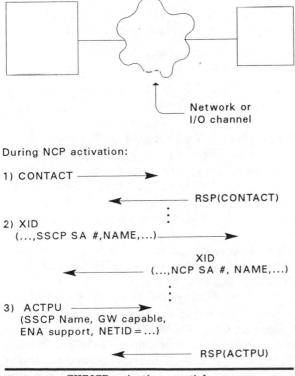

Figure 11.7 GWNCP activation—partial sequence.

exchange their node names and subarea numbers, as well as other information.

It is in the ACTPU command (step 3) that follows a successful XID exchange where the GWSSCP identifies itself as the gateway by setting a flag called *gateway-capable* equal to yes in the ACTPU parameters. After the ACTPU, the GWNCP knows the name, subarea numbers, and the network ID of the GWSSCP. At this point GWSSCP-GWNCP session establishment is complete.

11.4.2 Overview of Cross-Network Sessions

To understand the rest of the session establishment flow, the reader must be familiar with the role of the following commands in establishing cross-domain sessions: ACTCDRM, CDINIT, and CDCINIT. These are explained in Chap. 9 and you may wish to review them before proceeding further. The major tasks to be completed during session establishment include:

1. The SSCP that owns the LU initiating the session request (called the initiating LU) receives the session initiation request.

2. The SSCP owning the initiating LU requests the SSCP owning the destination LU to return the address of the destination LU.

3. The SSCP owning the destination LU returns the address of the LU (if such an LU is available).

4. The SSCP owning the initiating LU sends the logon request for the destination LU to the destination LU's owner.

Assigning real and alias addresses. As discussed earlier, an LU is known by an alias address in a foreign network and by its true address in its native network. As messages cross the network boundary, it is the responsibility of the GWNCP to switch between true and alias addresses. The alias addresses are assigned by the GWNCP dynamically at session establishment time. The true addresses are provided by the GWSSCP.

During a cross-network session establishment, the request network address assignment (RNAA) SNA command is used by the GWSSCP to request a pair of alias addresses from the GWNCP. When the GWNCP returns the two alias addresses, the GWNCP does not yet know the resources with which these addresses would be associated.

Following the RNAA command, the GWSSCP uses the set control vector (SETCV) command to return the true addresses of the session partners to the GWNCP. (SETCV is a multipurpose command and is also used for purposes other than address assignment.) After a successful RNAA and SETCV exchange, both the GWSSCP and the GWNCP know the true and alias addresses of the session partners and the session initiation can move ahead.

11.5 SSCP-SSCP SESSION BETWEEN GWSSCP AND OTHER SSCPS

All SSCPs send cross-network LU-LU session requests to the GWSSCP over an SSCP-SSCP session. Just as the GWSSCP-NCP session, the SSCP-SSCP sessions, too, are established only once at network startup. The session is established by the exchanging ACTCDRM command between the two SSCPs. For a cross-network SSCP-GWSSCP session we need to establish an alias address before the ACTCDRM command can be executed.

In our example we trace the establishment of a session between the GWSSCP, NAH5, in NETA with NBH1 in NETB as shown in Fig. 11.8. The figure does not show complete details or format of various commands and responses. Where necessary, Fig. 11.8 shows subarea-element addresses, which are part of the TH as well as partial contents of the RU to show the command being transmitted. The TH address fields are listed as OAF (origination address field) and DAF (destination address field).

It should be noted that, as far as host NBH1 is concerned, it is participating in a normal cross-domain session and knows nothing about multiple networks.

1. In preparation for setting up a cross-network session, the GWSSCP, NAH5, requests a pair of "alias" addresses from the GWNCP via an RNAA command.

   Aliases requested are for NAH5 (real address SA5, element 1) in NETA and NBH1 (real address SA1, element 1) in NETB.

2. GWNCP returns two addresses in response (RSP) to the RNAA command.

   Even though the GWNCP does not know it yet, SA8, element 4 is to be the alias address for NBH1 in NETA and SA7, element 2 is to be the alias address for NAH5 (GW) in NETB.

3. GWSSCP passes real and alias address pairs back to GWNCP via SETCV as follows:

   "My real address in NETA is (5,1) and I shall be known through a fake address of (7,2) in NETB. I intend setting up a session with an NAU known by an address (8,4) in my network (NETA) but known by an address of (1,1) in NETB."

4. GWNCP updates its tables with the addresses and acknowledges SETCV.

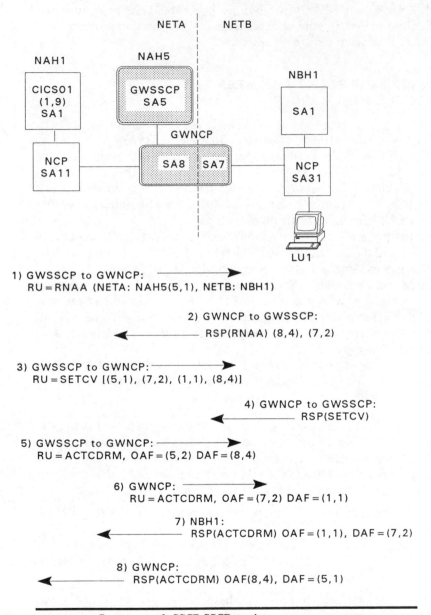

1) GWSSCP to GWNCP: ──────────▶
   RU = RNAA (NETA: NAH5(5,1), NETB: NBH1)

2) GWNCP to GWSSCP:
   ◀────────── RSP(RNAA) (8,4), (7,2)

3) GWSSCP to GWNCP: ──────────▶
   RU = SETCV [(5,1), (7,2), (1,1), (8,4)]

4) GWNCP to GWSSCP:
   ◀────────── RSP(SETCV)

5) GWSSCP to GWNCP: ──────────▶
   RU = ACTCDRM, OAF = (5,2) DAF = (8,4)

6) GWNCP: ──────────▶
   RU = ACTCDRM, OAF = (7,2) DAF = (1,1)

7) NBH1:
   ◀────────── RSP(ACTCDRM) OAF = (1,1), DAF = (7,2)

8) GWNCP:
   ◀────────── RSP(ACTCDRM) OAF(8,4), DAF = (5,1)

Figure 11.8 Cross-network SSCP-SSCP session.

5. GWSSCP, NAH5, sends an ACTCDRM command to NBH1 to start
   the SSCP-SSCP session. The OAF address is (5,1) representing
   NAH5 and the DAF is (8,4), the address by which NBH1 is known
   in NETA.

6. Address transformations by the GWNCP: Since NBH1 will not recognize either of the previous two addresses (or may confuse them with duplicate subarea numbers in its own network), the GWNCP intercepts the ACTCDRM command and modifies OAF to (7,2), the address by which GWSSCP is known to NBH1; and DAF to (1,1), which is the true address of NBH1 in NETB.

   GWNCP forwards the ACTCDRM to NBH1 after address translation.

7. NBH1 responds with a positive response to ACTCDRM; the response has an OAF = (1,1), which is NBH1's own address, and DAF = (7,2), the address by which GWSSCP is known to NBH1.

8. When this response arrives at the GWNCP, it must now convert OAF and DAF to addresses that are understood in NETA.

   GWNCP changes the OAF to (8,4) and DAF to (5,1) and forwards the response to GWSSCP, and the SSCP-SSCP session establishment is complete.

Similar address translations will be performed for all traffic between NAH5 and NBH1. Once the SSCP-SSCP session has been established, the GWSSCP can send or receive LU-LU session initiation requests to and from NBH1.

11.6 LU-LU SESSION BETWEEN CICS01 AND LU1 INITIATED BY CICS01

Figure 11.9 illustrates the flow for the following discussion.

1. The SSCP in NAH1 receives a request from CICS01 for a session with LU1. System tables in NAH1 would show LU1 to be owned by NAH5 (GWSSCP), i.e., CDINIT should be sent there and NAH1 sends the CDINIT to NAH5 (see Chap. 9 for a description of CDINIT).

2. The GWSSCP would forward this CDINIT to the true owner, NBH1, but it must first establish alias addresses for CICS01 and LU1.

   NAH5 requests alias addresses from GWNCP for CICS01 and LU1 through the RNAA command.

3. GWNCP uses its two pools of addresses, subareas 8 and 7, to select two available elements.

   In our example, selected addresses are (8,10) for LU1 for use in NETA and (7,12) for CICS01 for use in NETB. GWNCP returns these addresses to the GWSSCP.

4. NAH5 sends CDINIT to NBH1 on its SSCP-SSCP session with NBH1. CDINIT contains the alias address of CICS01 and the real names of both LUs. As this command passes through the GWNCP,

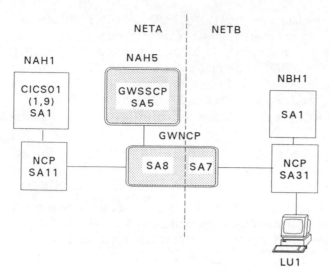

1) NAH1 to NAH5: OAF = (1,1), DAF = (5,1)
   RU = CDINIT (VAPPL1, OLU = (1,9), DLUN = LU1

2) NAH5 to GWNCP: OAF = (5,1), DAF = (8,0)
   RU = RNAA (VAPPL1, LU1)

           3) GWNCP to GWSSCP:
              RSP(RNAA): (8,10), (7,12)

4) NAH5 to NBH1: OAF = (5,1), DAF = (8,4)
   RU = CDINIT (OLU = (7,12), VAPPL1, DLUN = LU1)

   (After GWNCP changes DAF to (1,1) and
    OAF to (7,2), CDINIT goes to NBH1)

           5) NBH1 to NAH5:
              RSP(CDINIT), RU = DLU address(31,2C)
              (OAF and DAF changed at GWNCP to:
               OAF = (8,4), DAF = (5,1)

6) NAH5 to GWNCP: OAF = (5,1), DAF = (8,0)
   SETCV ((OLU: (1,9)/(7,12), DLU: (31,2C)/(8,10))

   (Address initialization complete now)

Figure 11.9 Cross-network LU-LU session (LU = originating LU,
DLUN = destination LU name).

the GWNCP changes the OAF address to the alias address and
DAF to the real address.

5. NBH1 responds to CDINIT with the real address of LU1 as (31,2C,
   assuming that LU1 is element 2C in subarea 31). Note that LU1 is
   attached to subarea 31 NCP.

6. NAH5 passes the addresses of CICS and LU1 to GWNCP via SETCV.

At this time both GWSSCP and GWNCP have complete addressing information, and cross-network address translations can be performed by the GWNCP.

Additional details, not shown in Fig. 11.9, would include a response to CDINIT (from the foregoing step 1) from the GWSSCP to NAH1. The response would identify LU1 as subarea 8, element 10. NAH1 can now send a CDCINIT for LU1 to NAH5, which would, in turn, forward it to NBH1. After the CDCINIT processing has been completed, the session traffic no longer has to flow through the GWSSCP but must flow through the GWNCP. The cross-network LU-LU session would continue even if the GWSSCP fails. However, no new cross-network LU-LU sessions can be initiated until there is an active GWSSCP.

The *class of service* (COS) resolution for the LU-LU session always takes place at the host where PLU resides, and in this case COS tables in NAH1 will select a *virtual route* (VR) to SA 5. Lastly, VRs cannot cross network boundaries, so GWNCP will be responsible for mapping the VR selected by NETA SSCPs into proper VRs in NETB.

11.7 DEFINING NETWORK IDENTIFICATIONS (NETIDs)

As we saw in Sec. 11.2.2, all cross-domain definitions in the GWSSCP are preceded by a NETWORK statement that identifies the network ID in which the resources reside. The network ID is assigned to the GWSSCP through the NETID parameter on the VTAM start list. Figure 11.10 shows a start list, ATCSTRnn, which assigns a network ID of NETA to NAH5's network. The second part of the table shows how network ID is used in the CDRM table to identify all CDRMs in NETA.

For the GWNCP, we still use the BUILD statement (Chap. 8) to describe its characteristics for the network where the GWNCP acts as a boundary node and the NETID for that network is defined on the BUILD statement. For each additional network, a NETWORK statement is coded in the NCP. The parameters on the NETWORK statement are similar to the BUILD statement and describe the network ID, subarea number for the NCP in that network, etc. We do not discuss NCP system generation tables in any further detail.

11.8 HANDLING DUPLICATE NAMES AND NETVIEW ALIAS FEATURE

Our discussions so far have looked at how SNI handles duplicate subarea numbers and addresses. However, SNA also requires that all

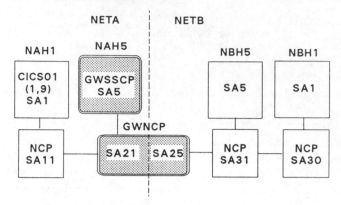

For GWSSCP:

1) ATCSTRnn:

    HOSTSA = 5,SSCPNAME = NAH5,HOSTPU = NAPU5,
    NETID = NETA,...

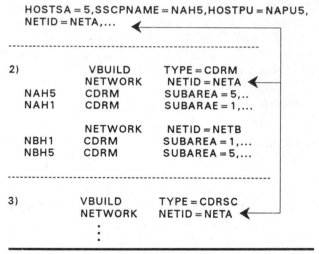

Figure 11.10   Defining network identifiers.

symbolic names be unique in a SNA network. Figure 11.11 shows a network in which we have an application called IMS in each network as well as a LU named LU1.

If our objective is to maintain network autonomy, then we do not want to change names of LUs or enforce unique names among the interconnected SNA networks. To handle duplicate names, the SNI function requires the use of the alias name translation feature in NetView. This NetView feature allows assignment of alias symbolic names to resources with duplicate names. The alias name table is defined in NetView in the GWSSCP host. In our example, we could as-

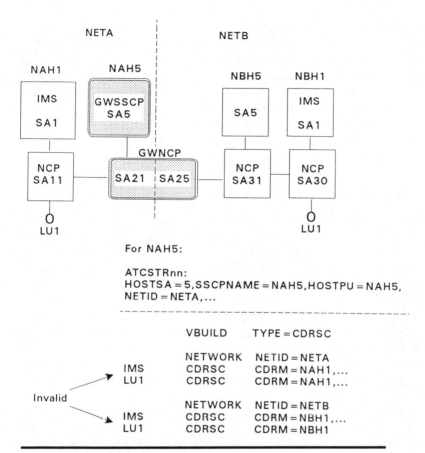

Figure 11.11   Invalid duplicate names.

sign an alias name of, say, IMSNETB for the NETB IMS system. This alias name would be used only by users in network A to log onto IMS in network B. Network B does not know that its IMS system is known as IMSNETB in network A. Similarly, alias names could be assigned by the GWSSCP host for other LUs that have duplicate names and eliminate the need to change any names in the connecting networks.

When a cross-network logon arrives at the GWSSCP, the GWSSCP passes the alias name to NetView and obtains the true name from it. The session partners do not know anything about the alias name translation.

11.9   SNI SUMMARY

SNI is another name for the IBM SNA-SNA gateway. It is implemented by a GWSSCP and a GWNCP. The GWSSCP and GWNCP can be in the same or separate networks and provide the gateway functions in addition to their normal functions. The GWSSCP is necessary during the processing of a cross-network session. After a successful session establishment, session data do not have to flow through the GWSSCP any more but must flow through the GWNCP. The GWNCP is responsible for providing alias addresses and switching alias and real addresses as PIUs cross the network boundary. NetView alias name translation feature may also be needed if the interconnected networks have duplicate names.

11.10   SNA-IBM TOKEN RING GATEWAY

LANs are the fastest growing segment of data networks. IBM's LAN architecture is IEEE 802.5-based Token Ring. The IBM cabling system for local area networking was announced in 1984 with the IBM Token Ring announcement following in the year 1985. IBM Token Rings can be operated at 4 and 16 megabits per second transmission rates. IBM's 8220 Token Ring to fiber converter can be used to extend Token Ring connections over optical fiber. Various bridge and routing products are available from IBM and other vendors to extend the range of Token Ring LANs.

At the ring itself, various IBM devices such as 3174, PS/2, AS/400, 3745, etc. can be equipped with a Token Ring adapter to attach them to the ring. As more and more PCs and other devices are being attached to Token Ring LANs, the ability to access applications in SNA hosts has become critical. This section discusses several IBM gateways to access host-based SNA applications from LAN stations.

To define the scope of gateway functions, let us start with a comparison of Token Ring and SNA architectures as shown in Fig. 11.12. In contrast to SNA (and OSI), LAN architectures deal only with the lowest two layers of the network architecture. The media access control (MAC) layer deals with the management of tokens, frames, station addresses, and certain types of errors. Logical link control (LLC) deals with sequential delivery of frames, transmission error recovery, and the interface with upper layers. Each station on the ring is assigned a unique MAC level address. In addition, within a ring station, each application must be identified by a unique LLC level address. The LLC addresses are called service access points (SAPs), shown as S1-S4 in Fig. 11.12. In this context, an application is any software that interfaces with LLC software/microcode and is, typically, not a customer-written application but a subsystem software such as APPC, 3270 emulator, NetBIOS, or a network management application. For example, in a PC using both NetBIOS and IBM SNA microcode to support two different types of sessions, NetBIOS and SNA interfaces would each

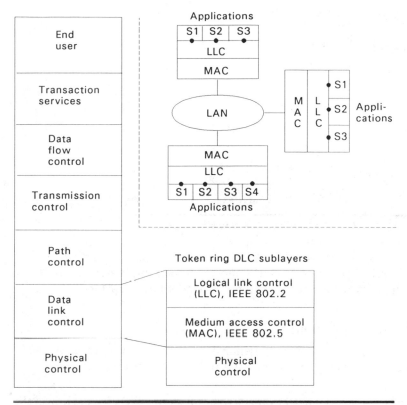

Figure 11.12 SNA versus token ring architecture [S1, S2, S3, S4 = service access point (SAP)].

be assigned a different SAP. SNA communications generally use a SAP of X'04' (the SAP used may be implementation defined). Thus, application subsystems are uniquely identified through a combination of their MAC/SAP addresses.

Architectures such as APPC and NetBIOS are capable of supporting multiple business applications concurrently. In this case a third level of address is provided by APPC or NetBIOS to uniquely identify the high applications.

Figure 11.13 contrasts data structure differences between Token Ring and SNA/SDLC. As can be seen, Token Ring has no impact on SNA levels 3-7. Token Ring does not get involved in any of the protocols above LLC, and SNA protocols and structures such as SSCP, PU, LU, and PIUs are transparent to it. The PIU (TH, RH, and RU) structure is carried in both architectures without any change. Nor is there any impact on the PU and LU protocols. As a matter of fact, LU 6.2

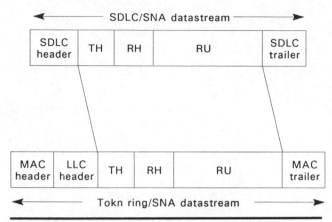

Figure 11.13   SDLC/SNA and token ring data structures.

with PU 2.1 is expected to be the most common implementation on the ring. The only difference is at level 2 headers and trailers.

11.10.1   Gateway Operation Overview

With the previous section as general background, we can now introduce various aspects of Token Ring to host communications.

Physical layer interface and data transformation.   This is, perhaps, the easiest function to describe. The gateway must have two adapters in it for physical connectivity—a LAN adapter on the ring side and another adapter for the SNA host side of the network. The host-network adapter can be SDLC or I/O channel.

Data transformation component deals with stripping MAC/LLC control information and replacing it with SDLC or I/O channel control information for ring-to-host traffic, and doing the reverse for host-to-LAN traffic. PIU itself does not require any transformation.

Address translation.   As MAC/LLC control information is replaced by SDLC or I/O channel control information for the host-bound traffic, LAN addresses (MAC/SAP) must be mapped into appropriate SDLC or I/O channel addresses. Reverse address translations occur for the LAN-bound traffic.

Gateway-provided SNA functions.   An important factor influencing gateway functions is whether the ring stations implement full PU/LU functions (such as with 3174, AS/400, OS/2 EE, and 9370) or only the

LU functions (such as with certain PC/DOS-based configurations). If the ring station implements only the LU function, the gateway has to provide PU functions on its behalf. In the other case, where LAN stations are configured with both PU and LU functions, the PU function is not required in the gateway. Thus, gateways are divided into two categories depending on whether they provide PU functions or not. We refer to these two types of gateways as PU passthrough and single PU gateways as shown in Fig. 11.14.

PU passthrough gateway. If the ring stations provide complete PU and LU functions, the gateway needs only to transform the MAC/LLC information into appropriate SDLC or I/O channel sequences. Beyond that the gateway is a transparent "passthrough" as far as PUs on the ring are concerned, and, therefore, the name PU passthrough. The

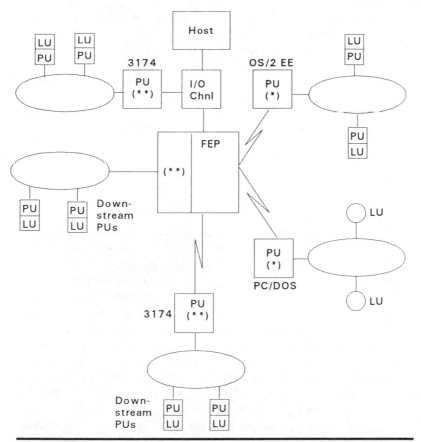

Figure 11.14 Multiple-PU (passthrough) and single-PU gateways [* = single PU gateway, ** = multiple PU (passthrough) gateway].

passthrough gateway can be provided by both the IBM 3174 and the NCP. To distinguish devices on the ring from the gateway device, the ring devices are referred to as the *down stream physical units* (DSPUs). Ring devices going through the multi-PU gateway do not use the NetBIOS interface. The DSPU uses MAC/LLC procedures to set up a connection between its PU and the gateway controller.

However, having PU and LU functions in each LAN station can significantly increase the host overhead of dealing with LAN stations, which is one of the disadvantages of the PU passthrough gateway.

Single PU gateway.   In this case, the gateway presents a single PU on behalf of all LAN devices. This approach is used by certain PC/DOS and OS/2 EE-based gateways. The communications between the gateway and the ring stations can be at the NetBIOS or MAC/LLC level. With some products, the gateway can provide the appearance of a single PU even with multiple PUs on the ring. One advantage of the single PU gateway approach is that it significantly reduces the number of PU definitions required in the host to represent the LAN stations. Specific implementations are discussed in Sec. 11.10.2.

Host (VTAM) view of the LAN.   VTAM has no direct support for Token Ring connections, which is one of the reasons for the gateway in the first place. The Token Ring-to-host gateway must emulate for the host one of the three configurations supported by VTAM:

1. A multidrop SDLC line

2. A switched SDLC line

3. I/O channel-attached device

The first two options are available if the gateway is connected to the host via a remote SDLC link, and the third option is applicable if the gateway is attached to the host I/O channel. The emulation choice is an important consideration in selecting the gateway product.

Figure 11.15 shows some of the major connectivity options for the IBM Token Ring gateway products. The IBM 3174 gateway can be directly attached to the I/O channel (box A) or can be attached via a remote SDLC link (box D). Similarly, the front end processor gateways can also be channel-attached (box C) or through a remote SDLC link (box E). With versions 4.3.1 and 5.2.1 of the NCP (or later release), it is also possible to go from one ring to another via the front ends as a bridge. For example, in Fig. 11.15, a user on ring TR-E could communicate with a user on ring TR-C with data moving through front ends E and C. OS/2 EE- and PC/DOS-based gateways can only be connected via SDLC links. Lastly, a ring can also be directly connected to the

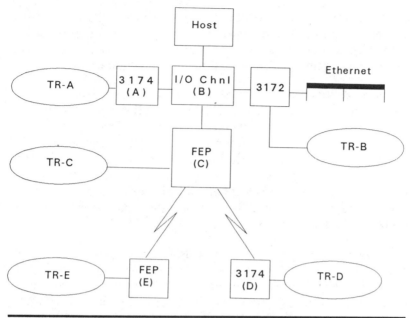

Figure 11.15   Token Ring LAN to IBM host connectivity (TR = Token Ring).

host I/O channel via the IBM 8232 LAN Channel Station or the IBM 3172 Interconnect Controller. Even though our focus here is IBM Token Ring, the IBM 8232 and 3172 can also be used as gateways between SNA and IBM PC Network Broadband or an Ethernet LAN.

11.10.2   Gateway Implementations

NCP as a gateway.   In this case the front end is configured with the NCP Token Ring Interface (NTRI) software and the Token Ring adapter. The FEP can be a channel-attached or remote FEP. NCP is a passthrough gateway, thus, one PU/LU pair must be defined in the host for each ring station. To the host, the downstream PUs appear as if they were on switched SDLC lines. Thus, one dummy switched port definition must be provided in VTAM for each concurrently active ring station. The MAC address of the ring stations is defined where normally one would define the telephone numbers for dial-out connections. When VTAM commands the NCP to set up a dial-up connection for one of the dummy dial-up devices, the NCP recognizes that the device is really a Token Ring device and uses MAC/LLC protocols to establish communications with the ring device. NCP gateway supports T5, T4, T2.0, and T2.1 nodes on the ring.

IBM 3174 SNA gateway. The 3174 gateway presents a different view of the LAN stations to the host depending on whether it is attached to the host via an SDLC link or the I/O channel. In either configuration, the 3174 gateway supports only T2.0 nodes as ring stations.

Channel-attached 3174 gateway. In this case each downstream PU appears to the host as a channel-attached controller and requires one subchannel address per ring station. Subchannel addresses are a precious resource and the large number of subchannel addresses required for this gateway configuration is one of its disadvantages. For the host-bound traffic, the gateway 3174 presents the information on the appropriate channel and subchannel and for the ring-bound traffic, the gateway sends the traffic to appropriate ring device with the proper MAC/SAP address.

Remote 3174 gateway via SDLC link to an NCP. In this case the downstream PUs are defined to the host as if they were on a multidrop SDLC line. The NCP executes normal SDLC operations such as polling for the ring stations. The polls are intercepted by the gateway PU, which responds to them on behalf of the downstream stations and passes the traffic to the real downstream PU. If there are 50 ring stations, NCP would actually go through the motions of polling 50 controllers on a multidrop line. This can cause excessive overhead on the NCP. To solve the problem of excessive polling, IBM introduced a group poll feature in SDLC whereby a group poll address can be assigned to a set of ring stations and a single poll can solicit information from the gateway on behalf of any of the ring stations.

Before we leave the PU passthrough gateway, let us briefly discuss the tradeoffs between using a 3174 or an NCP/3745 as a gateway. The 3174 is much smaller in capacity than 3745 and can connect to only one ring at a time. The 3745 can connect with multiple rings and can support a much greater number of ring stations and traffic. The 3745 can also support PU 2.1 on the ring (as of January 1991 IBM has no support for PU 2.1 through the 3174). The 3745, on the other hand, is a much more expansive gateway with elaborate administrative procedures including table definitions in VTAM. Depending on the product release levels of VTAM and NCP, a user may have to go through expensive product upgrades to support the 3745 gateway.

OS/2 EE SNA gateway. The OS/2 EE SNA gateway feature presents a single SDLC PU appearance on behalf of all ring stations. Ring stations are still required to implement a full set of PU/LU functions but are hidden from the host by the gateway. Since VTAM does not know about the LAN PUs, it does not send ACTPU commands to them to establish SSCP-PU session. However, since T2.0 nodes require an ACTPU command to be operational, the OS/2 EE gateway has to perform this function, which is otherwise performed by the SSCP. Thus, one advantage of the OS/2 EE gateway is that it requires only one PU definition in the host even though each LAN station has a PU implemented in it. Even though OS/2 EE supports T2.1 node functions in a nongateway configuration, it does not support T2.1 nodes as DSPUs as of the writing of this book.

IBM products Personal Communications 3270 and the PC 3270 Emulator program and a number of non-IBM gateways also work as single PU gateways. An added advantage with some of the non-IBM gateways is that they do not require a PU function in each LAN station, which can reduce the processing overhead in the station and also provide memory relief in 640K limited PC/DOS stations.

11.11 TOKEN RING GATEWAY SUMMARY

IBM devices and PCs can be connected to the IBM Token Ring using a Token Ring adapter and appropriate software and microcode. For accessing the wide area SNA networks, IBM provides gateways through the NCP, the IBM 3174 establishment controller, and OS/2 EE- and PC/DOS-based products. The gateways fall in two broad categories: PU passthrough and single PU gateways. Selecting a gateway can be a complex decision. Some of the factors influencing the gateway selection include gateway cost, capacity, host overhead to support a LAN configuration, LAN PU types, and the operating system and the PU/LU configuration in the LAN PC. The NCPs can also be used to go from one ring to another using SNA wide area network as a "bridge."

11.12 SNA AND INTERNATIONAL STANDARDS

While SNA may continue to be IBM's preferred architecture for wide area networks, it would also have to coexist with the local area networks and wide area networks conforming to international standards. IBM has emphasized that it views international standards such OSI primarily as gateway architectures and not as network-defining architectures and that IBM fully intends to provide gateways to these standard interfaces. X.25 gateways are provided by IBM through adapter cards and software in its workstations and minis and through NCP Packet Switching Interface (NPSI) and SNA X.25 Interface (XI) products in the front end. For higher layers of OSI, IBM has a number of products, discussed in Chap. 14. IBM also provides interfaces for Manufacturing Automation Protocols (MAP) and Transmission Control

Protocol–Internetwork Protocol (TCP/IP). As the trend continues toward international standards, IBM is expected to provide much more comprehensive gateways or native mode support for these architectures.

11.13   SNA-X.25 INTERFACE

SNA and X.25 are the two most common architectures for wide area networks, with the trend moving increasingly toward X.25. Even though most SNA networks tend to be self-sufficient, they may have to provide connectivity to X.25 interfaces for the following reasons:

1. Intercorporate or interdivisional communication via public networks such as Tymnet, Telenet, or Accunet Packet Service where X.25 is the most common interface. Outside the United States, X.25 is even more common.

2. Connectivity within corporations for subnetworks using non-IBM technologies—AT&T, DEC, HP, and numerous other vendors rely on X.25 as a standard interface.

3. Building multinational networks almost always requires the use of X.25 based public packet networks.

SNA and X.25 are inherently incompatible and an interface between the two requires a protocol conversion or enveloping. To explain the extent of conversion, Fig. 11.16 shows the scope of X.25 architecture. X.25 defines only network access transport protocols. When using X.25, you still require other architecture to cover session (higher-level) protocols, and it is not possible to replace the lower three layers of SNA by X.25 on a one-to-one basis. The implications of each X.25 layer are as follows:

1. *Physical control layer:*   This layer defines the interface to the physical medium including the modem (DSU) interface and has no conversion requirements, i.e., the same physical layer interfaces can be used in X.25 and SNA. IBM products also provide support for the CCITT X.21 interface.

2. *Link layer:*   In X.25 the link layer protocols are defined by link access procedure balanced (LAPB). The SDLC protocol is replaced by LAPB at level 2. In some circumstances SDLC commands have to be transported through the X.25 network. Since SDLC commands have the same appearance as the LAPB commands, they have to be transmitted using special packets created just for this purpose. The fact that these packets carry SDLC control information is transparent to X.25.

3. *Packet layer:*   These protocols define maximum packet size, desti-

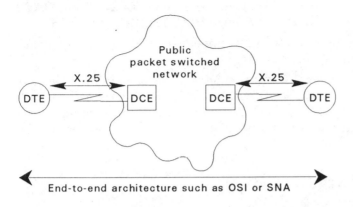

End-to-end architecture such as OSI or SNA

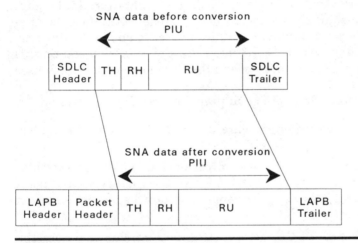

Figure 11.16 SNA to X.25 data mapping.

nation address, packet level flow control, etc. and procedures for establishing and terminating end-to-end connections. These protocols do not replace SNA path control or higher levels. While a packet header must follow the LAPB header, the remaining SNA headers—TH, RH, and FMH, if any—must be preserved. This is shown in Fig. 11.16, and this process is also referred to as protocol enveloping rather than as conversion.

Some of the specific differences between SNA and X.25 include:

1. SNA is not a packet architecture in the sense that it has no exact equivalent of X.25 packets, packet level sequencing, flow control, or end-to-end packet level assurance.

2. SNA and X.25 have different header structures: X.25 has LAPB and packet headers, and SNA has SDLC, TH, RH, and FMH.

3. SNA is a complete end-to-end architecture; X.25 is only the transport or the lowest three layers.

4. SNA and X.25 have different command structures. In SNA we have ACTPU, ACTLU, INITS, BIND, etc. In X.25 we have call request, call clear, etc. There is no X.25 equivalent for SNA session level flow control, responses, and other protocols such as brackets, chaining, etc.

11.14 SNA TO X.25 CONVERSION OPTIONS

As shown in Fig. 11.17, protocol conversion is needed at each DTE end. [For readers not familiar with X.25, DTE (data terminal equipment) is any machine that connects to an X.25 network; it can be anything from a simple terminal to a minicomputer to an IBM mainframe with a front end processor. DCE (data circuit termination equipment) is not a modem but a network node in the X.25 network to which user DTEs are connected.]

We have the following options in providing protocol conversion:

1. An X.25 adapter card or software in the DTE provides the conversion.

2. An external protocol converter, a packet assembler disassembler (PAD) is used. PADs are available for all terminal types and hosts in various capacities and price ranges and provide the best solution for a number of users.

3. The network node, DCE, accepts SNA data stream and does the protocol conversion into X.25 internally. In this case, the network is, in effect, appearing as an SNA network to the DTE. In the

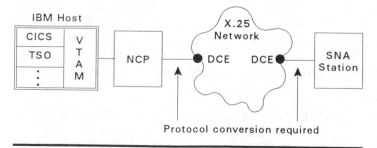

Figure 11.17   SNA to X.25 interface.

United States there are regulatory constraints on the extent of conversions that can be performed by various network providers (non-Bell corporations such as Tymnet and Telenet have more flexibility).

Our focus in the remainder of this section is on the IBM solution for SNA-X.25 interface. IBM has an extensive list of X.25 adapters for devices such as the IBM 3174, PCs (PS/2), AS/400, and S/3X machines. On the host end of the network we have the NCP Packet Switching Interface (NPSI) that can be installed in the IBM front end processor.

11.15   NCP PACKET SWITCHING INTERFACE (NPSI)

NPSI is the primary IBM product for connecting IBM SNA hosts with the X.25 networks. It is an extra cost product installed in the IBM front end processor in addition to the NCP. NPSI accepts X.25 data streams and converts them into SNA data streams for processing by NCP, VTAM, and host subsystems. The nature of conversion depends on the remote device (DTE) where the traffic originated and the type of PAD used by the device. NPSI support is divided into various categories, where each category is assigned a virtual circuit type. The virtual circuit types as defined here are IBM terminology and do not have any meaning under CCITT. Virtual circuits (VCs) defined by NPSI include Types 0, 2, 3, 4, and 5.

Virtual circuit Type 0. This virtual circuit type designation is used when the remote DTE is a true X.25 DTE and no PAD control is involved. Figure 11.18 shows such a configuration. In this case NPSI also provides PU/LU emulation on behalf of the X.25 DTE. SSCP-PU,

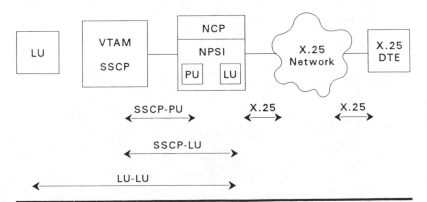

Figure 11.18   NPSI virtual circuit Type 0 - X.25 DTE.

SSCP-LU, and LU-LU sessions are with the emulated PU and LU. NPSI emulates a PU Type 1 and LU Type 1 as implemented in the now obsolete IBM 3767 terminal.

Virtual circuit Type 1.   No such virtual circuit type is defined by NPSI.

Virtual circuit Type 2.   This refers to SNA DTEs using the older IBM adapter for X.25 called the Network Interface Adapter (NIA). This has been replaced by virtual circuit Type 3, which is discussed in more detail.

Virtual circuit Type 3.   This circuit type is used to describe a remote SNA DTE, where the remote SNA DTE can be another front end processor running with NCP and NPSI or an SNA station using a PAD that is compatible with IBM PAD or adapter using qualified logical link control (QLLC). Figure 11.19 shows a configuration defined as *virtual circuit Type 3* to NPSI. In this case the SNA sessions are with the true SNA DTEs and NPSI provides only data transformations.

QLLC protocol is used to transport SDLC commands and responses across the X.25 transport. SDLC commands and responses are carried in special qualified packets as shown in Fig. 11.20.

Steps 2, 3, and 4 show QLLC commands where normally SDLC unnumbered frames would have been exchanged in a pure SNA network. QLLC_SM replaces a SNRM, QLLC_UA replaces UA and QLLC_RR replaces RR. These qualified packets are intercepted and processed by the IBM compatible PAD at the remote DTE to perform the equivalent SDLC function.

Following the packet header, the first character in the data field

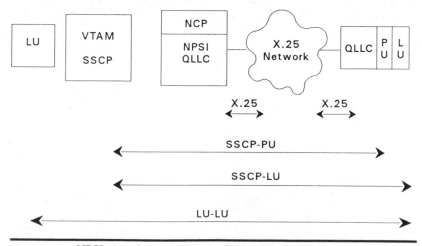

Figure 11.19   NPSI virtual circuit Type 3—SNA DTE (QLLC).

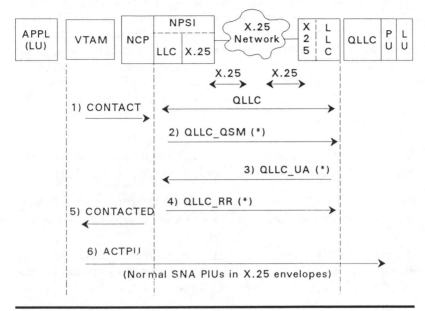

Figure 11.20 QLLC exchange for a PVC [(*) qualified packets containing SDLC control information].

contains the value from the address field in the SDLC header for the destination link station. The following byte contains the control byte value for the remote DTE. The following values are defined for the control field:

```
QSM      X'93'    QRD      X'53'
QDISC    X'53'    QUA      X'73
QXID     X'BF'    QDM      X'1F'
QTEST    X'F3'    QFRMR    X'97'
QRR      X'F1'
```

It should be apparent from the table that the QLLC control fields are selected SDLC commands and responses (e.g., QSM is for Set Mode, QDISC for DISC, etc.) and exist solely for the purpose of transporting these SDLC commands across an X.25 network as shown in Fig. 11.20.

Virtual circuit Type 4. IBM uses this circuit type to describe DTEs requiring handling of higher layers in the host and uses this virtual circuit type for supporting levels 4 and 5 of OSI. VC 4 is also used for BSC or other stations that do not conform to any other circuit defined by NPSI.

With VC 4, the user must write an application in the host to handle the details of the X.25 protocol instead of NPSI. This application is called the Communication and Transport Control Program (CTCP). This is a VTAM application and is written in the assembler language using VTAM application programming interface. The CTCP represents the host LU and is responsible for dispatching traffic to other host subsystems. NPSI component to support this configuration is also known as the General Access to X.25 Transport Extension (GATE).

For users with BSC stations, the use of virtual circuit Type 4 with CTCP is not an attractive solution due to its complexity. For them, a host PAD or an AT&T/NCR Comten NCP with X.25 support may be more appropriate.

Virtual circuit Type 5.   This option is used when defining remote asynchronous devices. There are two options within this virtual circuit type:

1. *Integrated PAD:*   This option is used when the remote DTE is supported via a PAD compatible with CCITT X.3, X.28, and X.29 specification.

2. *Transparent PAD:*   This option is used when the PAD does not conform to the CCITT specification. In this case the user has to provide a CTCP as with virtual circuit Type 4.

Figure 11.21 shows virtual circuit Type 5 support. As shown in the figure, the PU and LU support for the asynchronous DTE is simulated by NPSI. In addition, PAD control can be exercised by NPSI using X.29 procedures.

In summary, the NPSI support is divided into various categories depending on the remote DTE type. For SNA, X.25, or Asynchronous DTE, NPSI can provide a complete interface. For other DTEs, a host

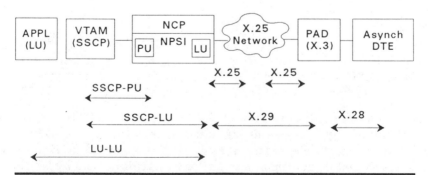

Figure 11.21   NPSI virtual circuit Type 5—asynchronous DTE.

application is needed to handle the X.25 details, and for such configurations NPSI may not be the best solution.

11.16 SNA X.25 INTERFACE (XI)

This IBM product, also used with NCP in the IBM front end processors, provides a different function than NPSI. As shown in Fig. 11.22 the SNA XI product enables the IBM front end processor to act as an X.25 DCE rather than an X.25 DTE as with the NPSI product. The transport network is still SNA. The XI product is not intended to build X.25 transport networks using IBM front ends. Its use is appropriate where a user has an SNA network in place but needs to provide X.25 access on an exception basis. XI can provide synchronous support for asynchronous devices attached to the network via X.25 PADs, or for devices that are inherently X.25.

The data is routed between XI nodes using SNA protocols. Intermediate NCP nodes through which XI data pass do not require XI products if they do not have any X.25 DTEs attached to them.

Perhaps, one application of XI would be attractive to users that have multivendor networks using both SNA and X.25 DTEs. Prior to XI, such a user would use SNA nodes and network to support SNA DTEs and a separate, probably a shared public, X.25 network for the X.25 DTEs.

Figure 11.22 shows such a network covering the United States and Europe. In this case, we assume that the user has SNA and non-IBM (DEC, HP, SUN, etc.) processors in New York and a set of users in London. SNA users are provided access to the network via a remote NCP in London using an extensive private line SNA backbone.

However, non-IBM users in the same building need an X.25 transport to reach New York and are, therefore, provided a separate X.25 access through a public packet switched data network (PPSDN). Due to protocol incompatibilities, customers are forced to use and pay for public network usage even though they already have a private (paid for) SNA network covering the very same locations.

The XI product can eliminate the need for a separate X.25 transport. With XI in the front end, in addition to the NCP and NPSI, X.25 DTEs in London can be directly connected to the existing SNA network as shown by dotted lines. Of course, we must also have a front end with NPSI and XI at the destination end, New York, to deliver the X.25 data to the destination DTE, again along the dotted lines in Fig. 11.22.

Another important characteristic of XI is that it resides in a private network and, therefore, provides no X.75 interface as a gateway be-

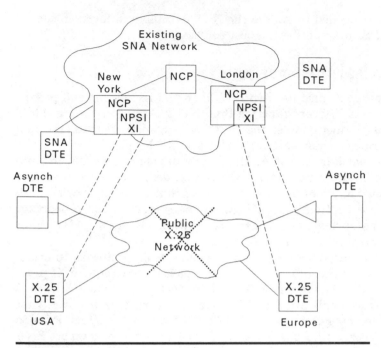

Figure 11.22   SNA X.25 interface (XI).

tween shared public networks (even though XI nodes use X.75-like protocols to communicate with each other). Since the CCITT does not permit data network identification codes (DNICs) for private networks, XI uses the Extended Addressing Facility of the 1984 recommendation to implement its gateway to other private X.25 networks. IBM also provides a network management application, Network Supervisory Function (NSF), that runs in the host with NetView and VTAM to monitor and control XI attached resources. NSF requires network management facility (NMF) in the XI product.

11.17   SUMMARY

We looked at three types of gateways in this chapter. The first, SNI, allows communications between LUs residing in independent SNA networks. Except for the gateway VTAM and the gateway NCP, the rest of the nodes are unaware of the fact that they are in a multinetwork environment. The burden of implementation details falls on the gateway nodes.

For sessions between Token Ring LUs and the wide area SNA LUs, gateways can be provided via 3174 controller, the front end processor, OS/2EE, or PC/DOS. The overriding factor in selecting a gateway is the capacity and cost—the FEP can handle a far greater number of ring devices and traffic volume but is also much more expensive. With NCP release 4.3 and 5.2, SNA subarea network can also be used as a bridge between Token Rings. The NCP also provides support for PU 2.1 (see Chap. 12), which is not available through the 3174 controller.

Finally we looked at the IBM NPSI and XI products. NPSI allows an IBM front end with NCP to connect to an X.25 network while acting as an X.25 DTE. The XI product allows a front end with NCP and NPSI to appear as an X.25 DCE, thereby permitting X.25 DTEs to communicate with each other over an SNA transport.

SNA Distributed Processing: LU 6.2 and PU 2.1

12.1 INTRODUCTION

One of the common criticisms of SNA in the early years was its host orientation with minimal provisions for distributed applications in the network. After some trial and error, IBM has settled on LU 6.2, also known as Advanced Program to Program Communications (APPC), as the architecture for generalized application-to-application communications. APPC architecture was announced in 1984 and is not tied into SNA transport. In addition to the SNA path control network, LU 6.2 can use IBM Token Ring, CSMA/CD, X.25, or any other transport for that matter. In addition, to facilitate host-independent sessions, IBM introduced PU 2.1, also known as Low Entry Networking (LEN) in 1985. PU 2.1, too, is discussed later in this chapter.

A third term, Advanced Peer to Peer Networking (APPN), is also mentioned often when discussing SNA distributed processing. APPN, an enhancement of LEN, was devised by IBM as a prototype architecture for small networks without any mainframes. After much procrastination, IBM finally designated APPN a part of SNA in 1991. APPN incorporates a number of features that are expected to impact significantly the future evolution of SNA. We also discuss APPN later in this chapter.

When discussing distributed processing under SNA we have to deal with two distinct aspects of the APPC environment. The first aspect deals with the internal architecture of the LU and its supporting node (PU). The second aspect deals with the transaction programs and their interface with the LU 6.2. In this chapter we discuss only the internal architecture of the LU 6.2 and the associated PU considerations. Transaction programs are discussed in Chap. 13.

12.2 DISTRIBUTED PROCESSING: TERMS AND CONCEPTS

To understand the scope and limitations of LU 6.2 or APPC, we need to understand the nature of distributed applications. There are no generally accepted definitions of some of the terms used in the following. The term *distributed processing* itself is too broad and can imply a wide range of requirements. For our discussions we would like to divide it into at least two categories: remote processing and cooperative processing. For both categories we also need to define the term *unit of work*.

12.2.1 Unit of Work

A unit of work can mean different things for different applications. In transaction processing parlance, a single transaction can equate to a complete unit of work (and often does) but does not have to. A transaction may consist of multiple units of work. A *unit of work* is an arbitrary amount of processing requested by one program from another program. Exactly what is accomplished by a unit of work, too, is application defined. If the unit of work involves altering data in tables or records on files or databases, then the work unit integrity would also involve functions such as commitment control, recovery, and resynchronization.

By *commitment control* we mean a mechanism whereby a target program can assure the requester that all changes to records have been completed successfully (data have been "safe-stored"). If the unit of work could not be completed, the program must "back out" partial changes to wipe out partial effects of a unit of work—in effect, that unit of work was never processed. A more serious system or application failure can affect multiple records including some from earlier work units, causing the integrity of multiple records to be questionable. In such cases recovery would involve resynchronizing to an earlier work unit by backing out multiple database changes until a point is reached where complete integrity of data is assured. Of course, transactions or units of work that are backed out are lost and would have to be reentered and reprocessed.

12.2.2 Remote Unit of Work

In this case one processing location requests some processing to be done at another (remote or target) site. The remote site may be geographically remote or could be within the same data center or could be another program on the same processor. What constitutes a remote program is determined by the local operating system and teleprocessing support system such as VTAM, CICS, and LU 6.2, etc. and may vary from vendor to vendor. One of the benefits of LU 6.2 is that it provides a uniform view of remote programs and a uniform way of communicating with them.

In any case, with a remote unit of work, as we define it here, all record processing and updates are done at the remote site, which is also responsible for commitment control and recovery. No file or data base updates are done at the requesting site.

An example of remote unit of work is shown in Fig. 12.1. A customer wishes to buy an air conditioner and charge the amount to a credit card. The sales clerk in the store enters information associated with the transaction at the local point-of-sale terminal. The transaction is routed by the store system to a headquarters system where all customer credit records are located. The headquarters system checks the purchase amount against credit available to the customer. If the purchase price is less than the available credit, the host application subtracts the purchase amount from the available credit and saves the result as the new amount of credit available. In addition, the application also sends back an OK for the sale to the point-of-sale system in the store so that the sales clerk can go ahead with the sale.

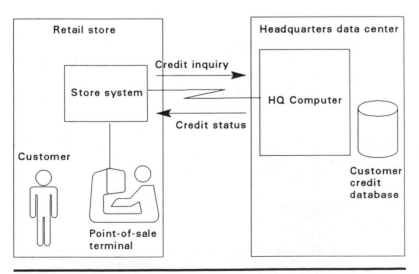

Figure 12.1   Remote unit of work.

The unit of work in the foregoing example was updating available customer credit amount and authorizing the credit card sale. All data updates were done at the target site and none at the source or requesting site. If there were any failure, the recovery would involve processing at the target site only.

12.2.3 Distributed Transaction Processing

We use the term *distributed transaction* to imply cooperative processing among multiple processes. Figure 12.2 illustrates an automated business system that ties together sales orders, manufacturing, and purchasing using distributed transaction processing. A salesperson receives an order for 1000 electrical motors and enters the order from a terminal connected to the order processing computer in Los Angeles. The system is not to confirm the order unless it is assured that the order can be fulfilled by the date requested. If the inventory on hand is insufficient to fulfill the order, the host computer in Los Angeles sends a request, in real time, to the manufacturing system in Chicago to schedule production of additional motors. The computer in Chicago checks the parts inventory and finds that they are short of coils for the motors and sends a transaction to the New York host for the purchasing department to place an order for the required number of coils. The New York host confirms to the Chicago host that the requisite coils are available. The manufacturing host in Chicago confirms to the Los Angeles host that the additional motors can be manufactured. The Los Angeles host at this time sends back a message to the person who entered the order, confirming the order.

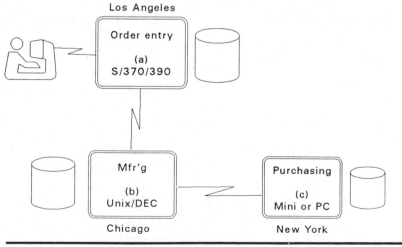

Figure 12.2   Distributed transaction processing (cooperative processing).

In this case three host machines were involved in processing the transaction: an IBM 370 system in Los Angeles, a DEC machine in Chicago, and an IBM AS/400 in New York. Files were updated in all three hosts to process the transaction. If the transaction fails in any of the three computers, the other computers would have to reset any changes to files associated with the transaction. Since several persons can be entering orders, there can be multiple concurrent transactions between the machines at any given time. Each machine must have the ability of differentiating among these transactions and the resources associated with each.

As can be seen, distributed transaction processing is much more complex than a remote unit of work. IBM intends that LU 6.2 protocols should be suitable for all of the foregoing requirements.

12.3 EVOLUTION OF DISTRIBUTED PROCESSING UNDER SNA

The ability to distribute work over multiple hosts predates SNA in the form of systems such as Network Job Entry where a job could be dispatched to one of several hosts. But it was a simple capability, basically, to route jobs as remote work units with no distributed transaction processing. In addition, there also existed systems that used custom made, one-of-a-kind software for distributed transaction processing—in effect, using a customer-defined architecture.

With the establishment of SNA, the Logical Units were supposed to support distributed processing, but in reality none could in the early years. LU Type 2 was suitable for interactive (display station) sessions and LU Types 1 and 3 for batch-type sessions. For applications in which none of the foregoing was suitable, LU Type 0 was provided as an open-ended LU whereby a product could define any LU protocol subset or superset. It was LU Type 0 that was used in early distributed applications such as the IBM 4700 for the banking industry and the IBM 8100 as a general-purpose distributed node. Early releases of NetView and IBM File Transfer Program (FTP) also used LU Type 0.

The first formally architected LU for program-to-program communications was LU Type 6. The architecture of LU Type 6 was heavily constrained by VTAM, which required that the Primary LU (PLU) be in the host and that only the PLU could support multiple concurrent sessions. The only implementation of LU Type 6 was in the CICS product as the Inter System Communications (ISC) feature.

In order to bring distributed transaction support under the other major host transaction processing system, IMS/DC, IBM had to modify LU Type 6 extensively and release it as LU Type 6.1. Even though LU 6.1 was formally architected, CICS and IMS implementations intro-

duced some mutual incompatibilities. CICS and IMS, both host resident, were the only two products in which IBM implemented LU 6.1.

The next objective for IBM was to allow distributed processing capability irrespective of whether an application ran in the host or in a
network application node (mini, PC, or communications controllers
such as IBM 3174). It turned out that LU 6.1 was not suitable for such
broad requirements.

By this time IBM had gained substantial experience in designing
protocols for distributed systems. To further enhance LU 6.1, IBM
came up with the following set of broad objectives for the new LU
architecture:

1. The architecture should be easy to implement in the mainframe,
   minicomputer, or personal computer. The required functions
   should not overwhelm a PC and yet must include sufficient functions to support complex mainframe-based transactions.

   To satisfy both ends of the spectrum, the architecture could be a
   set of minimal required functions with additional optional functions that may be implemented only if necessary for an application,
   such as in the mainframe (this decision to break up LU functions
   into required and optional sets would later cause compatibility concerns among different implementations of LU 6.2).

2. Since the future terminals would be intelligent work stations, the
   new LU could possibly be the only LU type in SNA.

3. As possibly the *only* LU type in the future, the architecture must
   also be suitable for interactive or batch processing.

With these requirements in mind, LU 6.2 was invented to allow generalized communications between programs running on different machines even while using different languages and operating systems. LU
6.2 is evolutionary with respect to LU 6.1 only in a functional sense. As
a protocol set, it is incompatible with LU 6.1, and a totally new LU type.
Even though early applications of LU 6.2 have been in the areas of file
transfers and message and software distribution, it is very much intended to support real-time distributed transaction processing.

12.4 OVERVIEW OF APPC AND LEN

Figure 12.3 shows an architectural view of distributed processing in
SNA. A distributed application program is supported by four
architected entities: the application, the LU, the PU, and the transport. This section introduces distributed aspects of each, except the applications that are discussed in the next chapter.

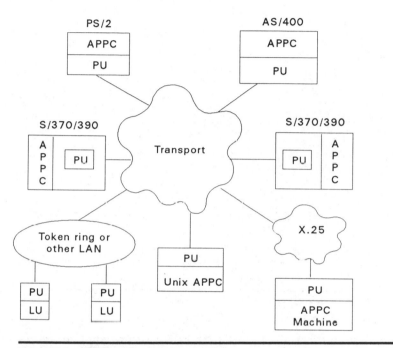

Figure 12.3 APPC environment—overview.

12.4.1 LU 6.2 Overview

Since LU 6.2 is one of the SNA NAU types, its functions are defined by the upper three layers of SNA (TC, DFC, and NAU Services). By definition, the users of LU 6.2 are transaction programs (LU 6.2 has no architected interface to a human operator). A single LU 6.2 can support multiple transaction programs (TPs) as shown in Fig. 12.4. Prior to LU 6.2, the SNA boundary was at the LU itself, and entities such as the transaction programs, called the end users, were outside the architected set. With LU 6.2, the architecture boundary has been extended to include the interface between transaction programs (end user) and the LU. This interface, called the LU 6.2 application program interface (API), is an architected SNA interface.

Sessions and conversations. An LU 6.2 enables communications between application programs, therefore, the name Advanced Program

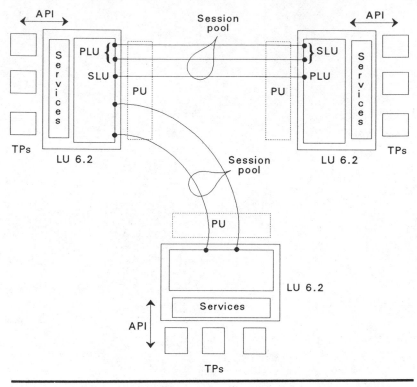

Figure 12.4 LU 6.2 overview (TP = transaction program).

to Program Communications (APPC). To differentiate application-to-application communications from LU-LU sessions, application-to-application exchanges are called *conversations*. A conversation is always associated with an underlying LU-LU session. An LU 6.2 can bind multiple sessions with other LUs and associate them with conversations as conversations are established (or "allocated" in LU 6.2 terminology). A session is exclusively allocated to only one conversation at a time. Once a conversation is over, the session becomes free and can be used for a different conversation. Multiple sessions between the same pair of LUs are also called parallel sessions.

LU services. The services provided by LU 6.2 are defined in the NAU Services layer. Its two sublayers—presentation and transaction services—include most of the new functions architected for LU 6.2. The sublayer transaction services did not even exist before LU 6.2.

SLU/PLU roles. In terms of session roles, we still have the Primary and Secondary LUs during LU-LU sessions, but LU 6.2 does not require that the Primary must reside in the host nor does it restrict the Secondary to a single LU-LU session at any given time. Specifically,

1. PLU can reside in a host or a peripheral node.
2. Even an SLU, host or peripheral node resident, can support multiple and parallel sessions.

In other words, PLU and SLU are finally peers.

Session pools and conversations. As stated earlier, in order to support multiple concurrent conversations, LU 6.2 needs multiple sessions. For multithreading transaction programs, one conversation and, therefore, one session, is required per thread. As shown in Fig. 12.4, these sessions are treated by the LU as a pool of serially reusable resources, i.e., a session is taken from the pool when needed and is returned to the pool when the conversation using the session ends.

The session pool can additionally be partitioned by partner LU name, session mode (bind image and class of service). The transaction programs can optionally specify session characteristics for their conversations or let LU 6.2 pick a session using default procedures. One of the design issues can be the timing of session initiation: Should you initiate sessions one at a time as needed or bind them all at startup and use them as needed? The answer is somewhat product dependent. For example, in a mainframe environment, VTAM has a very high overhead associated with starting new sessions compared with maintaining dormant sessions. In this environment it makes sense to bind sessions at startup rather than on an as-needed basis.

In addition, for each session we also have to define one of the two session partners as a contention winner. Contention winners are assigned to resolve deadlocks when both LUs try to allocate the same session for different conversations giving rise to a contention state. When contention occurs, session allocation succeeds for the designated winner and fails for the contention loser. The assignment of contention winner and loser is also called session polarity. The polarity of each session is defined at the bind time.

Change number of sessions (CNOS). Occasionally it is necessary for two LUs to change the size of the session pool between them. For this purpose LU 6.2 provides a control operator verb called change number of sessions (CNOS). CNOS is an optional LU 6.2 facility but is required for LUs implementing parallel sessions. Through parameters specified on the CNOS verb, a pair of LUs can increase or decrease the size of the session pool. The CNOS command itself also flows on an LU-LU session, and there must be a free session in the pool for a

CNOS to be exchanged. To ensure that such a free session is always available, it is recommended that two LUs bind at least one session using the bind image SNASVCMG (for SNA Service Manager) and not allow any user transaction programs to use this session for any conversations.

Using a CNOS verb, the LUs can change the number of sessions per mode name or the number of contention winners, or reset all sessions within a mode to zero.

LU bind image. LU 6.2 also has an impact on the bind image. With LU 6.2 we have an extended bind image to allow some of the newer features such as fully qualified names of the LUs, session ID, mode name, etc. Complete format of the bind image is shown in Appendix B. Some of the fields of particular relevance to LU 6.2 are pointed out in the following sections.

LU 6.2 bind image must indicate a negotiable bind in byte 1 to indicate that PLU/SLU roles are negotiable. The LU issuing the BIND command becomes the PLU. The FM profile number for LU 6.2 is 19, and the TS profile number is 7. Session contention winner is defined in byte 7 and adaptive pacing support is indicated in byte 9. Synchronization level support is defined in byte 24. Another unique feature of the LU 6.2 bind image is the use of structured data fields for defining such items as SLU name, SLU network ID, and the mode name.

12.4.2   PU Type Implications for LU 6.2

Each LU 6.2 is supported by a PU. It is the underlying PU that provides the directory services for local addressing (session IDs) and determines session connectivity options for the LU 6.2. In discussing connectivity options we would use the term *peripheral LU* for LUs that are not host resident. As stated earlier, in pre-LU 6.2 SNA, PLUs could only be host resident. With LU 6.2, SNA permits the peripheral LUs to be PLUs but only if the LU resides in a T2.1 node. The node type also determines whether a peripheral LU can support multiple sessions or have sessions with other peripheral LUs. T2.0 nodes represent the old SNA architecture and provide only SLU support. T2.1 nodes provide both PLU support and host-independent sessions. PU implications are discussed in more detail in Sec. 12.9. The interface between LU 6.2 and its controlling PU is product defined. A transaction program has no need to communicate with the PU or to invoke any of its functions. A user administers and controls the PU functions through product-defined interfaces.

12.4.3 LU 6.2 Transport Considerations

LU 6.2 does not require any particular transport type. The transport mechanism used is transparent to LU 6.2 and is product defined. Two of the most common transport implementations are the SNA Path Control and the IBM Token Ring. LU sessions can use any transport so long as nodes for both session partners support the transport. Transport protocols are not discussed in this chapter.

In the following sections we discuss the LU 6.2 internal architecture, PU 2.1 functions, and the Advanced Peer to Peer Networking (APPN). Following that we discuss the current state of VTAM/NCP support for APPC/LEN.

12.5 LU 6.2 LAYERS AND SERVICES

Figure 12.5 shows the layer structure for LU 6.2. The lower two layers, transmission control and data flow control, define the half session protocols. The upper layers, presentation services and transaction services, define the NAU services or, in this specific case, the LU services.

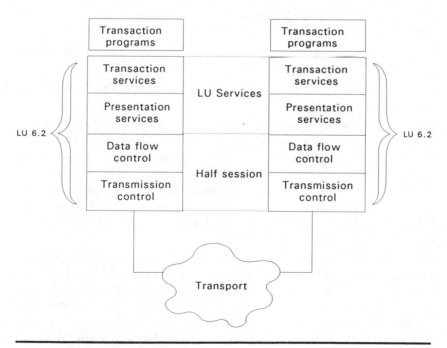

Figure 12.5 LU 6.2 layer structure.

12.6 LU 6.2 HALF SESSION

Half session protocols are defined by function management (FM) and transmission services (TS) profiles in the bind image as introduced earlier in Sec. 6.7. Half session protocols are transparent to the transaction programs, and their knowledge is not important to someone interested only in LU 6.2 transaction programs.

12.6.1 LU 6.2 FM PROFILE

The FM profile number for LU 6.2 is 19 and it allows the following functions:

Chaining: Both PLU and SLU can support chaining. The relationship between chain elements and transaction program data units is not defined by the architecture and varies from product to product.

Session request/response mode: Exception and definite responses are permitted. Both PLU and SLU use immediate request and immediate response mode. Immediate request mode means that no more than one definite response chain can be outstanding at any given time. The sender of a definite response chain would wait until a response has been received before sending any additional chains. The receiver of the chain, if in the immediate response mode, must send responses to the requests in the same order in which requests were received.

Data compression is not used (this capability is typically associated with RJE-type stations in a non-LU 6.2 environment).

Bracket protocols: Bracket usage is supported and required for LU 6.2 sessions.

In a broader SNA context an "in-bracket" state consists of one or more data chains exchanged between two half sessions while in a state bound by a begin bracket and an end bracket. The data exchanged during an in-bracket state are in some way meaningful to the LUs as a work unit. SNA does not define what a work unit is. For LU 6.2, an in-bracket state (or work unit) equates to a single conversation; i.e., begin bracket initiates a conversation and end bracket terminates a conversation.

The end bracket indicator (EBI) in the RH is not used for LU 6.2 and has been replaced by a new bit called conditional end bracket indicator (CEBI). PLU or SLU may send CEBI to terminate a conversation. Both PLU and SLU are authorized to initiate or terminate brackets. The begin bracket indicator (BBI) is used on the first element of the first chain and CEBI is used on the last element of the last chain. BBI and CEBI may both be set on the same chain or on the only element of a chain.

Bind parameters specify one of the two half sessions as the first speaker (or contention winner—see Sec. 12.4.1) and the other as the bidder. The first speaker can initiate a bracket state without requesting permission from the bidder, whereas the bidder must obtain permission from the first speaker to initiate a bracket. The bidder sends a bid simply by sending a request chain with BBI bit set to 1. The first speaker can accept the bid by sending a positive response to the bid or decline it by sending an exception response. When the first speaker declines a bid, it may indicate, through a sense code in the RU, that it would subsequently send a ready to receive (RTR) when it is ready to accept the bid. Not all first speakers support RTR. Whenever a bracket state terminates, the session returns to a contention state, i.e., either LU can initiate a new bracket.

In addition to the value of the CEBI bit, bracket termination is also determined by the setting of DR and ER bits in the RH. If the CEBI request is a definite response request with DR2 or DR1 and DR2 both set, the bracket termination is conditional and terminates only if a positive response is received but continues if an exception response is received.

A CEBI request with DR1 or ER is an unconditional termination of the bracket state. With ER set, the bracket state terminates with the sending of the RU and with DR1 the state is terminated on receiving a response, positive or exception, to the CEBI request. HDX/FF protocol is used for normal flow RUs within a bracket state. The LU initiating the bracket has the right to send data initially. When a sending LU has completed its data transfer, it places the partner half session in a send mode by setting the change direction indicator (CDI) to 1 in the RH on the last element of a chain.

Recovery is symmetric, i.e., the sender of an exception response is responsible for recovery irrespective of whether it is a PLU or SLU.

Function management headers usage.   FMHs 5, 7, and 12 are supported by LU 6.2. The detailed layout of LU 6.2 FMHs is shown in Appendix D.

FMH 5:   This header is also known as the attach header because it is used to "attach" a remote transaction, i.e., allocate a conversation. FMH 5 is used in conjunction with the BBI bit in the RH. The FMH itself contains information such as destination transaction program and LU name, etc.

FMH 7:   FMH 7 is also known as error FMH since it is used when an LU wants to terminate a chain due to some error condition. FMH 7 can occur in the middle of a chain and terminates the chain. The error condition can be an event recognized by the transaction program or an event discovered by the LU directly. FMH 7 also carries sense data in it.

FMH 12:   Also known as the security header, it is used to transmit enciphered data for LU-LU session password verification. The support for FMH 12 is optional under LU 6.2; when supported, it follows a successful BIND.

DFC requests (commands).   The following DFC requests are supported by LU 6.2 sessions:

Bracket initiation stopped (BIS): BIS is sent by a half session to indicate that it would not attempt to begin any more brackets on that session. BIS is normally used during a session termination phase and is sent optionally before an sending an UNBIND. The UNBIND is sent after a response to BIS has been received.

LUSTAT: In pre-APPC environment LUSTAT was used primarily to report whether an LU was available or not or any change in its status. With LU 6.2, LUSTAT is used during multiple conditions. It carries up to 4 bytes of status information in the RU and the only status value allowed for LU 6.2 in LUSTAT is X'0006', which is also known as a null RU and is essentially a no-op condition. The null LUSTAT is used by LU 6.2 when it is necessary for the LU to send some control information through the RH but there is no RU to follow the RH. Various conditions reported thus through LUSTAT are described in the following paragraphs. The conventions used in the following description are:

BBI: begin bracket indicator
CDI: change direction indicator
CEBI: conditional end bracket indicator
RQD1: definite response 1 (DR1) request
RQD2: definite response 2 (DR2) request
RQE1: exception response with DR1
RQE2: exception response with DR2

The meaning of LUSTAT with a sense code of X'0006' is interpreted in conjunction with other bits in the RH as follows:

1. (RQD1, BBI): The sending half session is bidding to begin a bracket without sending any data.

2. (RQE2,CDI): The sending half session transfers permission to send to the other half session to enable the other half session to do confirm processing and send a confirmation on the next request. Reply

to a confirm means that the transaction program connected to the other half session has received and processed the RU data successfully. (Confirm processing is done normally to synchronize completion of a work unit between distributed transaction programs.)

3. (RQD2,CDI): Same as in step 2 except that the completion of the confirm will be indicated by receipt of a positive response, DR2; i.e., this is definite response LUSTAT whereas the previous one was an exception response.

4. (RQE1,CDI): The sending half session transfers permission to send to its partner half session without requesting a confirmation. The intent here is to simply send a CDI without sending any accompanying user data in the RU.

5. (RQD2,CEBI): Same as in step 3 with the addition that the bracket state (conversation) will be terminated when a positive response is received.

6. (RQE1,CEBI): Terminates the bracket state unconditionally and puts the session back in a contention state.

Other DFC commands are:

Ready to receive (RTR): This is sent by a half session that had earlier rejected a begin bracket or a bid from its session partner. By sending RTR, the half session is telling its partner that it may now initiate a BBI.

SIGNAL: This expedited flow request is used by a half session in a receive state during a HDX/FF session (LU 6.2 sessions are always HDX within a bracket state) to request permission to send normal flow RUs. The target of SIGNAL may withhold permission or grant it by sending a CDI.

12.6.2 LU 6.2 TS Profile

TS profile 7 is used for LU 6.2, which provides the following functions:

Pacing: Both Primary-to-Secondary and Secondary-to-Primary normal flows can be paced.

Sequence numbers are used on the normal flows.

SNA commands SDT, CLEAR, RQR, and STSN are not supported.

Cryptography verification (CRV) is used when session level cryptography is selected (via a BIND parameter).

Additionally, the TS usage subfields in the BIND can define the following values:

Pacing windows for both PLU-to-SLU and SLU-to-PLU flows

Maximum RU sizes on the normal flows (to determine maximum chain element size) for PLU and SLU

12.6.3 Half Session Summary

Half session protocols define session flow control and error recovery protocols. With the exception of CEBI, the LU 6.2 differs from other LUs only in the protocol subset that it implements—the meaning of the specific protocols does not change for LU 6.2. These protocols are not visible to transaction programs, though in many cases they are invoked due to a higher-level request by a transaction program. The supported half session protocols are identified in the bind image. The interface between half session and the path control and PU functions is implementation defined.

12.7 LU SERVICES

LU services are provided by the upper layers and consist of presentation services and transaction services.

12.7.1 Presentation Services (PS)

Presentation services define the interface between LU 6.2 and the transaction program (TP) in the form of the LU 6.2 Application Program Interface (API), and define protocols for program-to-program communications. Transaction programs make their requests to LU 6.2 through program calls to PS. PS are responsible for loading, calling, and managing transaction programs and for controlling conversations between TPs.

As TPs make API calls, PS are responsible for verifying conversation state (send/receive, etc.), enforcing correct usage of API verb parameters, and providing the actual service requested in the verb. TPs can use basic or mapped conversations to invoke LU 6.2 services (conversation types are discussed in more detail in the next chapter). PS also define the meaning of mapped and basic conversations and LU 6.2 base (required) and optional functions. When TPs make requests for data transfers, PS are also responsible for buffering data into blocks for ensuring efficient transmission by half session.

12.7.2 Transaction Services

Transaction Services can be broken into two categories:

Common services. This category of services is common to all SNA NAUs and deals with services required to control and manage the operation of the network. These services are part of LU to SSCP (or T2.1 node control point) sessions and do not use LU-LU sessions or TP conversations. These services deal with three types of functions: configuration services, session services, and management services.

Configuration services apply only to SSCP-PU sessions. Session services, in association with LU resource manager and LU network services, provide functions in support of session initiation and termination functions. Management services apply to communication network management application (CNMA) such as NetView and, again, do not apply to normal transaction programs. In any case, this whole set of services is transparent to transaction programs.

Service transaction programs. This second category of transaction services, provided by entities called service transaction programs (STPs), is quite relevant to other transaction programs (user applications). From a user's point of view, LU 6.2 transaction programs are divided into two categories: application transaction programs (ATPs), which are the normal transaction programs and are discussed in the next chapter, and the STPs discussed here:

As shown in Fig. 12.6, STPs are transaction programs built as an integral part of the LU 6.2 and provide services to other ATPs. Services provided by STPs are unique to the STP and, strictly speaking, not a part of LU 6.2 protocol set. The fact that an STP uses LU 6.2 is

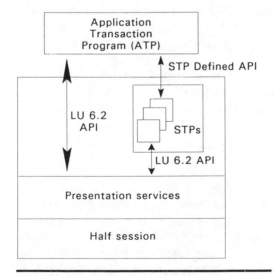

Figure 12.6 Service transaction programs.

transparent and mostly irrelevant to the STP user. The STP user does not have access to the LU 6.2 API. Examples of STPs include SNADs, DIA, and DDM.

Another way to look at an STP is as an IBM-architected application integrated within a specific LU 6.2 implementation. ATPs request the services of an STP using an STP-defined programming interface, not the LU 6.2 API. For that reason STPs are also known as "closed" APIs (as against the standard LU 6.2 API which is also known as the "open" API). As of January 1989, only the following STPs have been defined: DIA, SNADS, DDM, CNOS, and RSYNC. This list will grow in the future. CNOS was introduced earlier in this chapter and is discussed in further detail in the next chapter. A brief description of DIA, SNADS, and DDM is provided later in this chapter.

12.8 LU SERVICES MANAGER

Each SNA NAU contains an NAU Services Manager that manages services provided by the NAU. For LU 6.2 this manager is the LU Services Manager. Functions of the manager are invisible to a transaction program or an external user. Most implementations do not define a distinct software or microcode module to implement the managers, and their function is simply lumped together with the other LU functions.

The LU Services Manager, shown in Fig. 12.7, consists of two managers: the LU resource manager (RM) and the LU network services (note that the word *manager* is not used with respect to LNS).

The RM manages services provided by the services layers (PS and TS) by creating control blocks for a conversation, selecting free sessions, changing session pool sizes, requesting its half session to bid on a session, etc.

LNS deals with half session services in support of functions such as activating the LU and binding and terminating sessions. We do not discuss the functions of the managers in any further detail.

12.9 PU AND LEN CONSIDERATIONS
FOR LU 6.2

An LU 6.2 can reside in a Type 5, 2, or 2.1 node. (Even though we say that LU "resides" in a node, we do not mean that the PU and LU functions necessarily reside in the same machine or box. The term *node* is used broadly to include a PU and its associated LUs.) T5 node represents a host, and T2 and T2.1 nodes represent peripheral nodes that can be cluster controllers, minicomputers, personal computers, or

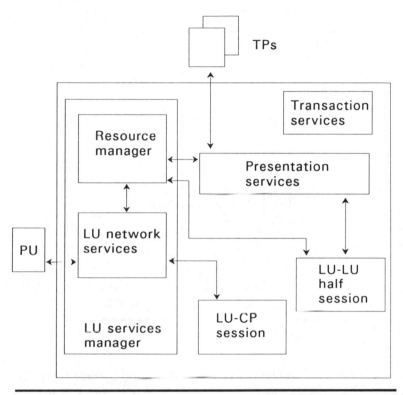

Figure 12.7 Service managers (CP = control point, e.g., SSCP).

other processor types such as PBXs. This section discusses the evolution of LU 6.2 support among the aforementioned three types of nodes. When LU 6.2 was announced, T5 was the only node to support it; then came T2.0 nodes and finally the T2.1 nodes.

12.9.1 Early LU 6.2 Support (Pre-VTAM Version 3.2) in T5 Nodes

As shown in Fig. 12.8, in a pre-T2.1 node environment, LU-LU sessions could exist either between LUs residing in Type 5 nodes or between one LU residing in a Type 5 node and the other in a Type 2 node. For host-to-host sessions, either LU could be the PLU, and both PLU and SLU could support multiple and parallel sessions. However, for the host-to-peripheral-node LU-LU sessions, the PLU had to be in the host.

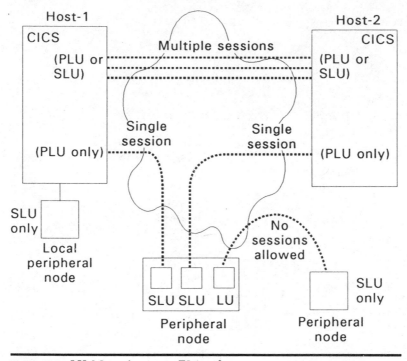

Figure 12.8 LU 6.2 sessions—pre-T2.1 nodes.

VTAM was involved in session establishment and no sessions could be established if VTAM were not available, which was the normal case in SNA.

12.9.2 Early LU 6.2 Support in T2.0 Nodes

As shown in Fig. 12.8, LUs in T2.0 nodes could have sessions only with host LUs and those, too, only as SLUs. Second, since the Type 2 node architecture allowed only one address per LU (and VTAM also allowed only one session per SLU), no parallel or multiple sessions could be established by LUs residing in T2.0 nodes.

12.9.3 Low Entry Networking (LEN)

When announced in 1986, the primary motivation for T2.1 nodes was to allow the same capabilities to LUs in peripheral nodes as the host LUs, in effect making them peer entities. Specifically, T2.1 nodes allow peripheral node LUs to be PLUs, support multiple sessions, and engage in host-independent sessions.

Host-independent sessions are allowed between LUs that reside in directly attached (on the same circuit) T2.1 nodes. Such nodes are called peer-coupled T2.1 or adjacent nodes and it is this configuration that is referred to as low entry networking (LEN). No sessions can be held between T2.0 and T2.1 resident LUs.

Figure 12.9 shows a LEN configuration along with a subarea network. This particular example assumes L1 to be a multidrop SDLC link (it could have been a LAN), and in SDLC there must be a primary station to perform polling and link level control functions; such a station is known as the *primary link station* (PLS). Normally PLS functions are provided by the NCP, but in low entry networking there may not be any NCP involved and the SDLC polling function must be provided by a T2.1 node. In our example we assume that this function is being provided by node A, shown as the primary link station (PLS); nodes B and C are shown as secondary link stations (SLS). (One should not confuse PLU and SLU roles with primary and secondary link stations. A PLU can reside in a secondary link station, and an SLU, in a primary link station.)

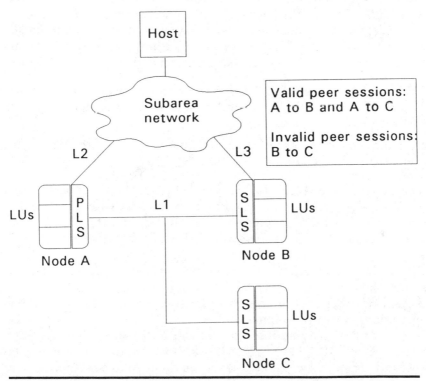

Figure 12.9 Low entry networking (LEN), pre-VTAM 3.2 (PLS = primary link station, SLS = secondary link station).

In LEN, the primary and secondary link station designations play an important role in determining the LUs that can have a session with each other. The rule is that LUs residing in an SLS node can have sessions only with LUs residing in a PLS node. In our example, LUs in nodes B and C can have sessions with LUs in node A. However, LUs in nodes B and C cannot have sessions with each other (one could technically get around this restriction by writing a switch transaction in LUA that routes data between LUs in nodes B and C). In other words, nodes A and B as well as A and C are peer-coupled (or adjacent) nodes, but B and C are not peer coupled. LEN is, therefore, also described architecture for sessions between adjacent nodes only.

12.9.4   LEN Support via Subarea (VTAM/NCP) Network

During the early days of T2.1 nodes, VTAM and NCP did not support LEN architecture and T2.1 nodes were treated simply as T2.0 nodes. However, starting with VTAM version 3, release 2 and NCP version 4, release 3 (3725) or NCP version 5, release 2 (3720 and 3745), IBM started introducing LEN support in T5 and T4 nodes.

To understand the need for these enhancements we need to understand the limitations of LEN support in earlier SNA products as discussed in the previous sections. To summarize the major constraints:

1. VTAM did not permit a PLU role for peripheral LUs; therefore, there were no multiple or parallel sessions, either, for peripheral LUs.

2. Circuits that were used for LEN traffic could not carry traffic for subarea networks and vice versa.

As shown in Fig. 12.10, LUs associated with nodes A and B—both Type 2.1 nodes—could not act as PLUs on sessions with LUs residing in hosts H1 and H2. The link between node A and the subarea network is L1, and the link between node B and the subarea network is L2.

Even though connectivity exists between node A and node B through the subarea network, the LUs on the two nodes could not use this path for their session because the subarea architecture forbade any sessions between peripheral LUs.

Let us further assume that node A and NCP1 are in Los Angeles, and node B and NCP2 are in New York. If we did need a LEN session between LUs on nodes A and B, these would have to be established on a separate link, L3. This extra link was needed solely because the

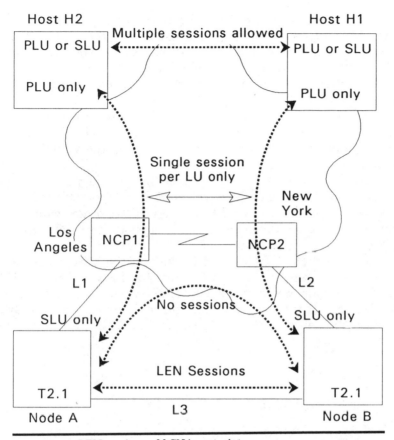

Host H2   Host H1

Figure 12.10   LEN sessions, old SNA contraints.

subarea network did not allow LEN (or host-independent) traffic to flow through it.

VTAM/NCP as 2.1 node.   The current versions of VTAM and NCP can together look like a composite LEN node and therefore allow LEN traffic to flow through the SNA subarea transport.

To show the impact of the new enhancements let us look at Fig. 12.12 in this section under "Session request flow." In this case we do not need a link L3 between nodes A and B as is necessary in Fig. 12.10. NCP1 appears to nodes A as an adjacent T2.1 node, and NCP2 appears to node B as an adjacent T2.1 node. Let us remind ourselves that LEN permits LU-LU sessions only between adjacent nodes.

In order to permit LU-LU sessions between nodes A and B via the subarea network, all LUs associated with node B would be defined in node A as if they resided in the NCP1. Similarly, LUs associated with node A would be defined to node B as if resident in the NCP2. Both nodes A and B would forward their session requests to their adjacent NCP. The NCP, with the assistance of VTAM, would determine the location of the destination LU and forward the session request to the proper PU.

The key point is that by opting to share the subarea network for LEN sessions we have to give up host independence—no LEN sessions can be established across the subarea network unless the VTAM owning that domain is running.

In the example shown in Fig. 12.12, only the boundary NCPs and the VTAM owning the domain have to have LEN support. If the LEN traffic has to flow over multiple NCPs to reach the other boundary NCP, the intermediate NCPs do not have to support the LEN feature or be at the current software release level.

Now let us look at the VTAM and NCP view of the LEN resources. In the NCP tables, Fig. 12.11, we still define the LEN node as a PU Type 2 but there is a new parameter called XID. We show partial NCP definition statements for nodes A and B and their associated LUs. By coding XID = YES on the PU profile we are indicating to the NCP

```
For NCP1 attached node:
               .
               .
LINE01    LINE ....
          SERVICE ....
NODE A    PU    PUTYPE=2, XID=YES, ....
LU A      LU    LOCADDR=0, ....
               .
               .
               .


For NCP2 attached node:
               .
               .
LINE02    LINE ....
          SERVICE ....
NODE B    PU    PUTYPE=2, XID=YES, ....
LU B      LU    LOCADDR=0, ....
               .
               .
               .
```

Figure 12.11 VTAM/NCP view of LEN resources.

that this is a T2.1 node and NCP must go through an XID-3 sequence with this node. The XID-3 sequence is executed when VTAM issues a CONTACT command to the NCP during the node activation sequence. As a result of the XID exchange, NCP tells VTAM that the peripheral node is a LEN node and does not require an SSCP session and VTAM does not issue an ACTPU command for the PU.

The LUs associated with the LEN nodes also require special handling by VTAM. There are two types of LU 6.2 from VTAM's points of view:

1. *Dependent LUs:*   These LUs represent the old architecture; i.e., they can only be SLUs (support only a single session). They can participate in sessions with other peripheral LUs only if the other LU is an independent LU (or a host-resident LU) and BIND must be issued by the partner LU (dependent LUs cannot issue BIND). No special definition is needed for these LUs in VTAM.

2. *Independent LUs:*   These are the new LEN-attached LUs. They can be PLUs and can support multiple and parallel sessions.

In our example, VTAM needs to know whether the LUs associated with nodes A and B are independent LUs. This is indicated by a local address (LOCADDR) of 0 (Fig. 12.11) on the LU profile (an address of 0 is an invalid value for other LUs). Independent LUs do not require an SSCP-LU session. Therefore, a local address of 0 also tells VTAM not to send an ACTLU command to this LU. However, VTAM still must "know" about this LU so that it can provide appropriate directory information (mapping LU symbolic name into a network address when a session request is received for an independent LU). VTAM gathers directory information during LU activation processing. In other words, for independent LUs, VTAM would go through LU activation process in a manner similar to other LUs in its domain, add the independent LU to its Resource Definition table, but would not actually send an ACTLU command to the LU.

Session request flow.   Figure 12.12 shows how a LEN session request is processed in the subarea network. In this case LUA on node A is requesting a session with LUB residing in node B. However, in node A, LUB is defined as if it resided in the NCP1, which is an adjacent LEN node to node A. LU1 initiates the logon request by issuing a BIND for LUB. The BIND request is forwarded by the PU in node A to NCP1. NCP1 cannot map the symbolic name LUB into a network address and so sends it to host H1 (assuming that H1 is the host that had issued the CONTACT for node A and therefore became a pseudoowner of all its resources). A new SNA command called the

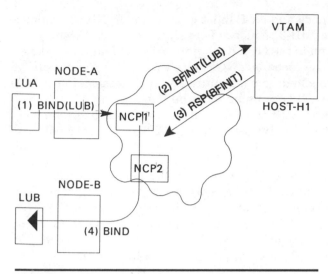

Figure 12.12   LEN sessions over subarea network.

boundary function initiate (BFINIT) is used by the NCP to request necessary information from VTAM to process the session request (including the network address). Response to BFINIT from VTAM provides the NCP with the information required to route this logon to node B via NCP2. When NCP2 forwards this session request to node B, it appears to node B that LU1 resides at NCP1. VTAM was required only during the session setup and is not necessary after that.

LEN and network management. In the pre-1991 SNA all network management data flows on SSCP-PU sessions and then is forwarded to network management application such as NetView. SNA does not allow any network management flows without SSCP-PU sessions. In the LEN network we have no SSCP-PU sessions with nodes A and B in our example; therefore, no management information can be sent to NetView from LEN nodes. For those users for whom this is an unacceptable situation, the new VTAM/NCP support provides a facility whereby a LEN PU can indicate during the XID exchange, through a flag in the XID, whether it would like to establish an SSCP-PU session. If the node allows for such a session, then VTAM would send it an ACTPU and the node can participate in the host-based network management. Starting with version 2 of NetView, network management information can be sent directly to NetView over an LU 6.2 session, bypassing the SSCP-PU session.

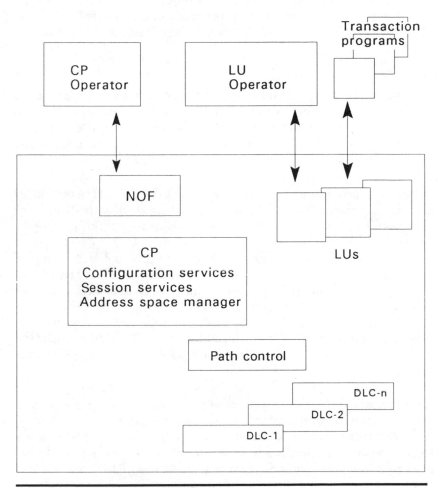

Figure 12.13   PU 2.1 node architecture.

12.10   PU 2.1 ARCHITECTURE

T2.1 node structure is shown in Fig. 12.13. Functions of various components shown are as follows.

12.10.1   Transaction Programs, LU Operator and the LUs

The transaction programs are the normal TPs supported by LUs on this node and are discussed in Chap. 13. The LU operator function is a part of LU 6.2. Even though generally a required function, LU 6.2 operator function is a product-defined interface and is not defined by the APPC/LEN architecture. Finally, the LUs are the local LUs Type 6.2.

12.10.2 Control Point (CP)

This component is responsible for managing the node resources. Its functions include session initiation and termination processing, creating path control and data link control instances in support of sessions, maintaining database of local resources, etc. Its functions are divided into the following three categories:

1. Configuration services. This component of the CP is responsible for maintaining configuration database, activating or deactivating links as requested by the node operator, and performing link failure processing.

The architecture provides no details on the protocol and format of the configuration database, or the information kept in its records. In some implementations this "database" may be a table that has to be created each time the node is activated.

One function that is discussed in detail and constitutes most of the configuration services specification is the DLC role negotiation via exchange ID (XID) and is discussed later in more detail in section 12.11.

2. Session services. Control point session services map destination LU names into the destination control point name and the link identification to reach the destination control point. Session services are also responsible for checking with configuration services that the required link is active and for controlling instances of LU sessions.

3. Address space manager. This component of control point is responsible for managing session addresses (IDs) for sessions initiated by this node. It is responsible for tracking which addresses in the address space have been allocated and for flagging addresses as free or available when sessions terminate. Session addresses are called local format session identifications (LFSIDs).

12.10.3 CP Operator and Node Operator
Facility (NOF)

The control point operator administers, monitors, and controls the node through interactions with the node operator facility. Specific commands, data structures, or flow sequences for CP operator and

NOF are not defined in the PU 2.1 specifications and are implementation defined.

12.10.4   Path Control

Path control is responsible for:

Routing PIUs between LUs: LUs may be in the same or different nodes. T2.1 nodes use FID2 transmission headers.

Interpreting session IDs and mapping them into routing elements. Segmenting session traffic if segmentation is supported: However, all implementations must allow 256-byte RU size as one acceptable value for the maximum segment size. RUs less than 11 bytes are never segmented. A node can support different maximum segment sizes in send and receive directions. Two T2.1 nodes exchange segment sizes are supported during XID-3 exchange.

12.10.5   Data Link Control

T2.1 nodes support SDLC (normal response mode), IBM Token Ring, and LAPB (X.25).

12.11   LINK CONTROL AND SESSION ADDRESSING IN LEN

As discussed in Sec. 12.9.3, one of the three link stations in Fig. 12.9 had to be the primary link station and would be responsible for initializing, polling, and performing other SDLC functions on the link. In a private line or in well-defined switched line arrangements, it is possible that primary and secondary roles are known at the system definition time and can be specified for each machine during system definition.

However, Type 2.1 nodes provide for a mechanism to decide primary and secondary link station roles dynamically at the link activation time. Since the primary is responsible for transmitting SNRMs, the role negotiation must be completed prior to sending SNRMs. SDLC command Exchange Identification (XID) is used for this purpose, and a new Type 3 XID command has been introduced in SDLC for this purpose. Figure 12.14 shows XID-3 exchange for role determination.

Primary and secondary link station roles are negotiated using the I field of the XID-3. The XID-3 contains information on the sender's characteristics, including link station capability (primary, secondary, or negotiable), node type, FID type supported, message size capability, and modulo (SDLC receive window) count, etc. The receiver of XID

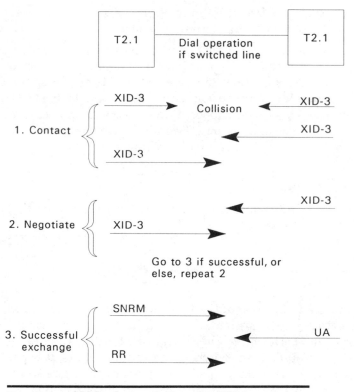

Figure 12.14   SDLC role negotiation using XID-3.

then transmits its own characteristics in an XID response that has a format similar to the XID command. There are two phases to the initial link level contact procedure used by T2.1 nodes:

1. *Contact phase,* culminating in an initial successful XID exchange: During this phase it is possible for XID collisions to occur if each station attempts to transmit an XID at the same time. This situation appears to each transmitting station as a time out, and is handled by the station by introducing a random delay before transmitting the next XID. A new random value is created as long as time outs recur, until eventually a successful exchange occurs.

2. *Negotiating phase,* resulting in the assignment of link station roles:
   a. First-order negotiation proceeds on the basis of the primary and secondary roles specified by each station in the XID-3. It is successful unless both stations have specified the same value for the primary and secondary roles. This outcome is pictured in Fig. 12.14.
   b. A link station can specify its primary and secondary roles as negotiable in XID-3. When both stations specify negotiable roles, second-order negotiation proceeds by comparing a pair of Role Negotiation Values. The field used for this purpose is the node ID field in the XID frame. Two node ID subfields, BLOCK NUMBER (12 bits) and ID NUMBER (20 bits), are used to complete the negotiation. If the node ID fields are unequal, the station with the higher value becomes the primary; and the other, the secondary. If node IDs are equal, the stations try a different random value up to 2 times. If by then the roles cannot be established, the XID exchange is terminated and communications cannot be established.

12.12 SESSION IDENTIFICATION ASSIGNMENT IN T2.1 NODES

T2.1 nodes allow their LUs to engage in both multiple and parallel sessions. It is the responsibility of the node to assign a unique ID to each session. Session IDs are carried in the FID2 transmission header.

Three fields are used to create unique session identification: ODAI, SIDL, and SIDH.

ODAI: OAF'/DAF' assigner indicator is a 1-bit field in the TH and is used as follows:

ODAI = 0 for all PIUs from the primary link station
ODAI = 1 for all PIUs from the secondary link station

Session ID low (SIDL) and session ID high (SIDH): These are the same two fields that carry destination (DAF') and origination (OAF') addresses in the FID2 for T2.0 nodes.

SIDL and SIDH are both assigned by the PU and, together with ODAI, are known as the local format session identifier (LFSID). As shown in Fig. 12.15, the ID assignment is very straightforward. A new ID is assigned for each new BIND issued by any of the LUs. In our example, node A on the left is assumed to be the PLS and therefore uses ODAI = 0. The ID assignments start with a session ID High, SIDH, with a value of X'01'. First BIND gets an SIDL of X'01'; the next, X'02'; then X'03'; etc.—until an SIDL of X'FF' is reached. Now

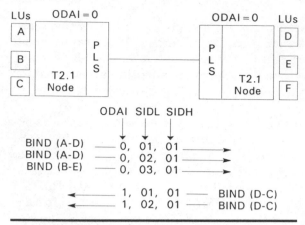

Figure 12.15 Session ID assignments for T2.1 node.

the SIDH is incremented to 02 and SIDL again goes from X'01'-X'FF'. Any values that are released by deactivation of a session are reused for new sessions. As seen in Fig. 12.15, when taken together with ODAI, each session has a unique ID.

Since the ODAI assignment is necessary to generate unique session IDs for LEN sessions, XID-3 is exchanged between LEN nodes even when they are connected via non-SDLC links such as the Token Ring.

12.13   ADVANCED PEER TO PEER NETWORKING (APPN)

After languishing for a number of years as a feature of S/36 and AS/ 400, APPN was finally designated a formal part of SNA and SAA by IBM in March 1991. APPN brings some sorely needed functions to SNA and sets the foundation for a new distributed SNA. Much of the early development on APPN was done by the IBM midrange systems (S/36 and AS/400) group in Rochester, Minn., but not by the IBM Communications Division in Raleigh, N.C., which perhaps explains some of the radical (by IBM standards) thinking that went into APPN design. The midrange systems group had a requirment to implement SNA networks consisting solely of minicomputers with no mainframes in the network. Such networks were not possible with the then SNA due to concepts such as SSCP and PU.T5 which could only be implemented in the mainframe-based VTAM.

With APPN, SNA for the first time starts asserting its independence from the host and the SSCP—neither of which is required under APPN. APPN also introduces major new concepts such as dynamic network directories and routing in SNA. It uses LEN (T2.1 nodes) as its foundation and defines "enhanced" LEN nodes which can act as network nodes, replacing SSCP, PU.T5, and PU.T4. There are no concepts such as subarea nodes, PUs, and SSCP in APPN. In contrast to APPN, the old SNA is now referred to as the "subarea SNA."

APPN concepts are introduced using LEN as a foundation.

12.13.1 LEN and APPN Configurations

Figure 12.16 shows three progressively richer APPN configurations. The first configuration is simply a LEN configuration with two T2.1 nodes, as discussed earlier, with no additional APPN features. All APPC/LEN functions are available here.

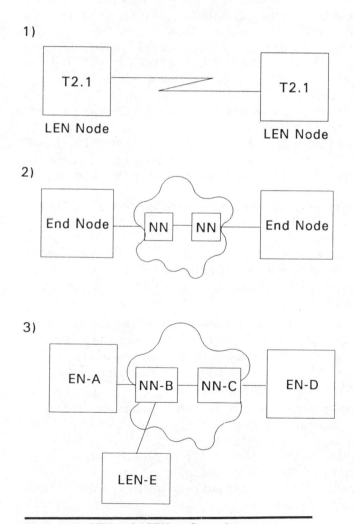

Figure 12.16   LEN and APPN configurations.

The second configuration shows two end nodes (ENs) instead of LEN nodes connected through an APPN network. The key difference between a LEN and an EN is that an EN is capable of building its directory dynamically. Since both nodes in this example are EN nodes, neither of the nodes has to predefine information about the LUs and TPs in the other node in its tables. ENs query the network nodes (NNs) in the network about location of remote LU. Once a resource has been discovered dynamically, the EN permanently adds the location of the resource in its directory, and subsequent references to the same resource do not cause any searches.

The third configuration shows a combination of LEN nodes and ENs on the same APPN nework. The NN provides distributed directory searches and routing capabilities in addition to the EN functions. While the ENs can obtain information from the NN dynamically, LEN nodes cannot. In our example, EN-A needs to define information only about the NN-B in its tables, and the EN-D only needs to define the information about the NN-C. The system administrator for LEN node E, however, needs to define all LUs at nodes A and D manually in order to have sessions with them. Since LEN is an adjacent node architecture, LUs at nodes A and D would be defined at LEN node E as if they resided at NN-B. NN-B would be responsible for routing data to the true LUs. NN-B is in this case the server NN for nodes A and E, and NN-C is the server for EN-D.

Let us summarize levels of functionality for each node type in the APPN environment as follows:

LEN node: A LEN node may participate in an APPN network by using the services of an attached network node (NN) server. However, the user at a LEN node must configure all the remote locations as if they existed at the server NN.

EN: An EN does not provide any network services to other nodes but may participate in the APPN network by using the services of an attached NN server. An EN operates in a peer environment similar to LEN nodes while providing additional functions such as automatic creation of configuration resources.

NN: A network node provides the following functions:
All functions performed by an APPN end node
Intermediate session routing function
Network server functions (perform directory searches and route selection) for attached APPN end nodes or low entry nodes
Can be defined as the management services focal point for network problem management.

12.13.2 APPN Services

Control point services. Provided by an APPN network node, these services keep track of the way nodes are linked in the network and also provide directory services. The control point session can be established only between adjacent NNs or an adjacent NN and EN. LEN nodes do not support control point sessions and therefore do not participate in dynamic directory searches and route selection. The control point session is used to exchange network topology information and to conduct directory searches. The results of the network topology information exchange are kept in a table called the network topology database.

Directory services. The directory services function in a node identifies remote systems that contain locations (LUs) for which a session has been requested. The identification consists of system's network ID and the control point name of the destination. End nodes use control point sessions with their adjacent network nodes to obtain directory services from the network node.

Each NN and EN contains a directory database that maps location names to the owning control point names. The directory database is built from configuration information contained in the node location lists, as well as from information obtained dynamically over control point sessions. The directory database is kept across system restarts, which means that the information is not lost when a system is restarted.

To minimize configuration information to be defined, APPN allows for generic location names and generic routing. Generic location naming allows you to configure a location name ending with an asterisk (*). This implies that any location name starting with the same characters preceding the asterisk match this entry. For example, if locations NYC01, NYC02, and NYC03 exist in an end node (with a control point name of NEWYORK), only a single entry NYC* need be configured as being located at NEWYORK.

Class of service. Each session initiation request is associated with a specific mode that has an associated class of service description (COS). The COS description defines the range of node and transmission group characteristics that are acceptable when determining the route to satisfy the session initiation request. In addition, the COS defines the transmission priority (high, medium, or low) at which data will be transferred through the network after the session has been established. If two routes within a class of service are equal, the network node will randomly choose the route taken.

APPN also supports other SNA concepts such as session pacing (with adaptive pacing window), intermediate routing nodes, and multiple transmission groups.

12.13.3   An Illustrative APPN Network

We show a more elaborate APPN network in Fig. 12.17. It shows two network nodes NN1 and NN2 connected to each other over a multilink transmission group (TG). NN1 has an end node, EN1, attached to it. EN1 also has a switched connection to NN2. NN2 has EN2 and a Token Ring LAN attached to it.

The services available to an EN from its server NN depend on whether or not the two nodes have been configured to have a control point session. If a control point session exists between EN and NN, the EN can ask for information such as the best route. Consider a session request from EN1 for a session with EN2. If NN1 and EN1 have a control point session, then EN1 can ask NN1 for the best route to EN2. NN1 will calculate the route and may tell EN1 that the best route is from EN1 to NN2 (over the switched connection) to EN2. All the data exchanged for the session will flow on this route.

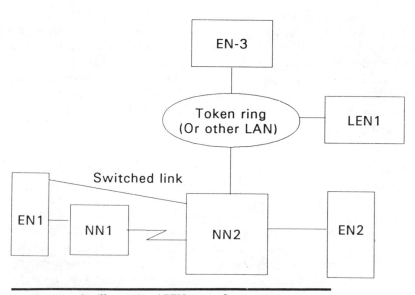

Figure 12.17   An illustrative APPN network.

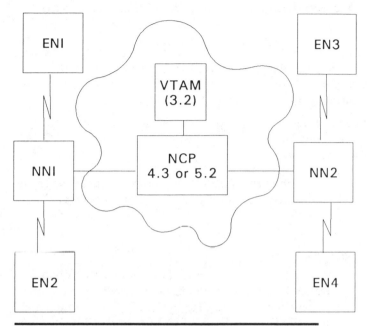

Figure 12.18 APPN and subarea networks.

On the other hand, if EN1 was not configured to have a control point session with NN1, but NN1 was still EN1's server, then EN1 would not ask NN1 for the best route to EN2. Instead, EN1 would simply use NN1 (its server) as the first hop in the route. NN1 would then calculate the best available route from that point. Therefore, the route would be EN1 to NN1 to NN2 to EN2. With the exception of the LEN node, LEN1, there is no need to manually define remote network locations at any of the nodes.

12.13.4 APPN and Subarea Networks

With the availability of LEN support in subarea nodes, we can also have the subarea network providing intermediate routing for APPN sessions. For this capability we must have at least VTAM version 3.2 and NCP version 4.3. or 5.2. Figure 12.18 shows an APPN network with part of it using the subarea transport. The subarea network appears as an LEN node to APPN nodes; thus it cannot participate in APPN control point sessions or directory searches. All locations in EN3, NN2, and EN4 would appear to NN1 as if they were resident in the subarea node. Conversely, all locations in EN1, NN1, and EN2 would appear to NN2 as if resident in the subarea node.

There are some restrictions with regard to this connectivity as follows:

1. An APPN network can have only one path connecting it to the subarea network. Therefore, in Fig. 12.18, there cannot be a direct line connecting any of the ENs (or other NNs if they were present) to the subarea network.

2. In order to communicate using the subarea network, nodes in the APPN network must have the same network name as the NCP to which they are connected.

It should be pointed out that the APPN support in subarea nodes is still evolving and the aforementioned restrictions may not apply in the future.

12.13.5 APPN Summary

APPN is an innovative extension of the LEN architecture. With dynamic directory searches and topology features it provides a number of services that users have been looking for in the SNA for a long time. With APPN support available on AS/400, OS/2EE, and IBM 3174, we should expect to see a greater number of APPN networks in the near future. As more and more APPN features are implemented in VTAM and NCP, the subarea SNA will be replaced by APPN over a period of time.

12.14 LU 6.2 and LEN SUMMARY

In this chapter we looked at the SNA components and the most recent SNA developments in support of distributed processing. We would look at distributed transaction programs in the next chapter. Although we have come quite a distance since the days of single-session secondary LUs, distributed processing under SNA—with various inconsistencies among subarea architecture, LEN, APPN and lingering VTAM insistence on staying in control—is still awkward at best. With the emerging trends towards OSI and the need for extensive gateways to interface with OSI, it will be a while before we have truly seamless, generalized distributed systems.

APPC Transaction Programs and API

13.1 INTRODUCTION AND REVIEW

In the previous chapter we introduced the LU 6.2 environment and its three major components: the transaction programs, the LU, and the PU. Having discussed the LU and PU architectures in that chapter, we now shift our focus to the transaction programs. As shown in Fig. 13.1, transaction programs communicate with the LU 6.2 through the presentation services using the LU 6.2 Application Program Interface (API). Rather than using the full name "LU 6.2 API," or "APPC API" we simply use the term *API* to refer to this programming interface. The reader is cautioned that the term *API* is, in general, used by numerous products and does not always mean the LU 6.2 API (VTAM API, CICS API, API for a driver on PC, etc.), but in this chapter, unless otherwise qualified, it means the LU 6.2 API.

Figure 13.1 reviews some of the important aspects of the LU 6.2 environment introduced in the previous chapter.

1. *Transaction programs:* Transaction programs, which include customer-written applications, are the users of LU 6.2 and are referred to simply as transaction programs (TPs) or sometimes as application transaction programs (ATPs). In contrast, as shown in Fig. 13.1, are the service transaction programs (STPs) that are, if present, contained within the LU 6.2 and provide value added functions that are not a part of the architected LU 6.2 services. The STPs provide their own programming interfaces which are called *closed* APIs as opposed to the LU 6.2 API which is also referred to as the *open* API.

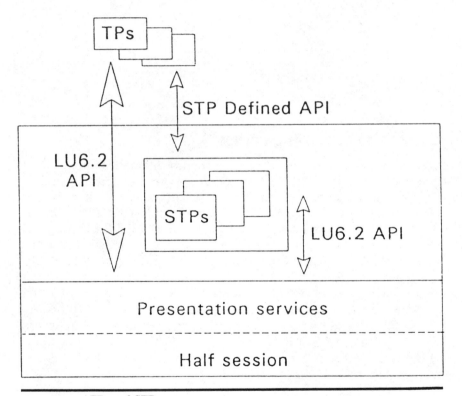

Figure 13.1 ATPs and STPs.

2. *Sessions and conversations:* An LU 6.2 can bind multiple sessions simultaneously with one or more LUs. As shown in Fig. 13.2, one session is required per active conversation. Sessions are treated as a pool of reusable resources. A transaction program can allow the LU to select a session using LU's own procedures or can specify its own requirements for the session to be used for the conversation.

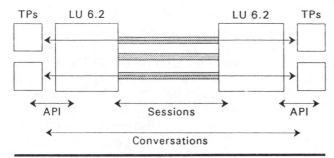

Figure 13.2 Transaction programs, LU 6.2, and API.

In terms of session protocols, one conversation equals one "in-bracket" state, a begin bracket starts a conversation and a conditional end bracket terminates it. Function management header 5 (FMH-5) in the RU carries the details of the conversation initiation request along with the BBI indicator in the RH.

In this chapter we focus on the details of the transaction programs and the API. At the end of the chapter we also look at three of the major IBM STPs.

13.2 INTRODUCTION TO TPs AND CONVERSATIONS

The stimulus that triggers a conversation normally comes from a source external to the LU or the TP, e.g., a control operator command to start a transaction program, arrival of a message, or events such as a timer-based task. The details of how an LU loads and manages transaction programs and handles error conditions (program checks, etc.) and program terminations are implementation defined. Not all LU 6.2 products may even handle all of the aforementioned conditions.

Before we look at the conversation establishment and flows, let us reiterate that a conversation represents cooperative distributed processing. Two transaction programs participating in a conversation cannot be designed entirely independently of each other. The design of the distributed transaction would specify application protocol requirements such as:

Who initiates the conversation?

What is an appropriate mode (bind image) for the conversation?

What are the rules for send and receive states?

Is the conversation going to be recoverable?

The overall design of a TP is much more complex than the details of the API. The broader issues of distributed design are, to a large extent, independent of LU 6.2 and have to be resolved by a designer in addition to the LU 6.2 considerations discussed here. LU 6.2 only facilitates exchange of information between two transaction programs. Any difficulties in the use of API are generally due to insufficient product documentation or inconsistent implementations across products. Therefore, it is important to emphasize that programming the API interface is only a minor part of the overall design and implementation of a distributed system.

A high-level API view is shown in Fig. 13.3. What we have been calling a transaction program may not be a single or simple entity. From a technical point of view, a transaction program is any software module that interfaces with LU 6.2 at the API level. A user may choose to separate business functions (the real application) from software that interfaces with LU 6.2 as shown in Fig. 13.3. In this case what is called a transaction program by LU 6.2 may be called a utility program by the real application to control commu-

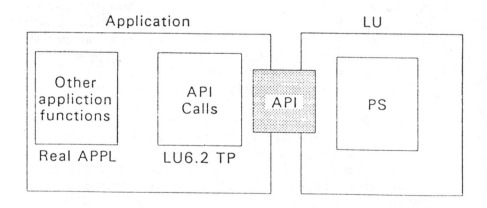

Figure 13.3   TP and API overview.

nications with remote programs. Such an architecture allows a designer to make even the LU 6.2 API transparent to application programmers.

The interface between the real application and the transaction program can be a "call" or any other structure allowed by the machine operating system and compilers. The application requests can be mapped into API verbs by the transaction program and passed over to the LU using the API data stream. The two LUs communicate information using SNA RU data streams and LU 6.2 protocols. At the destination end the process is reversed.

13.3 LU 6.2 API OVERVIEW

The API consists of a set of verbs that are invoked by the TP in the form of programming calls. The IBM publication *LU 6.2 Transaction Programmer's Reference Manual* documents the specifications of the API verbs, parameters for each verb, and return codes. The architecture does not require or recommend any particular programming language or compiler for the API. The language(s) supported is (are) defined by specific product implementations. Products, including IBM's own, implement verbs in syntax that is not exactly the same as in the *LU 6.2 Transaction Programmer's Reference Manual* or may use the same verb names but not perform exactly the same function. Unless there is a table mapping product specifications into the LU 6.2 API verb set, it becomes difficult to evaluate whether two implementations would be compatible. To be an open API, an implementation must define its syntax to semantic mappings unless it uses the same syntax as the LU 6.2 API. IBM has defined another programming interface for LU 6.2 under SAA called the common programming interface for communications (CPIC) which does define the programming syntax. CPIC is described in Chap. 14.

13.3.1 API Base and Option Sets

In Sec. 12.3 we introduced the notions of a base (minimally required) and multiple option sets of verbs within the API. To be called an open API, a product must at least support the base set. The base set is sufficient for general, basic communications, and option sets provide enhancements (e.g., security, recovery, etc.). At the time of this writing, IBM had defined a total of 50 different option sets—each set consisting of a specific set of functions. To maintain compatibility, APPC requires that when a particular option set is implemented, it must be implemented in its entirety or none of it can be implemented.

13.3.2 Verbs and States

Although verbs define the LU 6.2 functions being invoked, the states (of the TP) define the order in which the verbs may be issued at any given time (e.g., a TP may not issue a SEND verb while in a RE-CEIVE state; if it were to do so, the LU would reject the verb with a "state error"). LU 6.2 PS enforces the correct verb and state usage.

13.3.3 Basic and Mapped Conversations

In spite of the similarity of terms, basic and mapped conversations have no relationship to the base and option sets introduced earlier. These conversation types represent different levels of programming complexity of the verbs and the data stream that the TP presents to the LU. A basic conversation represents a low-level (more technical) API than does a mapped conversations. It is IBM's expectation that mapped conversation would be preferred and used by most application programmers. Basic conversations would be appropriate for system software vendors and, within IBM, for the development of STPs such as SNADS, DDM, etc.

The mapped conversation verbs are preceded by the prefix MC_. The verb to allocate a conversation, for example, is described as AL-LOCATE in basic conversation and as MC_ALLOCATE in mapped conversations. Some verbs have the same syntax (i.e., no MC prefix) for basic and mapped conversation. These are known as type-independent verbs.

We do not get to a level of detail in this book appropriate for discussing specific differences between each basic and mapped verb. As a matter of convenience, we use the mapped verbs' syntax in our examples, but the examples are meant to be generic and the information would apply to both basic and mapped verbs unless specified otherwise.

13.4 LU 6.2 DATA STREAMS

The structure of the data stream presented by the TP over the API is also defined by the conversation type used by the TP. The following data streams are defined by the LU 6.2.

13.4.1 Generalized Data Streams (GDS)

Generalized data stream is used by LU 6.2 internally to carry conversation data. It is also used by IBM Service Transaction Programs

(STPs). Information provided by TPs, whether using basic or mapped conversations is converted to GDS by PS for sending it over the half session.

Generalized data stream consists of multiple data units—each called a GDS variable. Each GDS variable consists of a header followed by variable data, as shown in Fig. 13.4. The header consists of a 2-byte length field defining the number of bytes in the variable field (including the 4 bytes for the length and the ID fields), followed by a 2-byte field ID. The minimum length value is 2 bytes (null variable) with values less than 02 reserved for internal use by the LU. For example, a value of 01 in length is used to indicate the presence of a presentation header (PH) used for certain SYNCPOINT functions. All TP data are identified by a variable ID of X'12FF'. Other GDS IDs are listed in Appendix D.

13.4.2 Logical Records

Logical record format is used by TPs with basic conversations. In this case the TP passes user data to the LU preceded by a 2-byte length field. A logical record is similar to a GDS variable except that it does not contain an ID field. Everything following the length field is treated by the LU as user data. Maximum length for a logical record is 32,767 bytes including the 2-byte length field.

If the transaction programs use any IDs following the length field, it is up to the TPs to assign and interpret the ID fields.

13.4.3 Data Records

Data record is the name given to TP message units when using mapped conversations. LU does not interpret any information in data

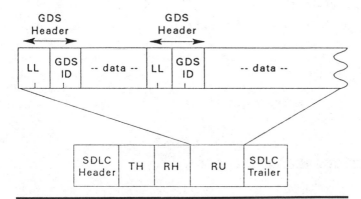

Figure 13.4 Generalized data stream (GDS)—basic conversations.

records and their content is relevant only to the TPs. There are no architected limits on the size of data records. If the data record exceeds the GDS variable maximum size, the LU will divide the record into multiple units and send them as multiple GDS variables along with a continuation bit in the length field. (We have not yet introduced the MC_SEND_DATA verb; a data record is the amount of data passed to the LU in a single MC_SEND_DATA verb.)

13.5   CONVERSATION SYNCHRONIZATION LEVELS

We need to discuss conversation synchronization, at least at a high level, before discussing various verbs, as a number of them refer to synchronization level. LU 6.2 allows three levels of synchronization:

1. NONE: This is a part of the base set and for conversations allocated with this level, no synchronization pointing (syncpointing) or recovery support is provided by the LU. This level is appropriate for conversations where no files or data are altered (e.g., inquiring/response).

2. CONFIRM: This is also a part of the base set and here, too, LU does not provide any syncpointing support. But in this case LU does permit a TP to issue a CONFIRM request, which requires a confirmation reply from the partner TP. In addition, the LU also enforces the confirmation-pending state (e.g., it cannot deallocate a conversation while a confirmation is pending). However, LU assigns no meaning to the CONFIRM and it is up to the TPs to perform any mutually agreed-on processing when a CONFIRM is requested. The intent is to allow the TPs to implement their own syncpointing protocol when the LU does not support full syncpointing and commitment control protocol.

3. SYNCPT: This is the highest level of synchronization and is available only as a part of option set 108. In this case LU supports a complete syncpointing and commitment control protocol. We do not go into the details for the rationale for logging and syncpointing and how they help in the design of recoverable transactions, assuming that a reader needing to use these capabilities knows when and how to use them.

13.6   MAPPED CONVERSATION VERBS

It is not our intention that one should be able to code the API verbs from information provided herein only. Not all parameters or return

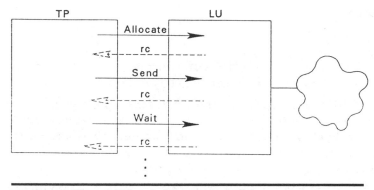

Figure 13.5 Flow of API verbs (rc = return code).

codes are shown for each verb. In any case, the syntax in this chapter is consistent with the *LU 6.2 Transactions Programmer's Reference Manual*. Product-specific publications should be consulted for actual programming-level details.

A typical high-level verb flow is shown in Fig. 13.5. For each request made by the TP, LU returns a return code indicating whether or not the request was successful. The timing of the return of control to the TP is dependent on the verb and the parameters selected: It can be immediate or dependent on completion of some event. Most verbs also return some parameters containing information pertaining to the verb.

For each verb in the following sections, we also show whether it is a part of the base set or an option set. If the verb belongs to an option set, the option set number is also shown.

13.6.1 Conversation Initiation and Termination

MC_ALLOCATE (base set). This verb is used by a TP to start a conversation with another TP. Some of the parameters for MC_ALLOCATE follow.

```
MC_ALLOCATE     LU_NAME (----),
                TPN(----),
                RETURN_CONTROL (----),
                SYNC_LEVEL (---),
                    :
```

LU_NAME: Identifies the LU where the intended conversation partner TP resides. The partner TP can be another TP on the same LU as the requesting TP, in which case the name of the LU would be the requesting TP's own LU. A remote LU may also be known locally by an alias name, in which case the LU_NAME would be an alias name.

Returned Parameters

```
RESOURCE, RETURN_CODE
```

TPN: Specifies the name of the TP with which a conversation is desired. The destination TP name can also be an alias name.

RETURN_CONTROL: Specifies the conditions under which the LU is to return control to the TP. The base set specifies that control be returned only after a session has been allocated. Two option sets provide immediate return, whether successful or not, or a delayed allocation if a session is not available immediately.

SYNC-LEVEL: Defines the level of recovery and is discussed as a separate topic in section 13.6.4. In addition to the parameters shown, mode name and security requirements can also be defined.

Two values are returned by the LU after processing an allocation request. The RESOURCE variable contains a resource ID that is a unique ID for this conversation. The program must specify this ID with all requests associated with this conversation. The length and actual format of the ID is product defined. The second value returned is the RETURN_CODE which indicates whether the allocation request was executed successfully.

MC_DEALLOCATE (base set)

```
MC_DEALLOCATE      RESOURCE
                   TYPE (----)
```

The RESOURCE parameter identifies the conversation to be deallocated by providing the conversation ID. The TYPE parameter specifies the type of deallocation to be performed. Values permissible in the TYPE parameter very much depend on the state of the conversation. For example, if a conversation was allocated with the syncpointing option, an attempt to deallocate without completing syncpoint processing would cause an error return code from the LU. Another option is to tell the LU to "flush" (transmit) any accumulated records and then deallocate the conversation. Another possibility is that the conversation is already in a deallocate state due to an earlier request and the TP had to complete some local processing, in which case the TYPE parameter would specify a LOCAL deallocation only. An ABEND option causes a flush function and abnormal termination. The return code specifies whether the deallocation was successful or rejected due to parameter or state errors.

13.6.2 Sending Data

MC_SEND_DATA. This verb is used to send data by a TP when it is in a send state. The issuance of a send verb does not necessarily cause a transmission on the underlying session. The LU tries to buffer data from multiple send requests before actually transmitting it. The objective is to optimize the use of the underlying transport. The amount of data that can be buffered depends on a specific implementation. Various parameters for the verb follow.

```
MC_SEND_DATA       RESOURCE (---),
                   DATA (---),
                   LENGTH (---),
```

Returned Parameters

```
RETURN_CODE
REQUEST_TO_SEND_RECEIVED
```

RESOURCE identifies the conversation with which this request is associated. DATA specifies the location of the area (buffer) containing the data, and LENGTH specifies the size of the data and can be 0.

RETURN_CODE indicates acceptance of the request or an error due to state or other execution error.

REQUEST_TO_SEND_RECEIVED indicates whether the partner TP has sent a request-to-send (a SIGNAL Command on the underlying session).

MC_FLUSH (option set 101)

```
MC_FLUSH RESOURCE (----)
```

As we stated in the previous paragraph, the issuance of a SEND request does not necessarily cause a transmission on a session. A TP can force its LU to transmit the accumulated data by issuing the FLUSH verb ("flush" does not mean "throw it away"). The only parameter on this verb is the ID of the conversation for which the verb is being issued. There are no return parameters for this verb.

13.6.3 Receiving Data

Receiving data has many more options than does sending data. The TP has to indicate whether it wishes to be put in a "wait" state while waiting for data or wants the control to be returned immediately. The verbs issued for receiving data also causes a change in the state of a TP from send to receive (the CDI bit is set to 1 in the RH at the session level). A

RECEIVE request also causes the transmission or flushing of any accumulated data by the LU. Some of the data receiving verbs follow.

MC__RECEIVE__AND__WAIT (base set). This is probably the most common way of issuing a RECEIVE request. With this verb the TP causes the accumulated data to be flushed, gives permission to the partner TP to send data, and goes into a wait state pending arrival of a reply from the partner TP.

```
MC__RECEIVE__AND__WAIT      RESOURCE (----)
                            LENGTH (----)
                               :
```

Returned Parameters

```
RETURN__CODE
WHAT__RECEIVED
   :
```

RESOURCE specifies the conversation ID for which the request is being issued.

LENGTH specifies the maximum amount of data expected. (Upon completion of the request, LENGTH contains the actual length of data actually received.)

RETURN__CODE indicates successful processing or the reason for failure.

WHAT__RECEIVED is a very important returned value on this verb and identifies the type of data or signal that has been received. Some of the values returned in WHAT__RECEIVED include:

DATA__COMPLETE: The TP has received a complete data record, which is usually the normal completion for this request.

DATA__TRUNCATED: Indicates that data returned to the TP is less than what was received by the LU. LU has thrown away the remainder of the data (most likely because the data exceeded the LENGTH specified in the RECEIVE request).

DATA__INCOMPLETE: Indicates that data received is not a complete record and the TP needs to issue additional RECEIVE request(s) to receive the remainder of the record.

SEND: The TP has received permission to enter a send state and the partner TP has entered a receive state.

Additional values deal with CONFIRM and SYNCPOINT protocols discussed later, or the LU Type 6.1 FMHs, which are not discussed in this book.

MC_RECEIVE_IMMEDIATE (option set 20). This verb, its parameters, and returned values are similar to the RECEIVE_AND_WAIT verb, and it also returns to the TP any data that are available for the specified conversations. However, unlike RECEIVE_AND_WAIT, this verb does not wait for the information to arrive and the control is returned to the TP immediately with NO DATA indication if no data have been received on this conversation. If data has been received, WHAT_RECEIVED identifies the type of data or flags (see RECEIVE_AND_WAIT for values returned in WHAT_RECEIVED).

MC_PREPARE_TO_RECEIVE (option set 106). This verb is used by a TP to change its state from send to receive (it causes a CDI to flow at the session level).

```
MC_PREPARE_TO_RECEIVE        RESOURCE (----)
                             TYPE (----)
```

The change to receive state can be immediate or deferred depending on the value coded in the TYPE parameter, which allows the following values:

SYNC_LEVEL: This specifies that the verb is to be executed based on synchronization level specified at conversation allocation. If the SYNC_LEVEL was NONE, the change in state is immediate and all buffered data is flushed by the LU. If the SYNC_LEVEL was CONFIRM, confirm processing is performed and then a receive state is entered. If the SYNC_LEVEL was SYNCPT, the TP enters a deferred state and the state is changed only when the TP issues a subsequent CONFIRM, FLUSH, or SYNCPOINT request.

FLUSH and CONFIRM: These other two options on the TYPE parameter cause execution of a flush or confirmation function, respectively, before the state is changed.

MC_POST_ON_RECEIPT (option set 104). This verb is issued by a TP in a receive state to request its LU to post a notification to the TP telling it that data has arrived for the TP. The TP must either issue a wait or test request to determine whether it has been posted. The type of information returned to the TP is the same as in the RECEIVE_AND_WAIT.

MC_TEST (option set 103). This verb is issued to test one of two conditions:

1. Whether an earlier post on receipt has been posted, i.e., if any data have arrived since.

2. Whether a request to send has been received from the partner TP.

There is no wait for the completion of the condition being tested. The return code indicates whether the tested condition has occurred or not.

WAIT (option set 104). This is a type-independent verb, i.e., it is used the same way in mapped and basic conversations (therefore, no MC_prefix). The verb puts the TP in a wait state, waiting for a posting (to an earlier POST_ON_RECEIPT) to occur on any of its conversations. The return parameters identify the results of the posting and the conversation ID for which the posting is being reported.

RECEIVE_AND_WAIT versus other receive options. Before we leave the topic of receive verbs, let us briefly look at how they may be used.

RECEIVE_AND_WAIT is most appropriate when a TP is engaged in a single conversation such as that shown in Fig. 13.6a. In this example, when TP has sent all data to its conversation partner and has no other processing to do, it issues a RECEIVE_AND_WAIT. Once this verb is issued TP-A is put in a wait state until some data arrive from TP-B or an abnormal condition occurs.

Such a design would be inappropriate for a TP engaged in multiple conversations as shown in Fig. 13.6b. In this case TP-A wants to send one or more data records to TPs B, C, and D and receive records in reply. If TP-A were to issue a RECEIVE_AND_WAIT after step 1, it would be placed in a wait state and not be able to send any records to TP-C and TP-D until a reply came from TP-B. By using PREPARE_TO_RECEIVE on each conversation, TP-A can enter a receive state on each TP without entering a wait state and be able to continue sending records as shown in steps 3-6. Finally, in step 7, TP-A issues a POST_ON_RECEIPT and WAIT to its local LU and enters a wait state. A message from any of the three conversation partners would get TP-A out of the wait state. In summary, TP-A sends data records to all three TPs, enters a receive state on each conversation and, finally, enters a wait state only after it has sent data records to all three conversation partners.

MC_REQUEST_TO_SEND (base set). This verb relates to a receive state and we have chosen to cover it as a part of receive verbs. REQUEST_TO_SEND is sent by a TP that is in a receive state but has a need to send records. The TP invoking this verb is requesting its partner to change the state of the conversation so that the requester can enter a send state. The target TP can choose to ignore the REQUEST_TO_SEND and the state does not change unless the remote TP grants permission to send. Circumstances under which a

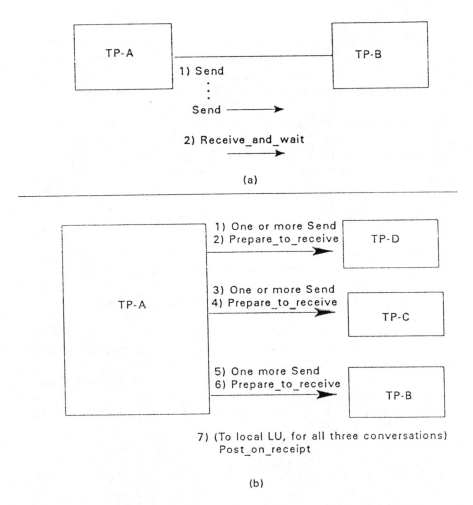

Figure 13.6   RECEIVE__AND__WAIT versus other option.

REQUEST__TO__SEND is sent or what to do on receiving it are issues that should be resolved during the application design. As a general guideline, REQUEST__TO__SEND can be thought of as a priority flag to be raised to report some special event such as an error or an exception requiring immediate attention.

13.6.4 Synchronization Verbs

The level of synchronization for a conversation is defined at allocation time and can be level 0 for NONE, level 1 for CONFIRM, or level 2 for SYNCPT. There are no synchronization verbs for level 0 since none are required. The verbs for the other two levels are described below.

MC__CONFIRM and MC__CONFIRMED (base set). MC__CONFIRM is issued by a TP during a conversation to ask its partner TP to perform some application-defined syncpointing and reply with a confirmation. The LU does not define the meaning of confirmation. CONFIRM implies a flush and puts the requesting TP in a wait and receive state. The target of the CONFIRM sends an MC__CONFIRMED when it has completed the processing required by a CONFIRM.

SYNCPOINT and BACKOUT (option set 108). This feature requires the implementation of the syncpoint manager in the underlying LU. Issuance of the SYNCPOINT verb causes a TAKE__SYNC__POINT notice to be posted to all TPs with which the initiating TP had allocated a conversation with level 2 synchronization. If the target TPs, in turn, have any additional conversations with other TPs with level 2 synchronization, the request to take a syncpoint would be forwarded to them also. In effect, the SYNCPOINT would cascade to all distributed TPs involved in the distributed transaction over multiple TPs and conversations. SYNCPOINT causes a number of exchanges among the LUs to assure that all TPs have successfully completed the SYNCPOINT processing and that protected resources have been safe-stored and all TPs have moved to the next synchronization point.

If any of the TPs is unable to complete the SYNCPOINT processing, it responds with a BACKOUT verb causing its local LU to restore the status of protected resources to the last successful synchronization point. The BACKOUT notification is then propagated to each TP as the return parameter BACKED__OUT and protected resources at each TP are restored to the last syncpoint.

It is also possible for an error to occur during the SYNCPOINT processing, which may cause some resources to be moved to the next syncpoint while other resources have been restored to the previous syncpoint. In this case, the return code is neither OK nor

BACKED_OUT but HEURISTIC_MIXED, and recovery is implementation defined.

13.6.5 Sending Error Information,
MC_SEND_ERROR (Base Set)

This verb is used by a TP to report an application level error to its partner TP. This verb can be issued in send or receive state.

If issued in a send state, whether the error message is sent immediately or accumulated by the LU in a buffer for later transmission is implementation defined. If the TP wants to make sure that the error notification is sent immediately, it may use the flush function after issuing SEND_ERROR. It is best to consult specific implementation documentation for details.

If SEND_ERROR is issued by a TP in a receive state, the LU purges all data received from the remote TP that has not been given to the TP. In addition, SEND_ERROR also cancels or resets all pending postings (POST_ON_RECEIVE) for any outstanding receive requests.

13.7 CONTROL OPERATOR VERBS

The verbs described in this section are not for use by the applications. These verbs are meant for system control programs to administer and control the LU 6.2 environment. Whether these verbs are supported or not is an implementation decision. Some implementations may also enforce the application authorization to issue these verbs.

13.7.1 Session Pool Control

There are four verbs to manage the size of the LU session pool and assign contention winners. They are supported through the change number of sessions (CNOS) STP (this support is required for LUs supporting parallel sessions). It is not clear why IBM classifies CNOS as a service transaction program and not just a verb. The initial operating environment is normally defined through tables using some implementation-defined procedures.

The CHANGE_SESSION_LIMIT verb is used to change session limits and contention winner polarity for parallel sessions with a specific partner LU. The new limit applies only to sessions with the mode name specified in the verb.

INITIALIZE_SESSION_LIMIT specifies the initial session limit for sessions with a particular LU and for a given mode name, and it also specifies the number of contention winner sessions.

RESET__SESSION__LIMIT resets the session limit to 0 for sessions with a specific LU for a given mode name.

Finally, the PROCESS__SESSION__LIMIT verb is used internally by the CNOS STP itself to process the session control verbs described in the foregoing paragraphs.

13.7.2   Session Activation and Deactivation

ACTIVATE__SESSION and DEACTIVATE__SESSION verbs are used to activate and deactivate sessions. The activation verb specifies the partner LU name and mode name for the session to be activated. The deactivation verb specifies the session ID of the session to be deactivated.

13.7.3   Defining and Accessing LU Characteristics

A number of verbs are available to a control program for defining LU operating environment or for interrogating values already defined.

Definition verbs allow definitions of local and remote LUs with parameters such as fully qualified LU names, session limits, and security requirements. Mode (BIND) parameters can be defined for use with a specific remote LU. Characteristics of local TPs can be defined with details such as TP name, conversation type supported (basic or mapped), sync level, security considerations, and authorization to issue control verbs.

A number of DISPLAY verbs are available to retrieve the aforementioned information from the LU tables. Finally, the DELETE verb can be used to delete entities defined by the aforementioned verbs.

13.8   CONVERSATION STATES

We noted earlier that LU presentation services are responsible for enforcing, not only correct usage of the API verb parameters, but also the proper states for the conversation. State transitions occur due to a verb issued by the local or the remote TP or error conditions. The TP states are summarized in the following.

Reset: In this state the TP can send data or request a confirmation or a syncpoint.

Receive: The TP can receive data from the remote TP.

Defer receive: The TP would go into a receive state following the execution of the next syncpoint, confirm, or flush verb. This verb applies only to conversations allocated with a sync level of SYNCPOINT.

Defer deallocate: The conversation would be deallocated following the next flush, confirm, or syncpoint. Applies only to conversations allocated with sync level of SYNCPOINT.

Confirm, confirm send, confirm deallocate: During these states a TP owes and sends a reply to a CONFIRM request.

Syncpoint, syncpoint send, and syncpoint deallocate: During these states a TP owes and sends a reply to a syncpoint request.

Pending deallocate: TP has issued a deallocate with CONFIRM, this is an intermediate state and changes to deallocate on receiving confirmation.

Deallocate: During this state the program can issue only deallocate-local request.

13.9   A SAMPLE CONVERSATION

Figure 13.7 shows a sample conversation. This is almost a trivial conversation in which a transaction allocates a conversation, sends a message, and deallocates the conversation without even finding out whether the message arrived at the destination (a more elaborate conversation is shown in the next section).

1. TP-a requests its LU to allocate a conversation with partner transaction program identified as TP-b.

   SYNC_LEVEL (NONE) means that confirmations and syncpoints will not be used in this conversation.

   LU acknowledges the ALLOCATE request with an OK return code and places the request in its buffer. The request is not transmitted to the destination LU (TP) at this point.

2. TP-a issues a SEND_DATA request. LUA appends the data in the buffer containing the ALLOCATE request from step 1, and nothing is actually transmitted.

3. TP-a issues a DEALLOCATE request. TYPE(SYNC_LEVEL) tells the local LU to use the synchronization level that was specified at the allocation time. This conversation was started with SYNC_LEVEL = NONE so no syncpoint is taken and LUA informs TP-a that the conversation has ended with a return code of OK.

4. As far as TP-a is concerned the conversation has ended.

5. However, no information was sent to TP-b so far. LUA will now transmit its buffer to LUB. The buffer contains data and control information from ALLOCATE, SEND, and DEALLOCATE requests.

   LUB recognizes the ALLOCATE request and loads and starts TP-b using implementation-defined procedures.

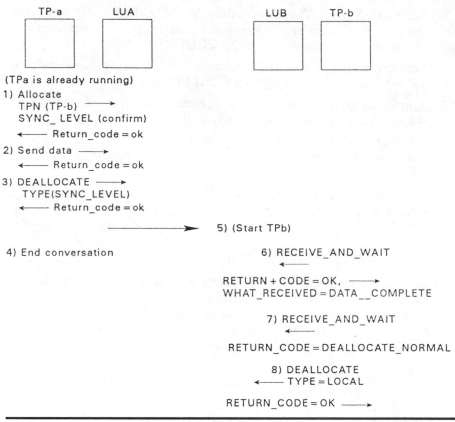

Figure 13.7   A sample conversation.

6. TP-b issues a RECEIVE__AND__WAIT and receives a complete record which was sent by TP-a in step 2.

7. TP-b issues another RECEIVE__AND__WAIT, and LUB passes it DEALLOCATE__NORMAL indication.

8. TP-b issues DEALLOCATE with TYPE(LOCAL) causing LUB to deallocate all resources associated with this conversation. Return code OK informs TP-b of successful termination.

13.10   API VERBS AND SESSION PROTOCOLS

In Fig. 13.8, we use a little more elaborate conversation and add the session level protocol details to show the relationship between conversation requests and session protocols. This conversation would be al-

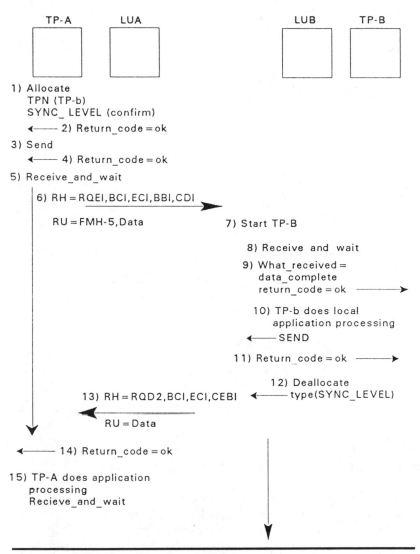

Figure 13.8 API verbs and session protocols.

located with SYNC_LEVEL (CONFIRM); the allocating TP would send a record; the receiving TP would process the record and deallocate the conversation after completing CONFIRM processing.

1. TP-a requests allocation of a conversation with TP-b with SYNC_LEVEL of CONFIRM.

2. LUA buffers the request and returns an OK code to TP-a.

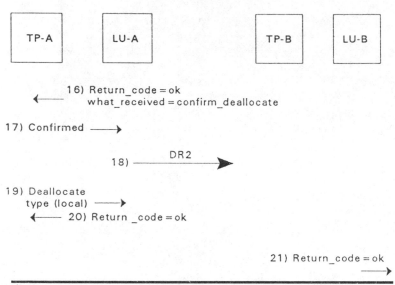

Figure 13.8   (*Continued*) API verbs and session protocols.

3. TP-a passes a record to LUA for transmission.

4. LUA accepts the record, appends it to the ALLOCATE request in the buffer and gives an OK return code to the TP.

5. TP-a issues a RECEIVE_AND_WAIT indicating that it now awaits data from TP-b.

6. LUA places TP-a in a wait and receive state and builds an SNA message consisting of an RH and an RU for transmission over the half session.

   The RU in this case would contain two logical records created by the LU—an FMH-5 from the ALLOCATE request in step 1 followed by the data from the SEND request in step 2. In this and the previous example we implied that ALLOCATE request was buffered and sent later with the data. Actually it is an implementation choice and some products may very well choose to send ALLOCATE as a separate transmission.

   The RH would have a number of bits set to 1 due to the TP requests as follows:

   RQE1 indicates that exception response with DR1 would be requested (most LU 6.2 flows use exception responses with DR1. DR2 is reserved for CONFIRM processing and DR1 is used in special control messages such as SIGNAL and BID).

   The begin bracket indicator (BBI) bit is set to 1 due to the enclosed ALLOCATE request. Since a function management header

(FMH-5) is also included in this transmission, the RH would also indicate that this is a formatted RU. The first part of the RU would be the FMH-5 carrying the details of the ALLOCATE request.

Notice that this RH also contains indicates beginning and ending of a chain (BCI and ECI). Each new conversation begins as a new chain. Even though this example shows only a single-element chain in step 6, it could have been a multielement chain depending on the length of data in step 3 and the size of LUB buffer. LU 6.2 has no specific chain element size requirements. However, the end chain flag is always used with a send-to-receive state change (RECEIVE, CONFIRM, or SYNCPOINT verb) or a verb that would cause a termination of the conversation.

The change direction indication (CDI) is set to 1 because TP-a changed its state from send to receive by issuing a RECEIVE_AND_WAIT.

7. LUB receives the composite message with multiple logical records in it. The LU recognizes the ALLOCATE request for TP-b and starts it using implementation-defined procedures.

8. TP-b starts in a receive state (the target of an ALLOCATE request always starts in a receive state) and issues a RECEIVE_AND_WAIT.

9. LUB returns to TP-b data passed by TP-a in step 3 and indicates that this is a complete unit of a data record.

10. TP-b performs local application processing with the data received, develops an output message for TP-a, and issues a SEND request.

11. LUB buffers the data and returns an OK return code to the TP.

12. TP-b has come to the end of this unit of work and issues a DEALLOCATE request with the prevailing synchronization level which requires CONFIRM processing (see ALLOCATE request in the foregoing). This causes TP-b to be placed in a wait state pending a confirmation.

13. LUB transmits the buffer, which includes both the data from step 10 as well as control flags from step 12. The RH would have the following indicators set to 1:

    RQD2: DR2 would be set to 1 to indicate that a CONFIRM has been requested.

    BCI and ECI flags would be set to indicate a complete chain.

    Since a DEALLOCATE was also issued, the CEBI flag is set to 1. CEBI always implies a change of direction; thus no CDI is set.

14. LUB parses the received transmission and posts the outstanding RECEIVE_AND_WAIT for TP-a with a complete data record.

15. TP-a performs local processing, and TP-a issues another RECEIVE_AND_WAIT.

16. LUA informs TP-a that it has received a request to deallocate with a confirmation.

17. TP-a does whatever processing is required to satisfy a confirmation and issues a CONFIRMED verb to its local LU.

18. LUA transmits a definite response 2 (DR2) to indicate that CONFIRMED has been issued.

19. LUB posts an OK return code to TP-b and the conversation has ended at LUB location.

20-21. TP-a issues a local deallocate, and the conversation terminates at LUA site also.

13.11   API IMPLEMENTATION—VTAM

LU 6.2 API became available under VTAM in late 1988. Prior to this interface, CICS was the only host product to offer an LU 6.2 API. Other major host subsystems such as TSO, JES, IMS/DC, etc. are expected to use the MVS APPC API to provide LU 6.2 support. The MVS APPC API became available in March 1991.

Figure 13.9 shows the overview of VTAM API support. Note that in this environment we have two types of LU 6.2 applications. One type is represented by CICS, which has its own API, and it does not use the VTAM 6.2 API (however, CICS does use the non-APPC VTAM API for its other communications functions as it always has). The second type of

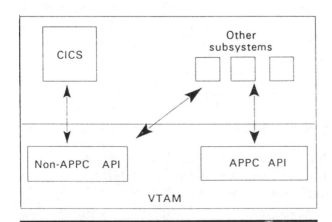

Figure 13.9   VTAM LU 6.2 API.

applications use both the old VTAM API for non-LU 6.2 applications and the LU 6.2 API for TP conversations requiring LU 6.2 support. With the new VTAM LU 6.2 API:

1. The old LU 6.2 subsystems such as CICS would continue to work as before using only the old API functions.
2. Subsystems using VTAM/APPC API may use the old API functions for communicating with LUs other than LU 6.2, and the VTAM/APPC API for LU 6.2 sessions. Starting with VTAM version 3, release 3, it provides support for both dependent LUs and independent LUs.

VTAM/APPC API supports only basic conversations and places some additional restrictions on its users. Therefore, it is not considered an open API. One example of VTAM limitations is that VTAM cannot start an application when it receives a BIND for one of its LUs, nor can it start TPs under specific LUs.

VTAM/APPC verbs are invoked through a new VTAM API command called APPCCMD. Various parameters on the APPCCMD specify the LU 6.2 verb and its associated details. Shown in the following is an APPCCMD prototype and an example.

```
APPCCMD CONTROL = verb, parameter 1, ---, parameter n
```

Example

```
APPCCMD CONTROL = ALLOC, LU_NAME = LUAPPLX, LOGMODE = MODE62,----
```

The rest of this section is written for those who have some familiarity with the old VTAM API. The old VTAM API control blocks such as RPL and ACB are used as before, as well as the LOGON and SCIP exits. However, the LOGON exit is not mandatory and VTAM can handle the binds automatically on the subsystems' behalf. In addition to the APPC API, VTAM applications still need to use the old API verbs such as OPEN ACB and SETLOGON to indicate their presence in the host and the ability to accept logons. The ATTN (attention) exit routine is used for processing conversation allocation (FMH-5) requests.

The APPCCMD in the foregoing example shows how an ALLOCATE request is issued through the CONTROL parameter on the APPCCMD command. Additional parameters are defined through the keyword parameters. Return values such as return code and conversation IDs are provided in the RPL and an extension called the RPL-extension. Applications may not issue other VTAM verbs such as SEND, RECEIVE, OPENDST, etc. on LU 6.2 sessions.

Applications using VTAM/APPC API are identified through the APPC = YES parameter in the applications node definition as follows:

```
(Node name)      VBUILD    TYPE = APPL
JES01            APPL      APPC = NO,PARSESS = NO,—
CICS02           APPL      APPC = NO,PARSESS = YES,—
APPLXYZ          APPL      APPC = YES,PARSESS = YES, —
                   :
```

The example shows three subsystems, the first is JES01 which uses neither the VTAM/APPC (APPC = NO) nor has its own LU 6.2 support, as indicated by its inability to support parallel sessions, PARSESS = NO.

CICS02 is an application with its own built-in LU 6.2 (PARSESS = YES) and does not use VTAM/APPC (APPC = NO).

The third application, APPLXYZ, uses the VTAM/APPC API.

Even though VTAM provides the LU 6.2 API and a number of half session functions, it is not the complete LU. Functions such as TP management, handling program checks, memory management, etc. are managed by the subsystem.

The following basic conversation verbs are supported by VTAM:

ALLOCATE

CONFIRM

DEALLOCATE

INITIALIZE_SESSION_LIMIT

CHANGE_SESSION_LIMIT

FLUSH

PREPARE_TO_RECEIVE

RECEIVE_AND_WAIT

REQUEST_TO_SEND

RESET_SESSION_LIMIT

SEND_DATA, SEND_ERROR

(Some parameters on ALLOCATE and DEALLOCATE are not supported. IBM publication should be consulted for further details.)

13.12 CICS APPC SUPPORT, INTER SYSTEM COMMUNICATIONS (ISC)

CICS was the first LU 6.2 implementation and in a number of ways is still the most comprehensive IBM implementation of LU 6.2. CICS is the only IBM LU 6.2 that provides level 2 synchronization (SYNC_LEVEL = SYNCPOINT). CICS also provides an open API.

APPC support under CICS is referred to by the name ISC. Two aspects of ISC include:

1. ISC environment definitions

2. API verbs

13.12.1 Defining the ISC Environment

ISC environmental definitions are provided in the CICS Terminal Control table (TCT). (The use of the term *terminal* here is a hang over from the days when the only resources in the network were terminals. LU 6.2 and other subsystems are defined using the same table, TCT, which is also used for terminals.)

CICS also implements more than one option for implementing distributed processing. One of the options is called the Multi-Region Operation (MRO) and is used between two CICS systems resident on the same computer. MRO uses operating system interprocess communications facilities rather than SNA or LU 6.2 facilities. The second option is the old LU Type 6.1 implementation, which is also called ISC. It is expected that all new implementations would use LU 6.2 rather than LU Type 6.1-based ISC. In any case, we do not discuss the LU Type 6.1 option. The third option is the LU 6.2. (Since it is used to refer to both LU Types 6.1 and 6.2, the term ISC is ambiguous in CICS. However, LU 6.2 is the only option that is referred to as APPC and, thus, APPC always implies LU 6.2 only.)

For the LU environment we basically define remote LUs to CICS and one or more session pools for each partner LU. An example of such a definition between two CICS systems is shown in Fig. 13.10 (various entries in the table start with the letters DFH, which is a prefix used by CICS with all its definitions and messages). We use the macro language syntax in this example. CICS Resource Definition Online is another method of defining these tables. It uses a different syntax but provides the same information. Even though our example shows both LU 6.2 systems to be CICS, it could have been any LU 6.2 product on the remote site. However, as of CICS version 1, release 7, CICS supports parallel sessions with other CICS systems only.

The entry that starts with TYPE = SYSTEM describes a remote LU 6.2 as indicated by TRMTYPE = LUTYPE62. SYSIDNT is the name by which this remote LU would be known internally by CICS, and NETNAME is the proper symbolic name for the same LU by which it is known to VTAM and SNA network at large. The reason for specifying the name twice is that CICS permits only four character names and SNA (VTAM) allows eight character names. In our example, the CICS system on the right side, system B, is known in SNA by its LU name CICSB but is known within CICSA as CS02. Conversely, CICSA is known within CICSB as CS01. We would need one TYPE = SYSTEM entry for each LU 6.2 with which a given CICS system is to have a session.

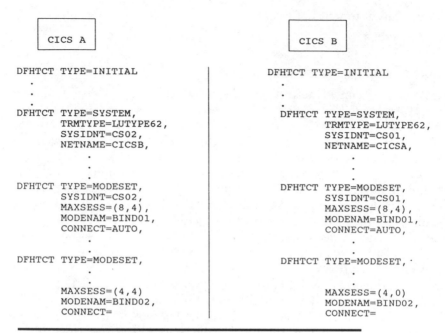

Figure 13.10 CICS ISC environment definitions.

Following each SYSTEM definition, we must define the session pool for each LU and it is done through the TYPE=MODEST (a set of sessions for a given mode) entries. The first entry defines the number of sessions for mode (bind image) name BIND01 (MODENAME). The MAXSESS parameter defines a total of eight sessions between CICSA and CICSB. The second value, 4, defines the number of sessions out of eight on which CICSA LU would like to be the contention winner. It should be obvious that these definitions must be coordinated between the two systems. We cannot have the two systems defining different numbers of sessions in the pools or contention winners that are not complementary of each other.

The second MODESET entry defines an additional four sessions between CICSA and CICSB in which the mode name is BIND02 and CICSA would be the contention winner on all four sessions [MAXSESS = (4,4) for CICSA] and CICSB would be the contention loser on all of them [MAXSESS = (4,0) for CICSB].

CONNECT=AUTO specifies whether CICS should automatically bind these sessions as a part of its initialization procedures.

13.12.2 CICS APPC API

CICS supports both mapped and basic conversations with full recovery. The programming syntax used is the CICS command (EXEC) level programming interface. Our intent here is not to provide an in-depth look at CICS programming interface but to point out some of the product-unique aspects of CICS implementation. The general structure of CICS commands (verbs) is as follows:

```
EXEC CICS Command parameters
```

Example

```
EXEC CICS ALLOCATE SYSID (CICS01)
```

While CICS provides functionality equivalent to LU 6.2 verbs, it does so using a different number of commands and a different syntax.

For example, the ALLOCATE command in CICS only reserves a free session, and, to actually allocate a session, the CICS ALLOCATE command must be followed by a CONNECT command. CICS commands ALLOC and CONNECT together do the equivalent of the LU 6.2 ALLOC.

CICS also allows for a command called CONVERSE which is a combination of LU 6.2 verbs SEND followed by a RECEIVE__AND__WAIT.

To obtain information about its conversation partner, a CICS TP can issue the command EXTRACT which returns information from FMH-5 and other CICS control blocks. A SEND INVITE in CICS is equivalent to MC__PREPARE__TO__RECEIVE. CICS does not support MC__POST__ON__RECEIPT. Deallocation of a conversation can be accomplished by the CICS command FREE or by using the parameter LAST (for "last exchange" in this conversation) on a SEND command.

CICS uses an internal buffer of approximately 4K in size for accumulating data. CICS would not do an automatic flush until this buffer is full. The chain element size is still defined in the bind image (256 bytes is a common value), and a 4K buffer can accommodate multiple chain elements.

CICS commands for LU 6.2 follow:

	SEND CONFIRM and ISSUE CONFIRMATION
ALLOCATE	
CONNECT PROCESS	ISSUE PREPARE
EXTRACT PROCESS	ISSUE ERROR
SEND, RECEIVE, and CONVERSE	ISSUE SIGNAL
WAIT	ISSUE ABEND
	FREE

Among the verbs not described so far, PREPARE is part of SYNCPOINT processing and the SIGNAL command is used in place of PREPARE__TO__RECEIVE.

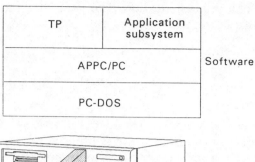

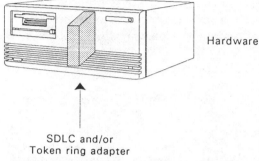

Figure 13.11 APPC/PC—hardware and software requirements.

13.13 APPC FOR THE PERSONAL COMPUTER (APPC/PC)

APPC/PC is an IBM product that provides LU 6.2 support on a PC (or PS/2) with the PC/DOS operating system. It is an open API and supports both mapped and basic conversations. Additional hardware required to support APPC/PC includes IBM SDLC or Token Ring Adapter. Both adapter cards can be installed but only one can be active at a time under PC/DOS. The hardware and software environment is shown in Fig. 13.11.

The software components required include:

1. PC/DOS, at least version 3.3 (See OS/2 enhancements at the end of this section.)

2. APPC/PC

3. Application subsystem—a user-provided system program

4. Transaction program—the application program, also user-provided.

The product APPC/PC contains both the LU and PU functions. It provides configuration screens to define link connections and link station address. Support for managing the SDLC and Token-Ring connections is also included with the product. APPC/PC, of course, also includes the LU 6.2 API.

Application subsystem.   In the PC/DOS environment there are a number of otherwise required functions that are not provided by the APPC/PC. They include system administration functions such as defining PU name, number of LUs and their names, session partner LU names, maximum number of sessions for each LU, etc. All of these functions must be user provided through the application subsystem.

APPC/PC activates its links only on receiving a request from the application subsystem. Handling or logging of errors (or forwarding alerts to NetView) is also a responsibility of the application subsystem. In addition, the application subsystem is responsible for loading and managing TP execution.

In view of all the functions that have to be provided by the application subsystem, it is fair to suggest that, in a PC/DOS environment, APPC/PC is not a complete product from a user's point of view.

Transaction programs.   These are the application programs that use the LU 6.2 API for conversations. These transaction programs can use basic or mapped functions and, until higher-level language support is available (see OS/2 EE), the API calls must be coded in the PC assembler language. APPC/PC supports the following LU 6.2 verbs:

ALLOCATE	PREPARE_TO_RECEIVE
DEALLOCATE	CONFIRM
SEND_DATA	CONFIRMED
FLUSH	SEND_ERROR
RECEIVE_AND_WAIT	POST_ON_RECEIVE
RECEIVE_IMMEDIATE	GET_ATTRIBUTES
REQUEST_TO_SEND	GET_TYPE

GET_ATTRIBUTES is used to retrieve attributes associated with the conversation such as fully qualified LU names, mode name, sync level, etc.

GET_TYPE is used to find whether the conversation is basic or mapped. Support is also provided for user ID verification.

Additional control verbs are provided for communications between the application subsystem and APPC/PC. These verbs provide functions such as activating and deactivating PU and LUs, managing session pools (CNOS), and receiving conversation initiation requests. The verb TRANSFER_MS_DATA is provided to send management services (MS) data to other locations such as NetView.

APPC/PC is not considered a good platform for developing APPC applications and PC/DOS users should consider one of several non-IBM solutions.

13.13.1 APPC Under OS/2 EE

APPC is a standard feature bundled with the OS/2 Extended Edition Communications Manager (none is available with the standard edition). A significant number of enhancements have been provided for APPC under OS/2.

A significant benefit of the OS/2 EE APPC is that the application subsystem, a user-provided function under APPC/PC, is supplied as a part of the OS/2 EE APPC function. Functions of control verbs and user exits, required in PC/DOS, have been eliminated since these functions have been directly integrated within OS/2 EE. In addition, applications can also be coded using any of the high-level languages supported by OS/2 EE.

13.14 APPC API AND CPIC

While APPC API defines the standard LU 6.2 interface, the overall long-term IBM standardization is defined through the System Applications Architecture (SAA).

SAA covers a wide range of interfaces. The one that particularly applies to LU 6.2 programming interface is the SAA Common Programming Interface for Communications or CPIC. CPIC is a subset of LU 6.2 and is intended to provide uniformity in APIs and portability across SAA environments. For designers planning distributed applications in a standard (common) programming environment, it would be important to conform to CPIC. CPIC is discussed in more detail in Chap. 14 under "SAA."

13.15 APPC ATPs SUMMARY

In the previous few sections we focused on Application transaction programs, open APIs, and characteristics of some of the products that offer them. As noted, each of the products discussed had a different programming environment, syntax, and restrictions. In discussing these diverse environments and product idiosyncrasies, the importance of CPIC becomes very clear and until it becomes available ubiquitously it would be difficult to implement LU 6.2 applications over different types of processors and operating systems.

In the next few sections we discuss a different type of LU 6.2 application—the service transaction programs (STPs), i.e., programs that run as an integral part of the LU and provide product-defined enhancements and application interfaces.

13.16 DOCUMENT INTERCHANGE ARCHITECTURE (DIA)

Even though referred to as a transaction program, DIA is an architecture that in turn gets implemented via products such as the IBM Distributed Office Support System (DISOSS), Professional Office System (PROFS), the recently announced OfficeVision, and various Personal Services products from IBM. Inclusion of DIA as an LU 6.2 service transaction program (STP) is an anomaly since it predominantly uses non-LU 6.2 protocols.

DIA is one of the three IBM architectures (the others being DCA and SNADS) that jointly constitute what IBM calls Office Information Architectures. These architectures deal with exchange of information between office users.

DIA defines a set of services to allow access to a centralized, DIA-managed library and to distribute documents to other users. DIA uses the term *document* very broadly and includes text documents, data documents, images, digitized voice, etc. So long as the "document" has been structured according to the rules of document content architecture (DCA, which deals with document formatting rules and has no direct LU 6.2 or communication implications) the document can be stored and retrieved from the DIA library and distributed by DIA.

DIA defines the following types of services for its users:

Document Library Services can be used by DIA users to file, retrieve, change, and delete documents from a central public library. In addition, users can also search for documentation based on keywords.

Document Distribution Services are used to send documents to other users. If other users are not resident within the same DIA system, DIA uses SNA Distribution Services (SNADS) to send documents to other DIA systems. SNADS functions are described in more detail in the following sections.

DIA Session Services are used to allow users to log onto DIA and use its services. Session services assign unique identifications to DIA users and define DIA functions that these users can invoke (not all DIA products necessarily support the same set of functions). The users that are assigned names by a DIA system, i.e., are known to

that DIA, are called "local" users or resident at that node. This no-
menclature will become important later when we compare DIA distribution with SNADS.

DIA also defines other functions such as file transfer services (to file
and retrieve documents from a user-specified library rather than the
DIA library—it is not a generalized file access or transfer utility) and
application processing services for performing maintenance tasks on
document profiles or changing their formats, etc.

13.16.1 DIA Users and Office Systems Nodes

Figure 13.12 shows the relationship between DIA users, services, and
Office Systems Node (OSN).

DIA users: A DIA user is a person who uses DIA services. Creating, editing, retrieving, and deleting documents and sending and receiving distributions from other users are some of the functions that
a user may perform. To use DIA services, a user must logon to a DIA
server (a product such as DISOSS) in an office system node (OSN).

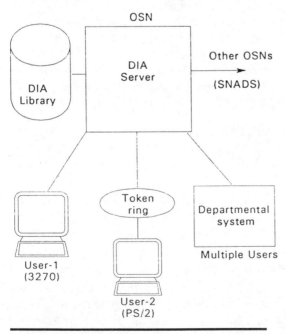

Figure 13.12 DIA users and office systems node.

The user can be an operator on a PC or a 3270 display station or any other terminal supported by the DIA product. No direct sessions are required or supported between users of DIA.

Because DIA users have to log onto the DIA server, DIA is also described by IBM as a "synchronous" architecture (synchronous = requiring logon). Since there are no sessions between users, user-to-user communications are called asynchronous.

DIA server: This is a product that actually provides DIA services to its users. The processor where a DIA server resides is called an Office System Node (OSN). Example of DIA OSNs are an IBM mainframe with DISOSS or PROFS product or an IBM AS/400 with OfficeVision.

An office information system network can be built by connecting multiple OSNs, each serving its local users, and making distributions across OSNs. Communications between OSNs are not defined by DIA; additional protocols are needed for that.

13.16.2 Communications Under DIA

Products implementing DIA do not necessarily use LU 6.2. Especially in the early implementation of DISOSS, LU 6.2 was used only by its SNADS component. Even today communications between end user node and OSN are more likely to be LU Type 2 (IBM 3270) or some product-defined interface other than LU 6.2. In any case, to a DIA user, the LU 6.2 aspects of DIA are transparent and irrelevant and the user deals with DIA through a product-defined interface.

13.17 SNA DISTRIBUTION SERVICES (SNADS)

SNADS is used by a DIA node to distribute documents to other (remote) DIA nodes. If distribution is to a local user, DIA handles it entirely on its own. Both DIA and SNADS require that documents conform to the DCA-defined structure.

Other than our discussion of local versus remote delivery, the following are some additional differences between DIA and SNADS:

1. DIA is synchronous; i.e., a user has to log onto DIA to send or receive distributions. SNADS is asynchronous; i.e., a user never logs on to SNADS or, for that matter, is even aware of SNADS. SNADS deliveries can be delayed depending on when the recipient logs on to its DIA node.

2. DIA, in addition to local distribution, also provides library, session,

and application services. SNADS provides only distribution function.

3. SNADS implementations always use LU 6.2; DIA protocols are product defined.

4. Using SNADS, applications such as file transfers and software distributions can be provided independently of DIA; i.e., SNADS does not require DIA.

DIA and SNADS also have their naming conventions. DIA directory contains only the local users and SNADS directory contains users in all DIA nodes as well as routing tables on how to reach them. As is shown in a few moments, with proper naming conventions we can significantly reduce the number of entries needed in the SNADS library.

13.17.1 SNADS Terminology and Concepts

In LU 6.2 terms, the unit of work performed by SNADS is a *distribution*. A distribution consists of multiple steps: accepting a distribution request, generating and distributing the distribution object, and delivering the object to specified destinations.

The entity being distributed is called a distribution object. These distributed objects are called Distribution Interchange Units (DIUs). Architecture specifies no limitation on the size of an object but does provide for a means to divide very large objects into multiple related segments. Lower layers of SNA may further break these DIUs into multiple PIUs.

The users of SNADS are divided into originating users and destination users. Users of SNADS are other STPs or ATPs such as DIA, NetView, and CICS etc. The real users (human beings) are provided access to SNADS through an agent (DIA, NetView, etc.).

A logical network of interconnected SNADS nodes is a SNADS network. Figure 13.13 shows such a SNADS network. The network shown consists of three OSN nodes, two of which provide both DIA and SNADS functions. Whereas DIA contains a directory of only the local users, SNADS includes a complete network-wide directory and routing tables.

Each node that contains a SNADS function is called a Distribution Services Unit (DSU). Each node in the SNADS network has a unique address and each user within a node has a unique name (some products require that names be unique across the total network, not just within a node). Both the node address and the user name consist of two fields.

User node address. The node address of a user is the DSU node where the user lives. This address is called the Distributions Services Unit

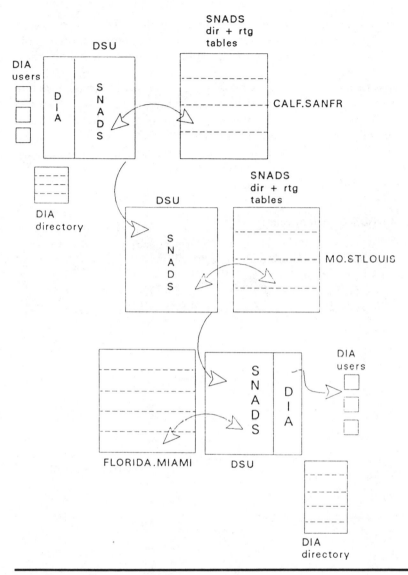

Figure 13.13   A SNADS network.

name and consists of a routing group name (RGN) and a routing element name (REN).

In our example, the three node address are CALIF.SANFR, MO.STLOUIS, and FLORIDA.MIAMI. In the first address, CALIF is the routing group name or RGN, and SANFR is the routing element name or REN.

User name. Each user resident in (or attached to) a DSU has a unique name called the distribution user name (DUN). Users or their agents must know the names (DUNs) of all other users to whom a distribution is to be sent.

The user name consists of two fields called the distribution group name (DGN) and the distribution element name (DEN). In our example a user in San Francisco may have a name of SANFR.SMITH or a user in Miami may have a name of MIAMI.LOPEZ. If we can make the group name of a user the same as the REN (second part of the address) as in the two foregoing examples, SNADS directory and routing tables can be simplified very significantly.

13.17.2 SNADS Directory and Routing

Figure 13.14 shows a little more elaborate SNADS network with three nodes: US.DALLAS, US.NYCSYS1, and EUR.LONDON. The Dallas location has two users: DALLAS.EWING and DALLAS.PEROT. New York has NYCSYS1.CUOMO and NYCSYS1.KOCH. London has LONDON.WINTHROP and LONDON.HIGGINS. There is one more

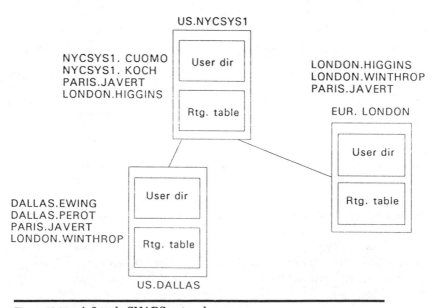

Figure 13.14   A 3-node SNADS network.

user defined as PAR.JAVERT in New York and Dallas, but we will see that this user really resides in Paris which is not shown in the network diagram.

The directories and routing tables for each node are shown in Fig. 13.15. In the Dallas node, Ewing and Perot are shown as local users and, thus, the OSN delivers their mail using DIA procedures. For all users in NYCSYS1 we have a single entry shown as NYCSYS1.* and, according to the tables, their mail is to be forwarded to US.NYCSYS1, a known destination to the SNADS node. If user name or address is not in the tables, the distribution fails with an error return code.

Now let us look at an example of indirect routing. In Dallas and New York nodes we have a user defined as PAR.JAVERT and routing

```
          US.DALLAS                              US.NYCSYS1
        USER DIRECTORY                          USER DIRECTORY

Destination│Destination              Destination│Destination
DUN        │DSUN                     DUN        │DSUN

DALLAS.*   │local                    DALLAS.*   │US.DALLAS
NYCSY1.*   │US.NYCSYS1               NYCSY1.*   │local
LONDON.*   │EUR.LONDON               LONDON.*   │EUR.LONDON
PAR.JAVERT │EUR.LONDON               PAR.JAVERT │EUR.LONDON


-----------------------              -----------------------
     ROUTING TABLE                         ROUTING TABLE

Destination│Connection               Destination│Connection
DSUN       │  Next DSUN              DSUN       │  Next DSUN

EUR.LONDON │EUR.LONDON               EUR.LONDON │EUR.LONDON
US.NYCSYS1 │US.NYCSYS1               US.DALLAS  │US.Dallas
-----------------------              -----------------------

                   EUR.LONDON
                 USER DIRECTORY

            Destination  │Destination
            DUN          │DSUN

            DALLAS.*     │US.Dallas
            NYCSY1.*     │US.NYCSYS1
            LONDON.*     │local
            PARIS.JAVERT │EUR.PARIS


            -----------------------
                 ROUTING TABLE

            Destination  │Connection
            DSUN         │  Next DSUN

            US.CHISYS2   │US.Dallas
            US.NYCSYS1   │US.NYCSYS1
            EUR.PARIS    │EUR.PARIS
            -----------------------
```

Figure 13.15 Directory and routing tables for Fig. 13.14.

tables show that this user is resident in EUR.LONDON. Thus, the two nodes would forward all mail for Javert to London. However, when we look at the London node tables, we realize that this mail would be forwarded to a node called EUR.PARIS by the London node. Indirect routing is necessary when there is no direct path between two SNADS nodes.

13.17.3   DSUN Internal Structure and Flows

Figure 13.16 shows the details of a DSU and its internal flows. Internally, SNADS is structured as a set of multiple STPs and queues. The internal STP, called the DS_ROUTER_DIRECTOR, is responsible for servicing distributions by looking up their addresses and placing them in appropriate queues based on information in the SNADS directory and routing tables. Various components shown in the figure are described in the following list:

1. *The users:*   They are outside SNADS; thus they are shown above the SNADS protocol boundary. A user can be an originating user who initiates a distribution, or a destination user to whom the distribution is directed. We can also have users who control and manage the DSU. The users access SNADS services through other transaction programs.

2. *The SNADS transaction programs:*   These are also above the SNADS protocol boundary. They interact with SNADS using the SNADS API and use SNADS verbs such as DISTRIBUTE_DATA and RECEIVE_DISTRIBUTION, etc., to send or receive distributions. SNADS places local distributions on the appropriate local delivery queue according to contents of the directory, and schedules the specified transaction program such as DIA for actual delivery.

3. *The SNADS protocol boundary:*   This defines the interface between the transaction programs and SNADS.

4. *SNADS presentation services:*   The set of programs that validates the requests from the transaction programs, schedules further distribution functions, and provides return codes and parameters to the transaction application programs.

5. *The router-director queue:*   This queue contains locally originated distributions and distributions received from other DSUs. The local distributions are placed on this queue by presentation services and those from remote DSUs are placed on this queue by another STP called DS_RECEIVE. This queue is serviced by DS_ROUTER_DIRECTOR.

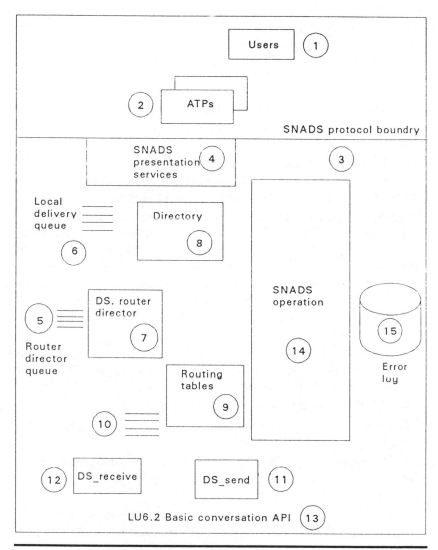

Figure 13.16   DSUN—internal structure and flow.

6. *The local delivery queues:*   These queues contain distributions for local users in this node. The directing part of DS_ROUTER_DIRECTOR places distributions on the queues. The appropriate queue is selected based on parameters in the directory and information in the distribution. These queues are ser-

viced by presentation services when an application transaction program issues RECEIVE_DISTRIBUTION.

7. *The router-director queue:* DS_ROUTER_DIRECTOR, a service transaction program, services this queue, accesses the directory and the routing tables, and places distributions on the local delivery queues or next-DSU queues.

8. *Directory:* This component contains information that enables DS_ROUTER_DIRECTOR to associate a destination DSU name with a destination user and local delivery parameters with a local user.

9. *Routing tables:* These tables contain information that enables DS_ROUTER_DIRECTOR to select the appropriate next-DSU queue for outbound distributions.

10. *Next-DSU queues:* These contain distributions to be transmitted to remote DSUs. Entries are placed on the queues by DS_ROUTER_DIRECTOR. The queues are serviced by DS_SEND.

11. *Send:* DS_SEND, a service transaction program, performs the functions required to send a distribution to an adjacent DSU. It safe-stores the distribution objects and places distributions on the router-director queue.

12. *Receive:* DS_RECEIVE, a service transaction program, performs functions required to receive a distribution, as a DIU, from an adjacent DSU. It also safe-stores the distribution objects and places distributions on the router-director queue.

13. *The LU 6.2 basic conversation protocol boundary:* This is the protocol boundary between SNADS and LU 6.2.

14. *SNADS operations:* These programs perform functions required when errors are detected, or when a control operator displays or changes DSU information.

15. *Error log:* This log contains information concerning errors detected by SNADS and is created and accessed by SNADS operations programs.

13.17.4 SNADS Summary

Along with DCA and DIA, SNADS completes the IBM office automation architectures. As we stated earlier, while SNADS requires conformance to DCA data formats, it can run independently of DIA. IBM product NetView Distribution Manager uses SNADS for distributing software to remote SNA nodes.

13.18   DISTRIBUTED DATA MANAGEMENT (DDM)

DDM is the last of the STPs that we discuss in this chapter. DDM, too, like DIA and SNADS, is an architecture. The purpose of DDM is to allow access to records on files on remote systems in a manner transparent to the application. The intent is to allow for the development of applications without regard for the physical location of the data.

It is important to emphasize the difference between a file and a database in this context. DDM is appropriate for those applications that need access to remote "flat files" such as Virtual Storage Access Method (VSAM) files on the mainframe. It cannot be used with relational or hierarchical databases.

DDM supports an extensive range of file models such as sequential, direct, and keyed access files.

DDM support is defined in terms of source and target systems. A source DDM system is the system that originates the data request, and a target system is one that contains the target file. This terminology is important since some of the products support only source DDM function and others support only target DDM, and some support both. The products that support DDM are shown in Table 13.1. Also shown for each product are the source and target modes supported. DDM/PC requires APPC/PC for its communications support.

Whether or not DDM is applicable depends very much on the application requirements since there are a number of alternatives available from IBM to access remote data. Extended Connectivity Facility (ECF) product allows a wide range of access to files, including on the VM system, for devices emulating IBM 3270 display stations (ECF does not use LU 6.2). APPC/PC itself can be used to retrieve information from any other system that supports APPC and has a complementary transaction program. However, this last approach does not provide transparent access, which is the strong point of DDM.

TABLE 13.1   DDM Product Support

Product	Source DDM	Target DDM
CICS/OS/VS	No	Yes
AS/400	Yes	Yes
S/36 AND 38	Yes	Yes
DDM/PC	Yes	No

13.18.1 DDM Operation Overview

As mentioned earlier, DDM obtains remote records for a program in such a way that the application does not have to learn the idiosyncrasies of the file management system of the remote machine, and, if implemented carefully, need not even be aware of the fact that a record came from a remote site. Figure 13.17, to which the following descriptions refer, illustrates such a flow.

1. The requester application codes its request for the record using the normal local data management interface (LDMI).

2. In a DDM environment, the LDMI recognizes that the data record is on a remote file and traps the request and forwards it to the source DDM server in the local machine.

3. The local DDM source server converts the request into a standard

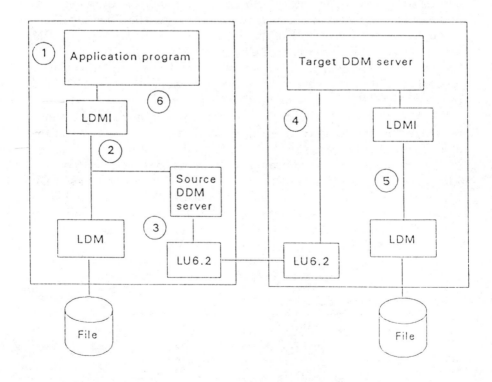

Figure 13.17   DDM flow.

DDM command and transmits the command to the target DDM system over an LU 6.2 session.

4. At the target system, the target DDM server interprets the command, locates the file, and converts the DDM command into a target LDMI request.

5. The request is executed by the target LDMI and the target DDM returns the data to the source DDM over an LU 6.2 session.

6. The source DDM forwards the data to the source LDMI, which in turn passes it on to the application that originated the request.

In summary, DDM is another useful tool to enable distributed applications along with ECF and APPC. DDM is also a part of SAA.

13.19   APPC APPLICATIONS SUMMARY

In this chapter we took an in-depth look at transaction programs and the APPC API—the basic and mapped conversations and base and options sets. With different syntax and idiosyncrasies of various products, there is no such thing as a standard API. IBM has finally introduced a standard in the form of CPIC under SAA. In addition to CPIC, we also need common database standards for distributed applications. From all indications IBM is hard at work to provide these enhancements.

We also looked at a number of service transaction programs. Their primary importance is in the services they provide to the application transaction programs and their LU 6.2 usage is mostly irrelevant to their users.

OS/2 EE has very rich set of functions—both in communications and data management—and should satisfy a number of outstanding requirements for developing PC-based distributed applications.

SNA and Future Trends

14.1 INTRODUCTION

In this chapter we discuss a number of enhancements to SNA expected over the next few years. Three of the significant factors influencing SNA's evolution would be IBM's System Applications Architecture (SAA), the popularity of international standards, and the evolution high bandwidth transports. We look at the state of each in an SNA context. We also look at the SNA transport and network management. Finally, we speculate briefly on how ISDN may impact users with large SNA networks.

14.2 SYSTEM APPLICATIONS ARCHITECTURE (SAA)

IBM announced SAA in March, 1987, as its strategy to provide consistency of applications across its diverse range of hardware and software platforms.

We should emphasize that SAA is an *applications* architecture that deals primarily with software architecture and is intended to make the underlying hardware and system software transparent to applications. With SAA, IBM intends to refocus a user's attention on IBM solutions as a family of software systems and to deemphasize the hardware aspects (of course, each software solution would require the use of some hardware and from IBM's point of view, preferably, IBM hardware).

For our purposes here, the question is: What is the impact of SAA on SNA or communications? To answer that, let us first define the objectives and scope of SAA. Software portability is often described as an objective of SAA. While SAA does facilitate the development of portable applications, SAA does not promise portable applications, nor is portability its primary objective. In describing SAA, the term IBM emphasizes most is *consistency*. The focus of SAA is applications programs and people who use these applications. SAA does not really care whether our network uses SNA at the lower layers (SNA is only one of several SAA transports); nor is SAA an architecture in the sense that it defines any new protocols. It is a set of software interfaces for providing consistency in the following three areas:

1. Application development
2. End user's view of the system and applications
3. Connectivity among applications

Figure 14.1 illustrates the scope of SAA. Besides defining interfaces and functions to standardize, IBM also defines the hardware and software platforms over which this standardization would occur.

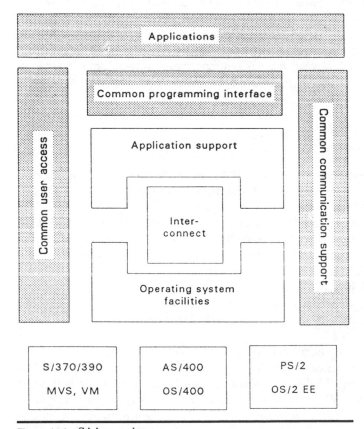

Figure 14.1 SAA overview.

14.2.1 SAA Platforms

The SAA processors include the System 390, System 370 (309x, 43xx, and 9370), AS/400, and PS/2. The operating systems for these platforms that are a part of SAA include:

MVS and VM for the S/390 and S/370 families

OS/400 for AS/400

OS/2 Extended Edition (EE) for the PS/2

Processors and operating systems associated with the RS/6000 are not included in SAA. However, SAA is still evolving and it would be interesting to know how long IBM can postpone the inclusion of UNIX or its own AIX in SAA. Another significant omission as of this writing is the VSE, but there is some speculation that it may be included in SAA in the future.

14.2.2 SAA and the Status of Teleprocessing Monitors

For the mainframe teleprocessing applications developers, the operating system is of secondary importance, or even irrelevant to some extent, since their applications run under the control of teleprocessing monitors such as CICS and IMS/DC. As many as 90 percent of teleprocessing applications in the mainframes may run under the control of these TP monitors. IBM uses the phrase "designated to participate" in SAA when it comes to TP monitors, which means that these subsystems would provide facilities so that SAA compliant applications could run on these subsystems.

14.2.3 SAA Components

SAA focuses on the application programmer, the end user, and standardized connectivity. The control programs will continue to be machine dependent (to exploit hardware specific features), and the system programmers and administrators would also continue to be specialists in their machines. The four major components of SAA are described in the following sections.

14.2.4 Common User Access (CUA)

The intent of this function is the easiest to describe but perhaps the most difficult to achieve. The CUA is intended to provide a common view of the system and applications for the users by standardizing features such as keyboards, colors, icons, panels, pull-down menus, windows, the use of the mouse, etc. To fulfill this objective, SAA assumes that all terminals in the future would be intelligent work stations or PCs (or PS/2s as IBM would insist). Features would be provided in microcode, hardware, operating systems, and support subsystems so that applications could be developed to provide a common system and application access and view. The primary vehicle for providing CUA is the presentation manager in OS/2.

14.2.5 Common Communications Support (CCS)

For SNA, this component of SAA is directly relevant since it identifies the communications protocols permissible for communications among applications under SAA. The permissible protocols are all derived from SNA and international standards. The following protocols are included (OSI protocols included in SAA are discussed in Sec. 14.4):

Data streams: Document Content Architecture (DCA), 3270 Data

Stream: Intelligent Printer Data Stream (IPDS)

Session protocols: APPC (LU 6.2)

Network access: LEN (PU 2.1) and APPN end node (EN).

DLCs: SDLC and Token Ring LAN

Application services: DIA, SNADS, SNA Network Management, and Distributed Data Management (DDM)

14.2.6 Common Programming Interfaces (CPIs)

The common programming interfaces (CPIs) provide languages, database interfaces, communications interfaces, and application generators to enable development of consistent applications. The CPI components are divided into two categories:

1. Languages:

    High-level: COBOL, FORTRAN, C, and RPG

    Procedural: IBM REXX

    Application generator: IBM Cross Systems Product (CSP)

2. Services:

    CPI for dialog interface (CPI-DI):   Still evolving; interim interface based on EZ-VU and ISPF

CPI for database interface (CPI-DI):   SQL

CPI for query interface (CPI-QI):   QMF

CPI for presentation interface (CPI-PI):   Interim interface based on GDDM

CPI for communications interface (CPI-CI):   APPC subset, more commonly known as CPIC

From SNA and distributed processing points of view, the relevant interfaces here are the distributed database functions under Query Management Facility (QMF), Structured Query Language (SQL), and CPIC. For SNA-related interfaces, CPIC is the most important and we discuss it in more detail.

CPIC. CPIC is a subset of LU 6.2 API and defines a syntax that is different from the mapped and basic conversation verbs described earlier in Chap. 13, but provides the same semantics (most of the time). CPIC is crucial to writing any portable applications or for porting programming skills across IBM systems. In addition to the high-level languages mentioned in the previous section, CPIC functions can also be invoked from REXX.

CPIC functions are invoked using a programming language call structure, e.g., a function call in C or a subroutine call in COBOL. A CPIC verb or command always starts with the letters CM (for CoMmunications, we suspect—IBM provides no explanation). Some examples are CMALLC for ALLOCATE, CMDEAL for DEALLOCATE, and CMCFM for CONFIRM, etc. The syntax of these verbs would not change irrespective of the language or the subsystem used for programming.

Each CPIC function has a callable name and a pseudonym. For example CMALLC is a function call name and ALLOCATE is the pseudonym. Where there is an approximate equivalence between a CPIC function and an APPC verb, the pseudonym is the same as the APPC verb name. CPIC functions are further divided into starter set calls and advanced function calls for documentation purposes and do not imply any constraints on their usage.

CPIC also contains functions that are not a part of APPC API verbs. For example, the function CMINIT (initialize conversation) must be used to define characteristics of a conversation before a program can allocate the conversation. There is no such requirement in LU 6.2. Table 14.1 shows pseudonyms for APPC and other functions defined under CPIC. These are described in IBM publication SC26-4399.

TABLE 14.1   CPIC Functions-Starter Set and Advanced Functions

Starter set		
Initialize__Conversation		
Accept__Conversation		
Allocate		
Send__Data		
Receive		
Deallocate		
Advanced function		
Confirm	Set__Conversation__Type	
Confirmed	Set__Deallocate__Type	
Flush	Set__Error__Direction	
Prepare__To__Receive	Set__Fill	
Request__To__Send	Set__Log__Data	
Send__Error	Set__Mode__Name	
Test__Request__To__Send__Received	Set__Partner__LU__Name	
	Set__Prepare__To__Receive__Type	
	Set__Receive__Type	
Extract__Conversation__Type	Set__Return__Control	
Extract__Mode__Name	Set__Send__Type	
Extract__Partner__LU__Name	Set__Sync__Level	
Extract__Sync__Level	Set__TP__Name	

14.2.7   Common Applications

As a part of its SAA strategy, IBM also intends to provide off-the-shelf applications that are SAA compliant. The first such major application announced by IBM was OfficeVision. It is expected that over a period of time many more SAA applications will become available from IBM and other vendors.

14.3   SNA OPEN COMMUNICATION ARCHITECTURES (OCAs)

OCAs are a subset of SNA protocols that IBM calls "open." IBM's motivation for OCAs was to blunt the criticism that SNA, being a proprietary architecture, was incompatible with the age of open systems. In 1987 IBM designated a number of SNA protocols as open and placed their specifications in the public domain and recommended that IBM customers use these protocols to connect to IBM/SNA networks. The following protocols are on the IBM open list:

1. Node architectures: T2.0, T2.1, and APPN end node (EN)

2. LU types: LU 6.2 and LU 2

3. Transaction Services: SNADS, DIA, DCA, and DDM

4. Data streams: 3270, Intelligent Printer Data Stream (IPDS)

5. Data link control: SDLC and IBM Token Ring

6. IBM implementations of international standards

Note that the terms "open" and "SAA" are not synonymous. PU Type 2 and LU Type 2, for example, are on the open list but are not part of SAA. Conversely, nothing in SAA is open unless IBM puts it explicitly on the open list.

As of this writing, IBM seems to be leaning toward licensing SAA interfaces whenever it can rather than put them on the open list. Even as IBM announced its OCAs, it significantly reduced the number of interfaces whose specifications were historically available through public-domain IBM documents. To cite only two examples, specifications of FID 4 and commands exchanged between subarea nodes, which used to be available prior to the announcement of OCAs, are no longer available through public-domain documents.

14.4   SNA, SAA, and OSI

For some time now IBM has been seeking to include the support for international standards in its products and to assure its customers that the existence of SNA, IBM's proprietary and primary architecture, would not stand in the way of IBM's support for international standards. And as IBM would readily admit, the reason for this is more than altruistic—it is becoming increasingly difficult to do business without support for international standards.

In the recent past Europe has dominated the drive for conformance to international standards and IBM has released its gateways for CCITT and OSI standards either only in Europe or in Europe first and then in the United States. Now even in the United States, conformance to international standards has become critical. In addition to the largest corporate customers, IBM's single largest customer, the U.S. government, started requiring conformance to OSI beginning in 1990. Also in the United States, the academic world is implementing OSI much faster than IBM had expected.

In 1988, IBM began delivering products to support its oft repeated commitment to OSI. In that year, not only did we see the inclusion of OSI in SAA, but the first set of significant new OSI products was also announced, giving us a good insight into how IBM plans to support OSI interfaces.

When looking at IBM products and interfaces for OSI, it is important to understand that IBM views OSI as an interconnect architecture and not a native architecture for IBM products. Thus, IBM OSI products are intended to provide communications between IBM/SNA systems and other vendors' OSI systems. OSI would not be the preferred architecture for IBM-to-IBM communications. For example, IBM X.25 support (NPSI and XI) does not replace SNA transport. The quality of the early IBM gateways has been a cause of many a complaint from IBM customers, and, if one is to go by them, IBM has a long way to go before it can support OSI products with any acceptable level of performance. But IBM seems well aware of these problems and is looking beyond just enveloping SNA packets across X.25 gateways and reassessing the appropriate level of conversion between X.25 and SNA.

In addition IBM is also trying to eliminate the "announcement gap" between Europe and the United States. The most recent IBM OSI platform, Open System Interconnect Communications Subsystem OSI/CS, for example, was announced worldwide on the same day.

IBM is not limiting its work to OSI only—it is also providing extensive support for other major standards such as TCP/IP. On a broader scale, this support comes under the overall IBM interoperability strategy which includes providing gateways, not only for public standards, but also for other proprietary architectures such as DECnet.

IBM announcements and documentation for OSI are presented primarily within an SAA context with derivative SNA implications. We follow a similar model in our discussions of IBM OSI support. The two SAA areas most affected by the IBM OSI support are the SAA common communications support (CCS) and CPIC component of common programming interface (CPI). We look at the architectural issues first, then at specific implementations.

14.4.1 OSI and CCS

IBM has identified a number of OSI protocols that it intends to support within CCS. The OSI protocols announced for inclusion in CCS are shown in Fig. 14.2.

Level 2, data link control: LAPB (X.25) and Token Ring protocols.

Level 3, network layer: For connection-oriented network services (CONS), IBM supports X.25 (ISO 8878) and for connectionless networks services (CLNS) it would support Internet (ISO 8473).

Level 4, transport layer: CCS would provide support for classes 0, 2, and 4 (ISO 8073) for OSI transport layer.

Level 5, session layer: CCS would support all functions of session layer versions 1 and 2 (ISO 8327).

Level 6, presentation layer: CCS would support Kernel and ASN.1 (ISO 8823 and 8825).

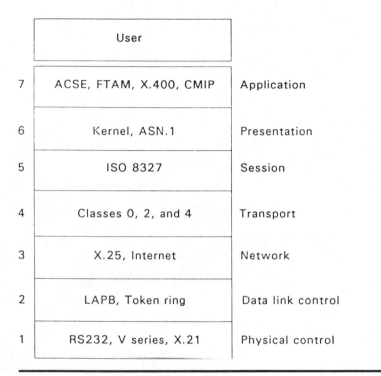

	User	
7	ACSE, FTAM, X.400, CMIP	Application
6	Kernel, ASN.1	Presentation
5	ISO 8327	Session
4	Classes 0, 2, and 4	Transport
3	X.25, Internet	Network
2	LAPB, Token ring	Data link control
1	RS232, V series, X.21	Physical control

Figure 14.2   Standard protocols included in CCS.

Level 7, applications: CCS would provide support for:

Association Control Service Element (ISO 8650)
CCITT X.400 Message Handling
System ISO File Transfer, Access, and Management (FTAM, ISO 8571)
Common Management Interface Protocol, CMIP (Draft proposal 9596)

14.5   IBM OSI COMMUNICATIONS SUBSYSTEM (OSI/CS)

IBM provides a number of products to support OSI interfaces as shown in Fig. 14.3. We have already discussed IBM products NCP Packet Switching Interface (NPSI) and SNA X.25 Interface (XI) in Chap. 11. In this section we discuss the OSI/CS.

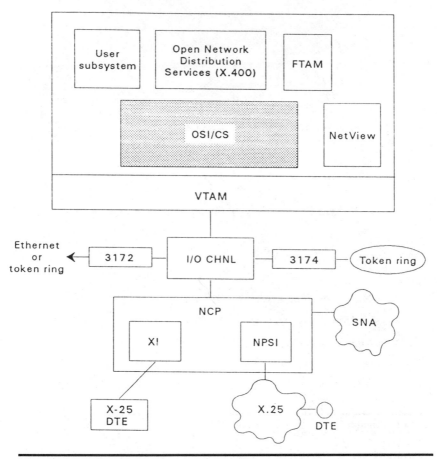

Figure 14.3 OSI/CS and other IBM products for non-IBM standards (*PROFS in VM systems).

OSI/CS has been characterized by IBM as its strategic foundation for providing OSI functions on various SAA platforms. It is really a family of products, one OSI/CS for each of the SAA platforms. It provides support for levels 3-7 of the OSI model. The product was first released for the S/370 MVS in 1990. In another first, OSI/CS is a common worldwide offering, erasing any differences between IBM products for different markets worldwide.

The product provides a common foundation for the development of OSI applications by users, IBM, and software vendors. OSI/CS consists of a base component that is machine- and operating-system-dependent and deals with environment-specific issues. The OSI layers are implemented in a machine-independent form using Pascal programming language. Thus, the same software is used for layer functions on all SAA platforms. Even though the software architecture of OSI/CS is generally transparent to the user, this approach, in IBM's view, provides for much more robust software and ensures uniformity across platforms. The application programming interfaces to invoke services of OSI/CS, too, are uniform across SAA platforms, enabling easier development of multiplatform OSI applications for IBM, customers, and other software vendors.

14.5.1 OSI/CS Connectivity

Figure 14.4 shows various connectivity options for accessing OSI/CS. For wide area connectivity to other IBM or non-IBM open systems, OSI/CS requires the use of X.25. IBM software product NCP Packet Switching Interface (NPSI), available since the late 1970s, provides X.25 gateway between mainframes and X.25 networks. Those familiar with X.25 may be wondering what level 3 functions does OSI/CS provide since X.25 already provides support for these layers. From an NPSI point of view, OSI/CS is implemented using the virtual circuit type 4 feature of NPSI so that it may exercise a greater control over

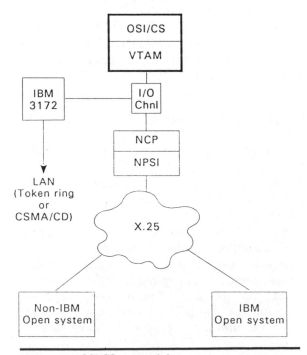

Figure 14.4 OSI/CS connectivity.

NPSI including its level 3 functions. AS/400 and PS/2 also provide X.25 support—with or without OSI/CS.

LAN connectivity is available for CSMA/CD (ISO 8802/3) and Token Ring LANs through the new IBM 3172 Interconnect Controller. The 3172 currently can connect only with an S/370/390 I/O channel. In September 1991, IBM also announced support for Ethernet connectivity to the 3745/NCP. Currently, this support is restricted to TCP/IP only.

Perhaps it should also be mentioned that the intended role of the IBM 3172 is much wider than just providing connectivity for LAN-based OSI applications. Independent of both OSI and TCP/IP, the 3172 Interconnect Controller may also be used for remote channel-to-channel connectivity between IBM mainframes over T1 node links.

14.5.2   OSI/CS Application Programming
Interface (API)

OSI/CS provides access to three levels of OSI functions: session, presentation, and application. The application and presentation programming interfaces are available in COBOL and C languages. The access to Session Services is available only in assembler language. The expectation is that most user-written applications would need to deal with only the upper two layers, and access to Session Services would be needed for more technical (system-type) programs where familiarity with assembler may be more common.

OSI/CS Session Services.   Applications using OSI/CS can allow it to manage underlying sessions or may control the sessions directly using the session level API. There is a one-to-one relationship between associations (an association is an application level connection in OSI analogous to the LU 6.2 conversation) and sessions. Using the OSI/CS services, a programmer can organize application processing in "events" and "dialogs." An OSI event is completed by the occurrence of a major synchronization point. An event can be further divided into multiple dialogs, where each dialog is bounded by minor synchronization points. Within an event, a session can be resynchronized to a specific dialog. However, the session may not be resynchronized beyond a single event. Events and dialogs thus define the scope of recoverability within a session. The use of events and dialogs is optional under OSI and OSI/CS permits development of programs with or without events.

OSI/CS Session Services provide support for session establishment, termination, events, dialogs, and FDX/HDX flows. Data flows outside formal events are permitted by the use of "capability" data. This feature is useful for transmitting small amounts of data, called capability data, without incurring the overhead of setting up an event. Support is also provided for expedited flows (high-priority data), and typed data (data units that can flow against the constraints of HDX session state) as defined under OSI. Tokens required for the aforementioned functions are also supported. Specific Session Services used depend on application requirements, and their selection is a part of the application design. Of course, both sides of a session must support the required function sets for a particular service to be available.

OSI/CS Presentation Services. Presentation Services under OSI/CS deal primarily with the management of OSI Abstract Syntax Notation 1 (ASN.1), where ASN.1 is the OSI method of defining data structures so that various open systems can interpret each other's data streams. Some examples of ASN.1 data types are: boolean, integer, bitString, OctetString, NumericString, PrintableString, etc. OSI applications must describe their data structures in conformance with the ASN.1 rules. One problem with ASN.1 is that ASN.1 data type declarations are not embedded in today's compilers and require application programmers to learn a whole new data-defining syntax. To help alleviate the burden of ASN.1 requirements, IBM provides an off-line utility called the ASN.1 Syntax Checker (ASC). With ASC, a person or a small group of people in an organization can provide ASN.1 expertise to application programmers. The application programmers provide their data details to the ASN.1 experts, who then encode the ASN.1 statements. The ASN.1 statements are then processed by the ASC which generates the appropriate C or COBOL data definitions that can be included directly in the application program.

OSI/CS Application Services. The OSI model is designed to facilitate communications between peer application entities. The logical connection between application entities is called an *association.* The term *application,* as used in the OSI model, is not a customer-written business application, but rather a software module that provides Application Services to the business application. The components of the application layer that provide these services are called application service elements (ASEs). The fundamental service element in the application layer is the association control service element (ACSE) which provides services to start and terminate associations. It is during the association formation that the association partners agree on the OSI subsets that will be supported during the association (a process similar to the

TABLE 14.2   Sample OSI/CS Verbs

Sample session layer verbs	
OSSEND:	Send Data
OSSENDX:	Send Expedited Data
OSSENDC:	Send Capability Data
OSSACT:	Start Activity
OSRESY:	Resynchronize

Sample presentation layer verbs	
OSPUT:	Forward Data to Presentation Layer
OSGETS:	Get Data from Presentation Layer

Sample application layer verbs	
OSBAEE:	Build Application Entity Environment
OSAAE:	Activate Application Entity
OSBASE:	Build Association Environment
OSLISN:	Listen
OSSEND:	Send Data
OSRCV:	Receive Data
OSRLSE:	Release Association

SNA bind process during LU-LU session establishment). Examples of OSI/CS Application Services verbs are shown in Table 14.2.

However, the task of developing OSI applications is much more involved than just learning the API. As noted before, OSI applications involve peer relationships, thus, implicitly, distributed processing. The greater part of designing OSI applications involves learning the implications of OSI protocols—session activities, dialogs, association control, who starts an association, who terminates it, full- versus half-duplex applications, etc. If it is a multivendor environment, it will also require ensuring compatible function sets and profiles. Finally, there is the actual distributed application design and software development, testing, and the need for problem determination tools that work across multiple platforms and cooperatively. Such tools are not available yet. These are some of the same factors that have inhibited the growth of APPC applications even in a fairly homogeneous SNA environment. Thus, the availability of OSI/CS alone may not be sufficient for the availability of distributed open applications across multivendor environments. Most early OSI applications will most likely be vendor provided.

OSI/CS systems management.   OSI/CS provides direct support for the OSI Common Management Information Protocol (CMIP), Common Management Information Service (CMIS), and a control operator interface. In addition, as shown in Fig. 14.5, it also provides an interface to NetView so that OSI alarms can be integrated with SNA alarms

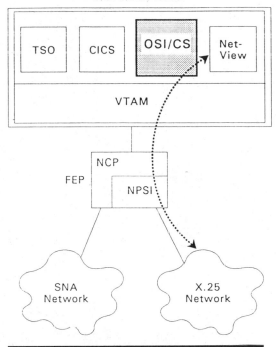

S/370/390 Host

TSO   CICS   OSI/CS   Net-View

VTAM

FEP   NCP   NPSI

SNA Network   X.25 Network

Figure 14.5   OSI/CS management and NetView.

under NetView. The NetView operator can also exercise control over the OSI resources.

However, as shown in Fig. 14.5, NetView does not support CMIP/CMIS directly. With OSI/CS, IBM also provides a NetView command processor (CP) which resides in NetView and processes NetView commands for OSI/CS as well as receives alarms from OSI/CS. The alarms received from OSI/CS are presented internally to NetView over the communication network management interface (CNMI) by the OSI/CS CP (CNMI is the same interface over which NetView receives SNA alarms). Translation of alarms from CMIP to SNA format is done by OSI/CS, so that OSI alarms appear to NetView as regular SNA alarms.

OSI, APPC, and CPIC.   OSI and APPC both permit peer applications development. It is conceivable that customers may wish to develop applications using both architectures depending on whether an application could run more optimally using APPC (predominantly SNA environment) or OSI (predominantly multivendor OSI environment).

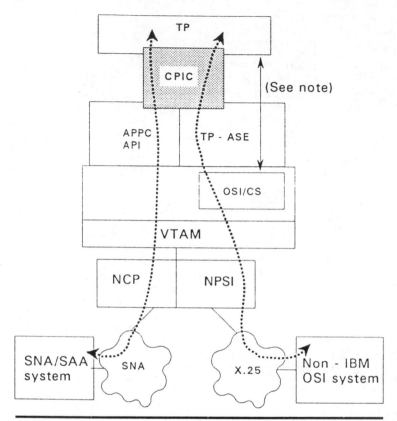

Figure 14.6   OSI and CPIC interfaces. *Note:* OSI/ACSE, PS or OSI session services API.

The IBM common programming interface for communication (CPIC) (Sec. 14.2.6.) can be used as a common interface for both APPC and OSI applications. Figure 14.6 shows how IBM intends supporting the OSI TP API [shown as TP Application Service Entity (ASE) in the figure]. Application programmers can use CPIC for requesting services from either APPC or ASE. CPIC would map application requests into APPC API or the TP ASE depending on whether the request is to flow over an SNA or OSI connection. One advantage of using the CPIC interface is that programmers can write applications that can work with both OSI and APPC environments without having to worry about protocols at lower levels.

Other OSI/CS platforms.   On September 18, 1990, IBM also announced OSI/CS/2 for the OS/2 EE, extending its OSI capability to the desktop. The product provides similar capabilities as the mainframe OSI/CS products described in the foregoing and is to be available on March 29, 1991. The product would require a minimum of 10 megabytes of main memory for a practical configuration. With the addition of other OSI applications such as FTAM, X.400, etc., the memory requirements are sure to increase.

On September 18, 1990, IBM also made a statement of direction stating that it intends to provide a similar product for the IBM AS/400.

OSI applications without OSI/CS.   The only way to run OSI applications on an IBM network is via OSI/CS. However, OSI/CS may not be available on each IBM host for one of two reasons. First, the cost: it just may not be economically feasible to put a copy of OSI/CS on each mainframe. The second reason is the VSE operating system. VSE is not a part of SAA and IBM has no commitment to provide OSI/CS for VSE systems.

When no OSI/CS is available on a host, IBM provides the VTAM OSI Remote Programming Interface (RPI) for OSI applications. Using this product, customers can run OSI applications on any host with the VTAM OSI RPI as long as there is at least one host in the network that contains OSI/CS. RPI-based applications can communicate with other OSI applications only via the OSI/CS host, with the OSI/CS host acting as a relay. Obviously, users will have to analyze cost vs. performance tradeoffs to determine whether this is a viable option.

14.6   X.500 DIRECTORY SERVICES

One of the key requirements for association management is the need for a directory that includes items such as descriptions of local and remote application entities, their addresses, etc. OSI/CS provides this function via its OSI-based X.500 Directory support. However, the IBM X.500 support is much broader than just for managing local and remote application directories. It provides support for centralized directory as well as distributed directory architecture and includes support for both client and manager functions. The central directory function of the IBM X.500 Directory can be accessed by both IBM and non-IBM X.500 products, and, conversely, IBM's X.500 support can act as a client function to obtain its directory information from non-IBM X.500-based directory services.

14.7   OSI/FILE SERVICES

This product provides file transfer and management functions between open systems as defined in the File Transfer Access and Management (FTAM) OSI standard. The product supports creation and deletion of files, file transfers, modification of file attributes, etc. It provides both client and server functions. OSI/File Services also provides programming interfaces in C and COBOL as well as a menu-driven version of the API. OSI/File Services also supports CMS file in VM and physical sequential files under MVS.

OSI/File Services uses OSI/CS as its interface to the operating system and other communications subsystems.

14.8 IBM OPEN NETWORK DISTRIBUTION SERVICES

In 1989, IBM announced two separate systems, the IBM Open Systems Message Exchange (OSME) and the IBM X.400 Message Transfer Facility (MTF), to support X.400 messaging services in the U.S. and non-U.S. markets. Neither of the two was based on OSI/CS. However, in September, 1990, IBM announced a single product, IBM Open Network Distribution Services, as a worldwide offering to support X.400 messaging services. The new product is OSI/CS-based and also provides interfaces to existing IBM electronic mail and office automation products such as PROFS, DISOSS, and OfficeVision. Application programming interfaces are available in C and COBOL.

14.9 TRENDS IN SNA ADMINISTRATION, TRANSPORT, AND SESSIONS

14.9.1 System Generation and Administration

One of the more annoying aspects of SNA (and IBM systems) has been the cumbersome system definition procedures. Traditionally, system generations or definitions had meant defining detailed characteristics of all resources in static tables using assembler language syntax. A large amount of information had to be defined to multiple products. Instead of coding such information once and providing administrative software that could automatically generate tables for each product, the customer had to code the same information multiple times, using different syntax and macros—and, again, with no tools for cross-checking across systems. Even minor changes to configurations could require a complete new installation of VTAM or NCP. Addition of a new VTAM or NCP to the network could require a new generation and installation of each VTAM and NCP in the network—a major undertaking in a large network. A common comparison used to be that if the telephone companies were to administer their networks the way

IBM did, they would have to shut the network down each time a new subscriber joined the network. However, now that SNA has been around for over 15 years, people have gotten used to its administrative complexity.

IBM has eased a number of constraints recently. It is a little easier to add terminals dynamically (dynamic definitions do not hold across system restarts). A number of internal VTAM tables can be changed without having to shut VTAM down. More significantly, new routing tables can be distributed without having to shut down the network.

Advanced peer-to-peer networking (APPN) would serve as a prototype and test bed in some of these areas. The whole area of dynamic definitions and an ability for the system to "learn" about the changes to the network topology is getting extensive attention within IBM. APPN has clearly illustrated the value of distributed directories and dynamic directory search feature in its Network Nodes. An important issue in including new features from APPN in subarea architecture would be: What works well for less than a hundred nodes and a few thousand terminals—would it work as well for hundreds of nodes and hundreds of thousands of terminals? Wherever features can be projected to work well (from performance, reliability, and serviceability points of view) with very large subarea networks, they may be incorporated in the subarea network. Selective convergence of SNA and APPN has started and will continue in an evolutionary manner—perhaps a two- to five-year roll-out of products. The future addressing scheme of SNA would use a combination of APPN qualified names and subarea-element addresses. Migration choices would be provided to a customer who may not want to migrate to the new dynamic definitions and may stay with the old static approach (for control, performance, and problem determination reasons).

14.9.2 Routing and Subarea Node Connectivity

IBM seems generally satisfied with the state of the transport. While there are requirements—they are generally evolutionary in nature. We need more flexible procedures for route selection in SNA so that networks cannot determine primary or alternate routes heuristically. Currently, alternate routes are used only when the route in use breaks; no congestion-based adaptive routing is used. More importantly, when a route fails, all sessions on that route are terminated. Maintaining session continuity across route failures would probably be among the early enhancements in SNA.

Some of the other requirements, such as connecting subarea nodes via switched and multipoint lines, have already been satisfied in the recent VTAM/NCP releases. As for intelligent physical layer (T1 node bandwidth management, alternate routing by T1 nodes, and ISDN, etc.), IBM has not given any indications if or when it might incorporate these technologies as a seamless, integrated part of SNA.

The emergence of fast packet technologies such as frame and cell relay and B-ISDN is another challenge that SNA must meet. For LAN interconnectivity, multiprotocol routers are being aggressively positioned as alternates to IBM's 3745-based SNA transports. As of 1992, IBM support for multiprotocol routers and frame relay has been announced for the 3745/NCP, IDNX bandwidth management system and the RS/6000.

14.9.3   LEN and Distributed Processing

Support for LEN architecture in the subarea architecture is a welcome development but comes at the cost of host independence. Until APPN replaces host-based SSCP, domains of control, and network directory, it is difficult to see how IBM could do much host-independent work.

While LU 6.2 provides a framework for session and conversation level security, this needs to be extended to file and record access for local and remote files. Also needed are dynamic directories so that the objects can be located dynamically.

Since CPIC is based on LU 6.2, it supports only half-duplex conversations. If CPIC is also going to support OSI communications, it would have to support FDX Conversations since the proposed OSI TP protocols support FDX communications. CPIC currently does not support level 3 (SYNCPOINT) synchronization for commitment control and resource recovery and needs to provide that in the future. There is also a need to provide local-remote transparency for transaction programs. For single message transmissions, a single composite function that could allocate, send a message, and deallocate the conversation would be useful.

14.9.4   Very Large Networks

Another area being looked at by IBM is very large SNA networks. Functions such as implementation, performance, problem determination, and network management take on an entirely new dimension of complexity in networks with several hundred network nodes, and the current multidomain architecture would probably break down with such large numbers. About 200 subarea nodes appear to be the practical limit for a single multidomain network. Today one of the choices is to break up the network into multiple SNA networks using SNI.

But SNI creates other problems in end-to-end network monitoring, problem determination, and integrated network management.

As a new concept, IBM is toying with the notion of "clusters" of networks—where each cluster is a multidomain network. The concept of clustering is based on the observation that, as a practical matter, most users predominantly use a well-defined set of applications; i.e., data from various users tend to stay within certain boundaries of the network. If such boundaries can be defined reasonably, the network can be divided into multiple clusters, and each user would stay mostly within his or her own cluster. The cluster would fall somewhere between MSN and SNI. Although SNI is opaque (entities across the gateway are invisible), clusters would be translucent. The primary motivation for the clustering concept is to improve performance and management in very large networks.

14.10 SNA NETWORK MANAGEMENT TRENDS

Significant enhancements have been made in the area of network management in the last few years. Major requirements that are still outstanding include:

14.10.1 Presentation and Graphics

Until recently the focus of NetView had been on gathering alert information, doing analysis, and providing probable cause and recommended action. Now the focus shifts to the presentation of information.

Given the state of the art in work stations and graphics, IBM's current level of graphics support is quite inferior. IBM is quite aware of this and will probably announce graphics capabilities similar to AT&T's Accumaster by the time this book reaches bookstores. As a stop-gap measure they have acquired the NetCenter graphics interface from US West which is to be replaced by OS/2-based NetView Graphic Monitor in 1992.

14.10.2 Centralized Versus Distributed Management

After some experience with centralized systems, it is beginning to become clear that totally centralized systems may be neither possible nor most desirable. It is also becoming apparent that the closer to the source, a problem can be resolved, the more efficient is the network management. Thus, we also need distributed management subsystems to supplement centralized systems.

With "focal point" NetView, a central site communicates with a number of NetViews at different sites that provide management for IBM as well as non-IBM elements in the network. Only such events should be reported to the central site that could not be resolved at the distributed management system. Means must be provided so that a customer can customize the criteria for when information would flow between distributed management systems and the focal point NetView. The criteria could be a mix of on-demand, severity level, or some automated procedures.

The need for distributed management systems and data exchanges among them also brings home the problem of using SSCP-PU sessions for network management data. The use of this session has become a bottleneck since it uses very primitive flow and session control protocols. The SNA CNM architecture is being revised to allow LU-LU sessions with LU 6.2 protocols for network management flows. Such a change would significantly enhance IBM's ability to develop new network management capabilities. NetView support for LU 6.2-based sessions for network management is scheduled to be available in 1992.

14.10.3 Automated and Remote Operations and Expert Systems

With the capabilities available to bring alarms and other network management information into a central site, it is also becoming obvious that dumping all this raw information on a console is as bad as having no information at all. The system must have intelligence to filter and automate alarms and manage itself.

Correlation and coordination of alarms, automation, remote and unattended operations, and expert systems are the language of future enhancements. With release levels 2 and 3 of NetView, a foundation for such developments is already in place.

To further augment IBM-provided functions, NetView customization can be done using high-level languages such as PL/1 and C, both of which are well suited for developing rule-based expert systems. The NetView command lists, another feature to ease and automate operations, can now also be written in REXX—an easy-to-use procedures language. However, a truly integrated and seamless expert system is not possible unless all participants in the integrated system conform to the same alarm structure, codes, and management architecture. Most vendors are willing to provide OSI or simple network management protocol (SNMP) compatible alarms only and, unless IBM can get all these vendors to somehow integrate their network management systems with NetView, it would be difficult for IBM to develop comprehensive expert systems.

14.10.4 Data Repository

Another prerequisite for the development of alarm correlation and co-ordination; expert systems; comprehensive change, problem, configurations and performance management is a comprehensive and common data repository for the network. The repository is also a prerequisite for the integration of functions such as network design and planning, automated system definitions, orders and contracts administration, etc. Figure 14.7 shows the planned structure of such a repository. As a first step towards implementing this concept, IBM has implemented resource object data manager in NetView (available in 1992 with NetView version release 3) which will have an in-memory database for network configuration, and the first application to use it would be the NetView Graphic Monitor.

Getting complete and accurate information in such a repository would be a challenge. Ability to maintain correct inventory should be enhanced with the availability of the asset management feature in 3174 which can report machine serial numbers, machine types, model number, and local connectivity. OS/2 EE would provide similar capabilities for PS/2.

14.10.5 Managing Non-SNA Systems

We already have NetView/PC as a vehicle to integrate non-IBM management systems with NetView. To further enhance support

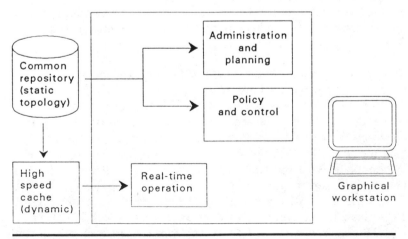

Figure 14.7 Network management data repository.

for hybrid environments, support for OSI's CMIP is being provided through OSI/CS and for simple network management protocol (SNMP) through the host TCP/IP products. In February, 1989, IBM also announced a PC-based voice-network design product. For additional voice-network management functions, IBM would provide interfaces to allow customers to build their own applications under CICS. IBM is also looking at intelligent common carrier networks and evaluating the role of NetView in managing services provided by these networks. Examples of such applications or services include 800 number services, call distribution, voice messaging, wide area Centrex, etc.

Automation of data center operations and remote management from NetView would continue to be another major focus in systems management.

14.11   SNA AND ISDN

To explore the possible impact of ISDN on SNA networks let us review some of the characteristics of SNA that are important in an ISDN context.

1. SNA is a private line architecture—designed to optimize large private line networks.

2. End-to-end connections in SNA are logical entities called sessions, and what we switch in SNA is a session, not a circuit. All switching is logical and done at subarea node level (hosts and front ends) in a "store and forward" manner.

3. The only physical links that SNA recognizes are dumb, "copper wire" circuits—with no multiplexing or physical switching in the backbone network. T1 node bandwidth management systems are implemented in a manner totally transparent to SNA.

So we have a very fundamental conflict between ISDN and SNA— SNA is a private-line-oriented architecture, whereas ISDN is switched services oriented. Given the nature of SNA sessions, it is difficult to develop scenarios, at least for the traditional Fortune 500 applications, in which they could benefit by ISDN switching. As an example let us look at a sample SNA network in Fig. 14.8. The network shows an SNA backbone with multiple front ends and mainframes. Let us look at terminal users at terminals T1-T6 in Los Angeles on the left side of the diagram. All six terminals are on the same multipoint link—shown as L1. Terminals T1-T3 are on the controller C1, and terminals T4-T6 are on controller C2. At any given time each one of the terminal users could be logged on to a different application in a dif-

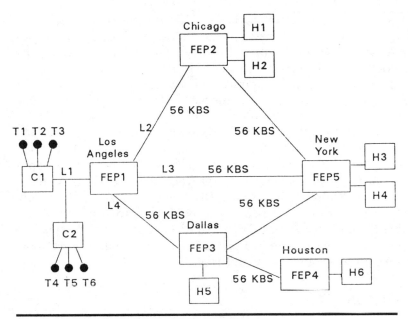

Figure 14.8   Sample SNA network.

ferent host in a different city. Terminal T1 user may be logged on to an application in H6 in Houston, while T2 user is concurrently working with host H5, and T3 with host H1, etc. Each message, as it arrives at FEP1, contains a destination address in the SNA header TH. The FEP interrogates that header and routes (switches) the message on to the appropriate link. Thus, traffic from each user on the same link can be switched to a different destination.

If we were to try to use ISDN circuit switched services, what would be the ISDN equivalent of L1? An ISDN B channel? If L1 maps into a single B channel, then ISDN switching would not work because it would switch all users T4–T6 to the same destination. We can develop some alternate scenarios such as each user having a separate B channel or sharing B channels with smart ISDN adapters, but in each case we run into functional inconsistencies or end up allocating a bandwidth of 64 KBPS to a user who cannot even justify 9600 BPS as a single user on the line.

If the motivation for ISDN is voice and data integration, then such integration is already being accomplished (independent of SNA) through highly optimized T1 node backbone networks with automatic rerouting around failing circuits. Here again, in the context of U.S. tariffs and customer control, it is difficult to make a compelling case for ISDN in the near future.

So, if we are looking at the existing SNA networks with only the traditional corporate applications—no, there does not appear to be much synergy. However, a number of new applications are emerging or the existing applications can be modified to take advantage of ISDN. Any customer service application (where customers call in for service) can benefit from the calling party ID feature of ISDN. Another change that could stimulate ISDN applications would be for IBM to incorporate features within SNA and its front ends that are designed specifically to exploit ISDN. IBM has been actively participating in ISDN trials and so far has not discovered any obvious applications to justify major changes to its front ends or SNA. A major thrust of early IBM participation in ISDN was through its Rolm subsidiary. With Rolm leaving IBM, we would have to wait for a new ISDN strategy to emerge from IBM. However, there do not appear to be any major market pressures on IBM to do so hurriedly. The impact of ISDN would be evolutionary, not revolutionary.

14.12 SUMMARY

No matter how you evaluate it, SNA has to be one of the most significant developments in the history of data networking. Surely it has blemishes—host orientation; strange routing algorithms and even stranger terminology; muddled layer structure; conflicting documentation; complex, inflexible, and cumbersome implementation procedures—we could go on and on. And yet it is by far the most successful architecture. To say that it is entirely due to IBM's marketing power gives far too much credit to IBM's sales prowess and too little to customers' intelligence. It also makes one wonder, if SNA were all that bad and still had the kind of success that it had—what was the competition doing? A fairer assessment would be that with all its flaws it was still a good and, in many cases, the only solution for customers using IBM mainframes.

IBM has never competed as a provider of cheapest technology or, MIP for MIP, the most efficient solution. However, IBM does provide pragmatic, perhaps not-so-revolutionary, but dependable, solutions with the assurance that it would be around tomorrow when the technology changes and provide, most of the time, a reasonable migration path and protect customer investment in existing systems. MIS managements tend to be conservative and do not necessarily want the most revolutionary solutions.

However, times are changing. The support for international standards is growing and customers are requiring compliance wherever useful and popular standards exist. IBM, too, recognizes that. With the age of international standards and high bandwidth LAN interconnect networks finally on us, one wonders whether SNA would have the same degree of success were it to be invented today. Perhaps SNA has served its purpose. But let us not forget that international standards do not specify internal protocols for networks—so proprietary architectures will continue to have a major role in corporate networks. So SNA will keep on evolving.

SNA Headers and Trailers

A.1 SNA DATA STREAM OVERVIEW

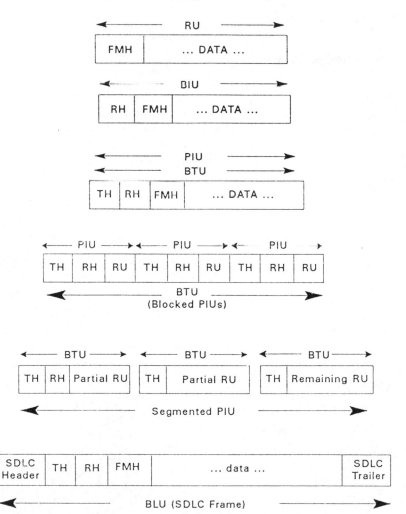

Figure A.1 SNA data stream overview (RU = request/response unit, FMH = function management header, RH = request/response header, TH = transmission header, PIU = path information unit, BTU = basic transmission unit, BLU = basic link unit).

A.2   SDLC HEADER AND TRAILER (SUMMARY)

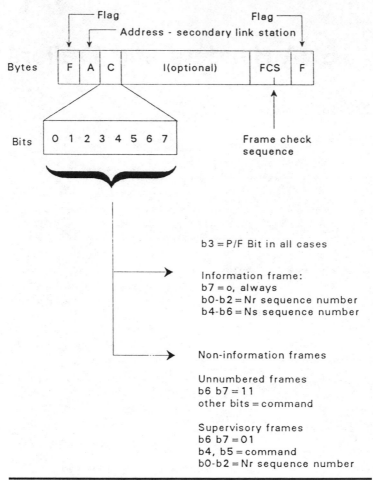

Figure A.2   SDLC summary (*Notes:* P/F bit = 1; from primary, primary is polling; from secondary, secondary has no more data. Ns = sequence number of frame being sent; Nr = sequence number of frame expected next).

A.3   TRANSMISSION HEADER

A.3.1   TH: FID Types

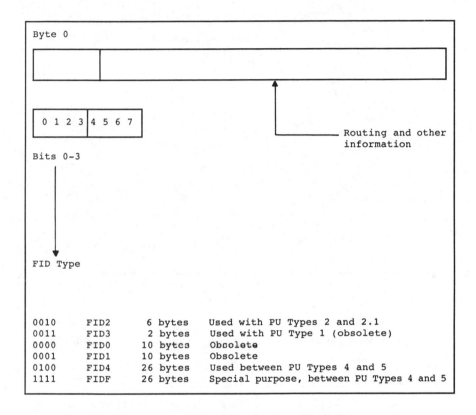

A.3.2   FID2

The FID2 TH is used between a T4 or T5 node and an adjacent T2 or T2.1 node, and between adjacent T2.1 nodes. See Fig. A.3. The FID2 field descriptions follow.

Byte 0

Bits 0-3—FID2 (format identification):   B'0010' or X'2'

Bits 4-5—MPF (mapping field):   This specifies whether the information field associated with the TH is a complete or partial RU, and, if a partial RU, whether it is the first, a middle, or the last segment. Bit 4 is the begin segments bit, and bit 5 is the end segments bit. The bits are used as follows:

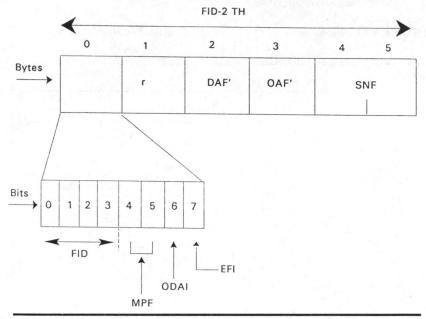

Figure A.3 FID2 TH (r = reserved, SNF = sequence number field).

10: First segment

00: Middle segment (There may be multiple middle segments.)

01: Last segment

11: Unsegmented whole PIU, also called only segment

Bit 6—ODAI (OAF'-DAF' assignor indicator): This is used by LEN, EN, and NN nodes; otherwise, it is reserved. Together with the DAF' and OAF' values, the ODAI value forms a 17-bit local-form session identifier (LFSID). ODAI usage is determined during XID-3 exchange between APPN nodes.

Bit 7—EFI (expedited flow indicator): The EFI designates whether the PIU is a normal or expedited flow PIU. Expedited flows are re-served for selected SNA commands and can pass normal flow PIUs flowing within half sessions. It has the following meaning:

0: Normal flow

1: Expedited flow

Byte 1. Reserved.

Byte 2. DAF'; destination address field, local ID.

Byte 3. OAF'; origin address field, local ID.

A PU Type 2.0 and the SSCP always use a local ID of X'00'. A PU Type 4 or 5 adjacent to the T2.0 node uses a local ID of X'FF'.)

Bytes 4-5. The SNF (sequence number field) contains the BIU sequence number. The sequence numbers range from 1 to 65,535 (incremented by 1 for each BIU, i.e., chain element) and wrapping through 0 thereafter; the responses echo the SNF values of the BIU to which they are responses. For LU 6.2 responses, the low-order 15 bits carry the SNF from the last successful BB. This ordering of sequence numbers applies only to normal flow chain elements.

A.3.3 FID4

The FID4 TH format is used between adjacent subarea nodes, provided that both support ER and VR protocols. (FID0/1 is used if either node does not support ER and VR protocols; only pre-1980 VTAM/NCP releases require FID0/1.)

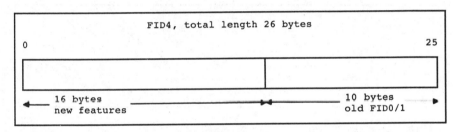

Byte 0

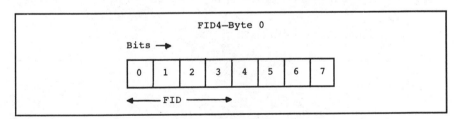

Bits 0-3—B'1000' (indicate FID4).

Bit 4—TG__SWEEP (TG sweep):

0: This PIU may overtake any PIU ahead of it in the transmission group.

1: This PIU does not overtake any PIU ahead of it in the transmission group.

Bit 5—VR, ER support indicator:

0: All nodes in the explicit route support VR/ER.

1: Not all nodes in the explicit route support ER/VR (FID 0/1 may have to be used).

Bit 6—VR pacing indicator:

0: Pacing window has not gone to 0.

1: Pacing window has gone to 0; VR pacing response must be received before additonal PIUs can be transmitted.

Bit 7—network priority use indicator:

0: Follow traffic priority in TPF (byte 3).

1: This PIU has network priority, which is the highest priority.

Byte 1. Reserved.

Byte 2

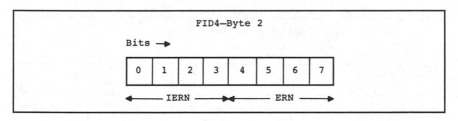

Bits 0-3—IERN (initial explicit route number): This contains the same value as VRN in byte 3.

Bits 4-7—ERN (explicit route number): ERN for the PIU.

Byte 3. VRID (virtual route ID).

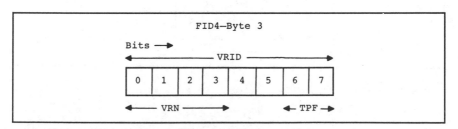

Bits 0-3—VRN (virtual route number)

Bits 4-5—reserved

Bits 6-7—TPF (transmission priority field): 00 = Low, 01 = Medium, 11 = High. (Also see bit 7, byte 0.)

Bytes 4-5

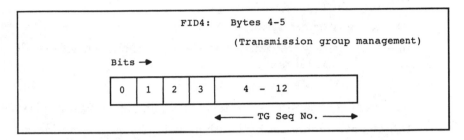

Bit 0—VR__CWI (virtual route change window indicator):

0:   Increment window size by 1.

1:   Decrement window size by 1.

Any congested TG in the route may turn this bit on; subsequent TGs leave it on.

Bit 1—TG__NONFIFO__IND:

0:   FIFO sequencing of PIUs required.

1:   FIFO discipline not enforced by TG. When set to 1, resequencing of PIUs may be necessary by the end user.

Bits 2-3—VR__SQTI (virtual route sequence and type indicator): Indicates an internal PIU type meaningful only to subarea nodes.

00:   NC PIUs, nonsequenced, nonsupervisory

01:   VR pacing response, nonsequenced, supervisory

10:   Others, single sequenced

Bits 4-15—TG-SNF (transmission group sequence number): Used when TG FIFO discipline is enforced. See bit 1, byte 4 above.

Bytes 6-7

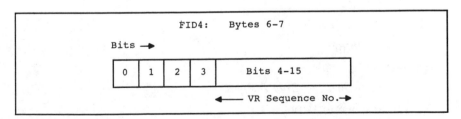

Bit 0—VRPRQ (VR pacing request):

0:   VR pacing response not being requested.

1:   VR pacing response is being requested.

Bit 1—VRPRS (VR pacing response):

0: Not a VR pacing response

1: VR pacing response to earlier VRPRQ

(Virtual route pacing, in contrast to the session pacing, affects all sessions on the virtual route.)

Bit 2—VR_CWRI (VR change window reply):

0: Increment window size by 1 without exceeding maximum window.

1: Decrement window size by 1 without going below the minimum.

Bit 3—VR_RWI (VR reset window indicator).

0: Do not reset window.

1: Reset VR window to minimum.

(This indicator is used when severe congestion occurs on a VR.)

Bits 4-15—VR_SNF_SEND (virtual route send sequence number field)

Bytes 8-11. DSAF (4-byte destination subarea address field).

Bytes 12-15. OSAF (4-byte origination subarea address field).

Byte 16

Bits 0-2—reserved

Bit 3—SNAI-SNA indicator:

0: PIU originated in a non-SNA device.

1: PIU originated in an SNA device.

Bits 4-5—MPF (mapping field, segmentation indicators):

00: Middle Segment

01: Last Segment

10: First Segment

11: Only Segment

Bit 6—reserved

Bit 7—EFI (expedited flow indicator):

0: PIU is normal flow.

1: PIU is expedited flow.

Byte 17. Reserved.

Bytes 18-19. DEF (*destination element field*): A 2-byte destination element address field. The complete network address results from the combination of DSAF and DEF. An element address of 0 denotes the PU Type 4 or 5 controlling the associated subarea.

Bytes 20-21. OEF (origin element field): A 2-byte origin element address field. The complete network address results from a combination of OSAF and OEF.

Bytes 22-23. SNF (sequence number field, session level); see SNF in FID2.

Bytes 24-25. DCF (data count field), the number of bytes in RH and RU that follow.

Note: Prior to the invention of FID4 TH, the TH used to be FID1 or FID0. Bytes 16-25 of FID4 contain information that formerly used to be in FID1/0, except the destination and origination subareas which are now in a different part of FID4.

A.4   REQUEST/RESPONSE HEADER

The request/response header (RH) is a 3-byte field that may be a request header or a response header. The RH control fields shown in Fig. A.4 are described below.

r: Reserved (not used).

RRI (request/response indicator):

0:   Request (RQ)

1:   Response (RSP)

RU category: Identifies one of the following categories to which the RU belongs: session control (SC), network control (NC), data flow control (DFC), or function management data (FMD). (The NC category is not supported by T2.1 nodes.)

00:   FM data (FMD), this category also includes user data

01:   Network control (NC)

10:   Data flow control (DFC)

11:   Session control (SC)

FI (format indicator): Indicates which of two formats, format 1 and format 0, is used within the associated RU. For SC, NC, and DFC RUs, this indicator is always set to format 1.

On FMD requests for SSCP-SSCP, SSCP-PU, and SSCP-LU ses-

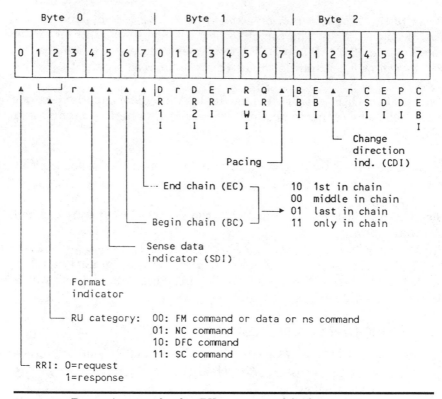

Figure A.4   Request/response header (RH; r = reserved for future use).

sions, format 1 indicates that the request RU includes a network services (NS) header and is field formatted.

For LU-LU sessions that support FM headers on FMD requests, format 1 indicates that RU begins with an FMH. Format 0 indicates that no FMH is present. The format indicator is always set to 0 on positive responses; negative responses are implementation dependent.

0:   No FM header, for LU-LU sessions; or character-coded data without NS header for network services (NS) RUs.

1:   FM header (FMH) follows, for LU-LU sessions; or field formatted with an NS header (NSH) for NS.

For LU-LU sessions that do not support FM headers, the meaning of this indicator is implementation dependent.

SDI (sense data included indicator): Indicates that a 4-byte sense data field is included in the associated RU. The sense data field (when present) always immediately follows the RH.

0:   No sense data included.

1:   Sense data included.

BCI (begin chain Indicator):

0:   Not first in chain

1:   First in chain

ECI (end chain indicator):

0:   Not last in chain (EC)

1:   Last in chain (EC)

An element with BCI = ECI = 0 is called a middle element and with BCI = ECI = 1 is called the only element in chain.

Responses are always marked "only RU in chain."

DR1I (definite response 1 indicator):

0:   Not DR1

1:   DR1

DR2I (definite response 2 indicator):

0:   Not DR2

1:   DR2

ERI (exception response indicator): Used in conjunction with DR1I and DR2I. In a request, indicates the form of response requested. On a response, indicates positive or negative response.

0:   Positive response

1:   Exception (negative) response

RLWI (request larger window indicator):

0:   Larger pacing window not requested

1:   Larger pacing window requested

(new function for adaptive pacing.)

QRI (queued response indicator):

0:   Response bypasses TC queues.

1:   Enqueue response in TC queues.

PI (pacing indicator):

0:   Not a pacing request or response

1:   Pacing request or response

BBI (begin bracket indicator):

0:   Not BB

1:   BB

EBI (end bracket indicator, non-LU 6.2 only):

0:   Not EB

1:   EB

CDI (change direction indicator):

0:   Do not change direction

1:   Change direction

CSI (code selection indicator): One of two codes, ASCII and EBCDIC, may be used. Each code is assigned a number 0 or 1 at session activation.

0:   Code 0

1:   Code 1

EDI (enciphered data indicator): For session level cryptography.

0:   RU is not enciphered

1:   RU is enciphered

PDI (padded data indicator): Indicates whether the RU has been padded to the next integral multiple of 8 bytes in length.

0:   RU is not padded.

1:   RU is padded (PD).

CEBI (conditional end bracket indicator, LU 6.2 only):

0:   Not conditional end bracket

1:   Conditional end bracket (CEB)

A.5   FUNCTION MANAGEMENT HEADERS

Function management headers, supported by various LU types, are shown in Fig. A.5. LU Type 6.1 is only of historic interest and we do not describe FMHs associated with it. FMHs 1, 2, and 3 too are less important given the trend towards LU 6.2. Therefore we describe FMHs 1, 2, and 3 qualitatively only. FMHs for LU 6.2 are described in Appendix D.

A.5.1   FMH-1

This header is used by multidevice LUs to select a destination within an LU. For devices such as RJE stations that consist of multiple devices such as a card reader, printer, console, and a floppy disk, the FMH-1 indicates the destination or the source of the message.

LU Type	FM Header type
0	None required, but may use any header
1	1, 2, 3
2	None
3	None
4	1, 2, 3
6.1	4, 5, 6, 7, 8, 10
6.2	5, 7, 12
7	None

Figure A.5   LU types and FMH usage.

A.5.2   FMH-2

For LUs using FMH-1, once a destination has been selected using FMH-1, this header is used to describe details of the data management task such as record ID, erase record, delete file, etc.

A.5.3   FMH-3

This header handles data management tasks that are common to all destinations in the LU-LU session. Its format is identical to FMH-2 except that FMH-3 applies to all destinations whereas FMH-2 applies only to the destination specified in a preceding FMH-1.

B

SNA Commands

B.1 SUMMARY OF SNA REQUEST RUs (COMMANDS) BY CATEGORY

Request RUs prefixed by an asterisk (*) require response RUs that contain some return values. RUs prefixed by a plus (+) sign indicate old commands being phased out or replaced by new commands. Selected commands are described in more detail in Sec. B.3. This is not an exhaustive list. Additional commands and responses are documented in IBM licensed document LY43-0081.

B.1.1 Network Control (NC) Commands

+LSA	NC-ER-TEST
NC-ACTVR	NC-ER-TEST-REPLY
NC-DACTVR	NC-IPL-ABORT
NC-ER-ACT	NC-IPL-FINAL
NC-ER-ACT-REPLY	NC-IPL-INIT
NC-ER-INOP	NC-IPL-TEXT
NC-ER-OP	

B.1.2 Session Control (SC) Requests

*ACTCDRM	DACTLU
*ACTLU	DACTPU
*ACTPU	RQR
*BIND	SDT
CLEAR	*STSN
CRV	*SWITCH
DACTCDRM	UNBIND

B.1.3   Data Flow Control (DFC) Requests

BID	RELQ
BIS	RSHUTD
CANCEL	RTR
CHASE	SBI
LUSTAT	SHUTC
QC	SHUTD
QEC	SIG

B.1.4   FMD Network Services—Configuration [NS(c)] Requests

ABCONN	INOP
ABCONNOUT	IPLFINAL
ACTCONNIN	IPLINIT
*ACTLINK	IPLTEXT
*ADDLINK	LCP
*ADDLINKSTA	LDREQD
+ANA	NS-IPL-NIT
CONNOUT	NOTIFY +VR-INOP
CONTACT	+NS-LSA
CONTACTED	NS-IPL-ABORT
DACTCONNIN	NS-IPL-FINAL
DACTLINK	NS-IPL-TEXT
DISCONTACT	PROCSTAT
DELETENR	REQACTCDRM
DUMPFINAL	REQACTLU
*DUMPINIT	REQCONT
*DUMPTEXT	REQDISCONT
+ER-INOP	REQFNA
ESLOW	*RNAA
EXSLOW	ROUTE-INOP
FNA	RPO
INITPROC	*SETCV

B.1.5   FMD Network Services—Maintenance [NS(m)] Requests

ACTTRACE	RECSTOR

DACTTRACE	RECTD
DISPSTOR	RECTR
ECHOTEST	RECTRD
ER-TESTED	REQECHO
EXECTEST	REQMS
NMVT	*ROUTE-TEST
RECFMS	SETCV
+RECMS	TESTMODE

B.1.6   FMD Network Services—Session [NS(s)] Requests

BINDF	CTERM
CDCINIT	*DSRLST
*CDINIT	INIT-OTHER
CDSESSEND	*INIT-OTHER-CD
+CDSESSSF	INIT-SELF
CDSESSST	NOTIFY
+CDSESSTF	NSPE
CDTAKED	SESSEND
CDTAKEDC	SESSST
*CDTERM	TERM-OTHER
*CINIT	TERM-SELF
CLEANUP	UNBINDF

B.2   INDEX OF COMMAND RUs BY NS HEADERS AND REQUEST CODES

In the previous section we looked at a breakdown of SNA commands by functional categories. The following request codes are arranged in the ascending order of hexadecimal codes for requests. The request codes are unique within their own categories (e.g., we can have a request code of X'04' in each category with a different meaning). These request codes are carried in byte 0 of the RU.

B.2.1   NC Request Codes

X'02'	NC-IPL-FINAL
X'03'	NC-IPL-INIT
X'04'	NC-IPL-TEXT
X'05'	LSA

X'06'	NC-ER-INOP
X'09'	NC-ER-TEST
X'0A'	NC-ER-TEST-REPLY
X'0B'	NC-ER-ACT
X'0C'	NC-ER-ACT-REPLY
X'0D'	NC-ACTVR
X'0E'	NC-DACTVR
X'0F'	NC-ER-OP
X'46'	NC-IPL-ABORT

B.2.2   SC Request Codes

X'0D'	ACTLU
X'0E'	DACTLU
X'11'	ACTPU
X'12'	DACTPU
X'14'	ACTCDRM
X'15'	DACTCDRM
X'31'	BIND
X'32'	UNBIND
X'33'	SWITCH
X'A0'	SDT
X'A1'	CLEAR
X'A2'	STSN
X'A3'	RQR
X'C0'	CRV

B.2.3   Data Flow Control (DFC) Requests

X'04'	LUSTAT
X'05'	RTR
X'70'	BIS
X'71'	SBI
X'80'	QEC
X'81'	QC
X'82'	RELQ
X'83'	CANCEL
X'84'	CHASE
X'C0'	SHUTD

X'C1'	SHUTC
X'C2'	RSHUTD
X'C8'	BID
X'C9'	SIG

B.2.4   FMD Network Services Requests

X'010201' CONTACT

X'010202' DISCONTACT

X'010203' IPLINIT

X'010204' IPLTEXT

X'010205' IPLFINAL

X'010206' DUMPINIT

X'010207' DUMPTEXT

X'010208' DUMPFINAL

X'010209' RPO

X'01020A' ACTLINK

X'01020B' DACTLINK

X'01020E' CONNOUT

X'01020F' ABCONN

X'010211' SETCV (FMDNS(c))

X'010214' ESLOW

X'010215' EXSLOW

X'010216' ACTCONNIN

X'010217' DACTCONNIN

X'010218' ABCONNOUT

X'010219' ANA

X'01021A' FNA

X'01021B' REQDISCONT

X'010280' CONTACTED

X'010281' INOP

X'010284' REQCONT

X'1010285' NS-LSA

X'010301' EXECTEST

X'010302' ACTTRACE

X'010303' DACTTRACE

X'010311' SETVD (FMD NS(ma))

X'010331' DISPSTRO

X'010334' RECSTOR

X'410220' NOTIFY (SSCP ↔ PU)

X'410221' ADDLINKSTA

X'410223' VR-INOP

X'410235' INITPROC

X'410236' PROCSTAT

X'410237' LDREQD

X'410240' REQACTLU

X'410243' NS-IPL-INIT

X'410244' NS-IPL-TEXT

X'410245' NS-IPL-FINAL

X'410246' NS-IPL-ABORT

X'410286' REQFNA

X'410287' LCP

X'410289' ROUTE-INOP

X'41028A' REQACTCDRM

X'410304' REQMS

X'410305' TESTMODE

X'410307' ROUTE-TEST

X'410384' RECFMS

X'410385' RECTR

X'410386' ER-TESTED

X'41038D' NMVT

X'410387' REQECHO

X'410389' ECHOTEST

X'410601' CINIT

X'410602' CTERM

X'410620' NOTIFY (SSCP ↔ LU)

X'410629' CLEANUP

X'410680' INIT-OTHER

X'410681' INIT-SELF (format 1)

X'410682' TERM-OTHER

X'410683' TERM-SELF (format 1)

X'010381' RECMS	X'410685' BINDF
X'010382' RECTD	X'410686' SESSST
X'010383' RECTRD	X'410687' UNBINDF
X'010604' NSPE	X'410688' SESSEND
X'010681' INIT-SELF (format 0)	X'410620' NOTIFY (SSCP → SSCP)
X'010683' TERM-SELF (format 1)	X'818627' DSRLST
X'410210' RNAA	X'818640' INIT-OTHER-CD
X'41021C' DELETENR	X'818641' CDINIT
X'41021D' ER-INOP	X'818643' CDTERM
X'41021E' ADDLINK	X'818645' CDSESSSF
X'818646' CDSESSST	X'818649' CDTAKED
X'818647' CDSESSTF	X'81864A' CDTAKEDC
X'818648' CDSESSEND	X'81864B' CDCINIT

B.3   DETAILS OF SELECTED SNA COMMANDS

This section contains a more detailed description of the content and structure of some of the common SNA commands. This is not meant to be an exhaustive treatment of SNA commands. Readers should consult appropriate IBM publications for a comprehensive detail.

The commands described are contained in the RU as shown in Fig. B.1. In the following descriptions, the numbers in the left column indicate the byte position in the RU of the field being explained. For example, in the ACTCDRM command, the first field described is as follows:

0   X'14'   Request code

The notation means that byte 0 (the first byte in the RU) contains a value of X'14' and it identifies the request as ACTCDRM.

Occasionally we would also show bit level detail. In such cases bits would be clearly distinguished from the bytes.

Each command name is followed by a notation such as the following:

(SSCP-SSCP, Exp, SC)

The first entry indicates the NAU types (SSCP, PU, and LU), between which the command flows. The example shows an SSCP-to-SSCP flow. The second word indicates whether the command is an expedited (Exp) or normal (Norm) flow PIU. Lastly, the third word shows the class to which the command belongs, e.g., SC for session control, NS for network services, etc.

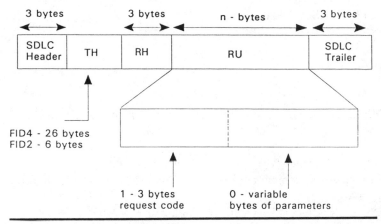

Figure B.1   SNA command overview.

ACTCDRM (activate cross domain resource manager)

(SSCP-SSCP, Exp, SC)

ACTCDRM is sent from one SSCP to another SSCP to activate a session between them and to exchange information about the SSCPs.

0	X'14'	Request code
1	Bits 0-3	X'0' is the only value defined.
	Bits 4-7	Type of activation X'1' cold X'2' ERP
2	FM profile number	
3	TS profile number	
4-11	Contents ID: An implementation-defined 8-character EBCDIC symbolic name representing information about the SSCP issuing the ACTCDRM.	
12-17	SSCP ID: A 6-byte field with the ID of the SSCP issuing the ACTCDRM. The ID field has the following structure: Bits 0-3 B'0000' - the only value defined Bits 4-7 PU type of the node containing the SSCP Bits 8-47 Implementation defined ID in binary	
18	TS usage Bits 0-1 Reserved Bits 2-7 Primary half session receive window size. 0 means no pacing requests may be sent to the primary.	
19-n	Control vectors: The following control vectors are allowed for ACTCDRM. X'06' CDRM control vector X'09' Activation request/response sequence ID control vector X'13' Gateway support capabilities control vector	

X'18'   SSCP name control vector

X'60'   Fully qualified PCID control vector

ACTLINK (activate link)

(SSCP-PU_T4 or 5, PUCP-PU, Norm, FMD NS(c))

ACTLINK initiates the link activation procedure in the link station attached to the link identified in the command.

0-2   X'01020A' NS header, request code for ACTLINK

3-4   Link address, element address of the link (ENA) or network address

5   Indicator field:
    Bit 0 Switched subarea support indicator
        0: Switched subarea not supported
        1: Switched subarea supported

ACTLU (activate LU)

(SSCP-LU, Exp, SC)

ACTLU is sent by an SSCP to establish a session with an LU and set up parameters for the SSCP-LU session.

0   X'0D'   Request code

1   Indicators:
    Bit 0   Enhanced address management indicator:
        0: Sender does not support enhanced address management.
        1: Sender supports enhanced address management.
    Bit 1   Static/dynamic address indicator, applies only if enhanced address management supported.
        0: Sender considers the LU address to be static.
        1: Sender considers the LU address to be dynamic.
    Bits 2-5 Reserved
    Bits 6-7 Type of activation requested
        B'10', ERP, the only value defined

2   Bits 0-3 FM profile
        X'0' FM profile 0
        X'6' FM profile 6
    Bits 4-7 TS profile
        '1' TS profile 1, the only permissible value

3-n   Optional control vectors; X'0E' is the only allowed vector.

ACTPU (activate physical unit)

(SSCP|PUCP - PU, Exp, SC)

ACTPU is sent by an SSCP to establish a session with a PU and set up parameters for the SSCP-PU session.

0	X'11'	Request code
1	Bits 0-3	Format X'0' Format 0 X'3' Format 3, sent only to PU Types 4 or 5 that supports ERs and VRs
	Bits 4-7	Type of activation requested X'1' cold X'2' ERP
2	Bits 0-3	FM profile X'0' FM profile 0 X'5' FM profile 5
	Bits 4-7	TS profile X'1' TS profile 1 X'5' TS profile 5
3-8	SSCP ID: A 6-byte field with the ID of the SSCP issuing the ACTPU. The ID field has the following structure. Bits 0-3 0000, the only value defined Bits 4-7 PU type of the node containing the SSCP Bits 8-47 Implementation-defined ID in binary	
9-n	Control vectors, only if format 3. Allowed vectors: X'09' Activation request/response sequence ID control vector X'0B' SSCP-PU session capabilities control vector X'0E' Network name control vector X'18' SSCP name control vector	

BFCINIT (boundary function control initiate)

`(SSCP-PU T4|5, Norm, FMD NS (s))`

This is a new command, part of the VTAM/NCP LEN support and requests a boundary function BF (PLU) to activate a session with the identified SLU.

0-2	X'812601' NS header, identifies the request as BFCINIT.
3-n	IBM restricted information

BFINIT (boundary function initiate)

`(PU T4|5 - SSCP, Norm, FMD NS (s))`

Another command that is a part of the new VTAM/NCP LEN support, this requests an LU-LU session initiation between two independent LUs identified in the request using the enclosed bind image.

0-2	X'812681' NS header, identifies the request as BFINIT.

3-n   IBM restricted information

BIND (bind)

(PLU-SLU, Exp, SC)

BIND is sent by a PLU to an SLU to activate an LU-LU session subject to acceptance of the enclosed bind image. The SLU uses the enclosed bind parameters to determine whether to accept or reject the bind request.

0   X'31'   Request code
1   Bits 0-3   Format, 0000 (only value defined)
           Bits 4-7   Type:
                       0000:   Negotiable (only value defined for LU 6.2)
                       0001:   Nonnegotiable
2   FM profile: Profile number
3   TS profile: Profile number
4   FM usage: Primary LU protocols for FM data
           Bit 0   Chaining use selection:
                       0:   Only single-RU chains allowed from primary LU half session.
                       1:   Multiple-RU chains allowed from primary LU half session (only value defined for LU 6.2).
           Bit 1   Request control mode selection:
                       0:   Immediate request mode (only value defined for LU 6.2)
                       1:   Delayed request mode
           Bits 2-3   Chain response protocol used by primary LU half session for FMD requests; chains from Primary will ask for:
                       00: No response
                       01: Exception response
                       10: Definite response
                       11: Definite or exception response (only value defined for LU 6.2)
           Bit 4   2-phase commit for syncpoint (reserved if any TS profile other than 4):
                       0:   2-phase commit not supported
                       1:   2-phase commit supported
           Bit 5   Reserved
           Bit 6   Compression indicator (reserved for LU 6.2):
                       0:   Compression will not be used on requests from primary.
                       1:   Compression may be used.
           Bit 7   Send end bracket indicator:
                       0:   Primary will not send EB (only value defined for LU 6.2)
                       1:   Primary may send EB.
5   FM usage: Secondary LU protocols for FM data
           Bit 0   Chaining use selection:
                       0:   Only single-RU chains allowed from secondary LU half session.

1: Multiple-RU chains allowed from secondary LU half session (only value defined for LU 6.2).

Bit 1   Request control mode selection:
0: Immediate request mode (only value defined for LU 6.2
1: Delayed request mode

Bits 2-3   Chain response protocol used by secondary LU half session for FMD requests; chains from Secondary will ask for:
00: No response
01: Exception response
10: Definite response
11: Definite or exception response (only value defined for LU 6.2)

Bit 4   2-phase commit for syncpoint (reserved if any TS profile other than 4):
0: 2-phase commit not supported
1: 2-phase commit supported

Bit 5   Reserved

Bit 6   Compression indicator (reserved for LU 6.2):
0: Compression will not be used on requests from secondary
1: Compression may be used

Bit 7   Send end bracket indicator:
0: Secondary will not send EB (only value defined for LU 6.2).
1: Secondary may send EB.

6   FM usage-common LU protocols:

Bit 0   Whole-BIUs required indicator (reserved in nonextended non-LU 6.2 BINDs):
0: The sending node supports receipt of segments on this session.
1: The sending node does not support receipt of segments on this session. The maximum sent-RU size, specified in bytes 10 and 11 of BIND and RSP(BIND), are negotiated so that BIUs on this session are not segmented when sent to a node requiring whole BIUs.

Bit 1   FM header usage:
0: FM headers not allowed.
1: FM headers allowed (only value defined for LU 6.2).

Bit 2   Brackets usage and reset state:
0: Brackets not used if neither Primary nor secondary will send EB, i.e., if byte 4, bit 7 = 0 and byte 5, bit 7 = 0. Brackets are used and bracket state managers' reset state is INB (1) if either Primary or Secondary, or both, may send EB, i.e., if byte 4, bit 7 = 1; or (2) if FM profile 19 is specified (only value defined for LU 6.2).
1: Brackets are used and bracket state managers' reset state is BETB.

Bit 3   Bracket termination rule selection (reserved if brackets are not used, i.e., if byte 6, bit 2 = 0, byte 4, bit 7 = 0, and byte 5, bit 7 = 0; and if FM profile is not 19):
0: Rule 2 (unconditional termination) will be used during this session.

	1:	Rule 1 (conditional termination) will be used during this session (only value defined for LU 6.2).

Bit 4   Alternate code set allowed indicator:
0:   Alternate code set will not be used.
1:   Alternate code set may be used.

Bit 5   Sequence number availability for syncpoint resynchronization (reserved if any TS profile other than 4 is used):
0:   Sequence numbers not available
1:   Sequence numbers available
Note: Sequence numbers are transaction processing program sequence numbers from the previous activation of the session with the same session name; they are associated with the last acknowledged requests and any pending requests to commit a unit of work. If no previous activation existed, the numbers are 0, and this bit is set to 0.

Bit 6   BIS sent (reserved for TS profiles other than 4):
0:   BIS not sent
1:   BIS sent

Bit 7   BIND queueing indicator:
0:   BIND cannot be queued (held, pending resource availability, thus delaying the BIND response).
1:   BIND sender allows the BIND receiver to queue the BIND for an indefinite period, thus delaying the sending of the BIND response.
Note: BIND sender may provide a timer or operator interface to send UNBIND if session activation time exceeds BIND sender's implementation-defined limits. BIND queueing is terminated by sending UNBIND to the BIND receiver.

7   Bits 0-1   Normal flow send/receive mode selection:
00:   Full duplex
01:   Half duplex contention
10:   Half duplex flip-flop (only value defined for LU 6.2)
11:   Reserved

Bit 2   Recovery responsibility (reserved if normal flow send/receive mode is FDX, i.e., if byte 7, bits 0-1 = 00):
0:   Contention loser responsible for recovery (see byte 7, bit 3 for specification of which half session is the contention loser.)
1:   Symmetric responsibility for recovery (only value defined for LU 6.2)

Bit 3   Contention winner/loser (reserved if normal flow send/receive mode is FDX, i.e., if byte 7, bits 0-1 = 00; or if the normal flow send/receive mode is HDX-FF, brackets are not used, FM profile is not 19, and symmetric responsibility for recovery is used, i.e., if byte 7, bits 0-1 = 10, byte 4, bit 7 = 0, byte 5, bit 7 = 0, byte 6, bit 2 = 0, and byte 7, bit 2 = 1):
0:   Secondary is contention winner and Primary is contention loser.
1:   Primary is contention winner and Secondary is contention loser.

Note: Contention winner is also brackets first speaker if brackets are used.

Bits 4-5   Alternate code processing identifier [reserved unless alternate code set allowed indicator (byte 6, bit 4) is 1]:

00:    Process alternate code FMD RUs as ASCII-7

01:    Process alternate code FMD RUs as ASCII-8 (only value defined for LU 6.2)

Note: When the alternate code processing identifier indicator is set to the value 01, the entire FMD request RU is to be translated using the transforms defined by the ANSI X3.26 Hollerith card code.

Bit 6   Control vectors included indicator:

0:    Control vectors are not included after the SLU name (bytes r + 1 − s).

1:    Control vectors are included after the SLU name (bytes r + 1 − s).

Bit 7   Half-duplex flip-flop reset states [reserved unless (1) normal flow send/receive mode is half-duplex flip-flop (byte 7, bits 0-1 = 10), and (2) brackets are not used or bracket state manager's reset state is INB (byte 6, bit 2 = 0)]:

0:    HDX-FF reset state is RECEIVE for the Primary and SEND for the Secondary (e.g., the Secondary sends normal flow requests first after session activation.)

1:    HDX-FF reset state is SEND for the primary and RECEIVE for the Secondary. (E.g., the Primary sends normal flow requests first after session activation, only value defined for LU 6.2.)

8   TS usage:

Bit 0   Staging indicator for session level pacing of the Secondary-to-Primary normal flow:

0:    Secondary send window size (byte 8, bits 2-7) and the Primary receive window size (byte 13, bits 2-7) are for one-stage pacing. (The Secondary send window size is always equal to the Primary receive window size.)

1:    Secondary send window size (byte 8, bits 2-7) and the Primary receive window size (byte 13, bits 2-7) are for two-stage pacing.

Note: The meanings of 0 and 1 are reversed from the corresponding staging indicator for the Primary-to-Secondary normal flow.

Bit 1   Reserved

Bits 2-7   Secondary send window size, in binary for session level pacing.

9   Bit 0   Adaptive session level pacing support (reserved for non-extended BIND, i.e., when control vector X'60' is not present):

0:    Adaptive pacing not supported by the sending node: Pacing window values in bits 2-7 of bytes 8, 9, 12, and 13 specify the fixed value implied in each pacing response; a zero value specifies no pacing.

1:   Adaptive pacing supported by the sending node: Pacing window values in bits 2-7 of bytes 8, 9, 12, and 13
specify the preferred minimum value for each *Isolated
Pacing Message.* A zero value specifies that the preferred minimum value is as large as possible. Each
adaptive pacing partner initializes its own send window size to 1 at session activation.
Note: Adaptive pacing is supported only in conjunction
with one-stage session level pacing. If the PLU specifies
adaptive pacing in BIND, and the SLU is able to support adaptive pacing, the SLU responds with this bit set
to 1 in RSP(BIND). If the PLU indicates it does not support adaptive pacing, or if the SLU does not support
adaptive pacing, this bit is set to 0 in RSP(BIND).

Bit 1   Reserved

Bit 2-7   Secondary receive window size, in binary, for session level
pacing

10   Maximum RU size sent on the normal flow by the Secondary half
session: If bit 0 is set to 0, no maximum is specified and the remaining bits 1-7 are ignored; if bit 0 is set to 1, and the byte is interpreted as X'ab' = a.2**b. (Notice that, by definition, a __ >8 and
therefore X'ab' is a normalized floating point representation.)

11   Maximum RU size sent on the normal flow by the Primary half
session: Identical encoding as described for byte 10

12   Bit 0   Staging indicator for session level pacing of the Primary-
to-Secondary normal flow:
0:   Primary send window size (byte 12, bits 2-7) and the
secondary receive window size (byte 9, bits 2-7) are
for two-stage pacing.
1:   Primary send window size (byte 12, bits 2-7) and
the secondary receive window size (byte 9, bits 2-7)
are for one-stage pacing. (The primary send window
size is always equal to the secondary receive window size.)
Note: The meanings of 0 and 1 are reversed from
the corresponding staging indicator for the
Secondary-to-Primary normal flow (byte 8, bit 0).

Bit 1   Reserved

Bits 2-7   Primary send window size, in binary, for session level
pacing

13   Bits 0-1   Reserved

Bits 2-7   Primary receive window size, in binary, for session level
pacing

14   PS profile
Bit 0   PS usage field format:
0:   Basic format (only value defined)
Bits 1-7   LU Types 0, 1, 2, 3, 4, 6, or 7
PS usage field

Note: The following format for bytes 15-25 applies only to LU 6.2.

| 15 | LU 6 level: |
| | X'02' level 2 (i.e., LU 6.2) |

| 16-22 | Reserved |

| 23 | Bits 0-2 | Retired |
| | Bit 3 | Conversation-level security support: |

0: Access security information field will not be accepted on incoming FMH-5s.

1: Access security information field will be accepted on incoming FMH-5s.

Bits 4-5   Reserved

Bit 6   Already verified function support:

0: Already verified indicator will not be accepted on incoming FMH-5s.

1: Already verified indicator will be accepted on incoming FMH-5s.

Bit 7   Reserved

24   Bit 0   Reserved

Bits 1-2   Synchronization level:

01: Confirm is supported.

10: Confirm, syncpoint, and backout are supported.

Bit 3   Reserved

Bits 4-5   Responsibility for session reinitiation (reserved unless bit 6 of this byte is set to 0):

00: Operator controlled.

01: Primary half session will reinitiate.

10: Secondary half session will reinitiate.

11: Either may reinitiate.

Bit 6   Parallel session support for LU-LU pair:

0: Not supported

1: Supported

Bit 7   Change number of sessions GDS variable flow support (set to 1 if byte 24, bit 6 = 1):

0: Not supported

1: Supported

25   Reserved

End of PS usage field

26-k   Cryptography options

26   Bits 0-1   Private cryptography options (reserved for LU 6.2)

00: No private cryptography supported

01: Private cryptography supported: The session cryptography key and cryptography protocols are privately supplied by the end user.

Bits 2-3   Session level cryptography options:

00: No session level cryptography supported

01: Session level selective cryptography supported: All cryptography key management is supported by the SSCP and LU; exchange [via +RSP(BIND)], and verification (via CRV) of the cryptography session seed value is supported by the LUs for the session.

All FMD requests carrying ED are enciphered/deciphered by the TCs.

10   Reserved

11   Session level mandatory cryptography supported: All cryptography key management is supported by the SSCP and LU. Exchange [via +RSP(BIND)] and verification (via CRV) of the cryptography session seed value is supported by the LUs for the session. All FMD requests carrying ED are enciphered/deciphered by the TC.

Note: Only values 00 and 11 are defined for LU 6.2.

Bits 4-7   Session level cryptography options field length:

X'0':   No session level cryptography specified; following additional cryptography options fields (bytes 27-k) omitted.

X'9':   Session level cryptography specified; additional options follow in next 9 bytes.

27   Bits 0-1   Session cryptography key encipherment method:

00:    Session cryptography key enciphered under SLU master cryptography key using a seed value of 0 (only value defined).

Bits 2-4   Reserved

Bits 5-7   Cryptography cipher method:

000:    Block chaining with seed and cipher text feedback, using the data encryption standard (DES) algorithm (only value defined).

28-k   Session cryptography key enciphered under secondary LU master cryptography key; an 8-byte value that, when deciphered, yields the session cryptography key used for enciphering and deciphering FMD requests.

k + 1-m   Primary LU name field (always present)

k + 1   Length of Primary LU name (Values 1 to 17 are valid.)
Note: Value 0 is retired.

k + 2-m   Primary LU name or, if the secondary LU issued the INIT_SELF (or INIT_OTHER), the uninterpreted name as carried in that RU (and also in CDINIT for a cross-domain session).

m + 1-n   User data field

m + 1   Length of user data
Note: X'00' = no user data field present. If unstructured user data present, values 1 to 65 are valid.

m + 2-n   User data

m + 2   User data key:

X'00':   Structured subfield follow (only value defined for LU 6.2)
Note: Individual structured subfields may be omitted entirely. When present, they appear in ascending subfield number order.

Not X'00':   First byte of unstructured user data
    • For unstructured user data:

m + 3-n   Remainder of unstructured user data
　　　　　• For structured user data:

m + 3-n   Structured subfields

n + 1-p   User request correlation field (present only if carried in INIT from SLU, or if secondary LU name field or control vectors are included)

n + 1   Length of user request correlation (URC) field (values 0 to 12 are valid)
　　　　Note: X‘00’ = no URC present.

n + 2-p   URC: LU-defined identifier (present only if carried in INIT from SLU)

p + 1-r   Secondary LU name field (present only for negotiable BINDs and for non-negotiable BINDs that include control vectors)

p + 1   Length of Secondary LU name (values 1 to 17 are valid)
　　　　Note: Value 0 is retired.

p | 2-r   Secondary LU name
　　　　Bytes r + 1 – s are included only if byte 7, bit 6 specified that control vectors are included after the SLU name.

r + 1 – s   Control vectors: The following control vectors may be included.
　　　　X‘0E’: Network name control vector: PLU network name, X‘F3’ (present in extended BINDs when bytes k + 2 – m contain an uninterpreted name)
　　　　X‘2C’: COS/TPF control vector (conditionally present)
　　　　X‘2D’: Mode control vector (conditionally present, used in non-LU 6.2 extended BIND)
　　　　X‘60’: Fully qualified PCID control vector (When present, the BIND is called an extended BIND.)
　　　　Note: The receiving LU simply ignores unrecognized control vectors.

Note 1: The length of the BIND RU cannot exceed 256 or 512 bytes. The length of the basic BIND RU is restricted to 256 bytes including the X‘0E, X‘2C’, X‘2D’, and X‘60’ control vectors; any additional control vectors may cause the length to increase up to 512 bytes.

Note 2: If the last byte of a format 0 request not having control vectors is a length field and that field is 0, that byte may be omitted from the BIND request.

CONTACT (contact)

`(SSCP-PU T4|5, PUCP-PU, Norm, FMD SC (c))`

CONTACT requests a PU to initiate a link level contact with the identified adjacent link station. For SDLC links it would cause the initiation of a SNRM (T2 nodes) or XID-3 (T2.1 nodes).

0-2   X‘010201’ NS header, identifies the CONTACT request

3-4   Address of the station to be contacted, element address if ENA supported, network address if pre-ENA

5   Bit 0   Network services available indicator:

  0:   Network services not available via CP-CP session
  1:   Network services available
Bit 1   Enhanced address management indicator:
  0:   Sender does not support enhanced address management.
  1:   Sender supports enhanced address management.
Bit 2   Static/dynamic address indicator, applies only if enhanced address management supported:
  0:   Sender considers the adjacent link station (ALS) address to be static.
  1:   Sender considers the ALS address to be dynamic.
Bits 3-7   Reserved

6   Transmission group number, used when route extension TGs supported

7-n   Control vector X'0E' (optional)

CONTACTED (contacted)

(PU T4|5 - SSCP, PU - PUCP, Norm, NS (c))

CONTACTED is issued by a PU to indicate that it has completed the DLC contact procedure initiated due to an earlier CONTACT request. Parameters indicate whether the contact was successful or not.

0-2   X'010280'   NS header identifying the CONTACTED request

3-4   Link station address of the station being contacted

5   Flags to indicate status of the link station/node and whether the contact was successful

6-n   Various supporting details, e.g.
        Detailed status of the adjacent link station
        Whether contacted station T2.1 node
        If a domain takeover, whether boundary NCP would report sessions with independent LUs in the contacted link station

DACTLU (deactivate LU)

(SSCP-LU, Exp, SC)

This command terminates an SSCP-LU session.

0   X'0E'   Request code

1   Type of deactivation requested:
        X'01':   Normal deactivation
        X'02':   Session outage notification (SON)

2   Cause (present only if SON):
        X'07'   VR inoperative
        X'08':   Route extension inoperative
        X'09':   Hierarchical reset, controlling PU has been activated with "cold" ACTPU.

X'0B':   VR deactivated

X'0C':   SSCP or LU unrecoverable failure

X'0D':   Session override: A new session is being established between SSCP and the subarea PU.

X'0E':   SSCP or LU recoverable failure

X'0F':   Cleanup

DACTPU (deactivate PU)

(SSCP|PUCP - PU, PU - SSCP, Excp, SC)

DEACTPU is sent to terminate an SSCP-PU session.

0   X'12'   Request code

1   Type of deactivation requested:
          X'01':   Final use, physical connection may be broken
          X'02':   Not final use, do not break physical connection
          X'03':   Session outage notification (SON)

2   Cause, present only if SON:
          X'07'-'0F':   Same as byte 2, DACTLU above

B.4   RECOGNIZING SNA COMMANDS—DEBUGGING TIPS

This section contains tips on how to recognize SNA commands in hexadecimal traces.

As mentioned earlier, SNA commands fall into four categories. It is the first byte of RH that indicates whether the RU contains an SNA command. For each of the command categories discussed, the first byte of RH contains a unique value. These values can be verified by using the detailed RH bit level description provided in Sec. A.3. Figure B.2 shows these values and associated command classes. Most of the protocol analyzers and IBM-provided trace analysis programs automatically interpret the PIUs and, generally speaking; it is not necessary for a user to interpret them at the bit level. In case it should be necessary, the interpretation can be done easily using Fig. B.2 as a reference.

To illustrate its use, let us look at the following examples:

RH/RU combination

```
0B 80 00    11 01 01 05 40 40 40 40 40
← RH →      ←————————— RU —————————→
```

The meaning of each byte follows:

RH

6B: The first byte of the RH contains a value of 6B, which, according to Fig. B.2, is a session control command.

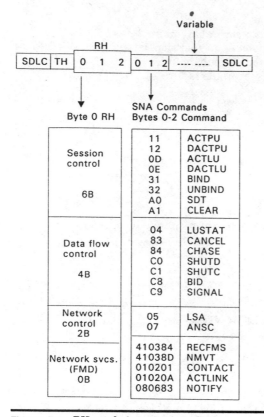

Figure B.2 RH and interpreting SNA commands, byte 0 in RH indicates SNA command class (*Notes:* Commands may be 1 or 3 bytes long; Variable number of parameters may follow).

80: Indicates DR1; all other values are set to 0

00: All values are set to 0.

That completes the three bytes of RH.

RU

11: This is the first byte of the RU and contains the command code. We already know that it is a session control request; so we can look at the SC request codes in Sec. B.2.2 or in Fig. B.2 and recognize that 11 is an ACTPU. Remainder of the RU consists of RU parameters, which we can interpret again using the detailed ACTPU description in Sec. B.3.

Parameters. Looking at the detailed description of ACTPU:

01:    The first digit 0 represents a format 0 command and the second digit 1 represents a cold start.

01:    Indicates an FM profile of 0 and TS profile of 1.

05:    Indicates that ACTPU originated in a T5 node and the five blanks following it are the implementation defined ID.

The next two examples should be self-explanatory when used with the references enclosed in various parentheses in the examples.

CONTACT example. See Fig. B.3.

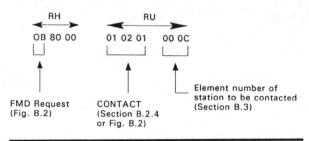

Figure B.3 CONTACT command.

A complete PIU with SIGNAL. See Figure B.4.

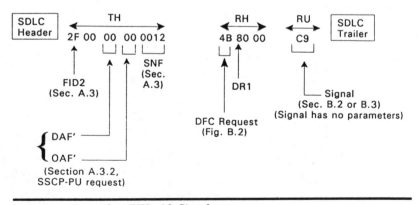

Figure B.4 A complete PIU with Signal.

C

Network Management RUs

C.1 OVERVIEW OF NMVT

Historically SNA has used numerous types of RUs for network management data. However, NMVT is the data structure that is being standardized for all future management RUs, including NetView/PC and OSI-generated network management data. This section presents an overview of of the NMVT structure.

NMVT (network management vector transport)

```
(SSCP-PU, Norm, FMD NS(ma))
```

NMVT carries management services (MS) requests and replies between an SSCP and a PU.

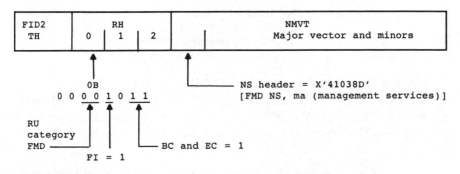

Byte 0, RH = X'0B'

1. RU category for NMVT = 00, FMD

2. FI = 1 means formatted RU or an FM header follows. For SSCP-PU session (used with NMVT), it means that an NS RU follows.

Byte 0-2, RU = X'41038D'. The NS header, X'41 03 8D', identifies the RU as an NMVT.

C.1.1 NMVT RU Detail

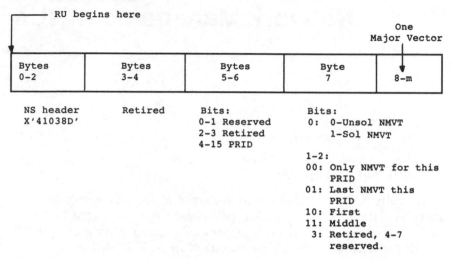

Meaning of values in various bytes

0-2: X'41038D'   NS header

3-4: Retired   Set to network address by subarea node sender; set to 0, the PU local address, by peripheral node sender; ignored by receivers implementing the current level of SNA.

5-6   Bits 0-1 Reserved
      Bit 2-3 Retired   Set to 01 by subarea PU sender; set to 00 by peripheral node sender; ignored by receivers implementing the current of SNA.

      Bits 4-15   Procedure-related identifier (PRID)

Note: For unsolicited replies (byte 7, bit 0 = 0), the PRID field contains X'000'. For solicited replies (byte 7, bit 0 = 1), the PRID field echoes the PRID from the NMVT RU request to which this is a reply. For requests that need no replies, this field contains X'000'.

7   Flags:
            Bit 0   Solicitation indicator: Used only for PU-to-SSCP flow (reserved for SSCP-to-PU flow)
                      0: Unsolicited NMVT
                      1: Solicited NMVT
            Bits 1-2 Sequence field: Used only for PU-to-SSCP flow (reserved for SSCP-to-PU flow)

00: Only NMVT for this PRID
01: Last NMVT for this PRID
10: First NMVT for this PRID
11: Middle NMVT for this PRID

Bit 3   SNA address list subvector indicator:

0: For the SSCP-to-PU flow: MS major vector in this NMVT does not contain an SNA address list subvector.

For the PU-to-SSCP flow: MS major vector in this NMVT does not contain an SNA address list subvector, or it contains an SNA address list subvector that does not require address-to-name translation by the SSCP.

1: For the SSCP-to-PU flow: MS major vector in this NMVT contains an SNA address list subvector.
For the PU-to-SSCP flow: MS major vector in this NMVT contains an SNA address list subvector that requires address-to-name translation by the SSCP.

Bits 4-7   Reserved

8-n   MS major vectors and unique subvectors: Each NMVT contains one and only one major vector and may contain more than one minor vector.
The following table shows, by key value, the MS major vectors:

8-9   Length of the major vector, including the length field

10-11   X'0000':   Alert, unsolicited
X'0010':   Trace data, solicited/unsolicited
  8010:   Trace request
X'0025':   PD statistics data, solicited/unsolicited
  8025:   PD statistics request
X'0080':   RTM data, solicited or unsolicited
  8080:   RTM, request
X'0090':   Prod set ID, reply
  8090:   Prod set ID, request
X'00A0':   Link resource control, reply
  80A0:   Link resource control, request

The description of each major vector includes a matrix indicating the subvectors that may be included within it.

Subvectors with keys X'80' through X'FE' have a meaning that is unique to the major vector in which they are used and are defined uniquely for each major vector.

Subvectors with keys X'00' through X'7F' are referred to as common subvectors. Their meaning is independent of the major vector in which they are used. They are defined in "MS common subvectors."

Subvectors may appear in any order within a major vector unless otherwise stated. IBM publication *SNA Formats* describes details of NMVT structure and detailed subvectors for each NMVT.

APPC and LEN Formats

D.1 FUNCTION MANAGEMENT HEADERS (FMHs)

D.1.1 FM Header 5: Attach

LU Type 6.2 uses this header to carry a request for a conversation to be established between two transaction programs. This header identifies the transaction program that is to be started and connected to the destination half session (LU).

When a transaction program issues an ALLOCATE verb naming a transaction program to be run at the other end of the conversation, an ATTACH FMH-5 carries the transaction program name (TPN) to the receiving LU.

BYTE

0	Length, in binary, of FMH-5, including this length byte	
1	Bit 0	Reserved
	Bit 1-7	FMH type: B'0000101' or X'05'
2-3	Command code: X'02FF' (ATTACH)	
4	Bit 0	Security indicator: 0: User ID is not already verified. 1: User ID is already verified.
	Bit 1-3	Reserved
	Bit 4	Program initialization parameter (PIP) presence: 0: PIP is not present following this FMH-5. 1: PIP is present following this FMH-5.
	Bit 5-7	Reserved
5	Length (j-5), in binary, of fixed length parameters field (currently 3—future expansion possible)	
6-j	Fixed length parameters	
6	Resource type: X'D0': Basic conversation X'D1': Mapped conversation	

7	Reserved
8(=j)	Bits 0-1 Synchronization level

                                                  00: None

                                                  01: Confirm

                                                  10: Confirm, syncpoint, and backout

                                                  11: Reserved

                                Bit 2-7   Reserved

j+1-p	Variable length parameters
j+1-k	Transaction program name field
j+1	Length (values 1 to 64 are valid), in binary, of transaction program name
j+2-k	Transaction program name: a symbol string identifying a transaction program name known at the receiver
k+1-m	Access security information field:
m+1	Length (0 or m-k-1), in binary, of access security information subfields (See "Access security information subfields" below.)
m+1-n	Logical-unit-of-work-identifier field: Length (values 0 and 10 to 26 are valid), in binary, of logical-unit-of-work-identifier field
m+2-n	Logical-unit-of-work identifier
m+2	Length (values 1 to 17 are valid), in binary, of network-qualified LU name
m+3-w	Network-qualified LU network name.
w+1-w+6	Logical-unit-of-work instance number, in binary
w+7-	
w+8(=n)	Logical-unit-of-work sequence number, in binary
n+1-p	Conversation correlator field
n+1	Length (values 0 to 8 are valid), in binary, of conversation correlator of sender
n+2-p	Conversation correlator of the sending transaction: a 1- to 8-byte symbol string identifier (unique between partner LUs) of the conversation being allocated via FMH-5 (An example construction of this field would be the composition of a transaction program instance identifier and a resource identifier.)

Note: Trailing length fields (bytes n+1, m+1, and k+1) that have value X'00' can be omitted.

Access security information subfields. The access security information subfields in FMH-5 have the following formats:

0	Length (valid values are 1 to 11), in binary, of remainder of subfield. Does not include this length byte.

1	Subfield type:
	X'00': Profile
	X'01': Password
	X'02': User ID
2-i	Data: A symbol string identifying access security information known at the receiver

Note: The access security information subfields may appear in any order in the access security information field of the FMH-5.

PIP variable. The PIP variable following FMH-5 ATTACH has the following format:

0-1	Length (4 or n + 1), in binary, of PIP variable, including this length field
2-3	GDS indicator: X'12F5'
4-n	Zero or more PIP subfields, each of which has the following format (shown in "PIP subfield" using zero origin)

PIP subfield. Zero or more of these subfields are contained in a PIP variable:

0-1	Length, in binary, of PIP subfield, including this length field
42-3	GDS indicator: X'12E2'
4-m	PIP subfield data.

D.1.2 FM Header 7: Error Description

LU Type 6.2 uses this header, following negative response (0846), to carry information that relates to an error on the session or conversation. For example, an FMH-7 and additional error information are sent when an FMH-5 (ATTACH) specifies a nonexistent transaction program name.

0	Length (7), in binary, of FMH-7, including this length byte	
1	Bit 0	Reserved
	Bits 1-7	FMH type: B'0000111' or X'07'
2-5	SNA-defined sense data (see below)	
6	Bit 0	Error log variable presence:
		0: No error log variable follows this FMH-7.
		1: Error log GDS variable follows this FMH-7.
	Bit 1-7	Reserved

Note: Only the following sense data (in hexadecimal) can be sent in an LU 6.2 FMH-7. Sense data carried in non-LU 6.2 FMH-7 varies by implementation.

Sense Data for LU 6.2

Sense data	Return code
1008600B	RESOURCE__FAILURE__NO__RETRY
10086021	ALLOCATION__ERROR--TPN__NOT__RECOGNIZED
10086031	ALLOCATION__ERROR--PIP__NOT__ALLOWED
10086032	ALLOCATION__ERROR--PIP__NOT__SPECIFIED__CORRECTLY
10086034	ALLOCATION__ERROR--CONVERSATION__TYPE__MISMATCH
10086041	ALLOCATION__ERROR--SYNC__LEVEL__NOT__SUPPORTED__BY__PGM
080F6051	ALLOCATION__ERROR--SECURITY__NOT__VALID
08240000	BACKED__OUT
084B6031	ALLOCATION__ERROR--TRANS__PGM__NOT__AVAIL__RETRY
084C0000	ALLOCATION__ERROR--TRANS__PGM__NOT__AVAIL__RETRY
08640000	DEALLOCATE__ABEND__PROG
08640001	DEALLOCATE__ABEND__SVC
08640002	DEALLOCATE__ABEND__TIMER
08890000	PROG__ERROR__NO__TRUNC or PROG__ERROR__PURGING
08890001	PROG__ERROR__TRUNC
08890100	SVC__ERROR__NO__TRUNC OR SVC__ERROR__PURGING
08890101	SVC__ERROR__TRUNC

D.1.3 FM Header 12: Security

LU Type 6.2 uses this header during LU-LU verification. This header is used to return to the partner LU the enciphered version of the clear random data received in +RSP(BIND).

The function management header 12 (FMH-12) has the following format:

0	Length (10 bytes), in binary, of FMH-12, including this length byte
1	Bit 0 Reserved Bit 1-7 FMH type, B'0001100' or X'0C'
2-9	Enciphered version of the random data received in RSP(BIND)

D.2 GENERALIZED DATA STREAM (GDS)

The structure of GDS is shown in Fig. D.1.

Length (LL) description. Bits 1 to 15 of the LL contain a binary number from 4 through 32767, which is the length, in bytes, of the variable-length field that follows plus two for the length field itself. Values 0 and 1 for LL are reserved for use as escape sequences; values 2 and 3 are not used. Bit 0 of byte 0 (higher-order bit) is used for a length continuation indicator, where a value of 0 means last GDS variable segment. Some data streams built from structured fields use

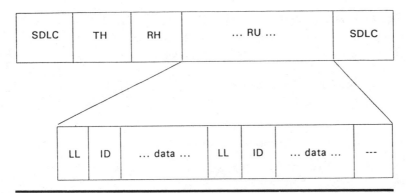

Figure D.1   Generalized data stream (LL = length, ID = GDS field identifier).

other methods to create data objects that are longer than a 15-bit length can specify.

Identifier (ID) description.   The 2-byte identifier that follows the length field describes the format and meaning of the data that follow. Sometimes additional values appearing in the information field are needed to completely specify the information field's content. Various IDs are listed below.

The code points used by LU 6.2 are:

X'1210'	Change number of sessions
X'1211'	Exchange log name
X'1213'	Compare states
X'12A0'	Workstation display passthrough
X'12E1'	Error log
X'12E2'	PIP subfield data
X'12F1'	Null data
X'12F2'	User control data
X'12F3'	Map name
X'12F4'	Error data
X'12F5'	PIP data
X'12FF'	Application data

D.3   LIST OF SNA SERVICES TRANSACTION PROGRAMS

LU Type 6.2 service transaction programs are identified by a transaction program name (TPN) that begins with a value of X'06'. Other SNA service transaction programs are identified similarly. The following table identifies the transaction program names that SNA currently defines. These TPNs are specified in FM header Type 5.

SNA Defined Service Transaction Programs

TP name	TP description	
X'06F1****'	LU 6.2 CNOS	
X'06F2****'	LU 6.2 Syncpoint resynchronization	
X'07F0F0F1'	DDM Synchronous conversation	
X'20F0F0F0'	DIA PROCESS destination TP	
X'20F0F0F1'	DIA SERVER TP	
X'21F0F0F1'	DS SEND TP	(SNADS)
X'21F0F0F2'	DS RECEIVE TP	(SNADS)
X'21F0F0F3'	DS ROUTER DIRECTOR	(SNADS)
X'21F0F0F6'	DS General server TP	(SNAPS)

**** = Any hexadecimal digit.

D.4 DESCRIPTIONS OF GDS VARIABLES FOR SNA STPs

D.4.1 Change Number of Sessions (X'1210') GDS Variable

0-1	Length (17 or n+1), in binary, of change number of sessions GDS variable, including this length field
2-3	GDS ID: X'1210'
4	Service flag: Bit 0-3 Reserved Bit 4-7 Request/reply indicator: 　　0010: Request 　　1000: Reply, function completed abnormal 　　1010: Reply, function accepted but not yet completed
5	Reply modifier (reserved if byte 4, bits 4-7 = 0010): 　　X'00': Normal—no negotiation performed 　　X'01': Abnormal—command race detected 　　X'02': Abnormal—mode name not recognized 　　X'03': Reserved 　　X'04': Normal—negotiated reply 　　X'05': Abnormal—(LU, mode) session limit is 0
6	Action: 　　X'00': Set (LU, mode) session limits 　　X'01': Reserved 　　X'02': Close
7	Drain immediacy: Bits 0-2 Reserved

	Bit 3 Source LU drain (reserved if byte 6 not = 02): 0: No (Send BIS at next opportunity.) 1: Yes
	Bits 4-6 Reserved
	Bit 7 Target LU drain (reserved if byte 6 not = 02): 0: No (send BIS at next opportunity.) 1: Yes
8	Action flags:
	Bits 0-6 Reserved
	Bit 7 Session deactivation responsibility: 0: Sender of change number of sessions request (source LU) 1: Receiver of change number of sessions request (target LU)

Note: Bytes 9-14 are reserved if byte 6 not = 0.

9-10	(LU, mode) session limit: Bit 0 Reserved Bits 1-15 Maximum (LU, mode) session count, in binary
11-12	Source LU contention winners: Bit 0 Reserved Bits 1-15 Guaranteed minimum number of contention winner sessions at source LU, in binary
13-14	Target LU contention winners: Bit 0 Reserved Bits 1-15 Guaranteed minimum number of contention winner sessions at target LU, in binary
15	Mode name selection: Bits 0-6 Reserved Bit 7 Mode names affected by this command: 0: A single mode name is affected. 1: All mode names are affected.
16	Length (Values 0 to 8 are valid; reserved if byte 15, byte 7 = 1), in binary, of mode name
17-n	Mode name (omitted if byte 16 = X'00')

D.4.2   Exchange Log Name (X'1211')
GDS Variable

0-1	Length (p+1), in binary, of exchange log name GDS variable, including this length field
2-3	GDS ID: X'1211'
4	Service flag: Bits 0-3 Reserved Bits 4-7 Request/reply indicator: 0010: Request 1000: Reply, function completed abnormally 1001: Reply, function completed normally

5	Syncpoint manager flags:
	Bits 0-6 Reserved
	Bit 7 Log status:
	          0: Cold
	          1: Warm

6	Length (Values 1 to 17 are valid), in binary, of network-qualified LU network name
7-n	Network-qualified LU name
n+1	Length (Values 1 to 64 are valid), in binary, of log name
n+2-p	Log name

D.4.3   Compare States (X'1213')
GDS Variable

0-1	Length, in binary, of compare states GDS variable, including this length Field
2-3	GDS ID: X'1213'

4	Service flag:
	Bits 0-3 Reserved
	Bits 4-7 Request/reply indicator:
	          0010: Request
	          1000: Reply, function completed abnormally
	          1001: Reply, function completed normally

5	Syncpoint manager state:
	          X'01': RESET
	          X'02': SYNC_POINT_MANAGER_
	                  PENDING
	          X'03': IN_DOUBT
	          X'04': COMMITTED
	          X'05': HEURISTIC_RESET
	          X'06': HEURISTIC_COMMITTED
	          X'07': HEURISTIC_MIXED

6	Reserved
7	Length, in binary, of logical-unit-of-work identifier field (Values 10 to 26 are valid.)
8-n	Logical-unit-of-work identifier
8	Length, in binary, of network-qualified LU name (Values 1 to 17 are valid.)
8-w	Network-qualified LU name
w+1-w+6	Logical-unit-of-work instance number, in binary
w+7- w+8(=n)	Logical-unit-of-work sequence number, in binary
n+1	Length (Values 0 to 8 are valid.), in binary, of conversation correlator

n+2-q	Conversation correlator of transaction program that allocated the conversation that failed
q+1	Length (Values 2 to 8 are valid), in binary, of session instance identifier
q+2-p	Session instance identifier of session being used by conversation at time of failure

E

Acronyms

(Acronyms are here spelled out without a full explanation of their meaning—which should be sought through the Index.)

ACF	Advanced Communications Function
ACK	Positive Acknowledgement in BSC
ACSE	Association Control Service Element (OSI)
ACTLU	Activate LU
ACTPU	Activate PU
AIX	Advanced Interactive Executive, IBM's version of Unix
API	Application Program Interface
APPC	Advanced Program to Program Communications (another name for LU 6.2)
APPN	Advanced Peer to Peer Networking (new enhanced SNA)
AS/400	Application System 400 (midrange processor from IBM)
ASN.1	Abstract Syntax Representation One (OSI)
BB	Begin Bracket
BC	Begin Chain
BCC	Block Check Character
BIS	Bracket Initiation Stopped
BIU	Basic Information Unit
BMS	Basic Mapping Support (CICS)
BNN	Boundary Network Node
BSC	Binary Synchronous Communications
BTAM	Basic Telecommunications Access Method
BTU	Basic Transmission Unit
CCITT	Consultative Committee for International Telephone and Telegraph

CCS	Common Cummunications Support (SAA)
CCW	Channel Command Word (an instruction for I/O channel)
CDI	Change Direction Indicator
CDRM	Cross Domain Resource Manager
CDRSC	Cross Domain Resource
CEBI	Conditional End Bracket Indicator
CICS	Customer Information Control System
CLIST	Command List
CLNS	Connectionless Network Service (OSI)
CMC	Communications Management Configurations
CMIP	Common Management Information Protocol (OS)
CMOL	CMIP Over LLC
CMOT	CMIP Over TCP/IP
CMIS	Common Management Information Service (CMIS)
CMS	Conversational Monitor System
CNM	Communication Network Management
CNMI	Communication Network Management Interface (VTAM)
CNOS	Change Number of Sessions
CNT	Communications Name Table (IMS)
CONS	Connection Oriented Network Service (OSI)
COS	Class of Service (SNA), *also* Corporation for Open Systems
CP	Control Point, *also* Control Program
CPE	Customer Premises Equipment
CPI	Common Programming Interface
CPIC	Common Programming Interface for Communications
CPMS	Control Point Management Services
CRC	Cyclical Redundancy Check
CTC	Channel to Channel
CTCP	Communication and Transport Control Program
CTS	Clear to Send
CUA	Common User Access (SAA interface name for user access standard)
CUT	Control Unit Terminal
DAF	Destination Address Field
DATE	Dedicated Access to X.25 Transport Extension in NPSI
DCA	Document Content Architecture
DCE	Data Circuit Termination Equipment, *also* Distributed Computing Environment (OSF)
DDM	Distributed Data Management

DFC	Data Flow Control
DFT	Distributed Function Terminal
DIA	Document Interchange Architecture
DIU	Distribution Interchange Unit
DLC	Data Link Control
DLU	Destination Logical Unit
DOS	Disk Operating System (not the same as PC/DOS)
DR	Definite Response (LU level response in SNA, two types called DR type 1 and 2)
DSU	Digital Services Unit
DSUN	Distribution Services Unit Name
DTE	Data Terminal Equipment
DTR	Data Terminal Ready
EB	End Bracket
EIA	Electronic Industries Association
ENA	Extended Network Addressing
EOT	End of Transmission
EP	Emulation Program
ER	Exception Response, *also* Explicit Route
ESA	Enterprise Systems Architecture, *also* Enhanced Subarea Addressing
ETB	End of Text Block
ETX	End of Text
FCS	Frame Check Sequence
FEP	Front End Processor
FID	Format ID
FM	Function Management
FMH	Function Management Header
FRMR	Frame Reject
FTAM	File Transfer and Access Management (OSI)
FTP	File Transfer Protocol (TCP/IP)
GATE	Generalized Access to X.25 Transport Extention in NPSI
GDS	Generalized Data Stream
GWNCP	Gateway NCP
GWSSCP	Gateway SSCP
HDLC	High Level Data Link Control
IBM	International Business Machines Corporations
ILU	Initiating Logical Unit
IML	Initial Machine Load

IMS	Information Management System
INN	Intermediate Network Node
IPDS	Intelligent Printer Data Stream
IPL	Initial Program Load
IPR	Isolated Pacing Response
ISC	Inter System Communications in CICS
ISCF	Inter Systems Control Facility
ISDN	Integrated Services Digital Network
ISO	International Standards Organization
IXC	Interexchange Carrier
JCL	Job Control Language
JES	Job Entry Subsystem
LAN	Local Area Network
LAPB	Link Access Procedure Balanced
LEC	Local Exchange Carrier
LEN	Low Entry Networking
LLC	Logical Link Control
LPDA	Link Problem Determination Application in IBM modems
LRC	Longitudinal Redundancy Check
LU	Logical Unit
MAC	Media Access Control
MFS	Message Formatting Services in IMS
MRO	Multiregion Operation in CICS
MS	Management Services
MSN	Multiple Systems Networking (formerly known as MSNF)
MSNF	Multiple Systems Networking Facility
MSU	Management Services Unit
MVS	Multiple Virtual Systems
NAK	Negative Acknowledgement in BSC
NAU	Network Addressable Unit
NCCF	Network Communications Control Facility
NCP	Network Control Program
NJE	Network Job Entry
NLDM	Network Logical Data Manager
NMVT	Network Management Vector Transport
NPDA	Network Problem Determination Application
NPM	Netview Performance Monitor
NPSI	NCP Packet Switching Interface

NRZ	Non Return to Zero
NRZI	Non Return to Zero Inverted
NTO	Network Terminal Option
OAF	Origination Address Field
OCA	Open Communication Architectures
ODAI	OAF/DAF Assignment Indicator
OLU	Originating Logical Unit
OSF	Open Software Foundation
OSNS	Open Systems Network Services
OSI	Open System Interconnect
OSI/CS	OSI Communications Subsystem
PAD	Packet Assembler Disassembler
PC	Path Control, *also* Personal Computer
PCNE	Protocol Conversion for Native Equipment in NPSI
PDN	Public Data Network
PEP	Partitioned Emulation Program
PIP	Program Initialization Parameters
PIU	Path Information Unit
PLS	Primary Link Station
PLU	Primary Logical Unit
POI	Program Operator Interface in VTAM
PPO	Primary Program Operator in VTAM/NetView
PPSDN	Public Packet Switched Data Network
PS	Presentation Services
PSDN	Packet Switched Data Network
PU	Physical Unit
PUCP	Physical Unit Control Point
PUMS	Physical Unit Management Services
PVC	Private Virtual Circuit in X.25
QC	Quiesce Complete
QEC	Quiesce at End of Chain
QLLC	Qualified Logical Link Control in NPSI
QMF	Query Management Facility
RECFMS	Record Formatted Maintenance Statistics
REJ	Reject
RH	Request/Response Header
RIM	Request Initialization Mode
RJE	Remote Job Entry

RNAA	Request Network Address Assignment
RNR	Receiver Not Ready
RPC	Remote Procedure Call in DCE
RR	Receiver Ready
RTM	Response Time Monitor
RTR	Ready to Receive
RTS	Request to Send
RU	Request/Response Unit
SA	Subarea
SAA	System Applications Architecture
SABM	Set Asynchronous Mode Balanced
SAP	Service Access Point
SAW	Session Awareness Data
SBI	Stop Bracket Initiation
SDLC	Synchronous Data Link Control
SIM	Set Initialization Mode
SLU	Secondary Logical Unit
SNA	System Network Architecture
SNADS	SNA Distribution Services
SNCP	Single Node Control Point (replaces PUCP in PU Type 2.1)
SNI	SNA Network Interface
SNMP	Simple Network Management Protocol in TCP/IP
SNRM	Set Normal Response Mode
SQL	Structured Query Language
SSCP	System Services Control Point
STP	Service Transaction Program in LU 6.2
SVC	Switched Virtual Circuit
SYN	Synchronous Character in BSC
TCAM	Tele-Communications Access Method
TCT	Terminal Control Table in CICS
TG	Transmission Group
TH	Transmission Header
TP	Transaction Program in an APPC or OSI context, *also* teleprocessing
TS	Transaction Services
TSCF	Target System Control Facility
TSO	Time Sharing Option
TTY	Teletype

UA	Unnumbered Acknowledgement
UOW	Unit of Work
USS	Unformatted System Services
VAN	Value Added Network
VSAM	Virtual Storage Access Method
VM	Virtual Machine
VR	Virtual Route
VS	Virtual Storage
VSE	Virtual Storage Extended
VTAM	Virtual Telecommunications Access Method
VTAME	VTAM Extended (now obsolete)
XI	SNA X.25 Interface
XID	Exchange ID

Bibliography

Architecture Publications[*]

SNA Format and Protocol: Architecture Logic (SC30-3112) [This voluminous manual is the reference manual for SNA. It defines SNA protocols and architecture logic. It does not include newer enhancements such as LU 6.2, LEN, and APPN which are documented in other manuals listed below.]

SNA Sessions Between Logical Units (GC20-1868) [This manual describes LU-LU protocols for LUs other than LU 6.2.]

SNA Technical Overview (SC30-3073) [A brief but very useful manual describing basic SNA definitions, control, and flow sequences. One of IBM's better publications.]

SNA Format and Protocol Reference Manual, Architecture Logic for LU 6.2 (SC30-3269) [This manual describes architecture for LU 6.2.]

SNA Type 2.1 Node Reference (SC30-3422) [This manual describes APPN, LEN, and node architecture. There is no additional APPN reference manual published by IBM. IBM does not publish APPN network node architecture and protocols.]

SNA LU 6.2 Reference, Peer Protocols (SC31-6808)

SNA Transaction Programmer's Reference Manual for LU 6.2 (GC30-3084) [This manual describes APPC API.]

SNA Distribution Services (SC30-3346)

SNA Management Services (SC30-3346)

SDLC Concepts (GA27-3093)

SAA, an Overview (GC26-4341)

SAA Common Communications Support (CCS) (GC32-6810)

SAA Common Programming Interface for Communications (CPIC) (SC26-4399)

Product Publications[†]

VTAM, Version 3, Release 3.

VTAM Network Implementation Guide (SC31-6404)

VTAM Resource Definition Reference (SC31-6412)

VTAM Programming (SC31-6409) [VTAM API except APPC]

VTAM Programming for LU 6.2 (SC31-6410) [VTAM APPC API]

---

[*]IBM publication numbers, such as SC30-3122, are listed in parenthesis next to the book titles. Publications are available through IBM.

[†]The publication numbers change with new product releases. The reader should check the latest publication numbers with IBM to ensure that the manuals correspond to their specific product release number.

NCP, Version 5.

NCP, SSP, and EP Generation and Loading Guide (SC30-3348)
NCP, SSP, and EP Resource Definition Guide (SC30-3447)
NCP, SSP, and EP Resource Definition Reference (SC30-3348)

NetView, Release 3.

NetView Installation and Administration Guide (SC31-6018)
NewView Administration Reference (SC31-6014)
NetView Customization Guide (SC31-6016)
NetView Operation (SC31-6019)
Console Automation Using NetView, Planning (SC31-6058)

OSI/CS.

General Information (GL23-0184)
Programming Reference (SL23-0190)

OS/2.

System Administrator's Guide for Communications (GO1F-0302)
APPC Programming Reference (SO1F-0295)
SAA Network Services Installation and Administration Guide (SC52-1110)
SAA Network Services APPC Programming Reference (SC41-1112)

IBM 3174.

3174 Introduction (GA27-3850)
3174 Functional Description (GA23-0218)

Index

(The *f.* after a page number refers to a figure; the *t.* refers to a table.)